The Philosophy of Psychology

What is the relationship between common-sense, or 'folk', psychology and contemporary scientific psychology? Are they in conflict with one another? Or do they perform quite different, though perhaps complementary, roles? George Botterill and Peter Carruthers discuss these questions, defending a robust form of realism about the commitments of folk psychology and about the prospects for integrating those commitments into natural science. Their focus throughout the book is on the ways in which cognitive science presents a challenge to our common-sense self-image – arguing that our native conception of the mind will be enriched, but not overturned, by science. *The Philosophy of Psychology* is designed as a textbook for upper-level undergraduate and beginning graduate students in philosophy and cognitive science. As a text that not only surveys but advances the debates on the topics discussed, it will also be of interest to researchers working in these areas.

George Botterill is Lecturer in Philosophy and a member of the Hang Seng Centre for Cognitive Studies at the University of Sheffield. He has published a number of essays in the philosophy of mind and the philosophy of science.

Peter Carruthers is Professor of Philosophy and Director of the Hang Seng Centre for Cognitive Studies at the University of Sheffield. His publications include *Human Knowledge and Human Nature* (' ' 1 *Language, Thought and Consciousness: An Essay :* *chology* (Cambridge University Press, 190⸀⸍

The Philosophy of Psychology

George Botterill

and

Peter Carruthers

PUBLISHED BY THE PRESS SYNDICATE OF THE UNIVERSITY OF CAMBRIDGE
The Pitt Building, Trumpington Street, Cambridge, United Kingdom

CAMBRIDGE UNIVERSITY PRESS
The Edinburgh Building, Cambridge CB2 2RU, United Kingdom
   http://www.cup.cam.ac.uk
40 West 20th Street, New York, NY 10011-4211, USA   http://www.cup.org
10 Stamford Road, Oakleigh, Melbourne 3166, Australia

First published 1999

Printed in the United Kingdom at the University Press, Cambridge

Typeset in Times 10/12pt [VN]

A catalogue record for this book is available from the British Library

Library of Congress cataloging in publication data

Botterill, George.
The philosophy of psychology / George Botterill, Peter Carruthers.
      p.   cm.
Includes bibliographical references and indexes.
ISBN 0 521 55111 0 (hardback) – ISBN 0 521 55915 4 (paperback)
1. Psychology – Philosophy.   I. Carruthers, Peter, 1952–   .
II. Title.
BF38.B63   1999
150′.1 – dc21   98–33301 CIP

ISBN 0 521 55111 0 hardback
ISBN 0 521 55915 4 paperback

for
Nick, Alex, and Dan
three's company

and for
Rachael
sugar and spice, and a will of steel

Contents

Preface

Audience

When we initially conceived the project of this book, our first task was to determine what *sort* of book it should be. The question of intended audience was relatively easy. We thought we should aim our book primarily at upper-level undergraduate students of philosophy and beginning-level graduate students in the cognitive sciences generally, who would probably have some previous knowledge of issues in the philosophy of mind. But we also hoped, at the same time, that we could make our own contributions to the problems discussed, which might engage the interest of the professionals, and help move the debates forward. Whether or not we have succeeded in this latter aim must be for others to judge.

Content

The question of the content of the book was more difficult. There is a vast range of topics which *could* be discussed under the heading of 'philosophy of psychology', and a great many different approaches to those topics could be taken. For scientific psychology is itself a very broad church, ranging from various forms of cognitive psychology, through artificial intelligence, social psychology, behavioural psychology, comparative psychology, neuro-psychology, psycho-pathology, and so on. And the philosopher of psychology might then take a variety of different approaches, ranging from one which engages with, and tries to contribute to, *psychological* debates (compare the way in which philosophers of physics may propose solutions to the hidden-variable problem); through an approach which attempts to tease out philosophical problems as they arise *within* psychology (compare the famous 'under-labourer' conception of the role of the philosopher of science); to an approach which focuses on problems which are raised *for philosophy* by the results and methods of psychology.

We have chosen to take a line towards the latter end of this spectrum, concentrating on cognitive psychology in particular. Our main focus is on the relationships between scientific (cognitive) psychology, on the one hand, and common-sense or 'folk' psychology, on the other. Since humans are such social creatures, one might expect psychology to be a subject in which people would start out with the advantage of being expert laymen. Yet there are various ways in which scientific psychology can easily seem to threaten or undermine our self-image either by raising doubts about the very existence of mental states as we conceive of them, or by challenging one or another cherished picture we have of ourselves (for example, as rational). And various questions can be raised concerning the extent to which folk and scientific psychology are attempting to do the same kind of job or achieve the same kind of thing.

What this means is that there is a great deal less in this book about levels of explanation, say, than certain pre-conceptions of what is required of a text on *Philosophy of X* (where *X* is some science) would suggest. There is also much less on connectionism than will be expected by those who think that philosophy of psychology just *is* the connectionism and/or eliminativism debate. And we say rather little, too, about a number of areas in which much scientific progress has been made, and which have been well worked-over by philosophical commentators – including memory, vision, and language.

Following an introductory chapter in which we review some background developments in philosophy of mind and scientific psychology, the main body of the book begins in chapter 2 with a discussion of the relationships between folk and scientific psychologies, and the proper interpretation of the former. Here we defend a robustly realistic construal of our folk-psychological commitments, which underpins much of what we say thereafter. Chapter 3 reviews the psychological arguments for nativism and modularity, raising the question whether modularism is consistent with our picture of ourselves as *unified* subjects of experience (and indicating a positive answer). Chapter 4 then considers what may be the best *scientific* view of the nature of our folk psychology, and the course of its development in the individual – arguing for a nativist/modularist 'theory-theory' approach, as opposed to either an 'empiricist' or a 'simulationist' one. Chapter 5 discusses the extent to which psychological evidence of widespread human irrationality undermines our picture of ourselves as rational agents, and considers the arguments of some philosophers that widespread irrationality is impossible. Chapter 6 takes up the issue concerning the appropriate notion of intentional *content* required by psychology (both folk and scientific) – that is, whether it should be 'wide' or 'narrow' – and defends the role of narrow content in both domains. (Here, in particular, we are conscious of swimming against a strong tide of contrary opinion.) Chapter 7 is concerned with the question of the *natural-*

isation of semantic content, discussing the three main programmes on offer ('informational', 'teleological', and 'functional-role' semantics). Chapter 8 discusses the connectionism–Mentalese debate, and considers a variety of ways in which natural language may be more closely implicated in (some of) human cognition than is generally thought. Then finally, in chapter 9, we consider the arguments for and against the possibility of integrating *phenomenal consciousness* into science. Here, as elsewhere in the book, we defend an *integrationist* line.

We think that the prospects for the future survival of folk psychology are good, and also for its relatively smooth integration into psychological science. And we think that the prospects for fruitful collaboration between empirically minded philosophers of mind and theoretically minded cognitive psychologists are excellent. These are exciting times for scientific psychology; and exciting times, too, for the philosopher of psychology. We hope that readers of this book will come to share some of that excitement.

Number of chapters

Not only did we face questions about *audience* and *content*, but we also faced a question about the *number* of chapters the book should contain; which is rather more significant than it might at first seem. Since lengths of teaching-terms can range from eight weeks up to fifteen in universities around the world, the challenge was to devise a structure which could be variably carved up to meet a number of different needs. We opted for a basic structure of eight main chapters, together with an introduction which could if necessary be set as preliminary reading before the start of the course proper (or skipped altogether for classes with appropriate prior knowledge). Then the two long final chapters were designed to be taken in two halves each, if desired. (Chapter 8, on forms of representation, divides into one half on the connectionism versus language-of-thought debate and one half on the place of natural language in cognition; and chapter 9, on consciousness, divides into one half on the 'new mysterianism' concerning phenomenal consciousness and one half on recent naturalistic theories of consciousness.) Moreover, chapters 6 and 7 both cover a great deal of much-debated ground concerning the nature of mental content (wide versus narrow in chapter 6, and the question of naturalisation in chapter 7); so each could easily be taken in two or more stages if required.

Acknowledgements

We are grateful to our students at the University of Sheffield (both under-graduate and graduate), on whom we piloted the text of this book at various stages of its preparation, and whose worries and objections did much to make it better. We are also grateful to Colin Allen for agreeing to use the penultimate draft of the book as a graduate-level seminar-text at Texas A&M, and for providing us with much useful feedback as a result; and to Thad Botham, one of the students on that course, for sending us his comments individually.

We are also grateful to the following individuals for their comments, whether oral or written, on some or all of the material in the book: Colin Allen, Alex Barber, Keith Frankish, Susan Granger, Christopher Hookway, Gabriel Segal, Michael Tye, and a reviewer for Cambridge University Press.

Thanks also to Shaun Nichols and colleagues (and to Cambridge University Press) for permission to reproduce their (1996) diagram of 'off-line processing', given here as figure 4.1; and to Alex Botterill for the art-work for figure 3.1.

Finally, we are grateful to our families for their patience.

1 Introduction: some background

Readers of this book should already have some familiarity with modern philosophy of mind, and at least a glancing acquaintance with contemporary psychology and cognitive science. (Anyone of whom this is *not* true is recommended to look at one or more of the introductions listed at the end of the chapter.) Here we shall only try to set the arguments of subsequent chapters into context by surveying – very briskly – some of the historical debates and developments which form the background to our work.

1 Developments in philosophy of mind

Philosophy of mind in the English-speaking world has been dominated by two main ambitions throughout most of the twentieth century – to avoid causal mysteries about the workings of the mind, and to meet scepticism about other minds by providing a reasonable account of what we can know, or justifiably infer, about the mental states of other people. So most work in this field has been governed by two constraints, which we will call *naturalism* and *psychological knowledge.*

According to *naturalism* human beings are complex biological organisms and as such are part of the natural order, being subject to the same laws of nature as everything else in the world. If we are going to stick to a naturalistic approach, then we cannot allow that there is anything to the mind which needs to be accounted for by invoking vital spirits, incorporeal souls, astral planes, or anything else which cannot be integrated with natural science. Amongst the thorniest questions for naturalism are whether thoughts with representational content (the so-called *intentional states* such as beliefs and desires, which have the distinctive characteristic of *being about something*), and whether experiences with phenomenal properties (which have distinctive subjective feels, and which are *like something* to undergo), are themselves suitable for integration within the corpus of scientific knowledge. We will be addressing these issues in chapters 7 and 9 respectively.

Psychological knowledge has two aspects, depending upon whether our knowledge is of other people or of ourselves. Different accounts of the mental will yield different stories about how we can have knowledge of it, or indeed whether we can have such knowledge at all. So a theory of mind ought to fit in with a reasonable view of the extent and nature of psychological knowledge. The details of the fit are a somewhat delicate matter. It must be conceded that both empirical evidence and theoretical considerations might force revisions to common-sense thinking about psychological knowledge. But the constraint of psychological knowledge does apply some pressure, because a theory is not at liberty to trample our common-sense conceptions without adequate motivation. In other words, there may be reasons to revise what we ordinarily think about psychological knowledge, but such reasons should be independent of the need to uphold any particular theory of the mind.

So far as knowledge of others is concerned, the constraint would seem to be as follows. In general, there is no serious doubt that other people do have thoughts and feelings just as we ourselves do (although we discuss the claims of *eliminativism* about the mental in chapter 2). And in particular cases we can know what it is that other people are thinking, whether they are happy or disappointed, what they intend, and what they are afraid of. Such knowledge is, however, not always easy to come by and in many instances behavioural or situational evidence may not be sufficient for any firm beliefs about another person's states of mind. Hence our psychological knowledge of others is not direct and immediate. It may or may not involve *conscious* inference about the thoughts and feelings of others. But even where no conscious inference is involved, our knowledge of other minds is dependent upon informational cues (from conduct, expression, tone of voice, and situation) – as can be seen from the fact that these cues can be manipulated by people who lie convincingly, pretend to be pleased when they are not, or make us forget for a while that they are just acting.

So far as knowledge of ourselves is concerned, while there can be such a thing as self-deception, we are vastly better informed than we are even about the psychological states of our nearest and dearest. In part this is because we have a huge store of past experiences, feelings and attitudes recorded in memory. But we would underestimate the asymmetry between self-knowledge and knowledge of others, if we represented it as just knowing *more*, in much the way that one knows more about one's hometown than other places. Self-knowledge differs from knowledge of others in that one seems to know in a different way and with a special sort of authority, at least in the case of one's *present* mental states. We seem to have a peculiarly direct sort of knowledge of what we are currently thinking and feeling. We do not seem to be reliant on anything in the way of evidence (as we would be if we were making inferences from our own situation and behaviour) and yet it hardly seems possible for us to be mistaken on such matters.

With the constraints of *naturalism* and *psychological knowledge* explained, we shall now review very briefly some of the main developments in twentieth-century philosophy of mind which form the back-drop to the main body of this book.

1.1 Dualism

Dualism comes in two forms – weak and strong. Strong dualism (often called 'Cartesian dualism') is the view that mind and body are quite distinct kinds of *thing* – while bodies are physical things, extended in space, which are subject to the laws of physics and chemistry, minds do not take up any space, are not composed of matter, and as such are not subject to physical laws. Weak dualism allows that the *subject* of both mental and physical *properties* may be a physical thing – a human being, in fact. But it claims that mental properties are *not* physical ones, and can vary independently of physical properties. Ever since Ryle's *The Concept of Mind* (1949) rejection of dualism has been the common ground from which philosophers of mind have started out. Almost everyone now agrees that there is no such thing as *mind-stuff*, and that the subject of mental properties and events is a physical thing. And almost everyone now maintains that mental properties *supervene on* physical ones, at least, in such a way that it is impossible for two individuals to share all of the same physical properties, but differ in their mental ones.

Much the most popular and influential objection to dualism (of either variety) concerns the *problem of causal interaction* between the mental and the physical. (Another objection is that dualism faces notorious problems in accounting for our psychological knowledge of others.) It seems uncontentious that there can be both physical causes which produce mental changes, and also mental events which cause bodily movements and, subsequently, changes in the physical environment. Perception illustrates the former causal direction: something happens and *you notice* it happening. Intentional action illustrates the mental-to-physical causal direction: after reflection you decide that the sofa would look better by the window, and this decision causes you to go in for some muscular exertions which in turn cause the sofa to get re-located. Such commonplaces are fundamental to our understanding of the relation between minds and their environment. But how such causal interactions could ever occur becomes mysterious on any consistently dualistic position, unless we are prepared to accept causal interaction between physical and mental events as a brute fact. And even if we *are* prepared to accept this, it is mysterious *where* in the brain mental events would be supposed to make an impact, given that enough is already known about the brain, and about the activities of nerve cells, to warrant us in believing that every brain-event will have a sufficient physical cause.

We cannot pause here to develop these and other arguments against dualism in anything like a convincing way. Our purpose has only been to give a reminder of why *physicalism* of one sort or another is now the default approach in the philosophy of mind. (Which is not to say, of course, that physicalism is unchallengeable. On the contrary, in chapter 9 we shall be considering arguments which have convinced many people that phenomenally conscious mental states – states with a distinctive subjective feel to them – are *not* physical.)

1.2 Logical behaviourism

The classic exposition of logical behaviourism is Ryle, 1949. His leading idea was that it is a mistake to treat talk about the mental as talk about inner causes and then go on to ask whether those causes are physical or not. To think this way, according to Ryle, is to commit a *category-mistake*. Talk about the mental is not talk about mysterious inner causes of behaviour, it is rather a way of talking about dispositions to behave and patterns of behaviour.

Behaviourism did have some attractions. It allowed humans to be included within the order of nature by avoiding postulation of anything 'ghostly' inside the organic machinery of the body. It also promised a complete (perhaps *too complete*) defence of our psychological knowledge of the minds of others, for knowing about others' minds was simply reduced to knowing about their behavioural dispositions. Furthermore, it seemed to be right, as Ryle pointed out, that people can correctly be described as knowing this or believing that, irrespective of what is going on inside them at the time – indeed, even when they are asleep.

The deficiencies of behaviourism were even more apparent, however. What always seemed most implausible about logical behaviourism was that *knowledge of one's own mind would consist in knowledge of one's behavioural dispositions*, since this hardly left room for the idea of first-person authority about one's thoughts and feelings. The point that *some* of our mentalistic discourse is dispositional rather than episodic had to be conceded to Ryle. But then again, some of our mentalistic discourse is episodic rather than dispositional. Surely a sudden realisation, or a vivid recollection, or a momentary feeling of revulsion cannot be treated as a disposition. There are, it would seem, mental *events*. What is more, the fact that beliefs, knowledge and desires can be long-standing rather than fleeting and episodic is by no means a decisive argument that they are dispositions to behaviour. Their durational nature is equally compatible with their being underlying states with a lasting causal role or potential (as argued in Armstrong, 1973).

Logical behaviourism was offered as a piece of *conceptual analysis*. It was supposed to be an account of what had all along been the import of our psychological discourse. Allegedly, theoreticians had misconstrued our talk about the mind and loaded it with theoretical implications of unobserved mental mechanisms never intended in ordinary usage. That being the Rylean stance, the most serious technical criticism of logical behaviourism is that it fails on its own terms, as an exercise in analysis. According to behaviourism what look like imputations of internal mental events or states should actually be construed as 'iffy' or conditional statements about people's actual and possible behaviour. The first objection to the pretensions of behaviourist conceptual analysis, then, is that nobody has ever actually produced a single completed example of the behavioural content of such an analysis. In itself, this objection might not have been fatal. Ryle suggested such cases as *solubility* and *brittleness* as analogous to behavioural dispositions. To say that something is soluble or brittle is to say something about what it would do if immersed in water, or if struck by a solid object. Now, admittedly, there is a disanalogy, because there is just one standard way in which such dispositional properties as solubility and brittleness can be manifested (that is, by dissolving and by breaking into fragments). But no doubt there are more complex dispositional properties, both psychological and non-psychological. If there are various ways in which a complex dispositional property can be manifested, then spelling out in terms of conditionals what the attribution of such a dispositional property amounts to might well be an exceedingly difficult and lengthy task.

There is, however, a follow-up to the initial complaint about behaviourist analyses (and their non-appearance, in any detailed form), which not only blows away this flimsy line of defence, but also reveals a deeper flaw in behaviourism. Suppose I am walking along and come to believe that rain is about to start bucketing down. Do I make haste to take shelter? Well I may do so, of course, but that all depends. It depends upon such things as how much I care about getting wet, and also upon what I think and how much I care about other things which might be affected by an attempt to find shelter – such as my chances of catching the last train, or my reputation as a hard-as-nails triathlete. As Davidson (1970) pointed out, a particular belief or desire only issues in conduct in concert with, and under the influence of, other intentional states of the agent. There is no way, there-fore, of saying what someone who holds a certain belief will do in a given situation, without also specifying what other beliefs and desires that agent holds. So analysis of a belief or a desire as a behavioural disposition requires invoking other beliefs and desires. This point has convinced practically everyone that Ryle was wrong. A belief or a desire does not just consist in a disposition to certain sorts of behaviour. On the contrary, our common-sense psychology construes these states as internal states of the agent which play a causal role in *producing* behaviour, as we shall go on to argue in chapter 2.

1.3 Identity theory

With dualism and logical behaviourism firmly rejected, attempts since the 1960s to give a philosophical account of the status of the mental have centred on some combination of *identity theory* and *functionalism*. Indeed, one could fairly say that the result of debates over the last forty years has been to establish some sort of functionalist account of mental concepts combined with token-identity theory (plus commitment to a thesis of supervenience of mental properties on physical ones) as the orthodox position in the philosophy of mind. There is quite a bit of jargon to be unpacked here, especially as labels like 'functionalism' and 'identity the-ory' are used in various disciplines for positions between which only tenuous connections hold. In the philosophy of mind, functionalism is a view about mentalistic concepts, namely that they represent mental states and events as differentiated by the functions, or causal roles, which they have, both in relation to behaviour and to other mental states and events; whereas identity theory is a thesis about what mental states or events *are*, namely that they are identical with states or events of the brain (or of the central nervous system).

There are two distinct versions of identity theory which have been the focus of philosophical debate – *type-identity* theory and *token-identity* theory. Both concentrate on an alleged identity between mental states and events, on the one hand, and brain states and processes, on the other, rather than between mind and brain *en masse*. Type-identity theory holds that each type of mental state is identical with some particular type of brain state – for example, that pain is the firing of C-fibres. Token-identity theory maintains that each particular mental state or event (a 'token' being a datable particular rather than a type – such as Gussie's twinge of toothache at 4 pm on Tuesday, rather than pain in general) is identical with some brain state or event, but allows that individual instances of the same mental type may be instances of different types of brain state or event.

Type-identity theory was first advocated as a hypothesis about correlations between sensations and brain processes which would be discovered by neuroscience (Place, 1956; Smart, 1959; Armstrong, 1968). Its proponents claimed that the identity of mental states with brain states was supported by correlations which were just starting to be established by neuroscience, and that this constituted a scientific discovery akin to other type-identities, such as *heat is molecular motion, lightning is electrical discharge*, and *water is H_2O*. In those early days, during the 1950s and 60s, the identity theory was advanced as a theory which was much the best bet about the future course of neuroscientific investigation.

Yet there were certainly objections which were troublesome for those who shared the naturalistic sympathies of the advocates of type-identity. A surprising, and surely unwelcome, consequence of the theory was an adverse prognosis for the prospects of work in artificial intelligence. For if a certain cognitive psychological state, say a thought *that P*, is actually to be identified with a certain human neurophysiological state, then the possibility of something non-human being in such a state is excluded. Nor did it seem right to make the acceptance of the major form of physicalist theory so dependent upon correlations which might be established in the future. Did that mean that if the correlations were not found one would be forced to accept either dualism or behaviourism?

But most important was the point that confidence in such type-correlations is misplaced. So far from this being a good bet about what neuroscience will reveal, it seems a very bad bet, both in relation to sensations and in relation to intentional states such as thoughts. For consider a sensation type, such as pain. It might be that whenever *humans* feel pain, there is always a certain neurophysiological process going on (for example, C-fibres firing). But creatures of many different Earthly species can feel pain. One can also imagine life-forms on different planets which feel pain, even though they are not closely similar in their physiology to any terrestrial species. So, quite likely, a given type of sensation is correlated with lots of different types of neurophysiological states. Much the same can be argued in the case of thoughts. Presumably it will be allowed that speakers of different natural languages can think thoughts of the same type, classified by content. Thus an English speaker can think that *a storm is coming*; but so, too, can a Bedouin who speaks no English. (And, quite possibly, so can a languageless creature such as a camel.) It hardly seems plausible that every thought with a given content is an instance of some particular type of neural state, especially as these thoughts would cause their thinkers to express them in quite different ways in different natural languages.

The only way in which a type-identity thesis could still be maintained, given the variety of ways in which creatures might have sensations of the same type and the variety of ways in which thinkers might have thoughts of the same type, would be to make sensations and intentional states identical, not with single types of neurophysiological state, but with some disjunctive list of state-types. So pain, for example, might be neuro-state H (in a human), or neuro-state R (in a rat), or neuro-state O (in an octopus), or . . . and so on. This disjunctive formulation is an unattractive complication for type-identity theory. Above all, it is objectionable that there should be no available principle which can be invoked to put a stop to such a disjunctive list and prevent it from having an indeterminate length.

The conclusion which has been drawn from these considerations is that type-identity theory is unsatisfactory, because it is founded on an assumption that there will be one–one correlations between mental state types and physical state types. But this assumption is not just a poor bet on the outcome of future research. There is something about our principles of classification for mental state types which makes it more seriously misguided, so that we are already in a position to anticipate that the correlations will not be one–one, but one–many – one mental state type will be correlated with *many different* physical state types. If we are to retain a basic commitment to naturalism, we will take mental states always to be realised in physical states of some type and so will conclude that mental state types are *multiply realised*. This is where functionalism comes in, offering a neat explanation of why it is that mental state types should be multiply realisable. Consequently, multiple realisability of the mental is standardly given as the reason for preferring a combination of functionalism and a *token*-identity thesis, according to which each token mental state or process is (is identical with) some physical state or process.

1.4 Functionalism

The guiding idea behind functionalism is that some concepts classify things by what they *do*. For example, transmitters transmit something, while aerials are objects positioned so as to receive air-borne signals. Indeed, practically all concepts for artefacts are functional in character. But so, too, are many concepts applied to living things. Thus, wings are limbs for flying with, eyes are light-sensitive organs for seeing with, and genes are biological structures which control development. So perhaps mental concepts are concepts of states or processes with a certain function. This idea has been rediscovered in Aristotle's writings (particularly in *De anima*). Its introduction into modern philosophy of mind is chiefly due to Putnam (1960, 1967; see also Lewis, 1966).

Functionalism has seemed to be the answer to several philosophical prayers. It accounts for the multiple realisability of mental states, the chief stumbling-block for an 'immodest' type-identity theory. And it also has obvious advantages over behaviourism, since it accords much better with ordinary intuitions about causal relations and psychological knowledge – it allows mental states to interact and influence each other, rather than being directly tied to behavioural dispositions; and it gives an account of our understanding of the meaning of mentalistic concepts which avoids objectionable dependence on introspection while at the same time unifying the treatment of first-person and third-person cases. Finally, it remains explicable that dualism should ever have seemed an option – although we conceptualise mental states in terms of causal roles, it can be a contingent matter what actually *occupies* those causal roles; and it was a conceptual possibility that the role-occupiers might have turned out to be composed of *mind-stuff*.

Multiple realisability is readily accounted for in the case of functional concepts. Since there may be more than one way in which a particular function, *φ-ing*, can be discharged, things of various different compositions can serve that function and hence qualify as *φ-ers*. Think of *valves*, for example, which are to be found inside both your heart and (say) your central heating system. So while mental *types* are individuated in terms of a certain sort of pattern of causes and effects, mental *tokens* (individual instantiations of those patterns) can be (can be identical to, or at least constituted by) instantiations of some physical type (such as C-fibre firing).

According to functionalism, *psychological knowledge* will always be of states with a certain role, characterised in terms of how they are produced and of their effects on both other such states and behaviour. Functionalism does not by itself explain the asymmetry between knowledge of self and knowledge of others. So it does need to be supplemented by some account of how it is that knowledge of one's own present mental states can be both peculiarly direct and peculiarly reliable. How best to deliver this account is certainly open to debate, but does not appear to be a completely intractable problem. (We view this problem as demanding a theory of consciousness, since the mental states one knows about in a peculiarly direct way are conscious ones – see chapter 9.) But if there is still unfinished business in the first-person case, one of functionalism's chief sources of appeal has been the plausible treatment it provides for psychological knowledge of others. Our attribution of mental states to others fits their situations and reactions and is justified as an inference to the best explanation of their behaviour. This view places our psychological knowledge of others on a par with theoretical knowledge, in two respects. Firstly, the functional roles assigned to various mental states depend upon systematic relations between such states and their characteristic causes and effects. So it seems that we have a common-sense theory of mind, or a 'folk psychology', which implicitly defines ordinary psychological concepts. Secondly, the application of that theory is justified in the way that theories usually are, namely by success in prediction and explanation.

We hasten to insert here an important distinction between the *justification* for our beliefs about the minds of others and *what causes* us to have such beliefs. In particular applications to individuals on specific occasions, we may draw inferences which are justified both by the evidence available and our general folk psychology, and may draw some such inferences (rather than others) *precisely because* we recognise them to be justified. But while our theory of mind can be justified by our predictive and explanatory successes in a vast number of such particular applications, we do not, in general, apply that theory because we have seen it to be justified. To echo Hume's remarks about induction, we say that this is not something which nature has left up to us. As we shall be arguing in chapters 3 and 4, it is part of our normal, native, cognitive endowment to apply such a theory of mind – in fact, we cannot help but think about each other in such terms.

So far we have been painting a rosy picture of functionalism. But, as usual, there have been objections. The two main problems with analytical functionalism (that is, functionalism as a thesis about the correct *analysis* of mental state concepts) are as follows:

(1) It is committed to the analytic/synthetic distinction, which many philosophers think (after Quine, 1951) to be unviable. And it is certainly hard to decide quite *which* truisms concerning the causal role of a mental state should count as analytic (true in virtue of meaning), rather than just obviously true. (Consider examples such as that *belief* is the sort of state which is apt to be induced through perceptual experience and liable to combine with *desire*; that *pain* is an experience frequently caused by bodily injury or organic malfunction, liable to cause characteristic behavioural manifestations such as groaning, wincing and screaming; and so on.)

(2) Another commonly voiced objection against functionalism is that it is incapable of capturing the felt nature of conscious experience (Block and Fodor, 1972; Nagel, 1974; Jackson, 1982, 1986). Objectors have urged that one could know everything about the functional role of a mental state and yet still have no inkling as to *what it is like to be in that state* – its so-called *quale*. Moreover, some mental states seem to be conceptualised purely in terms of feel; at any rate, with beliefs about causal role taking a secondary position. For example, it seems to be just the feel of pain which is essential to it (Kripke, 1972). We seem to be able to imagine pains which occupy some other causal role; and we can imagine states having the

causal role of pain which are not pains (which lack the appropriate kind of feel).

1.5 The theory-theory

In response to such difficulties, many have urged that a better variant of functionalism is *theory-theory* (Lewis, 1966, 1970, 1980; Churchland, 1981; Stich, 1983). According to this view, mental state concepts (like theoretical concepts in science) get their life and sense from their position in a substantive *theory* of the causal structure and functioning of the mind. And on this view, to know what a belief is (to grasp the concept of belief) is to know sufficiently much of the theory of mind within which that concept is embedded. All the benefits of analytic functionalism are preserved. But there need be no commitment to the viability of an analytic/synthetic distinction.

What of the point that some mental states can be conceptualised purely or primarily in terms of feel? A theory-theorist can allow that we have *recognitional capacities* for some of the theoretical entities characterised by the theory. (Compare the diagnostician who can recognise a cancer – immediately and without inference – in the blur of an X-ray photograph.) But it can be claimed that the concepts employed in such capacities are also partly characterised by their place in the theory – it is a *recognitional* application of a *theoretical* concept. Moreover, once someone possesses a recognitional concept, there can be nothing to stop them prising it apart from its surrounding beliefs and theories, to form a concept which is *barely* recognitional. Our hypothesis can be that this is what takes place when people say that it is conceptually possible that there should be pains with quite different causal roles.

While some or other version of theory-theory is now the dominant position in the philosophy of mind, this is not to say that there are no difficulties, and no dissenting voices. This is where we begin in chapter 2: we shall be considering different construals of the extent of our folk-psychological commitments, contrasting *realist* with *instrumentalist* accounts, and considering whether it is possible that our folk psychology might – as a substantive theory of the inner causes of behaviour – turn out to be a radically *false* theory, ripe for *elimination*. Then in chapter 4 we shall be considering a recent rival to theory-theory, the so-called *simulationist* account of our folk-psychological abilities. And in chapters 7 and 9 we consider the challenges posed for any naturalistic account of the mental (and for theory-theory in particular) by the intentionality (or 'aboutness') of our mental states, and by the phenomenal properties (or 'feel') of our experiences.

In fact one of the main messages of this book is that the theory-theory account of our common-sense psychology is a fruitful framework for considering the relations between folk and scientific psychologies, and so is to that extent, at least, a *progressive research programme* (in the sense of Lakatos, 1970).

2 Developments in psychology

We have to be severely selective in the issues in psychology which we examine in the following chapters. We have been mainly guided in our selection by two concerns: firstly, to examine aspects of psychology which might be taken as parts of the scientific backbone of the subject; and secondly, to address parts of psychology which are in a significant relation with common-sense psychological conceptions, either because they threaten to challenge them or because there is an issue about how well scientific psychology can be integrated with ordinary, pre-scientific thinking about the mind. Our general positions in relation to these two concerns are *realist* in regard to science and *Panglossian* on the relation between folk psychology and scientific psychology.

The term 'Panglossian' was coined by Stich (1983), recalling a character in Voltaire's novel *Candide* (called 'Dr Pangloss') who preached the doctrine that everything must in the end turn out for the best, since this world – having been created by a perfect God – is the best of all possible worlds. What Stich had in mind was that a modern Panglossian might *hope* that common-sense psychological conceptions would mesh quite well with what scientific psychology and cognitive science would reveal, but this was not much better than unfounded optimism in an easy and undisturbing outcome. However, we regard it as quite reasonable to hope for an integration of common-sense psychology and scientific psychology which will leave our pre-scientific psychological thinking substantially intact, although certainly enriched and revised. What chiefly supports the Panglossian prospect, in our view, is the fact that we are endowed with a highly successful theory of mind which has informative commitments to the causes underlying behaviour (a topic for chapter 2), and that this theory has developed as part of a modular capacity of the human mind which must be presumed to have been shaped by the evolutionary pressures bearing on our roles as interacting social agents and interpreters (themes for chapters 3 and 4). This falls short of a guarantee of the correctness of our native theory of mind, but it surely makes the Panglossian line worth pursuing.

We are also realists about the philosophy of science in general, and the philosophy of psychology in particular – which is not quite the same thing as being realist (in the way that we are) about *folk* psychology, since folk psychology is no science. What realists in the philosophy of science maintain is that it is the main task of scientific theories to provide a correct account of the nomological relations which genuinely exist between properties, and the causal powers of systems and entities, explaining these in terms of the generative mechanisms of the structures in virtue of which they have those powers. Anti-realists (such as van Fraassen, 1980) are apt to argue that no more can be asked of theories than that they should be empirically adequate, in the sense that they should be capable of predicting or accommodating all relevant observational data. The weakness of this anti-realist view is the assumption that there could possibly be a vantage point from which the totality of observational data is available. If it makes any sense at all to speak of such a totality, it is not something which is ever likely to be available to human investigators, who are continually finding novel ways of making relevant observations and devising new experimental techniques, without foreseeable limit. In fact, precisely one of the main advantages of realism is that it both allows and encourages an increase in the scope of observation.

Another major advantage of realism in the philosophy of science is that it gives a methodological bite to theorising, as Popper urged long ago (1956). If theories were merely instruments for prediction or the support of technology, then there would be no need to choose between different theories which served these purposes in equally good, or perhaps complementary, ways. But if we interpret theories as making claims about hidden or unobservable causal mechanisms, we will have to treat rival theories, not as different devices with their several pros and cons, but as mutually incompatible. This provides a spur to working out some way to decide between them – a spur to scientific progress, in fact. (See chapter 2 for more on different aspects of realism, and in particular for the case for realism about folk psychology.)

So much for our own general position. We now proceed to a swift survey of some very general trends in twentieth-century scientific psychology. Given the extent and range of recent scientific developments in this area, we must confine ourselves to some themes and topics which will recur in the following chapters. Some further areas of psychological research will then be surveyed, as appropriate, later in the book.

2.1 Freud and the folk

The theories of Sigmund Freud have attracted a degree of publicity which is out of all proportion to their actual influence within contemporary scientific psychology. In some respects Freud's theories have connections with themes of the present book which might have been worth pursuing.

For example, Freud clearly challenges some common-sense psychological conceptions. He is also clearly a realist both about intentional states and about his own theories. And he does make *use of* common-sense psychology, one of his major theoretical strategies being an attempt to extend ordinary styles of reason-explanation to novel applications – including behaviour previously considered to be unintentional, such as *Freudian slips*. It is also sometimes argued that some parts of Freud's theories have been absorbed by folk psychology, thus demonstrating that if folk psychology is a theory, it is not a completely fossilised or stagnating one. But this claim is questionable, since what folk psychology seems quite ready to acknowledge is the existence of unconscious beliefs and desires, rather than the distinctively Freudian idea of beliefs and desires which are *unconscious because repressed*.

The question of the methodological soundness of Freudian theory has been a matter of some controversy. Within philosophy of science it was given a special prominence by Popper (1957; 1976, ch.8), who treated Freud's theories (along with the theories of Marx and Adler) as a prime example of how theorising could go wrong by failing to satisfy the famous *Demarcation Criterion*. Genuinely scientific theories such as Einstein's theory of relativity were, according to Popper, distinguished by their falsifiability; that is, by there being tests which, if carried out, might possibly give results inconsistent with what such theories predicted, thereby refuting them. If theories could not be subjected to test in this way, then they were merely *pseudoscientific*. Popper's philosophy of science is now generally regarded as inadequate, because it fails to do justice to the role of auxiliary hypotheses and the long-term appraisal of research programmes. So the Popperian critique no longer seems so damaging. (Though see Cioffi, 1970, for an account of Freud's own defence of his theory of the neuroses which undeniably makes it appear worryingly pseudoscientific.)

We will not be engaging with Freud's ideas, however, or any issues concerning psychoanalysis in this book. Where Freudian theories do have any testable consequences they have consistently failed to be confirmed, and the overall degeneration of the Freudian programme has reached a point at which it is no longer taken seriously by psychologists who are engaged in fundamental psychological research. The tenacity with which these theories survive in areas of psychotherapy (and also in literary theory and other areas of the humanities), in increasing isolation from any research which might either justify their application or testify to their clinical effectiveness, is a matter of some concern. But we do not propose to go into this in the present work. (For discussion of the methodology and clinical effectiveness of psychoanalysis, consult Grünbaum, 1984, 1996; Erwin, 1996.)

2.2 Methodological behaviourism

We have already mentioned the arguments against *behaviourism in philosophy* (logical behaviourism). But there is also a behaviourist position in psychology. Indeed, for much of the twentieth century – under the influence of such theorists as Watson, Guthrie, Hull, Skinner, and Tolman – this was the dominant position in psychology, and it remains influential in studies of animal behaviour.

Although some theorists undoubtedly subscribed to both brands of behaviourism – methodological *and* logical – the two positions are distinguishable. A modest form of methodological behaviourism is not vulnerable to the arguments which sank logical behaviourism in philosophy. Methodological behaviourism need not deny that there are mental states and internal psychological mechanisms, it just declines to delve into what they might be – on the grounds that, being unobservable, they are not amenable to controlled scientific investigation. It proposes to treat the central nervous system as a 'black box', the contents of which are hidden from scrutiny. Rather than indulge in mere speculation about what goes on inside there, better to concentrate on what can be quantitatively measured and objectively analysed – the behaviour emitted by the organism in response to various stimuli. Stimuli and responses are undoubtedly observable, and stimuli can be controlled and varied to determine corresponding variations in response. So laws governing associations between stimuli and responses should make a respectable subject for empirical science.

We reject methodological behaviourism on two main grounds. Firstly, in terms of the philosophy of science it is a typically positivistic, anti-realist stance, confining the aims of inquiry to lawlike generalisations concerning what is – on a narrow view – taken to be observable. This we regard as unwarranted pessimism about the growth of scientific knowledge. Often scientific theory has been at its most progressive precisely when postulating previously unobserved entities and mechanisms. A self-denying programme which restricts us to studying associations between stimuli and responses is, in the long term, only an obstacle to progress. Secondly, there is a problem relating to psychological theory, and particularly to learning and cognitive development. Treating the central nervous system as a black box puts investigators seriously at risk of neglecting the extent to which cognitive functions and developmental profiles depend upon the internal structure of a complex system which is the product of evolutionary design. In so far as behaviourism neglects this structure by adopting an empiricist, associationist view of learning, we can leave the evidence against it to be presented in chapter 3, where we make out the case for the principles of *modularity* and *nativism*. The message, in brief, is that a significant part of our psychological capacities *mature without learning*.

Behaviourism would never have achieved the influence it did without having some paradigmatic experimental achievements to display, of course. Examples of *Pavlovian* or *classical conditioning* are well known: an animal responds to an *unconditioned stimulus* (such as the sight of food) with an *unconditioned response* (such as salivating); it is then trained to associate a *conditioned stimulus* – some other, initially neutral stimulus (such as a bell ringing) – with the unconditioned stimulus (sight of food); until eventually the conditioned stimulus (the bell) produces a *conditioned response* (such as salivating – though conditioned responses need not be identical with unconditioned responses). Behaviourists could also point to replicable instances of *Thorndikian* or *instrumental learning* in support of their research strategy. In one of the earliest of these experiments (Thorndike, 1898), hungry cats were placed inside a box with a grille on one side which afforded a view of some food. A door in the grille could be opened by pulling on a looped string within the box – a trick which the cat has to learn in order to get the food. On repeated trials, Thorndike found that cats did learn this trick, but on a trial-and-error basis and only gradually, with the number of fruitless attempts to get at the food steadily decreasing.

Such results prompted Thorndike to formulate the *law of effect*, according to which responses become more likely to recur if followed by a rewarding outcome, less likely if followed by no reward or discomfort. This law, in various formulations (such as Hull's *law of primary reinforcement* or Skinner's *principle of operant conditioning*), is the basic idea behind behaviourist learning theory. But although it certainly lent itself to attempts at experimental demonstration and quantitative measurement, behaviourist learning theory exhibited little in the way of genuine theoretical progress. It remained unclear how instrumental learning could be transferred, from methods of training animals to perform somewhat unnatural tricks in the laboratory, to yield an understanding of what controlled behaviour in natural environments. Above all, much of behaviour (human or non-human) seemed just too complex to be regarded as *a response*, or even a series of responses. Even a one-time behaviourist like Lashley questioned behaviourism's capacity to give an account of behaviour involving complex serial order, such as piano-playing (Lashley, 1951).

A very important kind of behaviour in which complex serial order is salient, of course, is linguistic behaviour. Chomsky's hostile review (1959) of Skinner's *Verbal Behaviour* (1957) was extremely influential. For it revealed just how inadequate are methodological behaviourism, and its learning-by-reinforcement, to the task of giving any account of the actual and potential verbal behaviour of an ordinary native speaker. On any view, it seemed clear that linguistic production and linguistic comprehension requires the presence of a rich knowledge-base in the ordinary human speaker.

Convinced of the degenerating trend of the behaviourist research programme, theorists increasingly turned towards hypotheses about what cognitive systems were at work inside the 'black box'. They have been rewarded by the sort of *expansion of evidence* about internal structure which, as we mentioned above, is one of the advantages of a realist approach to scientific investigation. Evidence concerning psychological mechanisms has now come to encompass such diverse sources as: developmental studies; population studies and their statistical analysis; the data concerning cognitive dissociations in brain-damaged patients; data from neural imaging; and many different sorts of experiments designed to test hypotheses about internal processing structures, by analysing effects on dependent variables. Examples of each of these sorts of evidence will be found in the chapters which follow (particularly in chapters 3–5).

2.3 The cognitive paradigm and functional analysis

The broad movement which superseded behaviourism, and which has, to date, proved far more theoretically progressive, is *cognitivism*. Cognitive psychology treats human brains and the brains of other intelligent organisms – as, at bottom, information-processing systems. It must be admitted that the emphasis on cognition in modern psychology has tended by comparison to leave aspects of psychology in the category of *desire* somewhat in the shade. We do actually offer a tentative suggestion as to how desire, conceptualised according to folk-psychological theory, may fit in with a modular cognitive architecture in chapter 3 (section 5.3). Whether this integrative effort is supported by future research remains to be seen. What is clear is that discoveries in cognitive psychology already constitute a fundamental part of scientific psychology, and will surely continue to do so in the future.

Yet again the word 'function' appears, though functional analysis in cognitive psychology is not the same thing as functionalism in the philosophy of mind. In cognitive psychology the object of the exercise is to map the functional organisation of cognition into its various systems – such as perception, memory, practical reasoning, motor control, and so on – and then to decompose information-processing within those systems into further, component tasks. Functional analysis of this sort is often represented by means of a 'boxological' diagram, or flow-chart, in which the various systems or sub-systems are shown as boxes, with arrows from box to box depicting the flow of information. We produce, or reproduce, a few such diagrams in this book (see figures 3.3, 4.1, 9.3 and 9.4). It might be complained of this style of boxological representation that, if not completely black, these are at least *dark* boxes within the overall container of the mind, in that we may not know much about how *their* innards work. This is true – but it is no objection to the project of functional analysis that there is still plenty more work to be done! Dennett (1978f) has likened this style of functional analysis to placing lots of little homunculi in the cognitive system, and then even more 'stupid' homunculi within the homunculi, and so on. The ultimate objective of the analysis is to decompose the processing into completely trivial tasks.

It is tempting to suppose that it was the advent of the computer which made modern cognitive psychology possible. This might be offered as some excuse for the limitations of behaviourism, in so far as this essential tool for investigating what intervenes between stimulus and response was not available until the later decades of the century. But despite the invaluable aid supplied by computer modelling, this is at best a half-truth. Thus Miller, in one of the most influential papers in cognitive psychology (1956), proposed the thesis that there is a severe restriction on human information processing, in that about seven or so items of information (7 ± 2) are the maximum that we can handle either in short-term recall or simultaneous perceptual judgements. Computer modelling would be of little help in establishing this feature of human information processing (which had, indeed, been partially anticipated by Wundt – 1912, ch.1). There have been many other test results which vindicate the cognitivist approach by relating human performance to an assessment of the processing task involved; for example, relating the transformations involved in production or comprehension of speech, according to grammatical theory, to the ease, accuracy, or speed with which subjects perform (see Bever, 1988, for references to several such studies).

So psychology has taken a cognitive turn, and there is very general agreement that it was a turn for the better. The result has led to fertile interconnections between cognitive psychology itself, research in computer science and artificial intelligence, neurophysiology, developmental psychology (as evidenced in relation to mind-reading in chapter 4), and evolutionary psychology (see chapter 5 for the example of *cheater-detection*). But within cognitivism there is a dispute between so-called *classical* and *connectionist* cognitive architectures.

2.4 Cognition as computation

According to the classical, or symbol-manipulation, view of cognition, the mind *is* a computer – or better (to do justice to modularity: see chapter 3), a system of inter-linked computers. Apart from the availability of computers as devices for modelling natural cognition and as an analogy for infor-mation-processing in the wild, there are a number of general consider-ations in favour of supposing that the mind processes information by operating on symbolic representations according to processing rules, in much the way that computers do when running programmes.

One sort of consideration concerns the processing task which perceptual systems must somehow accomplish. The role of these systems in cognition is to provide us with information about the environment. But the actual input they receive is information which derives immediately from changes in the transducers in our sensory organs. They must, therefore, somehow recover information about the environmental causes of these changes. How is that to be done? One answer which has been pursued within the cognitive paradigm is that these systems work by generating hypotheses about external causes of internal representations. Cognitive science can investigate this processing by first providing a functional decomposition of the processing task, and then working out algorithms which would yield the desired output. Perhaps this consideration in favour of the computa-tional view is no longer as compelling as it once seemed. *We* could not think of any other way in which the processing task could be accom-plished, but perhaps Mother Nature could. What is more, there is now a known (or so it seems) alternative to rule-governed manipulation of inter-nal representations in the form of connectionist networks. But even if information processing does not *have* to be done by means of symbol manipulation, the theory that it does operate in this way can claim such a considerable degree of empirical success in modelling perception and cognition that nobody would lightly abandon it (see, for example: Newell and Simon, 1972; Simon, 1979, 1989; Marr, 1982; Newell, 1990).

Another consideration in favour of a computational approach to cog-nition derives from Chomsky's seminal part in the cognitivist revolution. Chomsky maintains that both production and comprehension of utteran-ces (linguistic *performance*) depend upon the speaker's – and hearer's – *competence*; and that this competence consists in a tacit knowledge of the grammatical principles of the speaker's native language. So Chomsky is committed to linguistic processing on internal representations which is governed by these grammatical principles. And, as mentioned above, a body of empirical evidence does appear to show that Chomsky is right, by attesting to the psychological reality of this sort of processing (Bever, 1988; Bever and McElree, 1988; MacDonald, 1989).

Much the most vociferous advocate of classical computationalism, how-ever, has been Fodor, who has consistently argued, not only that cognition consists in computation over symbolic representations, but also that it requires an innate symbolic medium or *language of thought* (generally referred to as 'LoT', or 'Mentalese'). One of his early arguments for Mentalese was that it is required for the acquisition of any new word in a natural language, since in order to grasp a term one has to understand what it applies to, and one can only do that by means of a hypothesis which expresses an equivalence between the newly acquired term and a concept in some other medium – a medium which must precede acquisition of natural language concepts (Fodor, 1975). Few have found this particular argument convincing. But the conclusion might be true, for all that. Fodor has since offered arguments for computationalism combined with Mentalese which draw on quite general, and apparently *combinatorial*, features of thought and inference (Fodor, 1987; Fodor and Pylyshyn, 1988). In chapter 8 we will be considering the case for a language of thought and also exploring the extent to which natural language representations might be capable of serving some of the functions which computationalists have assigned to Mentalese.

In chapter 8 we also debate whether connectionism should be taken as a serious – or, as some maintain, superior – rival to the computational model of mind. Here we limit ourselves to some introductory remarks on how connectionism differs from the classical computational approach.

2.5 Connectionism and neural networks

One sometimes hears it objected, against the computational view, that brains do not look much like computers. This is a rather naive objection. There is no reason to expect computers fashioned by nature to be built of the same materials or to resemble in any superficial way the computers made by human beings. However, it is undeniably true that at the level of neurons, and their axons and dendrites, the structure of the brain does resemble a network with nodes and interconnections.

As early as the 1940s and 1950s the perceived similarity of the brain to a network inspired a few researchers to develop information-processing networks especially for the purposes of pattern recognition (McCulloch and Pitts, 1943; Pitts and McCulloch, 1947; Rosenblatt, 1958, 1962; Selfridge and Neisser, 1960). However, for some years work on processing networks was sidelined, partly by the success of the classical computational paradigm and partly by limitations of the early network models (as revealed in Minsky and Papert, 1969).

These limitations have since been overcome, and in the wake of Rumelhart and McClelland's work on parallel distributed processing (1986) there has been an upsurge of interest in connectionist modelling. The limitations of the early network models resulted mainly from their having only two

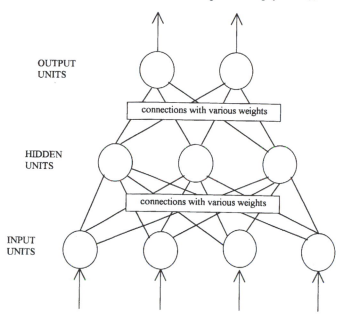

OUTPUT
UNITS

connections with various weights

HIDDEN
UNITS

connections with various weights

INPUT
UNITS

Figure 1.1 A simple three-layered network

layers of processing units ('neurons'). In principle, one can have as many layers in a network as desired, inserting *hidden units* between the input and output layers. But in order to get a multi-layered network to converge on anything like the reliable discharge of a cognitive function, appropriate training procedures or learning rules had to be available. It was the discovery of algorithms for modifying the set of weights and biases within multi-layered networks under training which has made recent progress possible. An illustration in terms of a simple, three-layered, feed-forward network (see figure 1.1) may help to make this comprehensible.

The network is feed-forward in that processing goes from input units through hidden units to output units, with no internal looping (a complication which could be added). The connections between units are assigned various weights, and there will usually also be some numerical bias assigned to each hidden unit and output unit. It may not matter very much what initial values are assigned to weights and biases before training up the network on some set of inputs and desired outputs. The important thing about the training process is that there should be a systematic way of modifying the set of weights and biases within the network, in response to discrepancies between the actual output and the desired output (see Bechtel and Abrahamsen, 1991, ch.3, for more information about the learning rules used to train up networks). After a number of trials on a given set of inputs and a series of modifications of the connection weights, the network *may* settle down and converge on a set of weights and biases which gives outputs reliably close to the desired values. (But it should be noted that this may require a very long run of trials, and it is entirely possible that the network will never converge on a successful set of weights and biases at all.) The creation of various connectionist learning-algorithms may thus be seen as attempts to model *learning* as a natural process, providing, in fact, a sort of low-level implementation of the behaviourist *law of effect*.

One of the chief attractions of the connectionist approach is that *we* do not need to work out in detail how a particular cognitive function is to be discharged before attempting to model it. For the algorithms used in connectionist modelling are not algorithms for solving the task being modelled, but algorithms of back-propagation, for modifying the processing connectivities in the light of output error. This spares us a difficult and sometimes intractable task of working out how a particular function could be discharged; for example, connectionist networks have been more successful at pattern-recognition than any programs specifically written to recognise patterns. It may also have the advantage of preventing us from imposing explicit cognitive structures on implicit, natural cognitive systems.

Above all, the chief difference between connectionist modelling and the classical computational approach is that there are no symbolic representations within the network. Rather, representation is *distributed* across the network, in such a way that the whole system can be said to be representing the content *the cat is on the mat*, say, while no particular *parts* of the network represent that content. Most networks operate by *superpositional storage*, in fact, so that a wide range of different items of information may be stored in one and the same set of weights and biases. This gives rise to further features of connectionist networks which many people find attractive. For example, connectionist networks (like many human cognitive systems) display *graceful degradation* when damaged – disabling a single node in a trained-up network may reduce the efficiency of its processing somewhat, but is unlikely to prevent it from functioning. In contrast, blocking a particular stage in the processing of a classical computer is likely to make the whole system crash, and removing any given symbolic structure from a data store will delete the corresponding item of information. Whether these features really do provide reasons for preferring connectionist modelling to the symbolic/computational approach is a topic for discussion in chapter 8.

3 Conclusion

The take-home message of this introductory chapter is that in the background to our discussions throughout the remaining chapters (mostly taken for granted, but also sometimes challenged or explicitly discussed) will be a combination of theory-theory with token-identity theory in the philosophy of mind, and cognitivism combined with information-processing models (classical or connectionist) in scientific psychology. In chapter 2 we will begin the real work of the book, where we start by considering the arguments for realism about folk psychology, and examining the threat of eliminativism.

SELECTED READING

For further background on dualism, behaviourism, functionalism and identity theory in the philosophy of mind, see: Carruthers, 1986; Smith and Jones, 1986; Churchland, 1988; Rey, 1997.

For texts which provide numerous examples of cognitive science at work: Luger, 1994; Gleitman and Liberman, 1995; Kosslyn and Osherson, 1995; Smith and Osherson, 1995; Sternberg and Scarborough, 1995.

For a lively discussion of theoretical issues in cognitive science and connectionism: Clark, 1989.

2   Folk-psychological commitments

How are folk psychology and scientific psychology related? Are they complementary, or in competition? To what extent do they operate at the same explanatory level? Should scientific psychology assume the basic ontology and some, at least, of the categories recognised by folk psychology? Or should we say that in psychology, as elsewhere, science has little to learn from common sense, and so there is no reason why 'a serious empirical psychologist should care what the ordinary concept of belief is any more than a serious physicist should care what the ordinary concept of force is' (Cummins, 1991)? The present chapter begins to address these questions.

1 Realisms and anti-realisms

Before we can determine what, if anything, scientific psychology should take from the folk, we must have some idea of what there is to take. This is a matter of considerable dispute in the philosophy of mind. Specifically, it is a dispute between *realists* about folk psychology and their opponents. The realists (*of intention* – see below) think that there is more to take, because they believe that in explaining and predicting people's actions and reactions on the basis of their intentional states (beliefs, desires, hopes, fears, and the like) we are committed *both* to there *being* such things as intentional states (as *types* or *kinds* – we return to this point later) *and* to these states having a *causal effect*. Opponents of this sort of folk-psychological realism come in various forms, but are all at least united in rejecting the claim that folk psychology commits us to the existence of causally efficacious intentional state-types.

Many different forms and varieties of both realism and anti-realism can be distinguished; but one of these is fundamental – this is the distinction between the realistic *commitments* of a body of belief (*realism of intention*), and the *truth* of those commitments (*realism of fact*). It is one thing to say that the folk are committed to the existence of causally effective mental state-types, or that the folk intend to characterise the real causal processes underlying behaviour; and it is quite another thing to say that those commitments are correct. Note that, as we are understanding these positions, realism of fact entails realism of intention – the folk could not be *correct* in their characterisations of the causal processes underlying behaviour unless they also *believed in* the existence of such processes. But one could endorse realism of intention about folk psychology while rejecting realism of fact, hence becoming *eliminativist* about folk-psychological categories.

Over the next two sections of this chapter we shall be concerned to argue the case in favour of folk-psychological realism *of intention*. Then in section 4 we shall turn to the issue of eliminativism, taking a preliminary look at the strength of the case in support of folk-psychological realism *of fact* – 'preliminary', because the question of the likely truth of our folk-psychological commitments will turn ultimately on the prospects for success of an intentionalist scientific psychology, and on the extent to which that psychology will endorse and validate the commitments of the folk. (These will be topics to which we shall return throughout this book.) Finally, in section 5, we return to the issue of realism of intention once again, considering the extent to which folk and scientific psychologies are engaged in the same *kind* of enterprise.

We should also declare that we adopt a realist (*of intention*) position about scientific theorising in general, on the grounds (a) that realism is the natural ontological attitude, (b) that it is methodologically more progressive because it sharpens the competitive conflict between theories, and (c) because it makes better sense of the role of experimental intervention in science (Hacking, 1983). But obviously we cannot just borrow arguments for scientific realism and apply them to folk psychology. Maybe as scientific investigators we ought to be as realist as we can be. But we cannot assume that *folk* psychology will conform to desirable scientific methodology.

In fact, it is important to appreciate that there is both a *normative* and a *descriptive* issue about realism. In adopting scientific realism, we stress that realistically interpretable scientific theories are possible, and where possible are methodologically preferable to other theories, particularly in relation to the progress of scientific knowledge. But that of course allows that other types of theory may also exist, and what those theories are like is a descriptive issue. Rather than telling us about underlying causal mechanisms or microstructural constitution (occupations favoured by the realist), such theories may just be devices which enable us to work something out or to solve a specific kind of problem.

For example, Ptolemy's astronomical theory, which attempted to predict and retrodict the movements of the heavens from a complex system of deferents and epicycles, was originally intended by him in exactly this spirit – to *save the phenomena*, with no commitment to the reality of the motions involved. Not all astronomers stuck to this modest and non-committal position. Many combined the representation of the sun, moon and planets as if circling round deferents which were circling round the Earth, with the idea that the Earth really was stationary and located at the very centre of the cosmos. That theoretical package was certainly refuted. But it remained possible to treat the apparatus of deferents and epicycles as merely a calculating device, without any pretensions to capture the way the universe is structured or what forces are at work. Clearly, while such an *instrumentalist* theory can be superseded, it cannot strictly speaking be refuted, any more than the abacus can be refuted by the pocket calculator.

By contrast, realists have more to be wrong about. They can be wrong, not only in their predictions concerning whatever phenomena are under consideration, but also about how those phenomena are produced. For this reason realism concerning folk psychology seems to leave room for a genuine challenge from eliminative materialism – folk psychology may turn out to be a false theory, and it may turn out that there are no such genuine kinds as *belief* and *desire*. But equally, instrumentalism concerning folk psychology may be vulnerable to a different sort of pressure from scientific psychology. For if the latter has to take some of its terms and principles from the folk (at least initially), and if science should assume realism on methodological grounds, then scientific psychology may well come to *enrich* the theoretical commitments of the folk. So we need to ask: to what extent are users of common-sense psychology engaged in a practice which has realist commitments?

2 Two varieties of anti-realism

Anti-realism (of intention) about folk psychology has been a popular view in the philosophy of mind, and has come in too many forms to survey exhaustively here. We will, however, indicate the ways in which we disagree with the positions of two influential philosophers, Davidson and Dennett. According to Davidson, folk psychology is not so much a theory as an interpretative schema which allows us to devise mini-theories of the psychological states of particular people, who are the targets of interpretation. According to Dennett, folk-psychological practice is a matter of adopting a certain kind of stance – *the intentional stance* – in order to predict the behaviour of other people. It is striking how these two approaches tend to concentrate on different folk-psychological tasks: interpretation and explanation after the act in Davidson's case, and expectation and prediction of coming conduct in Dennett's. Somehow folk psychology itself has to handle questions about why people did what they have done *and* about what they are going to do next.

2.1 Davidson

In a number of articles Davidson has insisted on the *anomalism of the mental* (see especially: 1970, 1974), by which he means that there can be no genuinely law-like generalisations framed in our ordinary psychological vocabulary. His main reason for thinking this, is that in interpreting the behaviour of others we attempt to make the best sense we can of them as rational agents, and that the best interpretation is therefore the one which best fits their behaviour subject to the normative constraints of rationality. Norms of rationality therefore play a constitutive role in determining which intentional states are to be attributed to other agents: what people believe and desire is just what the best normatively constrained interpretations of those people *say* that they believe and desire. The crucial point is that rationality plays a double role – not only do we as folk psychologists suppose that people will do what it is rational for them to do, given certain beliefs and desires, but what beliefs and desires they have is given by the rational interpretation of what they do.

Davidson is also a token-physicalist, however; and so in one (very weak) sense he endorses a form of realism. Davidson's view is that each particular (or 'token') belief or desire possessed by an individual thinker will be (will be identical to, or none other than) some particular state of their brain. So each token mental state or event will be a real physical state or event. And Davidson secures a causal role for the mental by maintaining that it will be these token brain-states which causally determine the person's behaviour. But for Davidson there is no *more* reality to the mental state *types* (for example, *belief* as opposed to *desire*, or *the belief that P* as opposed to *the belief that Q*) other than that they are involved in our interpretations of behaviour in the light of our normative principles.

On Davidson's view a good theory of interpretation must maximise agreement between interpreter and interpretee, and we must even 'take it as given that *most* beliefs are correct' (1975). Why? The thought is that in order to do so much as identify the subject matter of someone's beliefs we must attribute to them 'endless true beliefs about the subject matter'. Attributing false beliefs to an interpretee about some object undermines the identification of that object as the subject of their thoughts. For example, someone may have remarked on how blue the water of the Pacific is, leading us to attribute to them the belief that the water of the Pacific is blue. But if it turns out that they think the Pacific can be seen from the beaches of Spain, we will start to doubt whether that attribution was correct.

There must be something wrong with the Davidsonian view, however, because our overall project, as folk psychologists, is not just one of interpretation. We are just as much interested in generating predictions concerning people's likely behaviour, and in forming expectations as to what they may think or feel in various circumstances. The point here is not that, in laying so much emphasis on retrospective interpretation, Davidson's account makes folk psychology predictively useless. It is rather that it is a mistake to *prioritise* interpretation over prediction. One way in which this can be seen, is that we can surely have confidence in a great many attributions to someone of belief and desire, in advance of having observed any of their behaviour to form a target of interpretation. This is because our folk psychology provides us with many principles for ascribing mental states to others (such as: 'what people see, they generally believe'), which do not depend upon observations of behaviour.

Moreover, the constitutive norms of rationality which Davidson posits are somewhat mysterious. In attributing beliefs to others, is it agreement with our *beliefs* which should be maximised, or with *truth*? Of course, since we take our own beliefs to be true, we have no way of trying to maximise the latter without trying to maximise the former. But we do realise that there may be some divergence between our beliefs and the truth. So if we have some false beliefs about some objects, then *our* best interpretation may very well be one which misidentifies the subject matter of some better informed interpretee's thoughts. Besides, we can interpret and explain the actions of other people who hold theories and world-views which force us to attribute to them hosts of false beliefs. On our view Davidson makes the mistake of giving too central a place to the heuristics of folk psychology. What is right about his interpretationalism is a reflection of the extent to which *simulation* has a role to play in folk psychology, particularly in relation to inference (see chapters 4 and 5 for explanation of this point).

In addition, Davidson faces notorious problems in allowing for even so much as the possibility of irrational action. Since the norms of rationality are supposed to be constitutive of the possession of beliefs and desires at all, it is difficult to see how people could ever be credited with intentions which conflict with their goals. But we folk psychologists believe that this is a familiar (and all too depressing) fact of daily life. Consider, for example, the case of the man who knows that petrol is highly inflammable, and who knows that lighted matches ignite, but who nevertheless strikes a match over the mouth of his petrol tank in order to see whether or not it is empty – with disastrous results. In order to explain such cases Davidson is forced to say that they manifest two distinct *systems* of belief and desire within the one individual, each of which conforms to the norms of rationality, but which fail to interact (1982a). Now we do not deny that there may be many different parts and levels to human cognition – indeed we will make frequent use of this idea ourselves. But we do think it highly implausible that we should need to postulate divided persons or minds in order to explain irrationality. Rather, in many cases a belief can simply *slip our minds* – remaining real, but failing in the particular circumstances to become active in reasoning.

2.2 Dennett

Dennett's position (developed in his 1971, 1981, 1987, 1988a, 1991b) is a difficult one to grasp. Its front end appears unashamedly *instrumentalist*, but he adds a rider which appears to cancel out the anti-realism of his picture. We think his position is unstable, and that he really cannot have it both ways.

Presenting the boldly instrumentalist front end first, Dennett (1981) declares: '*What it is* to be a true believer is to be an *intentional system*, a system whose behaviour is reliably and voluminously predicted via the intentional strategy.' He appears to be maintaining that ascription of beliefs, desires, and so on, is produced by the adoption of a particular predictive/explanatory stance – a stance justified by nothing other than its predictive success and practical utility. He introduces the *intentional stance* by contrasting it with two others – the *physical stance* and the *design stance*. The physical strategy uses knowledge of laws of physics (and/or chemistry), combined with details of physical states and constitution, to predict outcomes. This may seem the most fundamental and scientifically well-founded approach. But it will rarely be the most convenient, and often is not feasible when trying to cope with a system of any degree of complexity. The *design strategy* predicts that something will behave *as it was designed to behave*. This strategy is obviously useful in relation to artefacts like motor cars, computers, and alarm clocks; and also to functional biological systems like hearts, livers, pistils, and stamens, which have acquired a design through evolution.

The *intentional stance* is a further option (and one might wonder why there should be just three):

Here is how it works: first you decide to treat the object whose behaviour is to be predicted as a rational agent; then you figure out what beliefs the agent ought to have, given its place in the world and its purpose. Then you figure out what desires it ought to have, on the same considerations, and finally you predict that this rational agent will act to further its goals in the light of its beliefs. (Dennett, 1981, p.57)

We can adopt the intentional stance very widely, even when we do not seriously suppose that we are dealing with a rational agent. For example, plants move their leaves, tracking the motion of the sun across the sky (*phototropic* behaviour). We can figure out the orientation of a plant's leaves several hours hence by supposing that it *wants* to have its leaves facing the sun and *believes* that the sun is wherever in the sky it in fact is. As a predictive strategy this has quite a lot to be said in its favour. In particular, it is marvellously economical. By contrast, the attempt to calculate the position of the plant's leaves by means of basic physics and chemistry, combined with information about the physico-chemical composition of the plant's cells, the intensity of photon bombardment from various angles, and so on, would be a hopelessly complicated task.

On the one hand, Dennett wants to maintain that there are 'true believers' (for example, people) *in contrast with* cases where we resort to useful metaphors and other non-serious attributions of intentional states (as with the phototropic behaviour of plants). On the other hand, he thinks that the difference between *true* believers and others is a matter of degree – it is just a difference in the volume and the detail of the predictions warranted by application of the intentional strategy. So it seems that there is a straightforward contrast between Dennett's position and ours. Dennett thinks that people have intentional states because (that is, *in so far as*) the intentional strategy works as a predictor of their behaviour. We think that the intentional strategy works as a way of predicting people's behaviour *because* (this is a causal-explanatory 'because') people have intentional states.

Yet Dennett also adds a pro-realist rider (1987, pp.29–35). The *true* believers are the systems whose behaviour is predicted both reliably, voluminously and *variously* – in contrast to things like thermostats and plants, whose behaviour is reliably predicted from the vantage of the intentional stance, but with little volume or variation. Now such a true believer must in fact be connected with its environment in a delicate and intricate manner, and in particular its behaviour must be regulated by *internal states* which are sensitive to the environment in which the intentional system is embedded. These internal states we treat as *representations*. So far as we can see, this concedes that true believers are the ones which *actually have beliefs*. Once the realist rider is added, Dennett's position becomes rather like Ptolemy's astronomy *plus* the claim that we would not be successful in 'saving the phenomena' unless planets really were circling on epicycles which were circling on deferents which were circling around the Earth. But we do not want to get bogged down in interpreting interpretationalists and other anti- or quasi-realists. (For more on Dennett's position see Dahlbom, 1993; especially the papers by

Haugeland, and Fodor and Lepore.) We must move on to making a positive case for realism about folk psychology.

3 The case for realism about folk psychology

It is not really enough to make out just a *general* case for some sort of realism (of intention) with respect to folk psychology. If you think, as we do, that folk psychology is built on a core theory, then what is really wanted is detailed information about its principles and commitments. One suggestion would be to follow Lewis (1966, 1970) in listing all the truisms of folk psychology (it seems likely that this list would be a long one) and saying that *that* then constitutes our folk-theory of the mind. Unfortunately, it is doubtful whether a list of truisms really constitutes a theory (Botterill, 1996); and it seems plausible that any such folksy list would be underpinned by a much smaller set of generative principles. However, providing these principles in the form of items of general propositional knowledge is likely to prove no easy task, since they may well be largely *implicit* rather than *explicit*. We return to this point in chapter 4.

It might seem, however, that the realist position is hopeless anyway, and that folk psychology is just obviously a very *shallow* way of thinking about human conduct and motivation. After all, there is no commitment in folk psychology to the brain being importantly involved in cognitive functions. Indeed, folk psychology is not even committed to people having brains at all! Notoriously, Aristotle and some of his Greek contemporaries supposed the brain to be an organ whose main function is to cool the blood. So far as we know, this made no difference to their interpretations and expectations of other people's conduct in the ordinary affairs of life. Nowadays bits of scientific knowledge are sufficiently well and widely communicated that most educated adults know something about the way in which regions in the brain are involved in various mental capacities. But this general knowledge also has very little impact on everyday interaction with other people – apart from making us more solicitous when someone has had a bang on the head, and perhaps more worried about whether there should be any such sport as boxing.

It is true that folk psychology is entirely silent about neural implementation. But it does have quite a lot to say about the way in which the mind *functions*. With the aid of just a little reflection on our folk-psychological practices we can tease out several significant implications, particularly concerning categorisation, causal activity, and conceptualisation. But before we go on to detail those, we will set out what we take to be a persuasive general reason for thinking that folk psychology is committed to a particular sort of inner organisation.

3.1 The Turing test

Turing (1950) proposed that instead of asking whether a computer could think, we should see if we could program a machine in such a way that its responses would fool interrogators into thinking they were dealing with a man or woman. This test he dubbed 'the Imitation Game'. Since then, several programs have been developed which have made a pretty good stab at passing the Turing test, at least with respect to question-and-answer sessions which are not too free-wheeling (for example, Weizenbaum's ELIZA, Winograd's SHRDLU, Colby's PARRY; Schank and Abelson, 1977: references to such attempted 'simulations of human thought' are legion). However, in spite of the ingenuity of the programmers, our in-tuitive reaction is surely that posing the Turing test really does change the question, because in order to engage in anything like human thinking it is not sufficient to *imitate the responses* a human being would make – one also needs to imitate the processes by which such responses are produced.

Thus, for example, using a lot of computing power to sort through a vast database of statistically sampled responses would be a sort of cheating, even if the responses did seem fairly natural. And as soon as we learn that a sophisticated chess-playing computer actually operates on a *brute-force algorithm*, searching through thousands upon thousands of feeble vari-ations which a human chess master would never bother to think about, we realise that attributions of intentional states such as 'wanting to avoid weakening its pawn-structure', 'trying to keep its king safe', 'intending to exploit the weakness on the light squares', and so on, cannot be true in the way that they might be true of a human player who had chosen the same moves.

In order to demonstrate this sort of point, Copeland (1993) constructs the following imaginary example of a computer which passes the Turing test by pattern-matching. There are a finite number of possible English conversations consisting of less than, say, 10,000 sentences, each of which consists of less than 200 words. Then imagine a computer in which all of these conversations are listed in a vast look-up table. The computer operates by matching a given input against its lists, and selecting one possible continuation at random. Call this computer (which may well be dependent upon computer technology far in advance of ours!) *Superparry*. It seems plain that Superparry would pass the Turing test in connection with any experimenter who did not actually know or suspect the details of its program. For we may suppose that no normal human conversation consists of more than 10,000 sentences, and that no normal human sen-tence consists of more than 200 words. But it is plain, is it not, that we would withhold mentality from Superparry as soon as we *did* learn that it operates by pattern-matching? We would no longer seriously suppose that Superparry *believes* what it says, or that its words are expressive of *thought*.

It is important to distinguish this example from that of the *intelligent robot*, however, if any realist conclusions are to be drawn. For if we withhold mentality from Superparry, not because it operates as a look-up table, but merely because it is a *computer*, then obviously nothing would follow about the realistic commitments of folk psychology. So, imagine that robots can be constructed which not only mimic human behaviours, but which share with us much of their inner architectures and modes of processing as well. Our view is that such a system should count as a thinker; and we believe that this intuition is shared by most of the folk.

Admittedly, many people also have the intuition that a robot could never be *phenomenally conscious*, or be subject to conscious feelings, experiences or sensations. But few would deny that a robot could ever have beliefs, perceptions, and goals. Thus the androids in science fiction stories, like the television series *Star Trek*, are standardly represented as being genuinely *thoughtful*, but as only simulating (that is, not really possessing) feelings. We shall return to the alleged mysteriousness of phenomenal consciousness in chapter 9, arguing that on this matter the folk have been misled. But for present purposes it is enough that people do not appear to be committed to the idea that genuine thought requires its possessor to have a biological constitution. In which case our point that people would withhold mentality whenever they discover that a computer operates by pattern-matching really does reveal something of their realistic commitments – only a system with the right sort of *inner organisation* can count as a thinker; or so we folk-psychologists believe.

3.2 Paralysis and other ailments

We are inclined to deny mentality where we know or suspect that inner organisation is very significantly different from the cases to which we standardly apply folk psychology (that is, human beings – although it seems very likely that many non-human animals should also have appro-priate inner organisation). If that is so, then it would seem that folk psychology must be committed to certain sorts of mental structuring, at least in functional terms. But a similar point can be made, we believe, by considering the readiness of the folk to countenance mentality in the *absence* of behaviour.

Consider someone who is paralysed, and has been so throughout his lifetime. Or consider someone with severe cerebral palsy, who has only minimal control of her movements. The folk are nevertheless quite pre-pared to entertain the idea that such people may be subjects of a rich mental life – with all of the experiences, and many of the thoughts and desires, of you or I. But there is no behaviour here to be interpreted, and there seems nothing to be gained by adopting the intentional stance towards such a person. How is this to be explained in other than the realist's terms?

(Of course it is very hard to *see* the behaviour of someone with cerebral palsy as imbued with mentality, and interacting with such a person is difficult – which is why such people face prejudice and discrimination. That is not the point. The point is that the folk are perfectly prepared to *believe* that there may well be a rich mental life behind the mask of disability.)

Davidson will have to say that the thoughts of the folk concerning the mental lives of the paralysed are *really* thoughts about how such people *could* be interpreted if they were *not* paralysed. But then such thoughts become either trivially true or covertly realist, depending upon how the antecedent of the conditional ('if he were not paralysed then he would. . .') is cashed out. They become trivial if the antecedent just means 'if he were behaving normally', for *of course* we would be attributing thoughts to him if he were! But they become covertly realist if the antecedent means 'if the physical obstacles to the expression of his beliefs and desires were re-moved', since this requires such states to be real, and to be operative – interacting with one another, at least – independently of the existence of any behavioural manifestation.

Dennett, too, will have problems with such cases. For the assumptions about optimal design and functioning which are supposed to underpin mental state attributions from the intentional stance (see the quotation given earlier) are plainly inappropriate here. And again the thoughts of the folk about the mental lives of the paralysed will have to be cashed as thoughts about the mental states we *would* attribute to them from the intentional stance if they *were* functioning normally. And again the di-lemma is that this becomes trivially true or covertly realist, in exactly the manner explained in the previous paragraph.

3.3 Inner commitments

We have argued that folk psychology is committed to certain sorts of mental structuring, or certain kinds of inner organisation. But just *what* is it committed to in the way of inner organisation?

(1) *Existence*: In the first place, folk psychology is committed to the *existence* of intentional states for people to have. This is fundamental, but it is also a hollow claim unless we say something more about what is involved. After all, the anti-realist can always agree, provided that it can be

added that this amounts to no more than the fact that there really are the appropriate patternings in people's behaviour.

(2) *Categorisation*: Secondly, and more interestingly, folk psychology is committed to the existence of a variety of *differences* between intentional-state attitudes of various kinds. Above all, folk psychology is committed to a broad difference between two major types of intentional state: belief-like states and desire-like states. Roughly speaking, the first kind are informational and *guide* conduct, while the second kind are goal-directed and *motivate* conduct. Common-sense psychology the world over recognises the difference between these two broad categories of intentional state, even though philosophers find it frustratingly difficult to articulate the difference. It is possible that scientific psychology might find no use for this broad division, but we think that it is a very good bet that it will.

(3) *Causation*: Thirdly, intentional states are causally active. Folk psychology is shot through with commitments to causal interaction, indeed. The best-known case – and also the most hotly disputed – concerns the relation between agents' actions and their reasons for so acting. The main argument for claiming that reasons are causes of actions (first presented in Davidson, 1963) is that an agent can have a reason to perform a given action, can perform that action, and yet that not be the reason for which the act gets done. So to account for the force of *because* in the standard folk-psychological explanatory schema 'X did it because X thought that . . ./wanted to. . .', we need to distinguish between a *possible* reason and the actually *operative* reason. And how can that distinction be made except in terms of the causal involvement of the intentional states which are the agent's reasons?

Suppose I agree to meet an old friend in an art gallery, for example. It may well be that there is, and that I know there is, a painting in that gallery by an artist whose work I admire; and I would like to see that painting. Getting to see that painting is undoubtedly *a reason* for me to go to the art gallery. But all the same, it may definitely be the case that when I go to the gallery I go *because* I want to meet my friend, and also that I would not have gone unless I had thought that I would meet him there. The fact that I have other attitudes which *might* make sense of my action does not suffice to make them my reason for acting unless they are causally involved in the right way. (Compare the 'Alice goes to the office' case in Ramsey *et al.*, 1990.)

This argument for a causal connection between reasons and actions has been fiercely resisted by many philosophers – particularly those in the Wittgensteinian tradition (Winch, 1958; Peters, 1958; Melden, 1961;

Kenny, 1963; and many others). Their complaints against the causal thesis, however, fail to impress us. They claim that offering reasons is a matter of providing justification for conduct. So it may be, particularly when you are offering reasons on your own behalf. But the reasons for which an agent acted may be disreputable enough to incriminate, rather than to justify. And even when agents are sincere in the justifications they offer, folk psychology is quite ready to believe they may only be *rationalisations*, and not the real reason.

Simplistic views about causation are often to be found lurking behind objections to the causal thesis. For example, it is sometimes said that beliefs and desires (agents' reasons) cannot be causes of action, because people who share the same beliefs and desires will often be found to act in different ways. This argument rests on the principle *like causes produce like effects*. But in that simple form the principle is not admissible: like causes only produce like effects *if relevant circumstances are the same*. Anti-causalists also often urge that the connection between an act and its motivation belongs 'in the logical space of reasons', alleging that reasons can be evaluatively good or bad, whereas causes just blindly cause. But this objection fails to observe the important distinction between an intentional state and its content. The content, 'Shares in this company are about to tumble' is a good reason for selling, but a particular sale will only be explained if that content is realised in a particular thought in a particular mind. Indeed, if agents capable of rational choice and deliberation are to be a causally unmysterious part of the natural order then it *must* be possible for what is in the logical space of reasons to be causally implemented.

As well as being committed to a causal connection between reasons and actions, folk psychology also takes *inference* to be a causal process (Armstrong, 1973). Ramsey *et al.* (1990) offer an example which illustrates this. On being questioned about his whereabouts the previous evening the butler testifies that he spent the night in the hotel in the village and returned to the château on the morning train. Inspector Clouseau concludes that the butler is lying. For Clouseau knows that the hotel is closed for the season and that the morning train is out of service. Now of course it is quite possible that Clouseau will realise that both these facts show the butler to be lying. But it is equally possible that only one of these beliefs will lead Clouseau to his conclusion. It is an empirical matter whether one or the other, or both, of his beliefs were engaged in his coming to believe that the butler is lying.

We can draw out some further causal commitments of folk psychology by invoking Grice's (1961) argument that there is a causal condition for *seeing*. Grice pointed out that looking in the direction of, say, a particular pillar and having a visual experience *as of a pillar* were not jointly sufficient conditions for seeing *that* pillar. For suppose there were a mirror, or some other device which reflected light, interposed between you and the first pillar, in such a way that the image of a second (similar but distinct) pillar was reflected into your eyes. Now, which pillar do you see? The answer, surely, is: the one which is causally involved in your having the visual experience – which in this case is *not* the one located in the direction of your gaze.

A similar, but more complicated, causal requirement applies to memory – more precisely to one sort of memory, namely personal recollection. Indeed, memory is worth special attention as an illustration of the relations between scientific and folk psychologies. Consider:

(a) She remembered the date of Shakespeare's death.
(b) She remembered how to pronounce it in Croatian.
(c) She remembered that long hot afternoon on the beach at Ynyslas.

As far as folk psychology is concerned these are all instances of remembering. But psychologists will want to distinguish between (a) factual memory (often called by psychologists 'semantic memory'), (b) procedural memory (abilities or skills), and (c) personal recollection (generally called by psychologists 'episodic memory'). Folk psychology is not inconsistent with these distinctions. It is just not very interested in them. As far as (c)-type memories, or recollections, are concerned the Grice-style argument goes like this: suppose she had spent *two* long hot afternoons on Ynyslas beach, and thought she was remembering one of them (five summers back, say), but her present memory experience was actually dependent upon the details of the other (six summers ago). Which day on the beach is she remembering? The answer would seem to be the day on which she had the experiences on which her present experiences are causally dependent. So if we do have any genuine memories of incidents, those memories are states which are causally related to the incidents of which they are memories.

(4) *Conceptualisation*: Fourthly – and most important of all, perhaps – intentional states have *conceptualised content*. When you think, you think that something is the case. When you hope, you hope that something will happen. Folk psychology regularly introduces content by means of an embedded sentence, or 'that-clause' (although there are other constructions). Two notable features of content, according to folk psychology, are (i) that a thinker can think in the same way of different things, and (ii) that a thinker can think about the same thing in different ways. Philosophers

have found (ii) a very interesting topic, especially in connection with names and definite descriptions. But let us consider (i) first.

Suppose that John thinks, plausibly enough, that grass is green. John also thinks that emeralds are green. Reflecting on this he concludes that both grass and emeralds are green, and that they have something in common – namely, greenness – with South African rugby jerseys, crème de menthe, and Granny Smith apples. According to the folk, John applies the same concept to all of these things. If you ask him whether any of these is red, of course he will say 'No'. And his reason will be the same in each case – that he thinks the item in question is green, and he also thinks that in general what is green cannot be red. A concept like *green* can feature in a particular thought (such as, 'Yuk, this cheese is turning green at the edges!'), but wherever it appears it has an implicit generality. In order to be thinking *green* of one thing you need to stand ready to think the same of anything else appropriately similar. So according to folk psychology concepts are linking capacities, and their application or tokening is constitutive of thoughts. (Compare Davies, 1991.)

As noted already, according to folk psychology someone can also think of the same thing in different ways. So if one has a thought about some item, it cannot be the item itself which is a constituent of the thought, but only the item-as-presented to the thinker, or the item-under-a-description. (See chapter 6 below for a much more detailed treatment of this point.)

We can sum all this up by saying that folk psychology is committed to people having intentional states, and to the claim that those intentional states are forms of intentional content in which actual or possible items are presented to a subject in various ways, and conceptualised in various ways. Moreover, there are characteristic causal connections between perception and some of these contentful states – so that, for example, a normal person is caused to acquire the belief that a room is empty, on coming into an empty room, by *seeing* it to be so. There are also – and this seems to be the very belief/desire core of folk psychology – characteristic causal connections between combinations of intentional states and actions. Thus if somebody wants to be alone and believes that the room at the end of the corridor is empty, then like enough this will cause that person to enter the room. In addition, there are characteristic causal connections between contentful intentional states themselves. Inference is a conspicuous example. You see someone going into the room at the end of the corridor. You are thereby caused to acquire the belief that this person has entered the room; and that belief will (usually) further cause you to acquire the belief that the room is no longer empty.

3.4 Varieties of realism

We have been defending realism of intention with respect to folk psychology. But what about the initial thought which we canvassed at the start of this section, concerning the *shallowness* of our folk psychology? Can what we have just been saying be reconciled with a lack of commitment to brains and their properties? Here it is important to distinguish between three different varieties of realism of intention about the mental, namely (1) *token physicalism*, (2) *compositional realism*, and (3) *nomic* (or causal) *realism*. Only (2) and (3) are committed to the reality of mental properties and mental state kinds, hence licensing the idea that mental states really do exist in the natural world as *natural kinds*. But (3) does this in a way which need not carry any commitments for the neural composition of mental state kinds. So it is (3) which we should endorse.

(1) Token physicalism has already been discussed in connection with Davidson's views in section 2 above, where we concluded that it could be classified as a weak form of realism. If each token mental state is identical with some token brain state, then mental state tokens really do exist in the natural world – for those brain states will certainly be real. But this is as far as it goes: there need be no reality to the various mental state *types*, and one could, consistently with token physicalism, deny that the world contains any psychological natural kinds.

(2) Compositional realism is perhaps the orthodox picture of what it takes to be a natural kind. Under the influence of Kripke (1972) and Putnam (1975a) we are tempted to think that what it is for a kind at the level of a 'special science' to be real is a matter of its having a common underlying structure – for example, water is real because it is H_2O. (The 'special sciences' are those which operate at a different level from, and have a more restricted range of application than, basic physics. Special sciences include chemistry, biology, psychology and economics.) But besides this being an over-simplification (for how tight does the basic similarity of constitution have to be? are gases not a real kind? and solids?), it is not the only way in which the reality of a kind can be vindicated. This is fortunate for folk-psychological realism, because folk-psychological states are not likely to be real in virtue of sharing a common composition (remember the multiple-realisation objection to type–type identity theory).

(3) Nomic realism is the sort we endorse. Kinds can be real in virtue of the fact that the terms for them mark things which are similar in their causal interactions in a law-like way. Fodor (1983) makes this point about aerodynamics and aerofoils: provided it is rigid enough, all that matters is that an aerofoil should have a certain shape, not what it is made of. The point should be obvious enough from physics, anyway (see Blackburn,

1991): the states which are nomically related may be role states, rather than realiser states. That is to say, the states which are important for the salient causal laws may be states which are distinguished from other states in terms of their functional characterisation, instead of their physico-chemical microstructure. Consider, for example, *mass* and *temperature*. Mass and temperature are nomically real all right, even though it is clear enough that both objects with the same mass and things at the same temperature *do not have to share a common microstructure*.

4 Realism and eliminativism

Realism (of intention) about folk psychology involves greater commitments and thereby also greater risks of getting things wrong than interpretationalism or instrumentalism. The methodological advantage of scientific realism is particularly connected with the *incompatibility* of theories which posit different underlying structures, causal processes, and generating mechanisms. By contrast, instrumentalism is more tolerant of the co-existence of different ways of problem-solving. Maybe my calculator enables me to work out the results more quickly than you can on your abacus. But that does not oblige you to abandon the abacus, if it serves your purposes well enough; and there may well be some circumstances (such as battery failure) when I will be quite happy to borrow a different device. But if, as we have argued, a strong form of realism about folk psychology is correct, and if – as we are going to argue in chapter 4 – folk psychology constitutes a sort of *theory*, then we have to acknowledge the possibility that folk psychology may be a *mistaken* theory.

Some people have argued *either* that folk psychology can already be seen to be an inadequate theory (Churchland, 1979, 1981) *or* that it is a good bet that folk psychology will be shown to be wrong by future developments in cognitive science and/or neuroscience (Stich, 1983, 1988; Ramsey *et al.*, 1990). Both of these claims are commonly referred to as 'eliminativism', but it is important to distinguish Churchland's 'elimination now' from Stich's less dogmatic 'elimination in prospect'. Either form of eliminativism is disturbing because it suggests that folk psychology is *radically* mistaken. What the eliminativists mean by this is not that folk psychology often makes us get things badly wrong, wildly misinterpreting each other, expecting people to do one thing and finding they do something quite other, and so on. It is not plausible that folk psychology is radically erroneous as a guide in practical affairs. Instead what is meant is that folk psychology is wrong about the sorts of internal states which lie behind our behaviour. Specifically, it is wrong in supposing that we have thoughts, wants, desires, beliefs, hopes, fears, and other intentional states. Note that only if realism (of intention) is right can folk psychology be *radically* incorrect in this sense. By contrast, there is nothing much for Dennett's intentional stance to be radically wrong *about*.

What the eliminativist proposes is sufficiently iconoclastic to seem absurd. How could it possibly be true that people do not have beliefs, fears, and hopes? Do we not know for certain in our own case that we do? Besides, is not the eliminativist view paradoxically self-refuting – daring to think the unthinkable; in particular, to *think* that there is no such thing as thought?

We reject eliminativism, but not for these considerations, which are not at all so compelling as they may seem at first. In fact they just beg the question. Suppose somebody insisted that we *know* the sun swings round the Earth through the sky because we can see it rising in the east and setting in the west. There is no doubt that when we see the sun rise and set we are observing some sort of phenomenon, a genuine change. We are observing a real process, but the question is how that process is to be interpreted. Similarly there is no doubt there are genuine differences between the internal states someone is in before thinking something and during the thought (as folk psychology might put it). To adopt a neutral vocabulary, we might say that we can be sure in our own case that we sometimes experience the changes involved in *cognitive processing*. But the fact that we are accustomed to describe such changes in the terms of folk psychology does not ensure that folk psychology correctly categorises and classifies them, any more than our lingering habit of talking about the sun 'rising' and 'setting' establishes anything about how the sun moves in relation to the Earth. Similarly, eliminativism might now seem to us to be self-defeating because it is something a few philosophers are crazy enough *to believe*. But that only shows that our conceptual resources in this area are limited by our old-fashioned theories. In time we might come to realise that there is a better way of understanding what goes on inside someone's brain when they are in the process of formulating a true hypothesis.

So that sort of argument does not knock out eliminativism. Nonetheless, we think eliminativism is mistaken. But we are more confident about this in relation to Churchland's brand of eliminativism than Stich's. We will take these in turn.

4.1 Churchland: elimination now

According to Churchland (1979, 1981), the defects of folk psychology should already be apparent to us, and we are already in a position to conclude that folk psychology is going to be replaced by a superior scientific understanding of human motivation and cognition. He claims we can judge folk psychology to be an inadequate theory – ripe for elimination and replacement by neuroscientifically informed theories – because of (1) its massive explanatory failure, (2) its record of stagnation, and (3) its isolation from and irreducibility to the growing corpus of scientific knowledge in psychology and the neurosciences. Several commentators have pointed out that these are far from convincing grounds on which to condemn folk psychology as a bad theory (Horgan and Woodward, 1985; McCauley, 1986; McGinn, 1989).

(1) Considering folk psychology's alleged explanatory (and predictive) failures first, the sorts of examples Churchland cites are folk psychology's failure to give us any grasp of how learning occurs, or of the mechanism of memory. But to raise this objection is just to forget that we are dealing with a common-sense or folk theory, which as such does not have the comprehensive and systematic concerns of scientific theorising. There are apt to be gaps in what common-sense theories explain, because there are limits to what common sense concerns itself with. But a failure *to* explain – where there is no serious attempt at explanation – is not at all the same as an explanatory failure. In the long history of folk psychology thousands of generations of children have grown up without their cognitive advances being tracked, probed and accounted for in the way that they have been by developmental psychologists in the last few decades. No doubt parents and elder siblings were too busy with other things to indulge any such curiosity in a similarly systematic way. They were missing much of interest, of course. But that only shows folk psychology does not go far enough, not that there is anything wrong with it as far as it goes.

(2) The second complaint against folk psychology – that its lack of change in essential aspects throughout recorded human history is a form of stagnation and infertility indicative of degeneration – strikes us as particularly perverse. We will accept that (while there may be degrees of cultural and historical variation – Hillard, 1997) the basic procedures for explicating and anticipating human actions and reactions through the attribution of contentful and causally efficacious internal states have remained stable for centuries. But why see this as a sign of decay and degeneracy? It seems far more reasonable to take it as a testimony to how well folk psychology has worked, at least for folk purposes. (As the old adage has it: *if it ain't broke, don't fix it.*) As to the point about infertility, this again misses the difference between folk theory and scientific theory. They have a different focus of interest. The *explananda* for scientific theories are themselves usually general, whereas folk psychology is designed for application to the conduct of particular individuals, allowing us to explore the details of their idiosyncratic attitudes, hopes and convictions. In a way, one might say that folk psychology is the most fertile of

theories, for it is re-applied countless times, with endless individual variation in each new generation.

(3) Churchland's (1979) claim that folk psychology stands in 'splendid isolation' and is not reducible to any scientific theory deserves careful consideration. It is substantially true, although the isolation is not so marked as it used to be. But does that count against folk psychology? We do not think so. As far as the isolation is concerned, there is a problem which needs to be solved – the problem of explaining how the sort of *intrinsic content* which intentional states have can be realised in naturally occurring systems. We will be grappling with this problem in chapter 7. It is a difficult problem, but there is no reason to abandon it as insoluble.

As to reducibility: why would anyone want to have it? We suppose that reduction requires the sort of type-identity which holds, for example, between the temperature of a volume of gas and the mean kinetic energy of its molecules, thus allowing an observational law at the macro-level (such as Boyle's law) to be derived from those at a lower level (in this case, statistical mechanics). But it should be realised that this sort of reduction is by no means the standard case in science. We can only obtain that sort of reduction where type-classifications at one level map tolerably smoothly onto theoretically significant type-classifications at a lower, micro-level. It just so happens that there is only one physical realisation of the difference between gases which differ in temperature, namely, a difference in molecular motion. But even in the case of temperature this neat micro-reduction only applies to a specific range of cases – not to the temperatures of solids and plasmas, in which differences in temperature are realised in different ways (see Blackburn, 1991). Usually we do not find a neat reduction, and it is not any threat to the unity of science or the ultimate sovereignty of physics that we do not. (We return to this important point in section 4 of chapter 7, in the context of our discussion of so-called 'naturalised semantics'.)

As Fodor (1974) points out, the normal situation in the special sciences is that we find autonomous law-like relations which hold *ceteris paribus*, and which are not simply reducible to (that is, *deducible from*) laws at more fundamental levels. The reason why this is so is that the special sciences deal with things grouped together as kinds which from other perspectives – and in particular in terms of their microstructural realisation – are heterogeneous. It is just not necessary to the viability of a theory that the kinds which it theorises about should correspond to classifications at a more general theoretical level. Thus there probably is not anything of neurophysiological significance which unites all and only those *who love bananas*, or all and only those *who cannot stand Wagner's music*, or all and only those *who have just realised that their current account is overdrawn*. But this lack of micro-congruity is no more bad news for folk psychology, than is the fact that money can be different sorts of stuff is for economics, or than is the fact that successful predators do not share a common and distinctive biochemistry is for zoology.

(Please do not suppose that in consequence we believe in emergent powers, or that psychology is a dimension of reality which does not supervene on physics. People sometimes take that as a consequence of irreducibility. But to do so is woolly thinking, failing to distinguish between type and token. Every *particular* event describable in psychological terms is, we presume, also an event which can be explained in terms of physics.)

4.2 Stich: elimination in prospect

We conclude that Churchland's case for 'elimination now' is weak. Stich's view cannot be dismissed in the same way. As a bet on future scientific developments it cannot be dismissed at all: we will just have to wait and see. Stich thinks that it is likely that what we will learn about the real underlying processes of cognition will show that folk-psychological categories, and in particular the category of *belief*, cannot be empirically defended.

As realists, we will have to grant that this is a possibility. A commitment to the causal efficacy of intentional states would be entirely hollow if it were consistent with any possible discoveries about internal psychological processes. So far the main concrete suggestion in this area has been that connectionism may be the correct model of cognitive processing, and that the way information is stored within connectionist networks is not consistent with those networks containing anything which could be a realisation of a belief-state (Ramsey *et al.*, 1990). But the alleged incompatibility between connectionism and folk psychology has been questioned (Clark, 1990; O'Brien, 1991; Botterill, 1994b). We return to this issue in chapter 8.

As yet we see no good reason to be so pessimistic as Stich about the prospects for a successful integration of folk psychology, scientific psychology, and neuroscience. On the contrary, we think that folk psychology works so well (admittedly, within its own limitations) that the causally efficacious intentional states with which it deals probably do approximate to the states which actually cause behaviour. Fodor (1987) puts this more boldly (as usual!), arguing that the 'extraordinary predictive power' of belief/desire psychology is an argument for taking folk psychology to be correct, at least in its major commitments.

We are in substantial agreement with Fodor's view, but a little needs to be said about assessments of predictive power. It is difficult to assess the 'predictive power' of folk psychology, since many of the reliable expectations we form about the conduct of others (including the example which Fodor cites, of arranging over the phone to meet someone at an airport) might appear to owe more to social rules and cultural order than they do to the application of folk psychology. (In this case the rule may just be: 'If someone utters the words "I will do A", then they generally do A' – nothing mentalistic is required.) Thus, when you hand over the money for your fare to the bus driver you expect to get something like the correct change back. But that expectation has little to do with any beliefs or desires you might attribute to the driver. Myriads of mundane personal interactions of this kind involve unthinking expectations to which social custom has habituated us. When we have to treat other people less superficially and make predictions on the basis of their attitudes and thoughts, our success rate may not be so spectacularly high.

To get a proper perspective on this matter one needs to appreciate that in applying any body of general theoretical knowledge, predictive success depends upon the quantity and quality of information available. Predictive ability is not likely to be good when information is inadequate or when reliance is placed on incorrect data. Living as modern humans do in vast (urbanised and industrialised) societies, individuals are repeatedly being brought into contact with strangers. There is not enough in the way of background psychological knowledge to allow folk psychology to work very well for many of these interactions. However, to a considerable extent settled social roles and practices enable us to cope with these situations, at least for a range of transactions which can be turned into social routines. (So we could add the *social-role stance* to Dennett's list of 'stances', and such a social role stance is very important to the way in which a large-scale society works.) But this does not reveal a defect in folk psychology; much less does it show that folk psychology is a false theory. All it shows is that folk psychology has its limitations, particularly in regard to the informational demands it imposes. These informational demands are, as noted above, very much less than those for the physical stance, but may still be overstretched in fleeting contacts with strangers. This does not give us any reason to think that we could not account for these strangers' actions and reactions in folk-psychological terms, if we only knew more about them and more about what they wanted, valued, and believed.

The home terrain for folk psychology consists in the purposes which it has evolved to serve, we believe (see chapter 4). Initially this would have been for purposes of both co-operation and competition between humans in the sorts of sizes of groups to be found, not nowadays, but hundreds of thousands of years ago (at least). The mind-reading basics of folk psychology needed to work well in small, tribal groups; and there is no reason to think that they do not. That makes it unlikely that its principles are radically incorrect.

But what if Stich turns out to be right? Would that mean that we should then abandon folk psychology, and agree that there are no such things as beliefs and desires? That really is more than implausible. The practical utility of folk psychology falls short of being a proof that it is actually correct. But it is a most persuasive reason for thinking that it is effectively indispensable – as Stich, too, acknowledges. So if the programmatic eliminativists turn out to be right, then the best bet about how we would react is this. We would concede that strictly speaking there are no such things as beliefs and desires, but most of the time we would not feel the need to speak strictly. On the contrary, we would need to speak loosely and roughly – so that we would become, so to speak, pragmatic instrumentalists. That may sound odd. But it is really much the same as physicists' attitudes to Newtonian mechanics. Theoretically it is false. But for most technological applications it gives results which are accurate enough, and is so much more convenient to use than relativistic theory.

5 Using folk psychology

Since we take folk psychology to be broadly correct in its major causal-functional categories, there is no reason for scientific psychology to ignore the intentional states it postulates. Scientific psychology tried to do just that during its behaviourist phase, and the results were not encouraging. We think that scientific psychologists should not be embarrassed about relying on certain aspects of the psychology of the folk.

It has been argued that folk psychology and scientific psychology are more or less unrelated, however – claiming that the latter can and should develop independently of the former; and that we need not concern ourselves about integrating folk psychology with cognitive science and neuroscience. On this view, what physicalists should assume is just an integration of *scientific* psychology with neuroscience, with folk psychology being left to the folk. This position has been defended in a number of places by Wilkes (1978, 1991a, 1991b).

One of Wilkes' main arguments is that folk psychology is quite a different *kind* of enterprise from scientific psychology, because it has diverse different purposes. For example, one needs to use folk psychology in order to persuade, cajole, threaten, warn, advise, seduce, and console others. This is certainly true, but we do not see it as a good reason for supposing that there will be no interconnections between folk psychology and scientific psychology. And in particular, it is very hard to see how folk psychology *could* serve all these purposes unless it were through having a theoretical *core* which can be used, quasi-scientifically, to generate predictions and explanations. In trying to seduce someone through words or actions, for example, one has to form *expectations* of the likely effects on the other of what one says or does; and one also has to be able to *interpret* accurately the other's initial responses to one's overtures.

Scientific theories, too, can be put to the service of all sorts of technological applications, quite apart from their pure central functions of explanation and prediction. This sort of 'technological impurity' surely is deeply built into the exercise of folk psychology, in its daily application. But that does not show that folk psychology is incorrect in many of the predictions and explanations which it yields, or in the theoretical framework which it uses to generate those predictions and explanations. On the contrary, it could hardly have served those other purposes so well for so long if it were not fairly effective in terms of prediction and explanation.

Certainly we may well find (or rather, we have already found) that in many ways folk psychology stands in need of correction. But as a starting point for scientific psychology, the human capacities recognised by folk psychology are more or less indispensable as subjects for investigation. The characteristic difference which we find between folk psychology and scientific psychology is that whereas the folk theory is geared to the minutiae of individual cases, scientific theory is interested rather in general *kinds* of process. Thus, I might be concerned whether that look on your face shows that you have recognised me as I attempt to sneak out of some disreputable haunt. What scientific psychology is interested in explaining is how our capacity for recognising faces operates in general.

Moreover, as we shall see in chapter 4, developmental psychologists have discovered a great deal, over the last two decades, about how 'theory of mind' (the basic mind-reading capacity of folk psychology) develops in children. But although the development of folk psychology (in the normal pattern, as contrasted with curious impairments and abnormalities) is the *subject* of this sort of developmental inquiry, it is notable that the developmental psychologists also have to make *use of* folk psychology in order to acquire empirical evidence. Thus the conclusion of these inquiries may be reported in the sort of general and systematic way appropriate to scientific psychology – as, for example, a conclusion about children's *meta-representational ability* at a certain age. But in order to gather the evidence for any such conclusions, developmental psychologists have to find out what individual children *believe* about the thoughts, desires and actions of others. In testing what beliefs children have about beliefs, they have to rely upon folk psychology in assessing what beliefs to attribute to their subjects. Whatever you might think about the long-term future of folk psychology, at the present time there is really no other alternative.

6 Conclusion

In this chapter we have made a start on investigating the relationships between folk psychology and scientific psychology. We have argued that folk psychology is *realist* in its commitments to inner organisation and the causal role of mental states. This opens up the possibility of elimination. But we have also argued that the prospects for a relatively smooth incorporation of folk-psychological categories into science are good – on this matter, it may well turn out that the folk have got things more-or-less right.

SELECTED READING

On the intentional stance see especially: Dennett, 1981, 1987, 1988a.

For Fodor's combination of nomological autonomy for special sciences and realism about folk psychology you might want to consult: Fodor, 1974, 1987. For further arguments for realism about folk psychology see: Davies, 1991.

Arguments for eliminativism are presented in: Churchland, 1979, ch.4, 1981; Ramsey *et al.*, 1990.

One of the first of many rebuttals of Churchland's version of eliminativism is: Horgan and Woodward, 1985.

Wilkes presents her case for the lack of connection between folk and scientific psychology in: Wilkes, 1978, 1991a, 1991b.

3 Modularity and nativism

In this chapter we consider how the human mind develops, and the general structure of its organisation. There has been a great deal of fruitful research in this area, but there is much more yet to be done. A fully detailed survey is far beyond the scope of a short book, let alone a single chapter. But one can set out and defend certain guiding principles or research programmes. We will be emphasising the importance of *nativism* and *modularity*.

We use the term 'nativism' to signify a thesis about the innateness of human cognition which does justice to the extent to which it is genetically pre-configured, while being consistent with the way in which psychological development actually proceeds. In terms of structure, we maintain that the human mind is organised into hierarchies of sub-systems, or *modules*. The chief advocate of the modularity of mind has been Fodor (1983), but our version of the modularity thesis is somewhat different from his. In one respect it is more extreme because we do not restrict the thesis of modularity to input systems, as Fodor does. But on the other hand, we think one needs to be a little more relaxed about the degree to which individual modules are isolated from the functioning of the rest of the mind.

The point of these disputes about the nature of modularity should become clearer as we go on. It ought to be stressed, however, that we think of modules as a natural kind – as a natural kind of cognitive processor, that is – and so what modules *are* is primarily a matter for empirical discovery, rather than definitional stipulation. When one hopes that articulation of a theory will latch on to the nature of a kind, theorising starts with an inevitably somewhat cloudy idea and then shapes it in response to growing empirical knowledge. For the time being, perhaps it will suffice to say that what we mean by a *module* is a causally integrated processing system with distinctive kinds of inputs and outputs – a sort of autonomous, or semi-autonomous, department of the mind.

1 Some background on empiricism and nativism

Issues of current interest concerning the extent to which human cognition is innately structured also exercised the philosophers of the scientific revolution in the seventeenth century. In one of the most influential philosophical texts written in English, *An Essay Concerning Human Understanding*, John Locke argued vigorously that there are 'no innate principles in the mind', and tried to show how all the materials of our thinking ('*ideas*', as he called them) are derived from experience (Locke, 1690). At that time Locke undoubtedly did a service to the advancement of science, since the sort of nativism advocated in his day was all too often associated with reactionary appeals to authority – 'it was of no small advantage to those who affected to be masters and teachers, to make this the principle of principles: *that principles must not be questioned*' (1690, I.iv.25).

What we want to insist on is that the merits of empiricism as an epistemological position (*epistemological empiricism*) – which is a view about how theories and knowledge claims are to be justified – should not be confused with its plausibility as a general hypothesis concerning cognitive development (*developmental empiricism*). In other words, claims to knowledge need to be defended by appeal to experience and experiment. But that does not mean that everything we know has been *learnt through* experience. On the contrary, one of the major insights of cognitive science has been the extent to which we depend upon a natural cognitive endowment, which assigns processing tasks to modular structures with quite specific and restricted domains and inputs. This makes excellent sense in evolutionary terms, as we shall see in a moment, and yet it remains difficult for us to accept about ourselves.

First, there is a natural inclination to suppose that cognition is integrated into a single system, available for the individual to survey. We are all subject to this illusion, the illusion of the 'transparent mind'. It is, indeed, a concomitant of consciousness, since as we shall be explaining in our concluding chapter, conscious mental states are surveyable and integrated in just this way. But a great deal of cognitive processing – in fact, most of it – goes on at a level beneath conscious awareness, and there is a considerable body of evidence testifying to its modular structure.

Moreover humans are, of course, intensely interested in differences between individuals. Some of our evolved special systems may themselves have the function of being sensitive to these differences. Social and economic competitiveness have also made us keen on grading slight differences in skills and intelligence. So when we think about thinking we are biased towards concentration on spectacular achievements paraded in a public arena. Yet if we consider the matter from a less partial and participatory perspective – as if we were alien scientists – we would see that all the basic cognitive capacities are shared by members of this species wherever they have spread over the planet, resulting from a common cognitive endowment (see, for example, Brown, 1991).

Whatever the merits of his arguments, Locke's *Essay* was very successful in establishing developmental empiricism as a dominant paradigm, first in philosophy and later in psychology. For this reason Chomsky's 'Cartesian linguistics' (1965, 1975, 1988) – the thesis that innate cognitive structures are required for the acquisition of grammatical competence in one's native language – has had a revolutionary impact throughout cognitive studies.

Before reviewing the central Chomskian argument, however, we ought to pause over the extent to which the developmental empiricist paradigm is rendered implausible by a more general theoretical perspective, namely that of evolution through natural selection. The essential features of the paradigm are these:

1 Human cognition is moulded in individuals through the experiential environment to which they are exposed.
2 There are only a small number of in-built mental capacities (such as selective attention, abstraction, copying, storage, retrieval, and comparison) for processing input from the environment.
3 These capacities are *general* ones, in that the *same* capacity can be applied to representations of many different kinds.

We will argue that cognitive science and developmental psychology have progressed far enough for us to judge the empiricist paradigm empirically inadequate to the facts within its own domain – mainly, facts about the development and functional organisation of cognitive processing. But there is also a serious question whether a system of such a kind – an empiricist mind – could ever have evolved in a species whose ancestors had more limited and inflexible cognitive systems.

Marvellous and intricate as evolutionary adaptation is, we need to remember that evolutionary development is constrained in terms of both its resources and its goals – it works on what it has already got (give or take the odd mutation) and what it 'designs' need not be a theoretically optimal solution. Now, it is clear that modern humans are descended from creatures with special systems for controlling behavioural responses to various kinds of environmental information. So we should expect to find that selective pressure has operated on a range of special systems in shaping human cognition, and hence that evolved special systems will structure human cognitive capacities. It is very hard indeed to understand how a big 'general-purpose computer' (which is the way in which developmental empiricists conceive of the human brain) could have developed from less powerful machines which were organised along modular lines – rather, one would expect these modular systems to have been altered, added to, and interconnected in novel ways (Barkow *et al.*, 1992). So even before looking at more direct evidence, modularity is what we should expect.

2 The case for nativism

The central argument against empiricist theories of learning is grounded in *the problem of acquisition* – also referred to as *Plato's problem* or *the poverty of the stimulus*. The problem is: how do children learn *so much, so quickly*, on the basis of *such limited and inadequate data*, if all that human children can bring to the task are general perceptual and cognitive abilities? Chomsky originally urged this argument in the case of acquisition of one's native language, but it applies with equal force to certain other domains (see chapter 4 on the development of our 'mind-reading' capacities). How forceful the argument is in any particular domain depends upon the facts – how much has to be known, how quickly the child develops a competence which requires that knowledge, and what relevant experiential input is available during the process of development.

Note that while we are committed to a general nativist research programme in psychology, we are *empiricists about our nativism*. Thus: there are grounds of coherence with general evolutionary theory for supposing that some of our psychological capacities deploy genetically inherited mechanisms; there are some cognitive domains in which the evidence for such inherited psychological mechanisms is extremely strong; but it remains to be seen what other areas of cognition depend upon genetic pre-programming. We are not denying that there is such a thing as learning from experience. One of the things to be learnt through the vicarious experience of psychological research is where we do and where we do not learn from experience!

As noted above, the Chomskian case concerning development is sometimes called 'the Poverty of the Stimulus' argument. However, that seems to us a misnomer which invites doubts about the strength of the reasoning. Are the data available to the learner really so inadequate? Have the Chomskians exaggerated the competence which is acquired? A further worry might be prompted by a parallel with speciation and environmental influences. A favourite argument of critics of evolutionary theory has been that environmental factors are neither strong nor specific enough to shape evolutionary development – that, in effect, there has been *a poverty of the environmental stimulus*. Yet Darwinians have never been much moved by such arguments, holding that they simply underestimate the selective efficacy of environmental pressures. So one might wonder whether empiricists could not avail themselves of a similar response and urge that, since children *do* learn, the stimuli to which they are exposed must be considerably richer than nativist theorists imagine.

However, there is a significant disanalogy between ontogeny and phylogeny which needs to be taken into account in these two areas of theoretical debate. The difference is that individual development (ontogeny) conforms to a cognitive pattern for the species as a whole, whereas there is no comparable phylogenetic pattern which constrains speciation. A well-known, yet only partly acceptable, dictum of evolutionary speculation has it that 'Ontogeny recapitulates phylogeny'. As far as the fundamentals of psychological development are concerned, it is a lot safer to say that 'Ontogeny recapitulates ontogeny' – that is, that the development of individuals follows a similar course to that of other individuals of the species.

Suppose, by way of thought-experiment, that we intervened in the evolutionary process to produce geographical isolation, taking similar stocks of a species and depositing them in quite different environments – sending one batch to Australia, another to a tropical rain-forest, a third to temperate grasslands, and so on. Assuming the shock of relocation does not lead to complete extinction, and allowing a short interval for speciation (say a million years or so), we return to survey the results. Supposing that the environmental conditions encountered by the several branches of the ancestral stock had continued to differ, would we expect to find parallel development and closely similar species in all those different environments? No, surely not. Geographical isolation leads to divergent speciation – as indicated by Darwin's study of the Galapagos finches, and by what has happened on Madagascar since it was separated from the African mainland.

If we were to find that while the species had evolved it had evolved in much the same way in those different locations, in apparent defiance of environmental variation, then we really might start to think there must be something in the idea of a pre-determined path for phyletic evolutionary development, somehow already foreshadowed in the experiment's initial gene-pool. Arthur Koestler believed that something like this is true, and that evolutionary development follows certain *chreods* (Greek for 'predetermined paths'; see Koestler and Smythies, 1969). There are indeed a few cases of remarkable similarities between species which are quite distant from each other in terms of descent – such as the Siberian wolf and the Tasmanian wolf. But only a few. So there is no good case for chreods in phylogenetic development. The strength of the nativist case, by contrast, derives from the fact that there really do seem to be *chreods* for human cognitive development. Nativism is primarily supported, not by the *poverty* of the stimulus, but by the *degree of convergence* in the outcome of the developmental process given varying stimuli.

This general point in favour of nativism is what we shall have in mind in speaking of *developmental rigidity*. Consider the case of language acquisition. In the industrialised West, parents tend to be assiduous in providing their offspring with helpings of 'Motherese', but there are many other communities in which adults take the view that there is little point in talking to pre-linguistic children – with no apparent ill effects (Pinker, 1994; especially chs. 1 and 9). In general the linguistic input to which a child is exposed makes all the difference to *which* language the child acquires. It also seems that a certain minimum level of linguistic input is necessary for the child's language to develop at all, as evidenced by rare cases of complete deprivation – such as wolf-boys (Malson, 1972), and the self-sufficient twins studied by Luria and Yudovich (1956). But the propensity to acquire *some* language is so strong that it can survive remarkably severe levels of degradation in input. For instance, children of pidgin-speakers spontaneously develop a Creole with genuine grammatical structure (Bickerton 1981, 1984; Holm, 1988); deaf children born to hearing parents and not taught any form of Sign manage to develop their own gestural languages ('*home-sign*' – Goldin-Meadow and Mylander, 1990; Goldin-Meadow *et al.*, 1994); home-sign-using deaf children brought together into communities spontaneously elaborate their gestural systems into fully grammatical sign-languages (Pinker, 1994); and some deaf-blind subjects can learn a language through the input they receive by placing their fingers on the throat and lower lip of a speaker (the Tadoma method: C. Chomsky, 1986).

There is much more evidence in favour of the Chomskian position on language acquisition (see Cook, 1988; Chomsky, 1988; Carruthers, 1992, ch.6). For example, the characteristic mistakes children make are not at all what would be expected if they were deploying a domain-general learning strategy without any pre-specified constraints on possible grammatical structures. Rather, the patterning in their mistakes shows that a rule-hungry, powerfully constrained, device for acquiring language has been at work. Moreover, a recent large twin-study by Plomin and colleagues found that the factors underlying severe language-delay are largely genetic, with three-quarters of the variance in delay amongst twins being attributable to genes, and only one-quarter to the environment (Dale *et al.*, 1998).

It is also instructive to contrast learning to speak (and to understand speech) with learning to read. Considering only what has to be learnt, learning to read should be assessed as a relatively trivial task for those with normal sight and hearing – for it is, essentially, just a *mapping problem*, whereas in learning a language one has to master complex phonetic and syntactic systems, and the rules which assign semantic properties to sentences, while also developing the physical skills necessary to articulate speech. Yet it is reading which requires tuition and special coaching, without which the ability will never be acquired; and many otherwise normal children never do acquire it. However valuable as a skill, reading is a learnt rather than a natural domain of human cognition. In contrast, capacities for speech are developed by all children in just a few years, in the absence of special disability.

We should stress, however, that the sort of developmental rigidity we have in mind as supporting nativism is entirely compatible with a considerable degree of developmental plasticity (*contra* the crude picture of innateness attacked by Elman *et al.*, 1996). This is because rigidity is a question of the *goal* towards which the normal development of cognitive organisation tends, whereas what can be plastic is the way such modular organisation is implemented in the causal processes of development. Some modules do seem to require dedicated neural structures – for example, vision and its various sub-systems. Others, while developmentally rigid in discharge of function, may be developmentally plastic in the way in which they are implemented. Handedness, for example, has a marked effect on hemispheric specialisation. Right-handers normally have their speech centres in the left hemisphere and left-handers in the right hemisphere. But for either handedness, if the region where speech centres would normally develop is damaged at an early age, then the corresponding area of the other hemisphere can be 'co-opted' for those modular functions. (An obvious speculation about the developmental process is that cognitive modules with irreplaceable and dedicated neural structures have a more ancient evolutionary history, dating back at least six million years to the common ancestor of ourselves and chimpanzees, in whom there was probably a minimum of hemispheric specialisation. See Corballis, 1991.)

Whatever the pathways of development, they are compatible with our position if in the normal case they lead to a common outcome in terms of modular cognitive organisation, from varied input. For it is this common outcome which will be innately pre-specified – at least in so far as genetic inheritance predisposes towards the development of such a cognitive system.

We should also stress that the sort of nativism defended here is not seriously threatened, we believe, by the progress made by connectionist modelling of cognitive processes. It is true that connectionism is often seen as an anti-nativist research programme. And at least in its early days, the hope was to discover systems which would learn to produce any output from any input, while mimicking human performance – that is to say, systems which would provide simulations of *general*, as opposed to do-main-specific, learning. But this hope has not been borne out. Most connectionist networks still require many thousands of training-runs be-fore achieving the target performance. This contrasts with human learning which, in many domains at least, can be one-off – human children will often need only a single exposure to a new word in order to learn it, for example. We predict that if connectionism is to achieve real success in domains which are most plausibly thought of as modular – such as various aspects of language-learning and language-processing, face-recognition, categorial-perception, movement-perception, and so on – it will be by devising networks with a structure which is specific to each domain, and which contain quite a high degree of pre-setting of the weights between nodes.

3 Developmental rigidity and modularity

In language acquisition and other areas of normal cognition, the one great and impressive regularity is both the similarity of developmental stages and the common adult capacity. We maintain that cognitive development is *rigid* in the sense that it tends to converge on specific and uniform capacities over a wide range of developmental experiences. The extent of this convergence is only becoming fully apparent in the light of research which has revealed the domain-specific and modular character of much cognitive processing.

Nativism and modularity are distinct, in that while nativism is a thesis about how cognition develops (involving the claim that it is independent of experiential input, to a significant degree), modularity is a matter of how cognitive processing is organised. But these two research program-mes are clearly mutually supportive. For it is not at all plausible to suggest that the same detailed modular organisation should be replicated in different individuals simply by the operation of general learning pro-cesses upon diverse experiential inputs. Modules seem to be special-pur-pose, dedicated cognitive mechanisms, and one of the major theoretical arguments in favour of modularity – at least in relation to perceptual input modules – is that there is adaptive advantage to having cognition structured in this way. If that is so, then the adaptive advantage will need to be replicated through genetic transmission of instructions for the growth of modular systems. In other words, part of the theoretical case for modularity depends upon nativism being correct at least as far as some modules – perceptual input modules – are concerned. Further, if cognitive processing is functionally organised in terms of modules which are domain-specific and also common to the human species, then the best explanation of how this organisation is replicated is that there are innate programs controlling the functional development of cognition.

So the case for nativism and the case for modularity are interconnected, and evidence which primarily confirms the one view may also indirectly fortify the case for the other. Recent research has supplied a great deal of relevant empirical evidence. This evidence is drawn from a number of sources, including early developmental studies, case histories of cognitive dissociations, and brain-scanning data.

3.1 Developmental evidence

Much of the developmental evidence has been gained by studies reacting against the seminal work of Piaget (1936, 1937, 1959; Piaget and Inhelder, 1941, 1948, 1966), although Piaget himself was not an extreme empiricist. In spite of Locke's striking metaphor of the *tabula rasa*, or initial *clean slate*, the idea of a cognitive subject as an entirely passive receptor holds out no hope at all of accounting for development. On any view the child must contribute a good deal to the developmental process. Developmental empiricisms can then be more or less extreme, depending upon the number and generality of the mechanisms they postulate for the processing of experiential input. The most extreme form of all is associationistic behaviourism, according to which learning is just a form of operant conditioning conforming to the general 'law of effect'. Piaget explicitly rejected this austere version of empiricism (1927, final ch.; 1936). Instead, he portrayed the child as an active learner who relies on general learning principles.

However, Piaget's methods for testing children's capacities were insufficiently sensitive, consistently overestimating the age at which a particular developmental stage is reached. Developmental psychologists have been able to lower – sometimes very significantly – the ages at which abilities can be demonstrated to emerge, by adopting more child-adequate techniques of investigation. (Early examples of the genre are Gelman, 1968; Bryant and Trabasso, 1971.) Moreover, development does not proceed on an even front across all domains, as Piaget believed, but follows different trajectories in different domains. (See for example Carey, 1985; Wellman, 1990; Karmiloff-Smith, 1992.)

As far as young infants are concerned, the techniques required for investigating their interests and expectations were simply not available in Piaget's lifetime. These techniques rely on the few things babies can do – suck, look, and listen – and on the fact that babies will look longer at what is new to them, and will suck with greater frequency on a dummy when interested in a stimulus. The experimenters who have developed these techniques (habituation and dishabituation paradigms) deserve recognition both for their extreme ingenuity and for the extraordinary patience they have shown in the service of cognitive science (Spelke, 1985; see Karmiloff-Smith, 1992, for surveys of much of the infancy data). In a typical case, an infant is repeatedly presented with a stimulus until 'habituation' occurs, and the infant's sucking rate returns to normal. Then new stimuli can be presented, varying from the original along a variety of dimensions, and the extent to which the infant is surprised can be measured by the change in its sucking rate.

The results of these studies show forms of awareness in infants so young that one can hardly speak of any plausible process of learning at all. This developmental evidence supports nativism because it greatly reinforces considerations of 'poverty of the stimulus'. At just a few months – or even merely a few hours after birth – babies clearly have very limited data! But it should also be noted that more child-adequate techniques involve investigating infants' awareness in the sort of domain-specific way which is highly suggestive of modularity. Thus, new-born babies show preferential interest in face-like shapes (Johnson and Morton, 1991). Neonates can also detect numerical differences between arrays with a small number of dots or shapes (Gelman, 1982; Antell and Keating, 1983), with control experiments indicating that it is the number of dots they are reacting to. And whereas Piaget thought that knowledge of basic properties of physical objects, such as their permanence, was only acquired slowly through sensory-motor interaction and certainly not before the end of the first year, habituation trials show that four-month old babies are already making inferences about the unity of partly obscured objects, and have expectations concerning the impenetrability and normal movements of objects (Spelke et al., 1994; Baillargeon, 1994).

3.2 Dissociation evidence

If the developmental studies have made the idea that we are entirely reliant on general learning mechanisms unlikely, evidence from dissociations – both genetically caused, and due to brain damage in adults – exhibits the modularity of the mind in a surprising but unequivocal way.

For example, compare and contrast four different genetically related conditions: specific language impairment, Down's syndrome, Williams' syndrome, and autism. (The last of these will receive extensive discussion in chapter 4.) First, children can exhibit a whole host of impairments specific to language, including comprehension deficits and various forms of production deficit, while being otherwise cognitively normal (see Rapin, 1996, for a review). Second, Down's children have general learning difficulties, finding the acquisition of new skills and new information difficult. But they acquire language relatively normally, and the evidence is that they have intact social cognition, or 'mind-reading' capacities, as well. (In fact, Down's children are routinely used as a control group in experiments on mind-reading impairments in autism, with most of them passing at a rate comparable to mental-age-matched normal children). Third, Williams children, too, have intact – indeed, precocious – social cognition and language, but do not suffer *general* learning difficulty. They acquire information without difficulty, but have severely impaired spatial cognition, and appear to have great difficulty in tasks which require theorising (Karmiloff-Smith *et al.*, 1995; Tager-Flusberg, 1994). Finally autistic children can have normal language (at least in respect of syntax and the lexicon, as opposed to pragmatics) but have poor communication skills, and have impaired social cognition generally (Frith, 1989; Baron-Cohen, 1995). It is very hard indeed to make sense of these phenomena without supposing that the mind is organised into a variety of pre-specified modules, which can be selectively impaired.

Turning now to brain lesions in adults, these have frequently been associated with special and unanticipated impairments, such as particular forms of agnosia or aphasia. Prosopagnosia, an inability to recognise faces, provides a good example (Bruce, 1988; Bruce and Humphreys, 1994). Subjects can be impaired in this ability without any corresponding decline in their ability to recognise other objects. In this case the dissociation evidence is supported by other reasons for supposing that we have a special processing system for dealing with facial recognition. The domain is one to which, as we have seen, infants display preferential attention from a very early age; and the adaptive importance of interaction with specific others ensures significant cognitive effects from spotting 'The same face again' or judging 'That's a new face I haven't seen before'.

Several other visual agnosias are well known, suggesting that visual perception is really a hierarchy of interconnected modules. For example, some subjects have been impaired specifically in their recognitional capacities: they could still visually delineate objects (as evidenced by their drawings), and they knew what a certain kind of object was (as evidenced by their ability to supply definitions) – and yet puzzlingly, they still could not recognise even the most familiar things. In other cases object-recognition may be unimpaired, but the subject is no longer able to perceive movement in the normal way. (See Sachs, 1985; Humphreys and Riddoch, 1987.)

The same general story – of various dissociations suggesting a variety of discrete processing systems at work – can be told in relation to speech and language-processing. Aphasia, which is an inability to produce or to

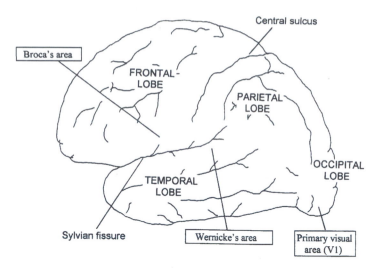

Figure 3.1 Some important regions of the human brain (left view of left hemisphere)

understand normal speech, comes in a great variety of forms. It is well known that Broca's area, a region of the brain close to the Sylvian fissure in the left hemisphere (see figure 3.1), seems to be important for grammatical processing. This is an area which brain-scans show to be activated when people are reading or listening to something in a language that they know. Patients suffering damage in this area are liable to suffer from *Broca's aphasia*, characteristically producing slow and ungrammatical speech. Yet damage to an area on the other side of the Sylvian fissure, Wernicke's area (see figure 3.1), can produce a completely different form of aphasia in which the patient produces speech which is fluent and grammatical but which fails to hit appropriate words, substituting instead inappropriate words or meaningless syllables. From this it seems that in most subjects Wernicke's area plays a crucial role in lexical retrieval: crudely put, while Broca's area is handling the syntax, Wernicke's area is doing the semantics.

However, lexical retrieval itself is not just a package deal which one either has or completely loses, as if the dictionary were either at one's fingertips or entirely lost. There are a variety of different deficits in lexical retrieval such as the various forms of anomia (impairments in the use of nouns). Patients have been found with specific deficits in the naming of living things, or abstract things, or artefacts, or colours, or bodily parts, or people, or fruits and vegetables – in fact, just about any category of items one can think of. These strange problems of mental functioning are far from being fully understood. But there does at least appear to be some

hope of understanding them on the hypothesis that the functional organisation of the mind is a hierarchy of modules.

3.3 Brain-scanning evidence

Our detailed understanding of how modules develop and function will
certainly be enhanced in the future by greater use of brain-scanning
techniques. But as yet this is not the most important source of evidence for
modularity. Partly this is because there are limitations on the tasks which
patients can perform while their brains are being scanned (their heads may
have to be motionless, for example; and obviously they cannot be playing
football!). But a more important problem for all scanning techniques is
that the resulting pictures of neural activation are always produced by a
subtraction of background neural activity. (A raw picture of brain activity
occurring at any one time would just be a *mess*, with activation of many
different areas around the cortex; for there is always too much processing
going on at once.) First a scan is taken while the subject is performing the
target activity (listening to a piece of text, say), and then a further scan of
the same subject is taken in which everything else is, so far as possible, kept
the same. The latter is subtracted from the former to obtain a picture of
those brain areas which are particularly involved in the target activity.

It is obvious that brain-scanning can only begin to be useful, as an
experimental technique, once we already have a set of reasonable beliefs
about the functional organisation of the mind and the modular
organisation of the brain. For otherwise, we cannot know what would be
appropriate to choose as the subtraction task. (For example, should the
subtraction task for text-comprehension be one in which subjects listen
to music, or rather one in which they receive no auditory input? The
answer will obviously depend upon whether speech-comprehension and
musical appreciation are handled by distinct systems; and upon whether
any 'inner speech' in which subjects might be engaging in the absence
of auditory input would implicate the speech-comprehension system.)
But as our knowledge advances, brain scans seem likely to prove an
invaluable tool in mapping out the contributions made by different brain
areas to cognitive functioning.

One further caveat to be entered about what brain-scanning can reveal
concerning modularity, is that one must be wary of assuming that a
module will always be located in a specific region of the brain. This is
because the notion of a module is itself essentially functional. What a
module *does* is more vital than *where* it gets done. Indeed, to philosophers
of mind brought up on orthodox functionalist accounts of the mind, such
as ourselves, it is somewhat surprising that cognitive functions should turn

out to map onto brain areas to the extent that they do. For we were long ago convinced of the falsity of type-identity theories by multiple-realisability arguments; and these arguments suggest that *where* in the brain a given function gets realised may be highly variable.

4 Fodorian modularity

The theoretical case for modularity has been presented with particular élan and energy by Fodor (1983, 1985a, 1989). According to Fodor, modular cognitive systems are domain-specific, innately specified input (and output) systems. They are mandatory in their operation, swift in their processing, isolated from and inaccessible to the rest of cognition, associated with particular neural architectures, liable to specific and characteristic patterns of breakdown, and they develop according to a paced sequence of growth.

Roughly, one can say that the domain of a module is the range of questions for which that processing system has been designed to supply answers. Putting this in terms of a computational/representational theory of cognition, Fodor suggests that modules are 'highly specialised computational mechanisms in the business of generating hypotheses about the distal sources of proximal stimulations' (1983, p.47). The important point to note is that if we take seriously both the idea of a cognitive architecture and the surprising evidence from dissociations, we will not in general be able to lay down *a priori* what the domains of modules are. It would definitely be an oversimplification to suppose that the traditional sensory modes of sight, hearing, touch, taste and smell are each separate input modules with single domains. The evidence of selective impairment suggests instead that hearing, for example, subdivides into the hearing of environmental sound, the perception of speech, and the hearing of music. The domain of a module is really its cognitive function. It is an entirely empirical matter how many modules there are and what their cognitive functions may be. We can get some insight into the domains of modular processing systems by asking top-down design questions about what processing tasks need to be discharged in order to get from the information in the proximal stimulus to the ultimate cognitive changes which we know to occur. But we cannot lay down the boundaries of domains before outlining the actual modular architecture of cognition.

The point which Fodor insists on, above all, is that modules are *informationally isolated* from the rest of the mental system. This isolation is a two-way affair, involving both *limited access* for the rest of the system and *encapsulation* from it. There is limited access in so far as the processing which goes on inside a module is not available to the rest of the mind; and there is encapsulation to the extent that modules are unable to make use of anything other than their own proprietary sources of information.

Limited access to the representations processed within input systems is taken by Fodor to be evidenced by the extent to which such representations fail to be available for conscious report. He suggests that the general rule is that only the final results of input processing are completely available to central cognition. So if we think of input processing as a richly mediated channelling in which information is filtered inwards from the sensory transducers, representations close to the sensory transducers will be completely inaccessible to the conscious mind. And for sure, we are not able to pronounce on the images formed at our retinas or the patterns of firing across our rods and cones. Moreover, both casual reflection and empirical investigation show that many informational details which must be represented at some level in the process of perception either do not consciously register at all or else are almost immediately forgotten. Thus one can tell the time without noticing details of the clock's dial or the watch's face; one can read words on a page without being able to say how some of the characters that composed them were shaped, or even how some of the words were spelled; and one can extract and remember the message which someone gave you while forgetting the exact words in which it was put.

The other aspect of the insulation of Fodorian modules, namely their *informational encapsulation,* is intimately connected with the dividing line Fodor draws between input-systems and central cognition. Central cognitive processes, for Fodor, are those which control such activities as decision-making, making up your mind about what beliefs to hold, and theorising. Fodor supposes that in order to work rationally such central systems must be capable of integrating all of the information available to a subject, in order to make the best decision considering all the circumstances, and to form the most reasonable belief on the balance of all the evidence. By contrast, the modular input-systems are blinkered and simply incapable of taking any account of other things which the subject may be well aware of.

The persistence of perceptual illusions provides Fodor with a striking illustration of his encapsulation claim. Consider, for example, the well-known Müller-Lyer illusion as displayed in figure 3.2. You must have seen this sort of thing before, and you would bet that the two horizontal lines are really of equal length. Perhaps you have even satisfied yourself of this by measuring them off with a ruler. But what you know about their relative length is quite impotent to alleviate the illusion – the line at the bottom still goes on looking longer than the line above, even though you are absolutely sure that it is not.

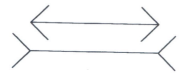

Figure 3.2 The Müller-Lyer illusion

Informational encapsulation is a key feature of modules in Fodor's account of the modularity of mind. It means that modular systems are blinkered, unable to make use of anything except their proprietary source of information. For some purposes this is exactly what is needed. It helps to explain how modules can process their input so quickly (speech perception is an impressive example of this). From the evolutionary perspective there is clearly value in having cognitive systems which are not 'dogmatic', which do not neglect environmental signals in cases where they conflict with previously stored information. To put it crudely, an animal had better be set up to react to movements or sounds or scents which may be associated with the presence of a predator, and it had better react sharpish. Sharpish counts for more than foolproof. Double-checking on whether it is really so gets you eaten, and so is a sort of behaviour which would not get repeated too often. In terms of survival costs and benefits, reacting to false alarms scores better than failing to be alarmed when you should be.

So modular input-systems have a sort of useful dumbness about them. As illustrated by perceptual illusions, they can quite easily be fooled by appearances, like a Venus fly-trap closing on a child's poking finger because it has been triggered to respond to the pressure of an alighting insect. Predation is not, of course, the only force shaping the evolutionary development of modular systems. Evolution has operated to recruit phenomenological features for their survival value: hence our fondness for sweet-tasting things, once a reliable guide to something it would benefit our ancestors to eat, and our revulsion at the taste of mouldiness, still an indicator of something liable to make you ill.

There is much in Fodor's account of modularity which we want to accept. His position has evolutionary plausibility on its side, and helps to explain what we know both about dissociations and the rigidity of normal development. However, we do not believe that all input modules are fully encapsulated. For example, it is known that visual imagination relies upon the resources of (shares mechanisms with) vision. Visual imagination recruits the top-down neural pathways in the visual system – which already exist in order to control visual search and to enhance object recognition – in order to produce secondary input, in terms of quasi-visual stimuli in the occipital cortex. These stimuli are then processed by the visual system in the normal way (Kosslyn, 1994). This means that the visual system *can* access centrally stored information to enhance its processing; and so modules need not be completely informationally encapsulated, after all. (Either that, or we arbitrarily confine the visual *module* to the processing which takes place in the occipital nerve, just as far as the initial cortical projection-area at the back of the brain, area V1 – see figure 3.1 above.)

Moreover, Fodor maintains that it is only input systems which are modular, whereas central cognitive processes are not. At this point, too, we feel we must part company with him, and reject the division between modular input systems and non-modular central systems. At the very least, a modular organisation for input systems and something completely different for central processes would be a theoretical awkwardness; and would also sacrifice much of the evolutionary plausibility of modular mechanisms, unless some special origin could be postulated for the divide. This might be something which could just about be accepted, if the non-modularity of central cognition promised to explain how central cognitive processes work. But it does not do so at all. On the contrary, Fodor is deeply pessimistic about our chances of understanding central cognition. So far as he can see, it is modular systems which we can investigate scientifically, both from the experimental angle and also from the direction of cognitive engineering (by figuring out how such systems might compute the output they need to deliver from their proprietary inputs). By contrast, central systems are intractable because they lack the limiting characteristics of modules – they are not domain-specific and they are not encapsulated.

It is important to note that in laying emphasis on the divide between input systems and central systems, Fodor is not simply acknowledging the problem of consciousness. To be sure, more of what goes on in central cognition is available to consciousness than the inaccessible processing within input modules. And certainly most people, on thinking about the matter objectively, would admit that consciousness is a queer phenomenon and a surprising one to find in a universe of physical causation. So: what is consciousness *for*? and: how could it possibly be implemented? are puzzling questions. We will be trying to give at least the outlines of answers to these questions in chapter 9. But the claim Fodor makes is that the sorts of processes which go on in central systems – conscious or not – cannot be devolved to modules. The next section considers whether the arguments for this are convincing.

5 Input systems versus central systems

Characterising their main cognitive functions in an ordinary and un-theoretical way, central systems operate to form beliefs and decisions. And forming both beliefs and decisions involves reasoning, whether the process of reasoning is conscious or not. But reasoning will often require one to bring together information from various different domains. In thinking about whether to take on a dog as a pet, for example, one will need to weigh up such disparate things as the appeal of canine companionship, the children's enthusiasm, and the health benefits of some obligatory walking against, on the other side, the costs and responsibilities of care, the increased dangers of infection and allergic reactions in the household, the emotional blow of bereavement, and so on.

In outline, then, Fodor's argument for the non-modularity of central systems goes like this. Central systems are the area of cognition in which we achieve integration of information from various domains. If they integrate information across domains, then they are not domain-specific. He also argues that they are 'in important respects, *un*encapsulated' (1983, p.103). If they are not domain-specific and not encapsulated, then they lack the main characteristics of modules. So the conclusion would seem to be that central systems are not modular.

Let us take this argument a bit more slowly, starting with the claim that central systems are not domain-specific. It seems obvious that information does get integrated, in terms of belief-formation, in terms of speech production, and in terms of the initiation of action. Surely this can only happen if separate information-processing streams deliver their output to systems which can somehow put the information together. So if I come to believe that there is a pig in my garden, I might well exclaim 'There is a pig out there!'. Prizing the condition of my lawn and flower-beds, I am going to take what steps I can to render the garden pig-free as soon as possible. Granted that I would not be in this pig-spotting state of alarm, if there was not something looking like a pig to me – and probably also sounding and smelling like a pig (as proof against hallucination) – but that is clearly not enough on its own to fix a belief and raise fears of its consequences.

Considerations of this sort do establish that central systems are not domain-specific in the way that input systems are. So, they are domain-general, then? No, that does not follow. As a number of recent thinkers have pointed out, this line of argument does not rule out the possibility of *conceptual modules* being deployed in thinking (Smith and Tsimpli, 1995; Sperber, 1996). Of course, if the conceptual modules simply duplicate the domains of the input modules, no integration could occur. But a certain degree of integration of information can be achieved via central conceptual modules provided their domains are different from the domains of input modules, and provided such conceptual modules can take the output from input modules as (part of) *their* input. We will first sketch out the case for believing in conceptual modules, before returning to Fodor's more formidable point about encapsulation.

5.1 The case for conceptual modules

As we have already noted, evolutionary considerations militate against the idea of an unstructured general intelligence. Rather, since evolution operates by effecting small modifications to existing systems, and by adding new systems to those which are already in place, one might expect to find cognition as a whole (and not just input and output systems) to be structured out of modular components. This is just the hypothesis which has been taken up and developed within the relatively new movement of *evolutionary psychology* (Barkow *et al.*, 1992; Hirschfeld and Gelman, 1994; Sperber *et al.*, 1995b). By speculating on the cognitive adaptations which would have been advantageous to humans and proto-humans in the environments in which they were evolving (as well as drawing on developmental and cross-cultural evidence), evolutionary psychologists have proposed a rich system of modular components, including systems designed for reasoning about the mental states of oneself and others; for detecting cheaters and social free-riders; for causal reasoning and inferences to the best explanation; for reasoning about and classifying kinds within the plant and animal worlds; for mate-selection; for various forms of spatial reasoning; for beneficence and altruism; and for the identification, care of, and attachment to offspring. This is the 'Swiss army knife' model of cognition (to be contrasted with the picture of the mind as a powerful general-purpose computer), according to which human cognition derives its power and adaptability from the existence of a wide range of specialist computational systems.

The case for a 'mind-reading' or social cognition module will be considered in detail in chapter 4. But two points are worth noting here. The first is that the mind-reading system must plainly operate upon conceptual inputs, rather than on low-level perceptual ones. For in general it is not bodily movements, as such, which are the targets of folk-psychological explanation, but rather *actions*, conceptualised as directed towards specific ends. Moreover, the mind-reading system can just as easily be provoked into activity by linguistic input (which is archetypally conceptual, of course), as when someone describes another's actions to us, or as happens when we read a novel and seek to understand the actions and motivations of the characters. The second point about the mind-reading system is that it does seem to be quite strongly encapsulated. Thus when watching a good actor on the stage, for example, I cannot help but see his actions as deceitful, jealous, angry, or whatever – despite knowing full well that he is really none of these things.

To take another example, Cosmides and Tooby (1992) have argued persuasively for the existence of a special-purpose 'cheater-detection system'. Since various forms of co-operation and social exchange have probably played a significant part in hominid lifestyles for many hundreds of thousands of years, it makes sense that these should have been underpinned by a cognitive adaptation. This would operate upon conceptual inputs, analysing the situation abstractly in terms of a cost-benefit structure, so as to keep track of who owes what to whom, and to detect those who try to reap the benefits of co-operative activity without paying the costs. Cosmides and Tooby also claim to find direct experimental evidence in support of their proposal, deriving from subjects' differential performance in a variety of reasoning tasks (more on this in chapter 5).

It is important to see that the *domain-specificity* of central modules is consistent with their having a variety of different input sources – perhaps receiving, as input, suitably conceptualised outputs from many of the various input-modules. For central modules may only operate upon inputs conceptualised in a manner appropriate to their respective domains, such as action-descriptions, in the case of mind-reading, or cost-benefit structures, in the case of the cheater-detection system.

If there are similarly conceptualised forms of representation produced as outputs by a variety of input-modules, then a module which took such outputs as its *in*put might appear to be less than fully domain-specific. But such a modular central-system might in fact be thought of as having both a fairly specific proximal domain (given by the terms in which its inputs are conceptualised) and also a more general remote domain. Consider, for example, the suggestion of a logic-module which processes simple inferences and checks for their validity (Sperber, 1997). These inferences could be *about* anything at all. So such a system has a remote domain of considerable generality. On the other hand, all it is doing is checking for formal validity and consistency in the representations which it takes as input. So its proximal domain would be quite limited and specific, being confined to a syntactic and lexical description of the input-representations.

Once we accept that a central module can take as input the output from various peripheral modules, then it should not be difficult to believe that it might also be able to make use of things known to some other parts of the cognitive system. In particular, it might be able to take as input the outputs of various other *central* modules (as when the output of the cheater-detection system is fed into the mind-reading system, say, to work out *why* a given individual has cheated); or it may be able to operate upon information called up from long-term memory (as when I recall and try to explain, for example, what someone may have done the last time we met). So in virtue of their centrality, central modules will not be so informationally isolated as peripheral input modules. But the important thing is that the way in which a module operates on this information should not be subject to influence from the rest of cognition. In any case, we at least need to enrich the Fodorian account of modularity by distinguishing *informational* encapsulation from *processing* encapsulation – whether information from elsewhere in cognition can *enter* a modular processor is a different matter from whether the *processing* which the module does can be influenced by other parts of the system.

5.2 Is central cognition unencapsulated?

We must now engage with Fodor's contention that central cognitive systems are capable of a kind of processing which is unencapsulated, and that they are therefore unlikely to be modular. A processing system, or module, is encapsulated if it processes its inputs in a way which is independent of the background beliefs of the subject. Perhaps everyone will be inclined to agree that central processes, such as conscious thought and decision-making, are not encapsulated in quite this way. But this should not lead us to conclude that *all* central processes are unencapsulated, of course. There might well be a whole host of central modules which perform their computations non-consciously.

One of the points which Fodor makes is that in decision-making the products of cognitive processing need to interact with utilities – that is, with what a person wants and wants to avoid. By contrast, Fodor insists that one of the functions of the encapsulated and mandatory operation of the input modules is to prevent them from being prone to what one might call 'wishful perceiving'. Selective pressures can presumably be relied upon to ensure that early stages of input processing are sufficiently unprejudiced not to be influenced by the pleasant or unpleasant character of distal sources of sensory stimulation. We can concede this, and also acknowledge the obvious point that desires and aversions must play a role in decision making. But this does nothing to show that a central process of decision making could not be modular. What it does show is only what one would want to maintain anyway, that the inputs to central processes are different from the inputs to perceptual input systems. That is no surprise. So far nothing counts against the idea of some sort of practical reasoning module, which takes as its inputs both current beliefs and current desires, and operates in such a way as to formulate as its output intentions to act.

Input systems can be very fast because of the limited source of their information. They do not incur the computational costs involved in taking account of background knowledge. But central processes do take background knowledge into account. However much it may look to me as if there is a pig in my garden, this is something I am going to find hard to believe, just because it is so surprising in relation to my background beliefs – for example, since there are no farms nearby it is difficult to explain how a pig could get to be there. Input systems may be designed to take the world at face-value, but central systems need to be at least somewhat dogmatic in order to avoid jumping straight from appearances to conclusions.

Fodor sometimes expresses this point by suggesting that whereas input systems have limited informational resources, a person's central cognitive processes only operate in a properly rational way if they take account of *everything that the person knows*. This seems to us a mistake. At least, it is a mistake if one takes potentiality for actuality. What we mean by this is that almost anything a person knows *might* be relevant to fixing upon a belief or making an inference. But clearly we cannot repeatedly be carrying out exhaustive surveys of our prior stock of beliefs. Even if this were part of an ideally rational, fail-safe procedure for belief acceptance, it clearly is not something that human beings, with limited processing resources and limited time, could possibly go in for. As we will be emphasising in chapter 5, it is important to distinguish between abstract ideals of rationality, and the sort of rationality appropriate to the human condition.

Fodor does have what seems like a better argument for supposing that central systems are unencapsulated, however, if one buys the idea that these systems are engaged in a sort of non-demonstrative fixation of belief which is analogous to the way in which scientific theories are confirmed. The inferences involved in belief-fixation are surely going to be non-demonstrative: in other words, they are not simply going to follow deductively valid rules. Inferences which do follow deductively valid rules can be as blinkeredly encapsulated as you like, because all that is needed to implement them is a system which advances in a reliable way from a list of premises to some of the conclusions which can be derived from those premises. Thus 'All robecks are thwarg', 'Omega-1 is a robeck', hence 'Omega-1 is thwarg' is an inference which can be drawn with absolute deductive security against a background of no matter what degree of ignorance on the topics *robecks* and *thwargness*. Some of our inferential capacities may rely on a topic-neutral logic module which works this way. But clearly that cannot be the general story, since it ultimately cannot explain where we obtain the premises, from which to run demonstrative inferences.

So how does non-demonstrative inference work? Well, if only we knew.

But at least there is a certain degree of consensus in the philosophy of science that Duhem and Quine were right to maintain that scientific theories and hypotheses form a sort of network in which there are reticular relations of evidential support (Duhem, 1954; Quine, 1951). This is a picture which appears to fit belief-fixation in general fairly well. A candidate belief gets accepted if it coheres sufficiently well with other beliefs. Although that seems right, epistemology has plenty of work to do in order to specify what exactly the relation of coherence consists in. For present purposes the moral to be extracted is that a candidate belief needs to cohere with other relevant beliefs, but what other beliefs are relevant depends on background knowledge and so cannot be given an *a priori*, system-external, specification.

As Fodor remarks 'in principle, our botany constrains our astronomy, if only we could think of ways to make them connect' (1983, p.105). This point can be illustrated by a supposed connection between solar physics and Darwin's theory of natural selection. Shortly after the publication of *The Origin of Species* a leading physicist, Sir William Thompson, pointed out that Darwin just could not assume the long time-scale required for gradual evolution from small differences between individual organisms, because the rate of cooling of the sun meant that the Earth would have been too hot for life to survive there at such early dates. Now we realise that the Victorian physicists had too high a value for the rate at which the sun is cooling down because they were unaware of radioactive effects. But at the time this was taken as a serious problem for Darwinian theory – and rightly so, in the scientific context of the day.

According to this argument, then – we will call it the *Network Argument* – what you come to believe depends upon your other relevant beliefs. But *what other beliefs are relevant depends in its turn upon what you believe.* Does this show that central cognitive processes, and in particular belief-fixation and non-demonstrative inference, cannot be encapsulated? Does the Network Argument refute the view that cognition is modular through and through? No. It cannot be the case that considerations drawn from epistemology and scientific practice (in fact the Network Argument is really founded on the case for a sort of *coherentism* in epistemology) should directly establish such a conclusion about psychology and the kinds of processing systems inside individual heads. There has to be a connection between epistemology and scientific confirmation on the one hand, and individual cognitive psychology on the other, because science has to be something individuals can do, and those individuals will be justified, and know that they are justified, in some of the things which they believe. But the transition from the epistemology of confirmation to the nature of central processing is by no means as smooth as the Network Argument would make out.

For one thing, it is quite possible for people to fail to appreciate the interconnections between their beliefs. So you may acquire a belief which conflicts with some of your other beliefs without being aware of the conflict, and you may fail to grasp that something you are inclined to believe is very strongly supported by something else you have believed all along. Those relevant interconnections will affect your beliefs, and the strength of your beliefs, *if* you notice them; but there is no guarantee that they will get noticed. We must not let the Network Argument fool us into thinking that they must inevitably get noticed by concentrating on the case of scientific practice, where there are always other people waiting to point out what we have missed.

Scientific enquiries are mostly conducted by people who have nothing else to think about, for most of the time. Professional scientists are employed to work back and forth between theory and data, checking against background information and evaluating alternative theories. And of course these activities will be conducted by a great many people simultaneously, often working in groups, normally with a great deal of overt discussion and mutual criticism. It is plainly a fallacy to think that the principles which are operative in such collaborative practices must transpose directly into the cognitive processes of individuals, as Fodor appears to do in his Network Argument. (See also Putnam, 1988, for a surprising convergence in views with Fodor here.)

Another point is that the Network Argument takes as its focus modes of belief-fixation which are paradigmatically conscious. Scientists formulate their theories explicitly and consciously, and explicitly consider their respective strengths and weaknesses, their relations with other theoretical commitments, and with other competing theories. And scientists also reflect consciously on the methodologies employed in their enquiries, and modify and try to improve on these as they see fit. But for all that the Network Argument shows, there may be a plethora of encapsulated belief-forming modules which operate *non*-consciously. Even if Fodor is right that conscious theoretical inference is radically unencapsulated, it may be the case that there also exist implicit, non-conscious, inferential systems which are modular, and fully encapsulated in their processing. We shall return to this idea in chapter 5.

We do think that it is one of the great challenges facing cognitive science *to explain how science itself is possible* – that is, to provide an account of the various cognitive systems involved in scientific enquiry, and to describe how they underpin the kinds of activities and inferences which we observe in scientific communities. But we are confident that progress with this question will only be made once it is accepted that central cognition comprises a variety of modular systems. It may even turn out that there is a dedicated science module, which operates non-consciously in ordinary individuals to generate at least some of the sorts of inferences which are conducted consciously and collectively by professional scientists.

5.3 Folk versus modular psychology

We have been urging the merits of modularism, not just in respect of input (and output) systems, but also in respect of central – conceptual – systems. Our view is that there are probably a good many modules of the latter sort, which take conceptual inputs and generate conceptualised outputs – including modules for mind-reading, for cheater-detection, for naive physics, naive biology, and others. But to what extent is modularism consistent with folk psychology? What becomes, in particular, of folk psychology's commitment to realistic construals of belief, desire, and various forms of reasoning (including practical reasoning), which we defended at length in chapter 2? Does central-process modularism entail *eliminativism* about the most important posits of folk psychology, in fact?

We believe that there need be no inconsistency here. One way to see this is to recall a point noted in chapter 2 (section 3.3), while discussing the causal nature of memory. We remarked that no particular problem is posed for folk psychology by the fact that scientific psychology posits (at least) three distinct kinds of memory – semantic memory, procedural memory, and episodic memory. For although folk psychology may not, itself, draw these distinctions, it is not inconsistent with them either – this is because *failure to draw* a distinction is not at all the same thing as *denying that there is* a distinction. Something similar may well be true in connection with such central-process posits as *belief*, *desire*, and *practical reasoning*. That is, it might be perfectly consistent with folk psychology that each of these should in fact subdivide into a number of distinct (modular) sub-systems. We shall consider one such possibility towards the end of chapter 5.

Another proposal for rendering central-process modularism consistent with folk psychology, would be to position the conceptual modules *between* the input (perceptual) modules, on the one hand, and systems of belief and desire on the other, as depicted in figure 3.3. In this diagram belief, desire, and practical reasoning remain untouched as folk-psychological posits on the right; and the various perceptual systems have been grouped together for simplicity into a single percept-box on the left (and included amongst these should be the natural-language comprehension-system, which counts as a distinct input module for these purposes). In between these are the various conceptual modules, some of which generate beliefs from the

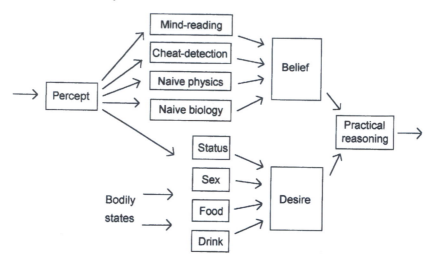

Figure 3.3 Modular central-systems and folk-psychological states

conceptualised outputs of the perceptual systems; and some of which generate desires (more on the latter in a moment). Note that – while we have not attempted to model this in figure 3.3 – the belief-generating modules *may* be able to take as inputs the outputs of other such modules. In chapter 8 we shall consider a hypothesis concerning how this might take place, according to which such inter-modular communication is mediated by language.

We have represented in figure 3.3 a variety of modular systems for generating desires. Since desires do not, on the whole, loom large in this book (nor in cognitive science generally), the existence and nature of such modules may bear some additional comment here. The modular systems which generate desires for food and drink will be at least partially responsive to bodily states such as levels of blood-sugar, we presume. But they may also take inputs from the various perceptual modules – think of how the mere sight or smell of chocolate cake can make you feel hungry, say, even if you are physically sated. And these modules may also effect more complex calculations, taking beliefs as inputs. Think, for example, of how one tends to get hungrier when on a long journey, even though the energy one expends while sitting in airport lounges is probably reduced from normal. Although the evidence is merely anecdotal, one can easily think of plausible evolutionary explanations for the existence of some such computational hunger-generating mechanism. The sexual-desire module, too, is likely to take a wide range of inputs, including sensings of internal bodily states, tactile and visual experiences of various sorts, and representations of complex social signals. And it also seems likely to engage in surprisingly complex computations using beliefs as inputs – for example, there is the startling finding by Baker and Bellis (1989), that the extent of sperm-production in men is proportional, not to the time elapsed since the last ejaculation (as might be expected), but rather to the amount of elapsed time for which the man has been physically separated from his partner (time during which she may have had other opportunities for mating), as predicted by sperm-competition theory.

We have also included in figure 3.3 a desire-generating module marked 'status'. It is a remarkable fact about human beings – which is not re-marked upon often enough in cognitive science, it seems to us – that human desires can encompass an astonishingly wide and varied set of objects, states and events. Something must act to generate such diversity, since it is mysterious how mere exposure to culture alone could produce a new set of desires. One plausible proposal is that we have a dedicated system which monitors others' attitudes to oneself, and computes which objects or events are likely to improve one's social status. Any such module would have to take beliefs as inputs, plainly – such as the belief, 'People who drive fast cars are admired', or the belief, 'People who are kind to animals are liked'. And it seems likely that one sub-goal in these modular computations would be *to stand out from the crowd* – hence giving us at least the beginnings of an explanation of why human desires tend to proliferate and diversify.

6 Conclusion

In this chapter we have presented the arguments for nativism, and for modular functional organisation of cognition, which are interlinked. We have also argued that modularity is probably not just confined to input and output systems, but characterises central cognition as well (belief-fixation of various kinds, practical reasoning, desire-generation, and so on). The resulting picture of the mind does not sit entirely easily with our conception of ourselves as integrated and unitary subjects of thought and experience. But it is at least consistent with the central commitments of folk psychology; and it does at least hold out the prospect of future scientific understanding. We shall return in chapters 8 and 9 to consider whether anything of our supposed cognitive unity can be preserved within a scientific account of consciousness.

SELECTED READING

For those seeking an introduction to the Chomskian inspiration behind modern nativism see: Cook, 1988 and Radford, 1997. Chomsky, 1988 is also quite accessible. See also Carruthers, 1992.

The seminal text on modularity is: Fodor, 1983. (His 1985a and 1989 are also well worth reading.) See also Shallice, 1988a; Sachs, 1989; Smith and Tsimpli, 1995; Segal, 1996; Sperber, 1996.

For arguments supporting both nativism and modularity from an evolutionary perspective, see many of the papers presented in: Barkow *et al.*, 1992.

A synthesis of developmental evidence in various domains is presented in: Karmiloff-Smith, 1992.

4   Mind-reading

We humans are highly social animals, unique in the flexibility with which we can adapt to novel patterns of interaction, both co-operative and competitive. So it is easy to see why our folk psychology, or capacity for mind-reading, is such an important psychological ability, both to individual lives and for our success as a species. But it is not only *other* minds which one needs to read. What should also be appreciated is that this very same capacity is used to think about what is going on in our own minds, as we shall see further in chapter 9. (One of the themes of this book is that this capacity for reflexive thinking greatly enhances our cognitive resources.) Other theses we argue for in the present chapter are that our mind-reading ability functions via *a central module*, that it operates by means of applying *a core of theoretical knowledge*, and that this core knowledge is *a product of maturation rather than learning*. In other words, we think that the 'theory of mind' module (often called 'ToM' in the literature on this topic) fits the general view on modularity and nativism which we outlined in chapter 3.

1   The alternatives: theory-theory versus simulation

Research into our mind-reading capacities has been assisted both by the investigations of developmental psychologists and by the debate between two rival views, theory-theory and simulation-theory.

1.1   Theory-theory

Theory-theory is a product of functionalism in the philosophy of mind. It proposes that core theoretical principles supply the descriptions of causal role (or function) which give us our conceptions of what different kinds of mental state *are*. Such principles might include elaborations on such truisms as, 'What people see, they generally believe', 'If people want something, and believe that there is something which they can do to get it, then they will generally do that thing, *ceteris paribus*' (see Botterill, 1996, for further discussion). According to theory-theory, this same general, theory-like, knowledge also enables us to attribute mental states in order to explain behaviour, and to predict behaviour from what we know about others' mental states.

While developmental evidence is undoubtedly relevant to resolving the debate between theory-theory and its opponents (as we shall see in section 4), the main point in dispute is how mind-reading ability fundamentally *operates* rather than how this ability is *acquired*. In particular, theory-theory as such is compatible with a range of possible methods of acquisition – such as by maturation of innate knowledge; through theorising upon data supplied by experience; or by grace of social instruction. It may sound paradoxical to claim that there could be such a thing as a theory which was not arrived at by theorising. If it strikes you that way, then forget about the word 'theory' and think of this position instead as the *core-knowledge-base* view. But we would actually suggest that, while it is true that most theories have to be earned by intellectual hard labour, this is hardly a conceptual truth. Elsewhere we have argued that, however acquired, this knowledge-base, as well as enabling us to explain and predict behaviour, provides just the sort of cognitive economy which is distinctive of theories – unifying, integrating, and helping to explain a diverse body of data (Botterill, 1996).

So theory-theorists may differ over how the theory is acquired. Gopnik and Wellman have argued that our theory of mind really does develop via a process of theorising analogous to the development of scientific theory: seeking explanations, making predictions, and then revising the theory or modifying auxiliary hypotheses when the predictions fail (Gopnik, 1990, 1996; Wellman, 1990; Gopnik and Wellman, 1992). The idea that folk psychology is the product of social instruction – probably the original default view amongst philosophers of mind in the days when they were deeply ignorant of empirical psychology – has found little favour with developmental psychologists (though see Astington, 1996, for a Vygotskian view of theory-of-mind development). Our opinion is that social instruction or enculturation surely does help shape the more sophisticated aspects of adult folk psychology, but contributes little to the formation of the core theory which is already employed by four-year-old children.

As we shall see in section 4, there are actually several reasons why we hold that the *correct* version of theory-theory – the only acquisitionally plausible one – is the nativist version, according to which we are innately predisposed to develop a theory-of-mind module. The fact that our mind-reading capacity exhibits developmental rigidity should, on its own, be strongly persuasive on this point. If mind-reading were the product of theorising or social instruction, then it would be quite extraordinary that all children should achieve the same ability at much the same age (about four years), independent of differences of intelligence and social input. Yet, give or take the usual variation to be found in any genetically controlled process of maturation, that is just what we do find.

Some people have pointed to the fact that wide cultural variations can seemingly exist in folk-psychological beliefs, as evidence for an account of theory-of-mind acquisition in terms of enculturation (Lillard, 1998). But almost all of this evidence relates to cultural variations in theory-of-mind *vocabulary*, and in variations in the beliefs about the mind which the folk will articulate, consciously, in language. Whereas, if there is a theory-of-mind module it is almost certain to be independent of language (see our discussion in chapter 9 below, section 3.9). Moreover, the basic internal operations of such a module may well be largely inaccessible to consciousness. What we would predict, from the perspective of nativism/ modularism, is that there should be a core mind-reading capacity whose developmental staging is the same across cultures, surrounded by a variable body of cultural accretions and concepts. And insofar as there is evidence bearing on this issue, this is just what we find (Avis and Harris, 1991; Naito *et al.*, 1995; Lillard, 1998).

Irrespective of their differences concerning the mode of theory-of-mind acquisition, theory-theorists have shown considerable convergence in respect of the different developmental stages traversed on route to the mature state, supported by an intriguing and diverse body of data (Wellman, 1990; Perner, 1991; Baron-Cohen, 1995). There would appear to be three main stages covered between birth and the age of four – stages which may correspond to increasingly elaborate theories devised by a process of theory-construction; or which may represent the maturational steps in the growth of an innate module, perhaps recapitulating the course of its evolution. The first stage – which is probably attained in the first eighteen months of life – is a simple form of goal-psychology. At this stage actions can be interpreted as goal-directed, and predictions can be generated from attributions of desire. (To see how this can work, notice that in general what is salient to you in your environment will also be salient to others; so if you attribute goals to others and work out what they will then do given their surroundings – in their environment as *you* represent it, that is – this is likely to prove reliable enough to be useful.)

The second stage – attained between the second and third years of life – is a kind of desire–perception psychology. As before, children can at this stage interpret and predict actions in the light of attributed goals; but they can now make some allowance for the presence or absence of perceptual contact with the relevant environmental facts. Yet there is no understanding of perception as a *subjective* state of the perceiver, which may represent some aspects of an object but not others, or which may represent wrongly. Rather, the principle seems to be: if someone has been in perceptual contact with the object, then they know everything which I know. (Perner, 1991, calls this a 'copy-theory of belief', since the idea seems to be that perception gives you a copy of the object as a whole, irrespective of which properties of it were available to you through perception.) This principle, while false, is close enough to being true, in most cases which matter, to be worth having – and certainly it is better than making no allowance for perceptual contact at all.

Then finally, during the fourth year of life, children attain a mature belief–desire psychology, or what Perner (1991) calls 'a representational theory of mind'. (This is not to say that there is no further development thereafter, of course – on the contrary, the theory continues to be elaborated, becoming considerably more subtle and sophisticated without altering its fundamentals.) At this stage children come to understand that people may have beliefs which are false, which *misrepresent* their environment. And they come to work with a distinction between appearance and reality, understanding that perception presents us with a subjective appearance of the world, which may sometimes be illusory. We shall return to consider in much more detail the tests for belief–desire psychology devised by developmental psychologists in section 4.1 below.

1.2 Simulation-theory

Simulationism challenges the above views by proposing that our mind-reading ability depends upon a process of simulation, rather than on the deployment of theoretical knowledge. Roughly, the idea is that we can pretend or imagine ourselves to be situated and motivated in just the way that other people are, and then go on to reason for ourselves within that perspective to see how we might then think, feel, and react. We then project our thoughts, feelings, and decisions onto the targets of our simulations. Simulation-theory might appear to be made plausible by the fact that we can, of course, quite consciously and deliberately adopt the strategy of supposing ourselves in the situation of others – or even, more dramatically, of re-enacting some episode in their lives – in order to help us anticipate their actions and/or appreciate their responses. But these are rather exceptional procedures, and simulationism needs a more low-key general account of simulation in order to deal with the mainly mundane business of mind-reading.

The leading advocates of simulationism have been the philosophers Gordon (1986, 1992, 1995) and Goldman (1989, 1992, 1993), and the psychologist Harris (1989, 1991, 1992). Like theory-theory, simulation-theory can take on a range of variations. One way in which simulationism may vary is by being more or less *radical* – being more radical if it relies exclusively on simulation, and less radical to the extent that it also depends upon the subject's use of general knowledge about mental states. Since a strongly radical form of simulationism is none too plausible, there is some danger of simulationism and theory-theory coalescing with each other. Indeed, since we do acknowledge that for one function our mind-reading capacity *must* rely upon a form of simulation, the position we advocate – limited simulation as an enrichment of the operation of an innate theory – is not too far away from a very *un*radical form of simulationism.

The main issue between theory-theory and simulationism concerns the sort of cognitive process involved in mind-reading – whether it is *knowledge-driven* or *process-driven*, to use Goldman's nice way of making the contrast. But we should remember that theory-theory not only furnishes us with a *philosophical* account of what conceptions of mental state types are: according to theory-theory, it is also the folk-psychological theory which supplies the ordinary human mind-reader with those very conceptions. Simulationism cannot very well just borrow this functionalist account, according to which such states as *belief, desire, hope*, and *fear* are understood in terms of their general causal interactions with other mental states, characteristic stimuli, intentions, and subsequent behaviour. Simulationism has to give up on the functionalist account of how we understand concepts in the vocabulary of propositional attitudes and intentional states – because such an account effectively involves implicit grasp of a theory. This looks like a serious gap unless the simulationist can come up with an equally plausible account of how we conceptualise the propositional attitudes.

So, can simulationists provide any adequate alternative story as to what our conceptions of mental states might consist in? This is clearly no easy task, given that some form of functionalist or theory-theory account is much the best that anyone has been able to come up with in the philosophy of mind (see chapter 1). Simulationists who have grappled with this task differ in the extent to which they have relied upon *introspection* as a possible source for knowledge of mental states. Our contention (see section 2.2 below, and also Carruthers, 1996a) is that, whether they invoke introspection or not, simulationists cannot give an adequate account of self-knowledge.

We noted above that if routine mind-reading runs on simulation, then simulation cannot be taken as full-blown, conscious pretending that one is in someone else's shoes. Such full-blown pretending occurs all right, but simply is not commonplace enough. So simulationists need a form of implicit, sub-personal pretending to match the theory-theorists' appeal to an implicit body of theoretical knowledge. Such an account has been

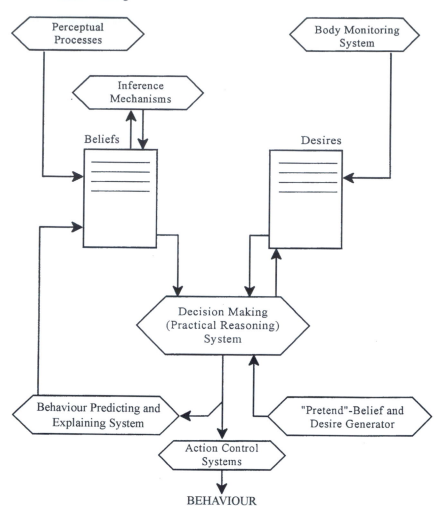

Figure 4.1 A simulation-based account of behaviour prediction

provided by suggesting that in solving mind-reading problems one simulates by running one's own decision-making or practical reasoning system 'off-line'. This suggestion is illustrated by the boxological diagram drawn by Stich and Nichols (see figure 4.1). They actually produced this diagram in the course of an attack on simulationism (Nichols *et al.*, 1996), but their elucidation of the idea of 'off-line' running has been found broadly acceptable by simulationists as well as their critics.

In the diagram the 'pretend'-belief/desire generator feeds inputs corresponding to the beliefs and desires of the target of the simulation into the mind-reader's own decision-making system. From then on this system operates just as it would have if the inputs had been the mind-reader's own beliefs and desires, rather than simulated beliefs and desires. The difference which makes this a case of off-line running comes in the output process. Whereas processing of the mind-reader's own beliefs and desires would eventuate in the formation of intentions and thereafter instructions to the motor-control systems leading to action, output of the processing resulting from 'pretend' inputs is side-tracked into a behaviour-predicting/explaining system. So instead of action, the result is expectations as to how others will behave, or attributions of intentions and other mental states to them.

Note from this how simulationism is liable to collapse into a hybrid view which also invokes theoretical knowledge. For in this scheme of processing both the *'pretend'-belief/desire generator* and the *behaviour-predicting/explaining system* clearly have important functions to discharge. The more those two parts of the processing system are given to do, the more it will seem that they must employ some body of tacit knowledge – an implicit *theory*, in fact.

2 Problems for simulationism

In section 4 we will be reviewing the evidence derived from developmental studies. We maintain that theory-theory does a better job of explaining this evidence than simulationism. But it should be acknowledged that current developmental evidence does more in the way of testifying to the modular and innately specified character of mind-reading than it does to discriminate between theory-theory and simulationism. Reflection on mature folk-psychological capacities reveals, however, a number of reasons why theory-theory should be preferred to simulationism, as we shall now see.

2.1 Simulation and explanation

Simulation is a feed-forward process. By feeding in 'pretend' inputs one can get an output or result. This seems quite acceptable if you want to *predict* what people will infer, or decide, or do, or how they will react. But it is quite unclear how such a process could generate interpretations or explanations of why someone has done something. Consider the analogy with a wind-tunnel, often used by simulationists themselves. By putting a model of a structure in a wind-tunnel you can find out how it will react to various forces. But it is no good putting in a model of a damaged structure (such as a broken aeroplane wing, or a collapsed bridge) in an attempt to find out why it incurred damage. In order to cope with explanation, simulation would probably have to resort to repeated iterations, trying first one 'pretend' input, and then another, until a match with the behaviour to be explained is achieved. This seems – unless it can somehow be constrained or accelerated – a slow, laborious and uncertain process. (You might *never* get a close enough match.) Yet interpretation and explanation do not appear to be more difficult for folk psychology to handle than expectation and prediction.

It seems plain, then – if simulation is to work effectively for purposes of explanation – that simulators will have to have a body of knowledge about the likely causes of action, and/or about the beliefs and desires which subjects are likely to possess in various circumstances. Simulationists generally appeal to a process of learning through development to explain our possession of such knowledge. The young child is said to begin with trial-and-error inputs to simulation, from which it gradually learns which are more likely to be successful in a variety of circumstances. In this way simulation is still held to be at the core of our mind-reading abilities. We think that this developmental claim is implausible. For the evidence is that young children begin successfully to *explain* what someone with a false belief has done at about the same age at which they first become able to make *predictions* from false-belief attributions, for example (Wellman, 1990) – there is no developmental lag, here, with explanation trailing behind prediction, of the sort to which simulationism is committed.

Since it is plain that simulation will have to be enriched with theoretical knowledge, we shall mostly focus on the claim that simulation is at the *core* of our mind-reading abilities, rather than on the more extreme claim that mind-reading is *exclusively* a matter of simulation. (In addition to the point made above, consider someone predicting how another will react when in a state of extreme fear – since it seems unlikely that the effects of extreme fear can be achieved by taking one's cognitive system off-line, this, too, will require theoretical knowledge.)

2.2 Simulation and self-knowledge

Our main argument against simulation-theory is that no version of it can give a satisfactory account of *self*-knowledge of mental states. According to theory-theory, self-knowledge will usually take the form of *theory-laden recognition*. But this does not mean that we work out what psychological states we are in by applying the theory to ourselves in a process of self-interpretation. (This does sometimes happen. In fact, there is evidence that it can happen so quickly and effortlessly that we are not consciously aware that this is what we have done; see Gazzaniga, 1994, for some remarkable examples of this in commissurotomised, 'split-brain', patients; and see chapter 8 below for some more discussion.)

On the theory-theory view, our concept of a certain kind of psychological state (*belief*, *desire*, *hope*, *fear*, *pain*, or whatever) is a concept of a state occupying a certain sort of causal role. But we can also *recognise* the occurrence of that sort of state in ourselves, recognising it *as* the state occupying that causal role. This kind of recognitional capacity is quite commonly found with theoretical concepts. For example, a diagnostician may recognise a cancer in the blur of an X-ray photograph; or when looking at the moon through a telescope we, like Galileo before us, may recognise *craters*. The possibility of the recognitional application of a theoretical concept is part of what philosophers of science have had in mind in talking of the *theory-ladenness of observation*.

As noted above, versions of simulationism differ over the role they assign to the recognition of mental states by means of introspection. According to Goldman and Harris, attributions of mental states to other people are grounded in first-person *acquaintance* with our own mental states. In order to predict what you will do in some situation, I *suppose* myself to be in that situation, making adjustments in my belief and desire set of which I am introspectively aware. I then let my practical reasoning system run 'off-line', concluding with a pretend intention of which I am also aware. I then attribute the corresponding action to the other person.

But when I am aware of these states in myself (pretend beliefs, desires, and intentions) *what am I aware of them as*? The simulationist cannot reply 'as states occupying a certain causal role', or this will become at best a version of simulation–theory mix (simulation used to enrich theory) – which would be to accept our own position, in fact (see section 3 below). So, presumably, we are supposed to be aware of them as states with a certain kind of *feel*, or introspectible phenomenology (as Goldman, 1993, has suggested).

We maintain that assigning this sort of role to phenomenological introspection is an alarmingly retrograde step in relation to the progress made in twentieth-century philosophy of mind. One thing which most philosophers of mind are agreed upon by now is that the idea that we learn what a mental state kind is from acquaintance in our own case is a complete dead-end. Quite apart from other objections, such an account imposes an overwhelming burden on learning: we must learn *which* feelings to induce in ourselves when simulating another; and we must learn which feelings to correlate with action-descriptions. Compare positivist accounts in the theory of perception, which say that we start from awareness of unstructured sense-data, and then have to learn how to construct on that basis representations of a 3-D world of tables, chairs, trees and so on. No one believes that any more; and introspectionist/simulationist accounts of mind-reading abilities look equally implausible. In each case the problem is to abstract an extremely rich causal structure on the basis of something which is a-causal.

If the argument so far holds, an important conclusion follows. This is that simulationist models of mind-reading mechanisms which *start out from distinguishable psychological states* are not genuine rivals to theory-theory. They only offer an account of how the processing for solutions of some mind-reading problems works within a general context of theoretical knowledge about the mind. On such an account, knowledge of causal and functional roles is needed to make the initial discriminations of different psychological states on which simulation might subsequently go to work. There is, however, a more radical form of simulationism, proposed by Gordon (1995, 1996).

Gordon thinks that we learn to mind-read by learning to pretend to *be* another person. He suggests that the default mode for simulation is 'total projection', just taking the person simulated to be exactly like yourself – without making any adjustment for situation, circumstances, or any other personal differences. However, we do gradually learn to make appropriate adjustments to match the situations of others. We also learn, more or less successfully, to make adjustments to our belief and desire set for the purposes of the simulation. And this need not involve any introspective awareness of what our own beliefs and desires are, Gordon thinks. Once we have achieved this sort of 'partial projection', we can then reason within the scope of that pretence, 'off-line'.

Gordon attempts to give a thoroughly principled and non-Cartesian account of self-ascription. The first step on the way to knowledge of one's own mental states is as easy as acquiring a simple linguistic habit. We start out self-ascribing a mental state of belief or intention by means of an *ascent-routine*: learning that where we are ready to assert 'P' we can equally well assert 'I believe that P'. Note that this is not intended by Gordon to require anything in the way of introspective awareness! The next step (on the journey to self-knowledge through simulation) is to combine the results of off-line simulation with the ascent-routine for belief. So we learn to transform pronouns in such a way as to ascribe a thought to the *other* person whenever we come out of the scope of a pretence – going from 'I believe that P' to 'He/she believes that P'. Finally, according to Gordon, we only learn to ascribe thoughts to ourselves (with understanding of the possibility that the thoughts may be false; that is, *not* just by means of an ascent-routine) by simulating another (or ourselves at a later time) simula-ting ourselves.

Gordon has constructed an ambitious and ingenious account of self-knowledge. But we do not think it will do. The problem here is to see how we could ever acquire the capacity which we surely do have: to ascribe, with understanding, occurrent thoughts to ourselves immediately, *not* on the basis of any sort of self-interpretation of our own behaviour. I can know what I am thinking even where those thoughts are unrelated to my overt behaviour or to my current circumstances. As I gaze silently out of the window I know that I have just entertained the thought, 'Avignon would be a good place for a holiday'. But I cannot have self-ascribed this thought by simulating another person simulating myself, since no one else could have ascribed such a thought to me in the circumstances. Simulation cannot take place under these conditions: there *has to be* some salient circumstance or behaviour to simulate.

2.3 The problem of mutual cognition

One way of approaching this problem is by wondering how simulationism can explain anyone as cunning as Iago, the villain of Shakespeare's *Othello*, who is hell-bent on bringing down his commander by making him think he has reason to be jealous of his wife (Desdemona) and one of his officers (Cassio). Suppose Iago can simulate what Cassio will think and want to do when he takes it that Desdemona is attracted to him. That is a first-level problem. But can Iago simulate what Othello will think Cassio will think and do in those circumstances? That is a second-level problem, and altogether trickier to model in terms of off-line processing. Suppose subjects can run their decision-making or inferential systems off-line. Then how can they do it *twice at the same time*, labelling one pass for Cassio and another pass for Othello-on-Cassio?

In fact *this* problem is not so very difficult for a simulationist, perhaps. For in one sense, in order to simulate Othello simulating Cassio, *you just have to simulate Cassio*. What can make your simulation of Cassio into a second-order one, is what initiates it, and what you do with it on completion of the simulation-process. To predict what Othello will think about Cassio's thoughts you begin (naturally enough) with a question about Othello. You then 'drop down' a level to simulate Cassio. And then on exiting the simulation you have to embed the resulting belief or intention twice over – first in the belief 'Cassio will think...', and then in the belief 'Othello will think that Cassio will think...'. Now there may well be a problem about how children could ever be supposed to *learn* how to execute this process. But the mature process itself seems an intelligible one.

There is, however, a real problem for simulation-theory in accounting for our ability to explain or make predictions concerning various forms of *mutual cognition*, such as mutual pretence, mutual jealousy, or mutual knowledge. Suppose that Peter and Pauline are mutually aware of the candle on the table between them – each can see the candle and can see that the other sees it; and this is mutually known to them both. This is surely a situation we can understand, and can begin to make predictions about. For example, we can predict that neither will find it necessary to comment on the existence of the candle to the other; that each would be surprised if the other *did* make such a comment; that each would be surprised if the other were *not* surprised if they themselves should make such a comment; and so on. But how can I simultaneously simulate Peter simulating Pauline, who is in turn simulating Peter simulating Pauline, and so on? Here if I try to do it by 'dropping down a level', I just simulate Peter and simulate Pauline – but that will not do at all, since it is crucial that I should simulate their reasoning about the mental states of the other, and their reasoning about what the other will reason about their own mental states.

It looks as if simulationists will have to concede that mind-reading of mutual cognition is handled by some sort of body of general knowledge, in addition to simulation. But then they may try to claim that this knowledge is learned through simulation in the course of normal development, hence preserving the view that simulation is at the core of our mind-reading abilities. But this looks pretty implausible when one reflects that children engage in, and understand, complex forms of mutual pretence, at least by the age of four (Jarrold *et al.*, 1994a). Since this is the age by which children acquire a properly representational conception of the mind (and hence can understand that beliefs can be false – see section 4 below), and since you cannot understand mutual pretence without such a conception, there is a real problem here for simulationism – namely, to explain how both competencies can emerge so close together in development.

2.4 Cognitive penetrability?

These three points against simulationism appear to us to be quite decisive; and to be a good deal more convincing than a rather technical line of argument which has been pressed by Stich and Nichols (1992, 1995; Nichols *et al.*, 1996). They dub their argument against simulationism 'the cognitive penetrability argument', but this is a rather confusing label (liable to be confused with another sort of penetrability, the sort which modules do not afford). So we prefer to think of it as 'the theoretical fallibility argument'. The thinking behind this line of argument is that if there is some area in which people regularly tend to behave irrationally in ways which are surprising to the folk, but where we consistently fail to predict this – wrongly expecting them to behave rationally – then we are probably relying upon theoretical knowledge. Theoretical knowledge might make mind-readers *consistently commit mistakes* about the products of quirks and flaws in human reasoning and decision-making systems. But if mind-readers were simulating and using their own reasoning and decision-making systems, they would *share* the quirks and flaws of their targets and so would *not* consistently mispredict their behaviour.

Taken in the abstract, this line of argument is impeccable. But it does depend upon being able to supply the requisite empirical evidence – namely, instances of surprising irrationality where we as observers also tend to make incorrect predictions. And it just is not clear that there are any examples which unequivocally fit this specification. Stich and Nichols' prime example is the Langer effect, which is a matter of subjects showing an unwarranted preference for lottery tickets which they have chosen themselves. But there is dispute over the conditions under which this preference is exhibited (Kühberger *et al.*, 1995). To be sure, there are plenty of examples of common irrationality, but the argument also requires that mind-readers should find these cases surprising, and should also get them wrong. That means *mis*predicting the responses of subjects: giving a wrong prediction, not just failing to predict by not knowing what to expect. Until clear-cut examples of this type are provided, the cognitive-penetrability/theoretical-fallibility argument remains an argument in search of its premises.

3 A hybrid view

So far our approach has been resolutely anti-simulationist. Yet we do want to acknowledge that there is a place for simulation, as an enrichment of the operation of theory. Note that sometimes the only way of dealing with a mind-reading question is to use your own cognitive resources. Suppose the question is: 'What will the President say when asked to name the state capital of Nebraska?'. It may be reasonable to assume that the President will know the answer and, given the context, be ready to give it. But your ability to predict *what* he will say depends, at least in part, on *you knowing* that Lincoln is the capital of Nebraska.

Heal (1986, 1995, 1996) has argued in favour of a mix of simulation and theory in folk psychology, with simulation handling the content-aspects of mind-reading problems while theory is required for non-content aspects (that is, for handling the types of intentional states and their relationships). We also want to accept this hybrid or mixed position, while stressing the fundamental role of theory in giving us our conceptions of the different mental state types. Specifically, we think that what simulation is involved in, is the process of *inferential enrichment* – that is, that we can input the 'pretend beliefs' of another person into our own system(s) of inferential processing, and then use the output of derived beliefs for attribution to the other; and that we can similarly start from an assumed goal and work out (on our own behalf, as it were) the steps necessary to achieve that goal, again then attributing the various sub-goals to the other.

There are at least three powerful reasons why an advocate of theory-theory should accept this much in the way of simulation:

(1) Anything like *a comprehensive theory of thinking* would be too large to handle, especially as a sub-system within a theory-of-mind module (this was Heal's original point). Much of human inference is *holistic* in character, at least to the extent that what inferences people will draw from what will depend, very largely, upon their perceptions of what other beliefs of theirs are relevant to the inferential steps in question. (This was the point discussed in chapter 3, section 5.2. We return to the issue of holism in chapter 7.) A comprehensive theory of thinking would then have to be, at the same time, a theory of *relevance*. In order to predict what someone will infer from some new belief of theirs, using theory alone, I would have to know, not just what their other beliefs are, but also which ones they will take to be relevant.

(2) We have to acknowledge, in any case, a capacity to process inferences on the basis of suppositions, because that is what hypothetical or counterfactual reasoning is. Much human reasoning can begin by *supposing* such-and-such to be the case, and reasoning from there. It is in this way that we can foresee the consequences of adopting a new belief in advance of accepting it, or of a new plan of action in advance of executing it.

(3) People's own inferential capacities impose limits on the inferences they can assign to others. Thus, in the case of belief-attribution we can hardly allow a cognitive mismatch such that the agent cannot see what to infer from *P*, but can perfectly well handle an inference from *P on someone else's behalf*. This is what we might call 'the Watson constraint': if Dr Watson cannot work out who the murderer must have been *for himself*, then he cannot work it out on Holmes' behalf, either. But if our theory of mind really did embody a complete theory of thinking, then it certainly ought to be possible, in principle, for people to *predict* thoughts in others which they cannot arrive at *in propria persona* by using their own theoretical or practical reasoning systems.

Theory-theory can quite happily make this much in the way of a concession to simulationism. What theory-theory should *not* concede is that simulation is needed for anything other than inferential enrichment, going from already attributed beliefs to further beliefs, or from already attributed goals to further sub-goals. In particular, theory-theory should deny that our conceptions of mental state types are provided by simulation, as well as denying simulation any role in the initial attribution of thoughts to others, and denying it any role in the prediction of action from intention and the prediction of intention from desire.

4 Developmental studies

During the last two decades there has been much ingenious and revealing research into the development of mind-reading in children. Ironically, it was an attempt to assess whether chimpanzees have mind-reading abilities which provided the spur to progress in the human case. Premack and Woodruff (1978) advanced evidence which might be interpreted as indicating that chimpanzees do have such abilities. Although there is considerable evidence – from both studies in the field and controlled experiments – which is at least suggestive of mind-reading abilities in some other primates besides ourselves (particularly chimpanzees and gorillas), the case remains far from conclusively made out (see Byrne and Whiten, 1988; Whiten and Byrne, 1988; Gomez, 1996; Povinelli, 1996). The problem with imputing mind-reading to chimps is that they might just be very adept at exploiting knowledge of correlations between situations, bodily cues (such as direction of gaze, bodily orientation and posture), and behaviour – without having a capacity for thought about the contents of another chimp's mind. In comments on Premack and Woodruff's seminal article Dennett (1978e) and Harman (1978) pointed out that what was required for a convincing demonstration of mind-reading was a test in which an expectation was formed on the basis of attribution of a *false belief.*

The idea behind the false-belief test is that cases in which conduct is appropriately related to *how things are* may be predictable simply on the basis of knowledge of regularities linking situation and conduct. For example, you may be able to predict that when there are ripe berries around people will pick and eat them, because you have noticed they tend to do so in that sort of situation. In general, where others have true beliefs about a situation a correlation with the situation can be substituted for a correlation with their belief about the situation. But if, instead, you predict that they will go looking for berries in a place where you know there are no berries, then that prediction is being made on the basis of *their misrepresentation* of the situation, their false belief that berries are to be found there. So far nobody has yet discovered a way of subjecting chimpanzees or gorillas to a clear-cut false-belief test. (The closest anyone has come so far, has been to devise an *ignorance* test – see Gomez, 1996; O'Connell, 1996 –

which tests, in effect, for the presence of desire–perception psychology, and which chimps and gorillas can pass. This suggests that great apes may have the mind-reading abilities of at least two- to three-year-old children.)

4.1 Normal development

It is possible to subject children to a false-belief test, however, as Wimmer and Perner (1983) showed. The paradigm such test features a character, Maxi, who places some chocolate in location A (a drawer in the kitchen). He then goes out to play, and in the meantime his mother moves the chocolate to another location, B (a cupboard in the kitchen). Maxi comes back feeling hungry after his exertions and wanting his chocolate. The children are then asked where Maxi will look for the chocolate. The correct answer, of course, is that he will look in location A *because that is where Maxi thinks it is*. In order to succeed in the false-belief task children have to appreciate that the actual location of the chocolate (B, in the cupboard) is something that Maxi does not know about. (Control questions are used to probe whether the children remember where the chocolate was originally located, and whether they recall where it was moved to.)

Most normal children are able to pass this test by about the age of four, whereas younger children say that Maxi will look where the chocolate actually is. This standard false-belief experiment has been repeated many times with many possible variations in the manner of presentation (such as puppet-characters, actors, story-books and so on). So the reliability of this watershed in mind-reading development has to be regarded as a highly robust finding. One can say of children that they start to 'do false belief' towards the end of their fourth year in much the same way that one can say that they start to toddle at the beginning of their second year.

Success on false-belief tasks at four years of age seems surprisingly precocious in relation to anything which might be expected on a Piagetian schedule of domain-general developmental stages. But in fact it may be that the request for a *verbal* response in standard false-belief tests actually inhibits a mind-reading ability which is already present. At least, this would seem to be the conclusion to draw from some research in which children's responses to false-belief tasks were assessed by noting the direction of their gaze, or by getting them to respond with very rapid motor activity (Clements and Perner, 1994). By these measures, children were succeeding on the tasks by as much as six months to a year earlier.

One variant on the original false-belief test is *the Smarties task*. In this experiment children are shown a container for a familiar type of sweet – a Smarties tube (the US equivalent is M&Ms) – and asked what the tube contains. The usual answer, as you might expect, is 'sweets' or 'Smarties'.

However, the experimenter had actually put a pencil inside the tube. These non-standard contents are now revealed to the child. The original point of the Smarties test had been to find out what children would say about another child who was going to be presented with the Smarties tube, with the pencil still inside – 'What will your friend say the tube contains?'. As in the Maxi-type false-belief test younger children, under the age of about four, erroneously attribute the knowledge they now have to other children – that is, they say the other child would *say there was a pencil in the tube*. But from about four years on, children correctly predict that the other child will get the contents wrong and say that the tube contains *sweets*. So results of the Smarties test corroborate the developmental watershed indicated by the original false-belief tests (Hogrefe *et al.*, 1986; Perner *et al.*, 1987).

But the really interesting finding on the Smarties test emerges from responses to a supplementary question: 'What did *you* think was in the tube?' It turns out that younger children – at an age when they are still failing the false-belief task – also fail to acknowledge *their own past false belief*. They answer the question by saying 'a pencil', even though only a few moments before they had said that there were sweets in the tube (Astington and Gopnik, 1988). Yet their failure is not merely one of memory – they can recall what they had *said* was in the tube, for example. Very similar results to those for the Smarties test have also been obtained on *Hollywood Rock* – sponges tricked out to look like rocks. When they see them, children will at first say they are rocks. They are then invited to handle them and discover, to their surprise, that they are not really rocks. Once again the younger children, not yet possessing a developed concept of (false) belief, will say that other children looking at them will think they are sponges; and they will also say that *they themselves thought they were sponges before too*! (See Gopnik, 1993, for a survey of test results and theoretical discussion.)

From the perspective of mature mind-reading, these may appear the strangest and most surprising results. In fact, they count heavily in favour of a nativist version of theory-theory and against the developmental *theorising* view. (So here is a second point to add to the argument from developmental rigidity advanced in section 1.1 above.) The theorising account must be that children learn to revise a more primitive theory, which uses conceptions of *desire* and *knowledge* and/or *perception*, to include possible *false belief* as well. Since children will sometimes have beliefs which are false, the suggestion could be that they will learn from their own case that there are such things as false beliefs. But natural as that thought might be, it is covertly Cartesian: it just assumes that introspection is a specially privileged form of observation, which is not theory-laden.

And the Smarties test provides us with a refutation of the suggestion. Children whose concept of false belief is not yet developed have difficulty recognising and recalling their own false beliefs. So children must somehow be revising their simple folk-psychological theory to include possible false belief, but without yet having any conception of false belief, and so without yet having access to their own false beliefs, either. This seems a difficult theorising task indeed!

This point may be worth elaborating further, since it has implications for philosophy of science. It is very difficult to understand how mind-reading could be a product of quasi-scientific theorising, given that children pre-four lack any concept of false belief. For what can motivate you to revise a theory in the face of recalcitrant data, if you cannot yet entertain the thought that the data suggest that *your theory is false*? In other words, we would argue quite generally that theory-of-mind development cannot be explained in terms of quasi-scientific theorising, because scientific theorising would be entirely impossible without mind-reading ability. This is clearly a theme which deserves treatment in its own right. For the time being we refer readers to some of Fodor's suggestive thoughts on the connection between experiments and the management of beliefs (1994).

So there is a strong case for the view that mind-reading ability is innate, rather than being the product of theorising. This has now been dramatically confirmed in a twin-study undertaken by Hughes and Cutting of the London Institute of Psychiatry (personal communication). They performed a whole battery of mind-reading tests on over 100 three-year-old twins, looking at differences in performance amongst monozygotic ('identical') twins, who share the same genes, as opposed to differences in the performance of dizygotic ('fraternal') twins, who have just 50 per cent of their genes in common. It turns out that two-thirds of children's variance on mind-reading tests is attributable to genetic factors, with only one third being attributable to environmental factors. Yet the genes in question turn out to be largely independent of those involved in the acquisition of other sorts of ability, such as language.

There is one piece of developmental evidence which might be thought to suggest that mind-reading ability is *not* innate: it is known that children with more siblings tend to pass the false-belief test earlier (Perner *et al.*, 1994). But we suggest that this is likely to be an instance of the general developmental principle that variation in opportunities to exercise a capacity can accelerate or retard the rate at which that capacity develops in a child. Co-variation of that sort is to be expected in development which is fundamentally a matter of *growth*, just as much as in cases in which children are learning from the input they receive. Moreover (as we noted in section 1.1 above) although some people may also be tempted to claim that cultural variations in folk-psychology count against the nativist hypothesis (Lillard, 1998), it does not really do so – on two counts. First, what evidence there is concerning mind-reading development in children cross-culturally suggests a common developmental trajectory (Avis and Harris, 1991; Naito *et al.*, 1995; Tardif and Wellman, 1997). Second, variable expression in varying circumstances is just what one might predict of an innate mind-reading module, in any case – just as the language-module develops differently in the context of different natural languages.

4.2 Abnormal development

If the human mind-reading capacity is indeed innate and domain-specific, then it is plausible – as argued in chapter 3 – that there is a modular processing system on which it runs. Where there are domain-specific modular systems, there are possibilities for special cognitive impairments. And there does indeed seem to be such an impairment in the case of mind-reading. It is known as *autism*, a developmental disorder first identified in the 1940s (Kanner, 1943; Asperger, 1944). Autism is known to have a substantial genetic component, and is clinically defined in terms of a triad of impairments:

(1) Abnormalities of social behaviour and interaction;
(2) Communication difficulties, both non-verbal and in conversation;
(3) Stereotyped, unimaginative behaviour and failure to engage in pretend play.

(Wing and Gould, 1979; American Psychiatric Association, 1987; World Health Organisation, 1987). Autistic children seem 'aloof', often treating other people as objects; they have difficulty in interacting socially with both adults and other children; and while many can successfully acquire language, they have difficulty with the pragmatic aspects of language-use (for example, not realising that when Mother asks whether the fridge is empty, you do not answer 'No' on the grounds that it contains a single mouldy lettuce leaf). They also have a tendency to become engrossed in repetitive and stereotyped tasks which normal children would find dull and monotonous. But their central problem seems to be *mind-blindness* – a specific deficit in mind-reading ability.

The difficulty that autistic children have with mind-reading has been revealed by their very low rate of success on the false-belief task, even at comparatively advanced ages (Baron-Cohen *et al.*, 1985). The poor performance of the autistic children in these tests can hardly be explained by any general learning difficulties or general cognitive impairments, since the autistic children do markedly less well than children with Down's syndrome, who in other respects have more severe cognitive impairments.

Autistic children's incomprehension of false belief is strikingly exposed by their inability to use deception. Anecdotal evidence concerning deception appears to confirm the normal developmental profile; and this placing of the ability to deceive within the child's mind-reading capacity has also been reinforced by tests such as 'the fairy and the stickers' (Peskin, 1992). A fairy-character (a puppet in a white dress) asks the child which is her (the child's) favourite sticker, and then takes the sticker that the child indicates. While four year olds quickly learn that the way to keep the sticker they want is to say that a different one is their favourite, three year olds seem unable to master this simple trick and keep on truthfully indicating *and therefore losing* their favoured stickers. In a similar experimental arrangement, even older (teenage) autistic children lose out in the same way as pre-four year olds. With Box B empty and Box A containing a goodie they want, even after repeated trials they are unable to work out the deceptive strategy of misdirecting to the empty box someone else who wants to take the sweet and asks them where it is (Russell *et al.*, 1991; Sodian, 1991; Sodian and Frith, 1992, 1993).

Autism is a developmental disorder. Long before four years of age there are differences between autistic and normally developing children. The staging of autistic deficits is summarised in the table below. (*Proto-declarative* pointing is pointing intended to direct another's attention to something of interest – as contrasted with *proto-imperative* pointing, which is pointing intended to obtain something.) Some of these differences have been used in screening tests, at 18 months, and have proved very reliable in identifying children subsequently diagnosed as autistic. The main features on the checklist (CHAT, or *Checklist for Autism in Toddlers*) are proto-declarative pointing, gaze monitoring, and pretend play (Baron-Cohen *et al.*, 1996; see also Baron-Cohen and Cross, 1992).

The autistic deficiencies are, of course, deficiencies in comparison with abilities of normally developing children. In adopting the nativist view that mind-reading is innate in humans we are not maintaining that mind-reading, or the hypothesised module through which it operates, is itself present from birth. Rather, we claim that there are genetic instructions which have been selected for precisely because in normal human environments those instructions generate processing systems with mind-reading abilities. Mind-reading is the long-range effect of those instructions and their biological function – it is the reason, or part of the reason, why they are in the human genome. If we are right about this, it still leaves many questions to be answered about what the shorter-range effects of those instructions are. Mapping of the normal developmental profile indicates that gaze-monitoring, and capacities for shared attention and pretend

Age	Autistic deficit
First year	• Little interest in faces • Failure to monitor gaze • Lack of sharing of attention • No proto-declarative pointing
c. 18 months	• Absence of pretend play
c. 4 years and later	• Failure on false-belief tests • Absence of deceptive behaviour/understanding of deception • Executive disfunction: problems with looking ahead and planning • Problems with pragmatic aspects of discourse

Figure 4.2 The staging of autistic deficits

play are among those effects. The nativist theory-theory is that mind-reading capacity *grows out of* these earlier capacities, or at least that its growth presupposes them. Baron-Cohen (1995) has suggested that this process of maturation towards the mature theory involves three precursor modules, an Intention Detector (ID), an Eye Direction Detector (EDD), and a Shared Attention Mechanism (SAM). (It may be that ID is the realiser of Wellman's simple-desire-psychology, and that SAM is the realiser of desire–perception psychology.) There is also some evidence of a dedicated neurological system for the mind-reading module, involving a circuit of interconnecting neural pathways (Baron-Cohen and Ring, 1994a: the circuit links the orbito-frontal cortex with the superior temporal sulcus and the amygdala).

The so-called 'executive function' deficits listed in the table above are experimentally tested on such tasks as the Towers of Hanoi. This involves transferring a set of discs of various sizes from one of three pegs to another, one disc at a time, without ever having a larger disc sitting on top of a smaller disc. Solving the task involves thinking about the positions of the discs a few moves ahead. Autistic subjects are much worse at this task than normal children, regularly repeating the same fruitless moves over and over again (Ozonoff *et al.*, 1991; Harris, 1993). This is taken to indicate a problem with the planning of actions which derives from difficulties with hypothetical and/or counterfactual reasoning – reasoning about what will happen *if I make that move* or about what might happen *if such-and-such were to be the situation.*

It should also be noted that those with clinical expertise in treating autistic children encounter a wide range of impairments and abnormalities – including, in addition to the mind-reading-related impairments already noted, such things as *impaired motor co-ordination, hyperactivity,* and *excessive thirst.* There is, therefore, certainly room for some scepticism as to whether the whole range of impairments observed in the autistic syndrome could be due to a single primary deficit, such as a deficit in mind-reading ability (Boucher, 1996). And it is indeed true both that the false-belief tests can only be carried out – given present experimental design, at least – on high-functioning autistic children with relatively good linguistic abilities, and that a certain proportion of these autistic children do pass the standard false-belief test. Are not these facts rather damaging to the *autism-as-mind-blindness* hypothesis?

Actually, all these facts are, on plausible assumptions, quite compatible with the mind-blindness hypothesis. In the first instance, the fact that a certain proportion of any group may pass a false-belief test should not be taken as indicating a similar percentage of mind-reading-derived understanding of belief in that group. There will be some lucky-guess 'passes' generated simply by noticing and mentioning a salient location or action. It is also probable that some high-functioning autistic children will have developed their own theories or heuristics – quite different from the innate mind-reading knowledge-base of normal children – which may be adequate for solving some psychological problems, though in a cognitively more demanding way. (Compare the effort involved in speaking a second language with the fluency of a native tongue.) Tests involving rather more difficult tasks (such as second-order tasks involving the attribution of beliefs about others' states of mind) seem to show that autistic subjects who pass on the first-order, Maxi-type, false-belief test do still have considerable difficulty in comprehending psychological states and motivation (Happé, 1994).

The second point which needs to be made is that whether we should expect to find a cognitive impairment such as *mind-blindness* depends upon the actual causal processes involved in generating the impairment. In general where an impairment results from incidents causing some sort of neural damage, the likelihood is that the extent of the damage will not be confined to the boundaries of a module or to neural circuitry with a particular functional role. So it is not particularly surprising that autistic children suffer from a range of deficits varying in extent and severity.

In addition to contrasting the autistic child with the normally developing child, we can also learn something by comparing autism with other developmental disorders, such as Williams' syndrome. As we noted in chapter 3, children with Williams' syndrome have poor practical intelligence, poor visuo-spatial skills, and poor theorising abilities. But they have good (in some ways precocious) linguistic abilities and are close to the normal developmental profile in mind-reading (Karmiloff-Smith *et al.*, 1995). The dissociation between theorising and mind-reading in Williams syndrome seems to support the hypothesis of a mind-reading module – and acquisition by theorising is surely ruled out in their case. Williams syndrome also poses a problem for simulationism. Simulationists say that autism is basically a deficit in *imagining*, or in *supposing*, which they say is crucially involved in pretend-play, in practical reasoning and problem-solving, and in mind-reading. But Williams syndrome children are normal at mind-reading, but have severe difficulties with practical reasoning and problem-solving. This strongly suggests that mind-reading and imagining/supposing dissociate.

5 Accounting for autistic impairments

Thus far in this chapter we have done two things. First, we have argued for the superiority of a modularist/nativist, maturational, form of theory-theory as an account of mind-reading development, as against the acquisition-by-theorising view. This has been on the grounds: (a) of developmental rigidity, (b) of the difficulties the child-as-scientist view has in explaining theory-change, and (c) that we find exactly the kind of genetically related deficit – namely, autism – which we would expect if the modularist account were correct. Then, second, we have argued for the superiority of theory-theory over simulationism as an account of the core, or basis, of our mind-reading abilities. This was on the grounds that simulationism: (a) has problems in explaining the parity of explanation with prediction, (b) that it can give no adequate account of self-knowledge, and (c) that it has problems in accounting for various forms of mutual cognition. Taken together, these arguments amount to a powerful case in support of nativistic theory-theory, it seems to us.

It has been claimed, however (notably by Currie, 1996), that the theory-theory view of mind-reading cannot offer such a good account of certain autistic impairments as simulationism can – particularly the absence of pretend play and deficits in executive function. Here our strategy will be to argue that theory-theory can offer explanations of these impairments which are *at least as good as* those offered by simulationism; leaving our earlier arguments to determine an overall victory for theory-theory.

5.1 Pretend play

During their second year normal children start to engage in play which involves some form of pretence. For example, a doll or teddy is treated *as if* it were a living companion. The increasing complexity of pretend-scenarios and the way in which children can become engrossed in their make-believe situations is a striking feature of early childhood, and a regular source of wonder to parents. Lack of interest in pretend play is an autistic impairment which may seem particularly problematic for the theory-theorist, and yet readily explicable for the simulationist. Normally developing children have usually started to engage in pretend play by about 18 months. As noted above, early absence of pretend play – along with absence of proto-declarative pointing and of gaze monitoring – is used as part of a checklist for autism in toddlers which has proved highly accurate in identifying children subsequently diagnosed as autistic. Autistic children *can be induced* to engage in pretend play if instructed to do so by others (Lewis and Boucher, 1988; Jarrold, *et al.*, 1994b), but hardly ever seem to do so spontaneously.

Superficially, it seems as if this supports simulationism: not going in for pretend play seems more like a deficit in simulation than something explicable by a lack of knowledge about minds. But we should not be too quick to assume that the deficit in pretend play is better explained by simulationism. To do so would be to fall victim to a sort of pun, or play on words. In so far as pretending actually is describable as engaging in simulation (so that 'pretending to be an airline pilot' is just another way of saying the same thing as 'simulating an airline pilot'), then there is a sense in which it is clearly true that children who do not go in for pretend play have 'a deficit in simulation'. But then that is just a redescription of the phenomenon. It is not an explanation of why autistic children should have this deficit in terms of the lack of some underlying capacity, on which pretend-play is causally dependent in normal children. If we think in terms of a simulationist mechanism at the sub-personal level such as the off-line running of psychological systems for practical reasoning and decision-making (see figure 4.1 above), then it is no longer so apparent that an inability to do *that* would provide a good explanation for failure to engage in pretend-play.

The question remains: how can theory-theory explain the autistic deficit in pretend play? One of us (Carruthers, 1996b) has suggested that autistic children lack any motivation to engage in pretend play because, being unable to detect and represent their own mental states (including the mental state of pretending), they cannot appreciate the fluctuating changes in mental state which provide the reward for pretend play. But this explanation seems to be pitched at too high a level. For recall that it is absence of pretend play at 18 months which is one of the trio of diagnostic criteria for autism. At that age it seems most unlikely, on a theory-theory account, that the child can represent any of its mental states *as such*. And at that age the sorts of pretence in which normal children engage are pretty simple – such as manipulating toy cars, or constructing towers out of building bricks – and hardly deserving of being called *imaginative* play. So it seems rather unlikely that the rewards of pretence, at that age, either derive from or involve the child *representing* their own mental state of *imagining*.

We are now inclined to propose that the rewards for simple forms of pretend play presuppose a capacity to detect and to represent *agency* – that is, that in normal children it implicates Baron-Cohen's (1995) 'Intentionality Detector' (ID) or Wellman's (1990) 'simple-desire-psychology'. To find the actions of manipulating a toy car rewarding, on this account, a young child must be capable of representing what it is doing as *moving the object like a car*, and of representing this as the goal of its action. For without at least this minimum degree of meta-representational ability, it is hard to see how pretend-actions could be differentially rewarding. (This is not to say that representations of agency or goal are *sufficient* for the rewarding nature of pretend play, of course; we only claim that they are necessary. Quite what it is that makes pretence enjoyable and intrinsically rewarding for young children is something of a puzzle. But note that this is *equally* a puzzle for simulationism.) Then, on the plausible hypothesis that autism will involve damage to, or a delay in the development of, the Intentionality Detector (or the mechanism responsible for simple-desire-psychology), we have a non-simulationist hypothesis to explain absence of pretend play in autism.

5.2 Executive function deficits and counterfactual reasoning

Executive function deficits involve some sort of problem with planning, and it is plausible to suppose that the problem is a lack of ability – or at least an inferior capacity – to think ahead. Not being good at thinking ahead is probably due to not being good at figuring out *what would happen or be the case if* such-and-such *were so*. This sort of reasoning has acquired the label of 'counterfactual reasoning'. It is not an altogether happy label, because the *such-and-such* set out in the *if*-clause might actually be, or come to be, factual. The point is not that the 'counterfactual' bit of counterfactual reasoning is not so, but rather that it is entertained merely as a supposition.

The idea that there is some peculiarly intimate connection between counterfactual reasoning and mind-reading ability is rather tempting. After all, the central representational capacity of mind-reading consists in handling representations which have the structure: *Agent – Attitude – Content*. In processing these triadic representations the very same contents can be embedded in different attitudinal contexts. Thus I can fear what you hope for; and I may not expect something to happen, but then be disappointed or pleasantly surprised that it does. In particular, people with a proper representational concept of belief will be able to avoid confusion between what they believe and the contents of beliefs attributed to others. Counterfactual reasoning involves something at least partially analogous, in the way of free-wheeling manipulation of contents accompanied by some way of marking off what is actually believed by the reasoner from what is merely being supposed.

Simulationists have urged that the use of suppositions involved in counterfactual and/or hypothetical reasoning fits their model of simulation. We know that people engage in this sort of reasoning, and so it is claimed to be an advantage of simulationism that we get an account of how mind-reading works, essentially for free. Further, they claim that in the case of the autistic impairment in executive function, what we are witnessing are the effects of a deficient ability to simulate.

We do not think that theory-theory is at any disadvantage in accounting for problems with counterfactual thinking, however. Remember that our hybrid view allows simulation to have a place within the application of theory of mind. We have explicitly said this in relation to *inference-enrichment* (section 3 above). We reject simulationism, but we do not reject simulation as a cognitive tool. Given that people can *first* distinguish between suppositions and their probable/possible consequences, on the one hand, and what they actually believe, on the other, then they can use the capacity to generate suppositions in order to simulate. But even if there is a case for thinking about counterfactual reasoning as a form of mental simulation, this should not be taken to exclude the sort of self-knowledge which on the theory-theory requires application of a theory-of-mind to one's own mind. For while counterfactual reasoning *may* involve simulation, it is even clearer that it involves the very sort of monitoring of psychological states for which a theory-of-mind system is needed – the ability to keep track of the scope of a supposition, to differentiate one's actual beliefs from the counterfactual supposition, and to make appropriate modifications in some of one's background beliefs (Carruthers, 1996b).

Indeed, our general view about executive function and counterfactual thinking is that simulation *may* be involved to a greater or lesser degree (depending on the sort of thinking required for solving different problems), but that theory-of-mind must *always* be involved, at least in a controlling or monitoring role.

To see the first point, consider someone wondering whether they can get a piece of furniture through a doorway or up a narrow staircase. Surely that will engage simulation. They are going to think, 'Suppose we have it this way round and then turn it like that' – and then imagine what would happen either from the perspective of an agent or of a spectator. But there are countless other cases of counterfactual reasoning in which processing is not going to be so closely tied to particular action-sequences. Very often the question, 'What would happen (or would have happened) *if* ...?' is going to be answered by combining the supposition in the if-clause with a rich set of background beliefs, some of which will have to be modified in order to secure coherence with the supposition being entertained.

To see the second point (that theory-of-mind must always be involved in complex counterfactual thinking), notice that as you think through, counterfactually, some complex problem, you will need to keep track of your own inferential moves – you will need to represent that at *this* stage you were supposing *this*, whereas at *that* stage you were supposing *that*, and so on. This requires a capacity to represent your own sequence of thoughts, thus implicating the mind-reading capacity. If autism is a deficit in mind-reading, as modularist theory-theorists suppose, then problems of executive function are precisely what we should expect.

6 Conclusion

We conclude that a modularist form of theory-theory stands as the most plausible account of human mind-reading abilities. While the spur provided by the contrast with the rival simulationist theory has been invaluable, we think it is clear that theory-theory is the more progressive and promising research programme – and that within this programme, it is the modularist/nativist version which should be preferred. There is, however, a role for simulation, in working out the consequences of, and relationships amongst, contents. In assessing the implications of developmental evidence, it is most important to remember that knowledge of minds is not only knowledge of *other* minds. Self-knowledge should not be taken for granted. This is an issue to which we shall return at length in chapter 9.

SELECTED REFERENCES

Three useful collections on the topics of this chapter are: Davies and Stone, 1995a (This reprints the papers from a *Mind and Language* special double-issue, plus

Heal, 1986; Gordon, 1986; and Goldman, 1989.); Davies and Stone, 1995b; Carruthers and Smith, 1996. (This also contains sections on autism, and on mind-reading in great apes.)

Two excellent books by psychologists on the development of mind-reading in children are: Wellman, 1990; and Perner, 1991.

Two useful books on autism are Frith, 1989; and Baron-Cohen, 1995.

5   Reasoning and irrationality

In this chapter we consider the challenge presented to common-sense belief by psychological evidence of widespread human irrationality, which also conflicts with the arguments of certain philosophers that widespread irrationality is impossible. We argue that the philosophical constraints on irrationality, such as they are, are weak. But we also insist that the standards of rationality, against which human performance is to be measured, should be suitably relativised to human cognitive powers and abilities.

1 Introduction: the fragmentation of rationality

According to Aristotle, what distinguishes humankind is that we are rational. Yet psychologists have bad news for us: we are not so rational after all. They have found that subjects perform surprisingly poorly at some fairly simple reasoning tests – the best known of which is the Wason Selection Task (Wason, 1968 – see section 2 below). After repeated experiments it can be predicted with confidence that in certain situations a majority of people will make irrational choices. Results of this kind have prompted some psychologists to comment on the 'bleak implications for human rationality' (Nisbett and Borgida, 1975; see also Kahneman and Tversky, 1972). Philosophers sometimes tell a completely different story, according to which we are committed to assuming that people are rational, perhaps even *perfectly* rational. There has, until recently, been almost a disciplinary divide in attitudes about rationality, with psychologists seemingly involved in a campaign of promoting pessimism about human reason, while philosophers have been trying to give grounds for what may sound like rosy optimism.

It would seem that one or other of these views about human rationality must be seriously wrong. But of course 'rationality' is hardly a well-defined notion, so when we look more closely into the matter the disagreement may turn out more apparent than real. Before considering the arguments and the evidence, we should notice that our pre-theoretical understanding of rationality suggests that people can be rational and – more saliently – fail to be rational in a number of different ways. Above all, a major division in forms of irrationality follows the distinction between *beliefs* and *desires*.

While much of interest might be said about the rationality of desires, we can only acknowledge how much we are neglecting in this area. For example, it is debated whether there is an issue of *rationality* as such concerning what people may or may not desire. If one moves from desires which are merely unconventional through the whole spectrum of possible eccentricities, to desires which are strange and 'unnatural', does one arrive at a point where desires become genuinely irrational rather than just extremely unusual and weird? Or should we accept the view famously expressed by Hume (1751, Appendix I), that rationality applies to means, not ends? This is a topic we shall not even touch on here.

Where desires conflict, there can certainly be a problem of sorts over the rationality of an agent who acknowledges one desire as more important, but in practice, in the heat of the moment, gives in to a contrary temptation – the notorious and familiar problem of *weakness of the will*. And even if desires cannot be rational or irrational when taken on their own, one can state certain formal principles about the rational structure and ordering of sets of desires. For example, preferences should be transitively ordered: subjects who prefer outcome A to outcome B and also prefer outcome B to outcome C, then *ought to* prefer outcome A to outcome C.

We will leave questions about the rationality of desire aside, however, and concentrate on belief, and irrationality as displayed in reasoning and inference – a topic more than large enough for the present chapter. But even when restricted to matters of belief, the question, 'Are humans rational?' makes doubtful sense. Rather like the question, 'Are humans tall?', it is radically incomplete without some specification of either a standard or a purpose. Moreover, as soon as one reflects, it becomes obvious that there are *many* different standards of rational belief-formation in different domains and different areas of enquiry. The norms governing reasoning with conditionals are different from those governing probabilities, and these are different again from the standards governing inference to the best explanation, such as might be involved in scientific enquiry – to name but a few. The question, 'Are humans rational?' needs either to be relativised to a particular domain, or to be understood as a generalisation across domains.

It is also worth noting, and briefly exploring the connections between, a number of different notions of epistemic rationality. We should distinguish between *creature rationality* (applicable to the person as a whole), *mental state rationality* (where it is a belief or other epistemic attitude which is being assessed), and *process rationality* (where it is the person's belief-forming processes which are at issue). And as we shall see, *state rationality* should probably be further bifurcated into *type-* and *token*-state rationality.

To say of particular people that they are rational (in the domain of belief) is, we think, to say that most of their belief-forming *processes* are rational ones. For imagine someone whose *beliefs* (or many of them) are clearly irrational, but where those beliefs were induced by hypnotic suggestion or brain-washing. Provided that the person 'keeps their wits about them', as we say, and that the processes by which they now evaluate and form beliefs are still rational ones, then we think their status, as a rational creature, remains uncompromised.

What is it to say of a belief that it is rational? Here we think a further distinction needs to be drawn. Imagine someone whose belief *that plants need water* has not been formed in the normal sort of way, but has been induced a-rationally by post-hypnotic suggestion. Here they have a belief which is rational, in the sense that it is a belief of a *type* which can be formed by rational processes. But *their holding* that belief – or that *token* belief of theirs – is *ir*rational, since it was *not* formed by a rational process. When we ask after the rationality of someone's beliefs, then, we need to be clear whether we are considering them as types, or as tokens.

It should be plain from the above that the most fundamental notion is that of a rational belief-forming *process*, since it is in terms of this notion that both creature rationality and state rationality are to be explained. What is it, then, for a belief-forming process, or a method of inference, to be rational? Plainly it would be a mistake to say, 'When it is a *valid* one, guaranteeing truth from truth'. For that would confine to the scrap-heap of irrationality all non-deductive modes of inference, including induction and inference to the best explanation. We might try saying that a rational process is, not just *reliable* (where 'reliable' means 'not leading from truth to falsehood'), but the *most* reliable available. Then where valid principles can be employed, the use of an invalid one would be irrational. But in other domains the use of an invalid principle of inference, such as induction, can be rational provided that it is more reliable than the competing principles on offer. Although tempting, to pursue this line of explication would be a mistake. For our goal as enquirers is not to form *only* true beliefs, but to form *enough* true beliefs in a short enough time-span. And the most reliable methods might be ones which hardly deliver any beliefs at all.

So standards of rationality for belief-forming processes should be relativised to our needs as situated, finite, enquirers after truth. This is an important point, to which we return at greater length in section 5. Others have suggested that there may be a multiplicity of purposes in relation to which our belief-forming processes can be assessed, besides those of *truth* and *speed* (Stich, 1990). We do not share this view, at least as an explication of our ordinary notion of 'rationality' – except in so far as what counts as *enough* true beliefs may depend upon our background needs and purposes as agents; but it would take us too far afield to argue for this here. In what follows we shall assume that processes should be assessed in relation to both *reliability* and *fecundity* (truth and speed). And for the most part we shall focus on just one belief-forming process in particular – namely inferences assessing the truth of conditionals – as an example from which, we hope, general morals can be drawn.

2 Some psychological evidence

There is a considerable body of evidence which shows that over a range of reasoning tasks people perform poorly. Reasoning about probabilities seems to be an area of particular weakness. The *gambler's fallacy* is a piece of probabilistic irrationality to which people seem strongly prone. This fallacy, of supposing that the probability of an independent event can somehow be affected by a series of previous occurrences (for example, the coin having just come up heads three times in a row), is strangely seductive even for those who ought to know better. Tests have also revealed the popularity of the *conjunction fallacy* – judging the probability of a conjunction, such as 'Albert is a physicist and an atheist', as being higher than the probability of either of the two conjuncts ('Albert is a physicist', 'Albert is an atheist') in relation to the same background information (Tversky and Kahneman, 1983). Other tests have been carried out to see how belief is affected by evidence which is subsequently discredited. If the question is put explicitly, probably everyone will agree that one ought to modify one's beliefs once the grounds for holding them are shown to be false – you ought not to go on believing something you no longer have reason to believe. However, though people might *say* they ought not to go on believing, it has been found they have a tendency to do just that, exhibiting *belief perseverance* even after the bogus nature of some concocted 'evidence' has been carefully explained to them in a debriefing session (Nisbett and Ross, 1980).

It might be questioned whether results such as these could reveal any general defect in human reasoning. For people can be taught reasoning skills, can't they? Once given adequate training, surely they will perform much better on reasoning tests than untutored and unsuspecting subjects? The answer is that they may well do so, but there is no guarantee they will not revert to bad habits of reasoning as soon as they start to deal with cases other than the examples on which they have been instructed. This is strikingly illustrated by one of the examples of *base-rate neglect*. Casscells *et al.* (1978) posed staff and students at Harvard Medical School with the question: what is the probability of a patient who tests positive for a certain disease actually having that disease, given that the prevalence of the disease in the general population is 1/1,000, and that the false-positive rate for the test is 5 per cent. Almost half of these highly trained people completely ignored the information about the base rate and said that the probability was 95 per cent. (Some way out, as the correct answer is 2 per cent! And on these sorts of judgements, life-and-death decisions get made!) This suggests some cause for concern about the way general defects in human reasoning may affect the decision-making even of those who have been given expensive professional training.

There is one particular sort of test which has become a dominant paradigm in the field of research on reasoning, much as the false-belief test has in research on mind-reading. It may be that this is because the test is uniquely well-designed as a way of probing the way conditional reasoning works. Or it may be that it just makes things easy for psychological experimenters because it is simple to carry out, suitable for the usual undergraduate body of subjects, and readily lends itself to variations which ring the changes. We have also heard it described as 'an obsession'. But in any case, it has definitely produced results which call for explanation, and which are illustrative of many of the issues arising in the debate concerning human rationality.

This test is the Wason selection task. In its basic form it goes like this. Subjects are presented with four cards, (a), (b), (c) and (d), as shown in figure 5.1 below, of which they can only see one face. They are told that each card has a letter on one side and a number on the other. They are then given instructions such as the following:

> Indicate which cards you need to turn over in order to decide whether it is true for these cards that *If there is an A on one side of the card, then there is a 5 on the other*. You should select only those cards which it is essential to turn over.

(If you like, pause to consider which cards you would select. Alternatively, get a group you can test, to see if previous results are replicated.)

About 75 to 90 per cent of subjects, given this style of presentation, fail to make the correct selection. This is because only about 10 per cent select the (d) card. Most people pick card (a) and card (c), or only card (a). The correct selection is card (a) and card (d), because only these two cards are potential falsifiers of the conditional, 'If there is an A on one side of the card, then there is a 5 on the other.' Whatever might be on the other sides of the (b) and (c) cards is irrelevant to whether that conditional is true or not.

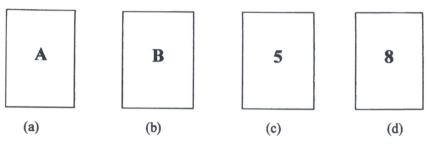

Figure 5.1 The Wason card-selection task

Judging from this version of the selection task it looks as if people are checking on the correctness of the conditional solely by checking for *positive instances*, as if seeking to confirm a rule 'All Fs are Gs' by examining the Fs and the Gs. Bad news for Popperians, you might think! Having accepted Hume's sceptical argument about inductive inference, Popper (1971) claimed that we do not rely on induction anyway. The impression that we do is a sort of 'optical illusion'. Instead, we start from some prior hypothesis and use the method of conjectures and refutations. The initial interpretation of the selection-task data would seem to be that the majority of people are, on the contrary, the most naive confirmationists, and that they are not at all alive to the crucial significance of the potentially refuting instance. Practically everyone chooses the (a) card, but on versions of the test like the one above few seem to grasp the significance of the (d) card as a potential falsifier of the proposed generalisation.

However, the results to be extracted from the selection task are more interesting and subtle than indicated so far. Changing the details of the task can change performance. You might expect that devising less abstract forms of the card-test, dealing with topics which are concrete and familiar to people, would significantly improve performance. But not so: familiarity turns out *not* to be one of the crucial variables. However, subjects do perform much better if they are dealing with what is called a *deontic* version of the task; that is, a case in which they are considering a normative rule which may be kept to or broken, rather than a factual generalisation. Thus, if the rule is *If anyone is drinking alcohol, then they must be over 18 years of age*, and the information about individuals' ages and drinks printed on cards reads: (a) *drinking a beer*, (b) *drinking cola*, (c) *26 years of age*, and (d) *16 years of age*, subjects see the importance of selecting the (d) card much more easily (Johnson-Laird *et al.*, 1972; Griggs and Cox, 1982).

So what needs to be explained is why people do badly at some versions of the selection task and not so badly at others. We will consider attempts to explain performance on this task in section 4. But it can hardly be denied that performance on the basic version of the selection task is very poor. Given that we are dealing with a general conditional of the form 'If anything is an *F*, then it is a *G*' ('If any card has an A on one side, then it has a 5 on the other'), this is logically inconsistent with the existence of something which is *F* and *not-G*. Surely, one might think, people ought to be capable of realising that it is just as relevant to examine items which are *not-G* as it is to examine items which are *F*. In the face of this sort of data, do we have to allow that people sometimes fail to make even very simple logical inferences? Or are there limits to be set on the degree of irrationality possible?

3 Philosophical arguments in defence of rationality

Like so many other things we do, reasoning would seem to be something we can do more or less well. So it should be possible to distinguish between *how one ought to reason* and *how people do in fact reason*. How one ought to reason (presumably, in order to arrive at enough true conclusions and to avoid false ones) is something studied by logic, an ancient branch of philosophy. How people actually do reason is something to be studied by psychology. Of course, it might be that people do reason – by and large – in the way that they ought to reason. But surely we cannot assume without investigation that this happy state of rationality prevails?

In general we are suspicious of the sort of conceptual analysis which would presume to lay down constraints on possible scientific enquiry in an *a priori* fashion. For the last thing philosophy should seek to do is impose a conceptual straitjacket on the growth of knowledge. In the end there are always going to be ways of breaking free from such restraints, such as devising new concepts which are liberated from the old conceptual necessities. Yet in the present instance there is undeniable plausibility in the thought that reasoning can only be *so* bad and still be *reasoning* at all. Despite the distinction between how people do reason and how they ought to reason, are there not limits to the extent that these two can differ? Must it not be the case that most of the time people reason as they ought to? After all, not just any old transition between thoughts can qualify as a piece of reasoning or inference. There must at least be some difference between a piece of reasoning and mere daydreaming! Or so it might seem. So we need to review arguments which seek to show that rationality is necessary or indispensable or otherwise guaranteed, and determine what they do establish.

3.1 The argument from interpretation

The most popular of such arguments has been the argument from *inter-pretation*. This has several variants, depending upon what sort of interpretation is claimed to require an imputation of rationality. It may be maintained that taking people to be rational is a precondition of considering their doings to be genuine instances of agency, or of making sense of their intentional states, or of taking them to be believers capable of entertaining both true and false thoughts at all.

Something which should be conceded to this line of argument is that genuine actions – as contrasted with bodily performances like snoring, hiccoughing and blushing – are things which agents do for reasons. Deeds of intentional agency all fall under the most general (and content-free) law of folk psychology, that agents act in such a way as to satisfy their desires in the light of their beliefs. So to take something a person does as an action is to assume that it is done for a reason, whether or not we can figure out what that reason might be. In taking something to be an intentional action we are assuming that it can be 'rationalised', in the sense that it can be explained in terms of the agent's reason for so acting. This point has been repeated very frequently in the philosophical literature. Unfortunately, many make the mistake of supposing that it establishes more than it really does. If an agent acts intentionally, then the agent has a reason for so acting. But that does not mean that the agent has a *good* reason. The action, or at any rate the attempt to act, needs to be appropriate in relation to (some of) the agent's own desires and beliefs. That gives no guarantee that the beliefs themselves are rationally held.

In order to establish a deeper root for a guarantee of rationality it is sometimes suggested that assuming subjects of interpretation to be rational is a precondition of engaging in the practice of belief-ascription (Davidson, 1973, 1974; Dennett, 1971, 1981). Taking people to be believers just is taking them to be rational. This claim is regularly presented under the guise of some such principle as the *principle of charity* – according to which attributions of unwarranted and irrational beliefs to the interpretee are to be avoided if at all possible. Our view is that any such principle has, at best, a heuristic role and a defeasible status. That, of course, is the realist view about intentional states. If anti-realism about beliefs were right, and what a person believed were fixed by the best available principles of belief-ascription, then we would have to accept a guarantee of at least limited rationality. But we have already found good grounds for rejecting anti-realism about beliefs. So if you agree with the arguments advanced in chapter 2, you will think that anti-realism has the relation of dependence the wrong way round. Beliefs are not generated by practices of belief-ascription. It is the practices of belief-ascription which need to track the actual content of beliefs. This they do fairly well, though far from infallibly, in ordinary folk psychology.

In the last chapter we touched upon an aspect of mind-reading which may account for the erroneous idea that rationality of belief is somehow guaranteed by being built into principles of interpretation. We propose an *error theory* which promises to explain why such an assumption of rationality might seem to be at work. The error arises from the need to use simulation as a way of enriching the stock of inferred beliefs which we attribute to others. As we saw in the last chapter, simulators will be relying upon their own inferential transitions. In any normal case (excluding short-term doubts about one's sanity) it must seem to simulators that their own inferential processes are rational, otherwise they would not be drawing the inferences they are. So it is true that simulators will generally (unless discounting for known foibles and idiosyncrasies) represent the target of their mental simulations as reasoning in a rational way *by the simulator's own lights*. The error which our error theory diagnoses is that of identifying rationality with the simulator's own inferential dispositions.

That is understandable, of course, if the business of belief-ascription is viewed from the perspective of the interpreter. But all that is required in order for the process of inferential simulation to work well enough for the purposes of folk psychology is that target and simulator should reason *in much the same way*. Correspondence may be achieved by their reasoning equally well, but for purposes of prediction and interpretation they can reason *equally badly* just so long as they make the same mistakes. So after seeing *Black* come up several times in succession an onlooker may be right in thinking that one of the gamblers will expect *Red* to predominate in the next few spins of the wheel – because they are both wrong in expecting this! So predictive and interpretative success may be achieved through common deficiencies, rather than perfect rationality.

Another variant on the argument from interpretation attempts to establish that believers' true beliefs must vastly outnumber their false beliefs (Davidson, 1975). The idea is that we can only ascribe false beliefs to thinkers in cases in which we can identify what it is that they have false beliefs *about*. So in order for someone to believe something falsely, such as that *the gun in Edgar's hand is unloaded*, they have to possess numerous true beliefs, such as that *there is a gun in Edgar's hand*, *Edgar has a hand*, and so on. However, this argument would only show that thinkers must have very many more true beliefs than false beliefs (true by *our* lights, that is), if we *have* to be able to identify and report what it is that they falsely believe in a referential vocabulary to which we, the interpreters, are committed. It does not eliminate the possibility of a thinker having indefinitely many false beliefs which other people cannot comprehend. We return to this point in chapter 6, when we discuss arguments for so-called 'wide content'.

We shall spend no more time on variants of the argument from interpretation. Realists will be more interested in arguments which impose limits on the extent to which beliefs themselves can be irrational, rather than on any heuristic considerations constraining the sorts of irrationality we can *ascribe*.

3.2 The argument from content

The argument from *content* is more effective and, in our view, does impose constraints on possible degrees of irrationality. This argument claims, firstly, that what it is for an intentional state to be the intentional state that it is, involves its having a specific content; and secondly, that in the case of beliefs, the content which they have depends, in part, upon their inferential role. The first of these claims is not in dispute. The second claim is more controversial, but since we shall recommend a (weak) form of functional-role semantics in chapter 7, we are committed to it.

The basic thought behind the argument from content can be presented like this. Suppose someone sincerely assents to the statement 'P * Q'. (Here the '*' is intended as a dummy sign, to be taken as a target of subsequent interpretation.) The person also comes to believe that P, but does not assent to the statement 'Q' and does not believe that Q even though still assenting to 'P * Q'. In such a case, if the thinker expressed any belief in assenting to 'P * Q', it cannot have been the belief that *if P then Q*. A thinker who believes *P* and fails to draw the inference to *Q*, cannot believe *if P then Q*, because it is *constitutive of having such a belief* that one should infer the truth of the consequent from the truth of the antecedent.

A similar point can be made using Stich's well-known example of Mrs T (1983). This old lady was ready to say that *President McKinley had been assassinated*. But when asked what had become of McKinley, she was not sure whether he was still alive or dead. The fact that she did not believe McKinley to be dead would seem to show that she had no stable belief that McKinley had been assassinated, rather than that she believed that, but was no longer rational enough to grasp that he must therefore be dead (Carruthers, 1996c). It seems appropriate to describe this case by saying that Mrs T had suffered a loss of memory. She remembered that 'President McKinley was assassinated' said something true, but she no longer remembered what that truth was.

In support of the argument from content, one can offer some persuasive examples of 'content-constitutive' inferential links. But a well-known voice has been raised against any form of inferential-role semantics. Fodor has repeatedly objected (1987, 1990; Fodor and Lepore, 1992) that in the light of Quine's attack on the analytic–synthetic distinction there is no principled way of distinguishing those inferential links which are constitutive of meaning from those which are not. (See Quine, 1951, who argues that there is no such thing as an inference which is valid in virtue of the meaning or content of its terms; rather, there is just a spectrum of inferences to which we are more-or-less firmly committed.) Fodor urges that the only adequate response to this point is to recognise the atomicity of representational content: that each particular belief has the content it has in virtue of its distinctive causal relationship with the world (see chapter 7). Otherwise we will be forced into the holistic absurdity of supposing a particular content to be constituted by the *totality* of its inferential links – in which case it must be doubtful if two thinkers can ever both have instances of a shared belief-type.

However, this line of argument involves an oversimplification. The question is: what inferential links *must* be in place if a thinker is to have a belief with a certain content? The answer, 'Those which are constitutive of content', is not unprincipled, even if it is not very informative. If you then go on to ask: 'How do you tell the links which are constitutive of content from those which are not?', you ask a difficult question. But one thing which ought to be clear is that there is no reason to suppose that there is going to be a single principle capable of delivering appropriate answers for all concepts, for all contents.

The problem with analytic inferential links, as determiners of content, is not that they are unprincipled, but that simple and transparent cases are in relatively short supply. Where we do have simple and transparent cases of this sort of inferential link, the source of the principle is usually easy enough to discern: we are dealing with a *derivative* concept which was linguistically introduced to thinkers via the inferential link in question. This applies to *assassinate*, and of course it also applies to the favourite philosophical example *bachelor* (therefore: *unmarried man*). These content-constitutive inferential links are readily accessible to us because they are the conduits through which we learnt the concepts in question. It is instructive to compare *bachelor* with *brother*. In terms of necessary and sufficient conditions 'male sibling' offers as good a definition of 'brother' as 'unmarried (adult) male' does of 'bachelor'. But a little girl can think that her brother has just come into the room without thinking that a sibling of hers has just come in.

It is quite evident that not all concepts are derivative: they cannot all be learnt through explicitly and prescriptively establishing an inferential link. Developmental studies suggest that our repertoire of conceptual contents is preconfigured by an intuitive metaphysics which sets firm divisions between such categories as *people*, *animals*, *plants*, and *artefacts* (Sperber *et al.*, 1995b). Such an intuitive metaphysics will at least associate with kind-concepts the sorts of inferential links which place them within an appropriate hierarchical category. So, for example, I will not be able to have such a belief as 'Algernon is a tortoise' unless I am ready to infer 'Algernon is an animal' and 'Algernon is alive'. If I think that it is really an open possibility that Algernon may turn out to be some sort of clockwork toy, then although I may *say* 'Algernon is a tortoise' I will not be sharing the belief which people usually have when they say that.

Admittedly, it does seem possible that someone – Sophie, say – should believe *of* tortoises that they are not animals, but rather some sort of mechanical device. But whether we can report her states of mind by using the concept *tortoise* depends upon the specific, purpose-relative interests which apply in a particular context. For example, we can certainly countenance the report, 'Sophie has noticed the tortoise in the garden', since this merely communicates the presence of a tortoise and Sophie's awareness – however conceptualised – of it. We can, perhaps, also report, 'Sophie has noticed that there is a tortoise in the garden', thereby attributing to Sophie a classification of the thing noticed in the garden as 'a tortoise'. But does Sophie *think* that there is a tortoise in the garden? The answer to this question hovers over the contexts in which content is attributed. For predictive purposes it is just barely acceptable (because she may *say*, 'A tortoise', if you ask her what it is), but also seriously misleading – because you cannot apply the strategy of *inferential enrichment* (see chapter 4, section 3), since Sophie will not share most of the beliefs which people normally do about tortoises. (We will be returning to the distinction between *communicative* and *predictive/explanatory* contexts of content-attribution in chapter 6, section 5.1.)

Where there are content-constitutive inferential links, there will be corresponding limitations on possible degrees of irrationality. To be sure, nobody can be so irrational as to think that Algernon is a tortoise and seriously doubt that he is an animal. (Nobody *including* Sophie – who is not irrational, but rather just does not understand what a tortoise is.) However, because only some inferential links are constitutive of content, the argument from content imposes no more than an ultimate backstop against possible degrees of unreason, leaving wide tracts of irrationality open to the ordinary thinker. At least, there is nothing in this line of argument which would lead us to question the interpretation of psychological experiments on reasoning and inference.

3.3 The argument from reflective equilibrium

If we ask what might be the source of our judgements concerning rationality and what gives them any authority they have, we may begin to see the force of the argument from reflective equilibrium (Cohen, 1981, 1982). In a debate on the philosophy of science Kuhn once remarked that if we suppose we have an authority for assessments of rationality independent of that supplied by reflection on the best scientific practice, then we are opening the door to cloud-cuckoo-land (1970, p.264). More generally, one might say that any theory of rationality must ultimately be answerable to human practices of reasoning. If that is so, then it must be doubtful whether we can bring in any overall verdict of irrationality on the way that people think.

It will help to bring matters into focus if we compare and contrast the issue concerning rationality, on the one hand, with ethics, on the other – an area in which a method of reflective equilibrium is widely accepted as the appropriate way to develop and refine moral theory. The idea behind the methodology of reflective equilibrium in ethics is that we should aim to find principles which systematise moral judgements which are held to be intuitively correct after due and appropriate consideration. What the ethical theorist is doing is dependent upon what ordinary thinkers are doing when at the top of their form. The theorist wants to arrive at principles which deliver, in general, just the same verdicts as ordinary thinkers, trying to minimise cases where the judgements of ordinary thinkers have to be rejected as erroneous.

There are morally difficult situations in which, with the best will in the world, one might be uncertain as to what one ought to do. We also use reflective equilibrium to assess principles against received judgement in less problematic cases, and then extrapolate the principles in the hope of resolving the difficult and contentious issues – rather as if we were building a *statute law* of moral theory on the basis of the *case law* of normal moral judgements. It is quite possible that we may not feel happy about the resolution of some moral dilemma when subsumed under a proposed principle. But in that case it is up to us to articulate the reasons for our unease – and these reasons for rejecting the proposed solution then become, in their turn, part of the data which a more refined moral theory needs to take into account. That is what the process of reflective equilibrium between general principles and particular judgements involves.

People are by no means always certain to make the right judgements, of course, even when they are trying to do the right thing. They may make mistakes because they are flustered, upset, confused, involved in too partisan a way with some of the people affected by a moral decision, and so on. So we need to make a distinction between people's *performance* as moral agents (which will most likely fall short of the ideal for a multitude of reasons) and their underlying *competence* in judging what is morally right and wrong. In a similar way, Cohen suggests that people may make performance errors on reasoning tasks, but this should not lead to a diagnosis of irrationality at the level of competence because the normative criteria of rationality which we (philosophers and psychologists included) may propound are all developed in an attempt to systematise and extend ordinary intuitions about reasoning.

Cohen therefore claims that psychological research on reasoning falls into four categories: (1) it may reveal conditions under which subjects are prone to genuine cognitive illusions, in which case special mechanisms must be postulated to explain them, and (2) it may investigate circumstances in which subjects reason poorly because of mathematical or scientific ignorance; but more commonly, fallacious or deficient reasoning may be wrongly imputed to subjects by experimenters because the latter (3) apply the relevant normative criteria in an inappropriate way, or (4) apply normative criteria which are not the appropriate ones.

However, there is an important metaphysical difference between reflective equilibrium in the case of ethics and in the case of rationality. In the moral case, the rightness or wrongness of conduct is (many believe) ultimately dependent upon what humans value. But in the case of rationality, the truth or falsity of beliefs about the world depends upon the way the world is, not upon how humans think. There is thus available a standard which is independent of people's intuitions of rationality (if not independent of their total belief-set), which can be used in assessing inferential norms. We can ask, 'Are they *reliable* norms, being such as to reliably generate truth from truth?' When we raise this question, we may discover that the norms ordinarily employed are highly *un*reliable.

Moreover, the argument from reflective equilibrium fails in a further respect. For it assumes an identity of purpose behind the standards governing ordinary competence and our normative – consciously developed – criteria. In the case of morality this assumption is justified. The moral theorist and the sincere, intelligent moral agent share the same concern to develop and apply principles which make clear how one ought to act and why. Indeed, whenever confronted by a moral dilemma a sincere and intelligent moral agent *becomes* a moral theorist. By contrast, we cannot assume that the objectives served by normative criteria of rationality are exactly the same as the constraints shaping the functioning of cognitive systems of reasoning. Normative criteria governing inference may place overriding importance on preserving truth and avoiding falsehood. Given sufficient time, investment, co-operative effort, education and study, we may be capable of thinking in this way. But much of the time, when relying upon our native resources, we may well depend upon mechanisms for cognitive processing which answer to other priorities. We shall return to develop these points in section 5 below. For the moment, our conclusion is that philosophers have failed to provide any good reason for rejecting the results of the psychological reasoning experiments.

4 Psychological explanations of performance

An idea shared at one time by several investigators was that what made variants of the selection task – such as that given in section 2 above – difficult for so many subjects, was that they were abstract and schematic, being about numbers and letters rather than more tangible or everyday materials. So perhaps the explanation for divergent performance on the selection task was that theorists classed variants of the task together because of their *formal* similarity, and yet these were different processing tasks for the subjects involved. According to the logician, the validity of an inference is a matter of the truth-preserving quality of a general pattern or schema which it exhibits, such as: *All Fs are Gs; all Gs are H; so, all Fs are H.* Instances of that pattern will be valid, no matter what 'F', 'G' and 'H' may be – whether the particular argument is about cabbages or kings.

But perhaps it matters to the ordinary reasoner's performance what a particular piece of reasoning is about. If she is familiar with cabbages and has had considerable practice in thinking about cabbages, perhaps she will perform much better on a test of reasoning about cabbages than on a similar test about kings (or triangles, or numbers, or sets). Several theorists (Manktelow and Evans, 1979; Griggs and Cox, 1982; Johnson-Laird, 1982; Pollard, 1982; Wason, 1983) have explored this basic idea by suggesting hypotheses concerning the way associational links might facilitate performance on reasoning tasks.

In fact it turned out that *mere* familiarity of subject matter has little effect upon task-performance. Although subjects do indeed perform better on some familiar versions of the selection task, it is always possible to find a version of the task which is equally familiar, but on which they perform poorly. Yet we need not give up on the idea that performance on such tasks is content-sensitive. Indeed, if we apply the general modularist research programme to results obtained on the selection task, we might expect that variation in performance on different versions of the task would be attributable to the operation of central modules specialising in different sorts of reasoning in different domains. This is an hypothesis which a number of investigators – most notably Cosmides and Tooby – have begun to explore.

4.1 Cheater detection: a module for monitoring social exchange

Familiarity of the subject matter may have some effect on performance, but it is swamped by the divergence on deontic (normative) and indicative (descriptive) versions of the selection task. Cosmides and Tooby (1992) have provided a decisive demonstration of this by testing subjects on tasks involving conditionals such as 'If you eat duiker meat, then you have found an ostrich eggshell' and 'If a man eats cassava root, then he must have a tattoo on his face'. Results showed that subjects performed better on deontic tasks than on indicative tasks concerning the same subject matter, whether that subject matter was familiar or not. Cosmides and Tooby's theory is that we have a specialised cognitive mechanism – a *cheater-detection module* – for reasoning about the sorts of deontic tasks on which subjects perform well. They consider these deontic tasks to engage a system of reasoning which is dedicated to normative conditionals concerning social contracts of the form 'If you have received the benefit, then you must pay the cost', or of the form 'If you have paid the cost, then you should receive the benefit'.

On a modularist and nativist approach of the type we advocate, there is a particularly strong case for postulating something like a cheater-detection system, on grounds of evolutionary selective pressures. For it is clear that human evolution has been heavily dependent upon novel forms of social co-operation. Yet along with all the advantages of co-operation comes an obvious danger – without special cognitive adaptations for monitoring social exchange, co-operative humans would offer to the free-riding cheat, who takes the benefits without paying the costs, an opportunity for exploitation. So, on game-theoretic grounds, a capacity to spot the cheater would be badly needed and likely to evolve. To do the job required, this would have to be a central module, capable of taking input from a variety of peripheral systems (such as hearing what people say and seeing what they are doing, as well as recollection of previous agreements). Hence the proposal of a special reasoning module for 'cheater-detection'.

Actually, this line of thought underestimates the evolutionary significance of such a special reasoning module. For it cannot be right to suppose that *first* there was contract-based social co-operation, *then* some individuals start to cheat, and *then* the others develop a capacity to detect cheating and take appropriate steps to exclude cheaters from the benefits. What is wrong with this picture is that innovative forms of social co-operation could not develop at all without a cognitive adaptation for social exchange. Before any worries about how to police a social contract arise, one needs a social contract to police. But that involves an understanding, on the part of contracting individuals, of what the contract implies. Those individuals need a way of working out and keeping track of the costs and benefits involved in social exchange. And then that very same mechanism will enable cheaters to be detected because it will be invoked both in working out what is required by way of fulfilment of an obligation and in discerning what is a case of defaulting. So perhaps it is something of a misnomer to call this module the 'cheater-detection module' – 'social-contract module' might be better. But we will retain the title since it seems to have become accepted. Besides, it may well be that what provided the initial impetus towards development of the module was selective pressure towards cheater detection in cases of social exchange which were *not* innovative (possibly early forms of food-sharing).

It is important that the special reasoning mechanism postulated as a cognitive adaptation for social exchange should not be (and is not taken by Cosmides and Tooby to be) a processing system for reasoning about prescriptive or deontic rules in general. For if all that we had in evidential support for the hypothesis of a cheater-detection module were considerations of evolutionary plausibility combined with data indicating a divergence in performance on deontic and indicative versions of the selection task, then the case for such a module would not be all that strong. This is because there is a potential alternative explanation as to why people do better on deontic tests. This is that deontic tests are easier because the deontic selection task is a *different* task, and one which is easier to process.

The reason why this might be so is that in the indicative versions of the task, subjects have to find the cards which need to be turned over in order to establish whether the 'rule' or generalisation *is true or not*. That is why the selection task is thought to show something about ability to test hypotheses. But in deontic versions of the task there is no question as to whether the rule is 'true' or not. In these cases it is a matter of stipulation that a certain prescriptive rule applies. The subjects' task is not to find out whether a certain rule obtains. (That really *would* be difficult. For while philosophers of science have laid heavy emphasis on the underdetermination of theory by evidence, it is far more obvious that observed conduct underdetermines prescriptive rules.) In the deontic cases subjects are asked to detect violations of a rule, but there is no doubt as to what the rule is. In the indicative cases, by contrast, subjects are presented with a rule or generalisation, but the truth-value of that generalisation is uncertain. So in effect subjects need to engage in an extra level of processing in the indicative selection tasks, because in order to solve them they have to ask themselves: 'Suppose this conditional applied. What would it rule out?' In the deontic tests that crucial first step is fed to the subjects, because they are told that the rule applies and asked to spot what it forbids. So if what was to be explained were just superior performance on deontic as compared with indicative versions of the selection task, it would seem that we could explain the difference very easily.

However, the hypothesis of a cheater-detection module suggests a more specific prediction than that deontic tasks will be easier than indicative ones. It predicts that, other things being equal, deontic tasks involving a trade-off between costs and benefits will be easier than both indicative tasks *and other deontic tasks*. For example, a social rule of the form 'If you are F, then you may do X', which permits something if a particular qualifying condition is satisfied, will be associated with improved performance on a selection task only if subjects take the doing of X to constitute a *benefit* (that is, not just a *good*, but an item in a cost-benefit social exchange). Cosmides and Tooby have devised a series of tests which confirm this novel and otherwise unexpected prediction (1989, 1992; Cosmides, 1989). For example, the very same statement of a rule – 'If a student is to be assigned to Grover High School, then that student must live in Grover City' – elicited better selection-test performance when it was explained that Grover High School was a superior school which citizens of Grover City had to pay for in terms of higher taxes (hence raising issues of fairness), even though in the control condition the importance of following the rule (in order to allow the right number of teachers to be put in a particular school) was given heavy emphasis.

We would add that it is also possible to detect this phenomenon retrospectively in tests carried out before the cheater-detection hypothesis was advanced, such as the postage stamp version of the selection task (Johnson-Laird *et al.*, 1972). In this test subjects had to decide whether the rule, 'If a letter is sealed, then it has a 5d stamp on it', was being observed in an array which showed: (a) the back of a sealed envelope; (b) the back of an unsealed envelope; (c) the front of an envelope with a 5d stamp on it; and (d) the front of an envelope with a 4d stamp on it. The experimenters described this conditional as 'meaningful', in contrast to an 'arbitrary' conditional which they used as a control. (In the control condition subjects were asked to decide whether the rule 'If a letter has a D on one side, then it has a 5 on the other' was being followed in an appropriate four-envelope array.) Of twenty-four subjects tested, twenty-one made the right selection in the case of the 'meaningful' rule, whereas only two got it right in the case of the 'arbitrary' rule. It was striking (and, we think, strikingly *modular*) that in spite of the formal similarity between the two conditions there was no transfer effect: having got the right answer on the 'meaningful' version did not help subjects to find the right answer in the control condition.

This was the sort of result which was interpreted as showing that reasoning is dependent on familiarity of content, with past experience

setting up some sort of associational link. However, a different interpretation of why the 'meaningful' rule is easier for subjects is possible in
the light of the cheater-detection hypothesis: the conditional may be
understood in such a way as to *prescribe* that the benefit of sealing the
envelope is only available if the (higher) 5d cost of postage is met. This
interpretation is confirmed by further tests comparing the performance of
subjects who varied in their knowledge of these postal arrangements.
American subjects did not perform as well on the test as subjects from
Hong Kong, where such a postal rule was enforced. But when the rule was
provided with a rationale – it was stated that sealed mail was treated as first
class – the American subjects did just as well on the selection task as Hong
Kong students (Cheng and Holyoak, 1985). We suggest that the rationale
served to aid subjects' reasoning by giving the task a cost-benefit structure,
hence bringing the cheater-detection module into play.

4.2 Relevance theory

The hypothesis of a cheater-detection module is strongly supported by the
fact that it is not only able to explain the divergence in performance
between deontic and indicative versions of the selection task, but also
yields a more precise specification of where the divergence is to be found.
Yet it cannot account for all the variation in performance to be found in
various versions of the selection task, since there is divergent performance
even on problems which do not differ in terms of possessing or lacking a
cost-benefit structure. Furthermore, even if we do have a special modular
capacity for reasoning about costs and benefits in social exchange, this
does not explain why we should be so surprisingly poor at many indicative
versions of the selection task, and in particular why we should find it so
difficult to spot the significance of the potentially falsifying (d) card. The
most impressive attempt to account for subjects' performance on these
indicative versions of the selection task involves the application of relevance theory, as advocated by Sperber and Wilson (1986/1995).

The thinking behind relevance theory is that new information presented
to an individual is always going to be processed in the context of previous
beliefs and earlier thought. The new information will be more or less
relevant to the individual depending upon the cognitive effects it produces,
in terms of new beliefs or modifications of existing beliefs. So *the greater
the cognitive effect, the greater the degree of relevance*. But a cognitive effect
will require processing, and heavy processing effort is likely to be too
expensive to indulge in. So *the greater the processing effort required to
extract a piece of information, the lesser its degree of relevance*. Sperber and
Wilson sum up their theory in terms of two general principles:

Cognitive principle of relevance: Human cognition tends to be geared towards the maximisation of relevance.

Communicative principle of relevance: Every utterance conveys a presumption of its own relevance.

In effect, they are offering an economics of cognition according to which human processing operates in such a way that the benefits of new cognitive acquisitions are balanced against the costs of the processing involved in their acquisition.

If we apply relevance theory to previously known results on indicative versions of the selection task, it immediately secures a promising success, by yielding an explanation as to why performance is improved if the conditional under consideration is of the form 'If F, then *not* G'. In such a case a majority of the subjects make the correct selection (Evans, 1972). For example, in a slightly altered version of the test presented in section 2, the conditional '*If there is an A on one side of the card, then there is* not *a 5 on the other*' would make the selection of cards (a) – containing an A – and (c) – containing a 5 – correct; and subjects do indeed tend to make this choice. Why?

Suppose that subjects check on the conditional by checking on what they take to be its consequences, relying upon the inferences they intuitively and unreflectively draw from it. Since any proposition has infinitely many consequences (from *P* we may infer *P or Q* and *P or Q or R* and so on), subjects must plainly stop when they judge that they have generated *enough* consequences to secure relevance. If the conditional is tacitly of the form 'For all x, if Fx then Gx' ('Every card is such that, if it has an A on one side then it has a 5 on the other'), then inferring that an instance *Fa* should, if the conditional is true, also be *G*, is the inference which costs subjects least in the way of processing effort. Hence the almost universal choice of card (a), which has *F* instanced (that is, having an A on it).

To make the other selection, subjects need to infer from the conditional a negative existential: that there is no instance such that it is *F* and *not-G*. But this inference involving negation is more costly for subjects in terms of processing effort (it is well known that inferences involving negation are more difficult). Instead, they tend to infer (non-deductively but reliably) from 'All Fs are Gs' to 'There are Fs and Gs', and so select the *F*-card and the *G*-card, rather than the *not-G*-card. However, with a negative version of the conditional, of the form 'For all x, if Fx then not Gx' ('Every card is such that, if there is an A on one side, then there is *not* a 5 on the other'), the burden of representing a negation within the scope of the negative existential has been lifted from subjects, and so the inference to 'There is no instance which is both an A and a 5' is more readily available to them. So on that version of the task they spot the significance of selecting the potentially falsifying *G*-card.

To avoid giving the impression that this is an easy, *ad hoc*, explanation of an already known result, Sperber and his collaborators have shown in detail how use of relevance theory can enable experimenters to manipulate subjects' performance on indicative selection tasks. In order to secure high levels of correct selections for conditionals of the form, 'For all x, if Fx then Gx' – making the selection task easy – one needs to increase the number of *F-and-not-G* choices, by reducing the required processing effort and/or by increasing the cognitive effect. To do the former, an experimenter could exploit a lexicalised concept which covers the *F-and-not-G* cases (for example, 'bachelor'; with *F*: 'male' and *G*: 'married'). To do the latter, one finds some way of making *F-and-G* cases less interesting to subjects than *F-and-not-G* cases. For full details of the experimental confirmation of these predictions of relevance theory, see Sperber *et al.*, 1995a.

The ability to control performance on a number of selection trials (although still requiring further replication) appears to be striking confirmatory evidence in favour of relevance theory. But a question arises concerning the relationship between relevance theory and the modularist research programme. For the relevance-theory explanation of results on indicative selection tasks is of a quite different kind from the postulation of a cheater-detection module dealing with deontic tasks which have a cost-benefit structure. Although different, it does not appear to be incompatible with modularity, however. For although the principles of relevance theory are intended to apply to cognitive processing in general, Sperber and Wilson are in no way committed to postulating a domain-general cognitive system or ability. It is entirely possible that relevance theory describes the constraints on cognitive efficiency which shape the functioning of a large number of distinct processing modules – although we would agree that how this might work out in a system of interacting central modules still remains fairly mysterious.

5 Practical rationality

Naive subjects attempting a selection task may not be following an infallible procedure for determining the truth-value of a conditional, but they may still (if relevance theory is right about this) be processing information in accordance with principles which secure a sort of efficiency worth having. We should expect ordinary human reasoning to be shaped by practical constraints which may not always elevate production of exactly the right answer above other considerations.

Consider once again the Wason selection task. What is generally described as 'confirmation bias' in the execution of this task – looking only at the *F* and *G* cases when testing a conditional of the form 'For all x, if Fx then Gx' – makes a good deal of sense when seen as a heuristic appropriate to most real-life cases. For suppose that the conditional in question is, 'For all x, if x is a raven, then x is black'. It makes sense to test this by looking for ravens, and perhaps by checking on the black things one comes across. But it makes no practical sense at all to conduct a search of *non-black* things, to try to find a potential falsifier; there are just too many of them! So confirmation bias can be seen, not as flat-out irrational, but rather as an overextension to the four-card case of a heuristic which is normally appropriate and rational. And given that the heuristic may in any case be implicit and non-conscious, it is easy to see how the overextension should come about.

Even if processing effort is available in abundance, pressure of time may make a partially reliable procedure which comes up with a conclusion swiftly of greater value than a slower but more exact computation. In other words, ordinary human reasoning may well use 'quick and dirty' methods for practical reasons. To give a simple example of a case involving explicit calculation: if one wants to convert a Celsius temperature into degrees Fahrenheit, the exact formula is: $F = 9C/5 + 32$. But if you are not too bothered to a degree or two and only want to know approximately how warm the weather is in terms of degrees Fahrenheit, then the approximation: $F = 2C + 30$ will serve well enough, while making the calculation so much quicker and easier to do in your head. Here is an instance in which those converting from one temperature scale to another will deliberately adopt a somewhat rough-and-ready approximation which is good enough for practical purposes.

If this kind of thing can happen at an explicit level of representation, something similar may occur at implicit levels of representation and within modular reasoning systems, as well. Tests of subjects on syllogistic reasoning, for example, suggest that assessments of validity by subjects without training in logic are indeed based on approximate principles which work fairly well, without being infallible (Oaksford and Chater, 1993, 1995). It is also well established that subjects exhibit 'belief bias' in assessing arguments – that is, they are much more willing to accept an argument with a believable conclusion, apparently using the likelihood of the conclusion as an index to the quality of the reasoning (Oakhill and Johnson-Laird, 1985; Oakhill *et al.*, 1989). Again, this is a fallible but quite reliable test, given that subjects will normally only countenance arguments whose premises they already believe.

5.1 Two notions of rationality

For these kinds of reasons, Evans and Over (1996) draw a distinction between two different notions of rationality, one of which is tied to general success, and the other of which employs whatever standards are derivable from normative systems of logic, probability theory and decision theory:

rationality$_1$: thinking which is generally reliable for achieving one's goals;

rationality$_2$: thinking which conforms with a (correct) normative theory.

Given the immense success enjoyed by our species (so far!), it seems very unlikely that ordinary human thinking should be lacking in *rationality*$_1$; but it may fail to exhibit *rationality*$_2$. Evans and Over have followed up this idea by proposing a dual process theory of thinking, according to which much of our thinking is carried out in terms of tacit and implicit processes. This can be accepted, with the modularist proviso that the level of implicit processing is itself multi-modular.

Evans and Over build up a powerful case that most human reasoning is governed by processes, such as those determining relevance and selective attention, which are implicit and inaccessible to the subject. Indeed, they report a particularly dramatic set of experiments in which subjects' choices in the selection task are manipulated by changing experimental variables, and where subjects are encouraged to verbalise the reasons for their choice (Evans, 1995). It turns out that eye-direction determines subsequent choice, with subjects choosing just those options which they initially attend to; and the explicit reasons subsequently offered are mere rationalisations of choices determined by a set of non-conscious heuristics. But Evans and Over do not deny that *sometimes* reasoning can be governed by processes which are explicit and conscious. Indeed, their dual-process theory of thinking maintains that both sets of processes can contribute to reasoning to a greater or lesser extent, depending on task demands. One of the distinguishing features of explicit (conscious) reasoning is said to be that it is verbally mediated, and that it is much more influenceable by verbal instruction. (We return to consider the possible connections between conscious reasoning and language in chapter 8.)

We therefore have two orthogonal distinctions in play: between two different notions of rationality, and between two different levels of cognition. Then one can (and should) ask of both implicit and explicit reasoning processes, to what extent they serve the subject's goals; and one can (and should) ask of both implicit and explicit processes, to what extent they approximate to valid logical norms.

First, as regards implicit processes, it seems plain that they must largely be rational$_1$, given that most reasoning is implicit, and given the practical success of our species. But it is also possible that some of these processes should be rational$_2$, involving computations which comply with valid norms, but driven by pre-logical judgements of relevance. (This seems to be the position adopted by Sperber *et al.*, 1995a.) Or alternatively, those processes may all be connectionist ones, as Evans and Over actually suppose, in which norms of reasoning find no direct application. Second, as regards explicit processes, the extent to which they are rational$_1$ may be highly variable, depending on what the subject's goals actually are. Similarly, one would expect that the extent to which they are rational$_2$ might depend upon the extent to which the subject has undergone appropriate training and instruction, since explicit normative criteria are usually arrived at through co-operative social enquiry.

To ask about the extent of human irrationality is to ask how often people reason as they *should*, or as they *ought*. But this question takes a very different colour when applied, first to implicit, then to explicit, processes of reasoning. For on reflection it is clear that, since implicit cognitive processes are outside of our control, it makes little sense to ask whether we *ought* to reason differently in respect of such processes. All we can really do is investigate the extent to which it is a good thing, from our perspective as agents, that those processes operate as they do. And as for explicit processes, it seems equally clear that there is unlikely to be any such thing as a basic reasoning *competence*, in the sense of an innate body of reasoning knowledge. Rather, explicit reasoning abilities will vary with subjects' different learning histories, and with subjects' differing theories of normative rationality. It does, however, continue to seem important to ask what norms *should* govern our explicit reasoning – but here it is vital to bear in mind the limits on our time, and the limitations of our cognitive powers.

5.2 Against the Standard Picture of rationality

If we ask how we *should* reason, when reasoning explicitly, most people assume that the answer is obvious – of course we should reason in accordance with norms derivable from valid logical systems. Call this the 'Standard Picture' of rationality, which sees rationality as coinciding with the set of norms derivable from more-or-less familiar principles of deductive logic, probability theory, and decision theory. We follow Stein (1996) in thinking that the Standard Picture is false, and should be replaced by a conception of rationality which is relativised to human cognitive powers. The main point is that it fails to take seriously the human *finitary predicament* (Cherniak, 1986). For example, the Standard Picture would seem to warrant normative principles such as this: 'If you believe some proposition *P*, then you should believe any valid consequence of *P*'; or this: 'Before you accept some new proposition *P*, you should check to see whether *P* is consistent with the other things which you already believe'.

These principles may seem reasonable enough, until one realises that compliance with them would be – to say the least – very time-consuming indeed! These are not in fact principles which finite beings could ever employ.

In effect, we need to incorporate the maxim '*Ought* implies *can*' into epistemology. The way in which we *ought* to reason is constrained by the way in which we *can* reason, and is relative to the powers and capacities of the human brain. Even where there is complete agreement concerning valid logical systems, it remains an open question how we *ought* (explicitly) to reason. But this is a question which has rarely been asked, let alone answered. So alongside the logician's project – and partially independent of it, at least – is the project of *practical epistemology*, or *practical rationality*. In fact there is not one project here but many. One task is to describe what principles of reasoning we should employ, given what is known or reasonably believed about human cognitive powers and functions, but assuming that our only goals are to obtain truth and avoid falsehood. But then there are a number of more complex subsidiary tasks which arise when we factor in the various other goals which people may legitimately have when reasoning, such as the desire to reach a decision within a given space of time. These tasks are largely unexplored, and cry out for further attention from epistemologists and philosophers of psychology (but see Cherniak, 1986; Stich, 1990; and Stein, 1996 for some discussion).

It is also important to remember that the development of normative standards for reasoning (the equivalent of the 'logician's task') is in some areas still very much work in progress. In philosophy of science, for example, the dominant tradition has, until recently, been the positivist one. This tradition – which is standardly both *instrumentalist* in relation to theories which go beyond what is observational, and *falsificationist* in its methodology – has provided the normative standards assumed by most psychologists investigating subjects' abilities to reason scientifically. But there have also been other, more realist, approaches to norms of scientific reasoning, derived from reflection on actual scientific practice as well as from armchair philosophical reasoning (Lakatos, 1970; Boyd, 1973, 1983). Naturally, as scientific realists ourselves, we favour this latter approach.

These disputes matter, because Koslowski (1996) has shown convincingly that a whole tradition of experiments which apparently reveal weaknesses in subjects' abilities to reason scientifically, may actually reflect a weakness in the positivistic philosophy of science upon which the experimental designs are based, rather than in the subjects' ability to evaluate hypotheses. So what, in a scientific context, may look like examples of unwarranted 'Confirmation Bias' or 'Belief Perseverance', may turn out to be appropriate epistemic practice, if the realist's approach is correct. For if scientific theorising is driven, not just by a concern to discover true generalisations, but to uncover real causal mechanisms, then it may be reasonable, for example, to revise rather than abandon a theory in the face of recalcitrant evidence, provided that some story about the different underlying mechanisms involved is available.

So our advice to the philosophers is: look to the psychological evidence of human cognitive powers, seeking to devise suitably *practical* epistemic norms; and our advice to the psychologists is: look to the best available philosophical account of the norms which are valid in a given domain, before devising tests of human rationality, and making pronouncements of irrationality. This is an area which is ripe for further inter-disciplinary collaboration.

6 Conclusion

In this chapter we have reviewed the philosophical arguments in support of human rationality, and have found that they are very limited in their effect. And we have reviewed some of the psychological evidence of human irrationality, from which a more complex picture emerges. In all likelihood human reasoning is conducted on a number of different levels in cognition, and within a variety of different modular sub-systems. What we do insist on is that questions concerning human rationality should be relativised to different domains – although until a reliable map of the modular structure of our cognition emerges, we can perhaps only guess at what the relevant domains are. And we also insist that if questions concerning rationality are to have normative *bite*, then they must become *practical*, being relativised to humans' limited powers and abilities.

SELECTED READING

For a general overview of philosophical issues concerning reasoning and rationality see: Stein, 1996.

For more details on reasoning tasks and experimental evidence consult: Manktelow and Over, 1990; Evans and Over, 1996.

For the argument from reflective equilibrium see: Cohen, 1981.

For criticism of philosophical attempts to secure a guarantee for human rationality: Stich, 1990; Stein, 1996.

On the cheater detection hypothesis: Cosmides and Tooby, 1992.

For the application of relevance theory to the selection task: Sperber, *et al.*, 1995a.

On the significance of human finitude: Cherniak, 1986; Stein, 1996.

6   Content for psychology

In this chapter we review, and contribute to, the intense debate which has raged concerning the appropriate notion of *content* for psychology (both folk and scientific). Our position is that the case for wide content (that is, content individuated in terms of its relations to worldly objects and properties) in any form of psychology is weak; and that the case for narrow content (that is, content individuated in abstraction from relations to the world) is correspondingly strong. But we also think that for some common-sense purposes a notion of wide content is perfectly appropriate.

1 Introduction: wide versus narrow

The main reasons why this debate is important have to do with the implications for folk and scientific psychology, and the relations between them. (But it will also turn out, in chapter 9, that the defensibility of narrow content is crucial to the naturalisation of consciousness.) For if, as some suggest, the notion of content employed by folk psychology is wide, whereas the notion which must be employed in scientific psychology is narrow, then there is scope here for conflict. Are we to say that science shows folk psychology to be *false*? Or can the two co-exist? And what if the very idea of narrow content is incoherent, as some suggest? Can scientific psychology employ a notion of content which is externally individuated? Or would this undermine the very possibility of content-involving psychology?

Some wide-content theorists, such as McDowell (1986, 1994), believe that the debate has profound implications for philosophy generally, particularly for epistemology. McDowell maintains that narrow-content theorists place an intermediary between the mind and the world, somewhat in the way that Cartesians and sense-data theorists did, making sceptical worries especially pressing. We believe that this is a muddle. The debate is about the individuation-conditions for content, not about referential semantics, or about the phenomenology of thinking. Narrow-content theorists should agree that each token thought *will have* truth-conditions, and those truth-conditions will standardly involve worldly items and states of affairs. Equally, a narrow-content theorist should agree that when one thinks a token thought, the whole focus of one's attention may be on the worldly items which the thought concerns. But narrow-content theorists deny what wide-content theorists assert, namely that the truth-conditions of thoughts are essential to their identity. A narrow-content theorist will say that the very same thought could have been entertained, in different circumstances, with different truth-conditions.

The theory of content which derives from Frege (1892), and which has dominated philosophical thinking for much of this century, distinguishes two different aspects of thought-content and sentence-meaning – there is *reference*, which is constituted by the states of affairs and objects in the world which our thoughts concern; and there is *sense*, which is the *mode of presentation of* or the *manner of thinking of* reference. The terms 'Venus' and 'The Evening Star' share the same reference but differ in sense. And the thoughts expressed by 'Venus has set' and 'The Evening Star has set' share the same truth-conditions, but differ in the manner in which those conditions are presented in thought. So one might, for example, believe the first thought to be true while denying that the second was, and vice versa.

As is suggested by this last remark, Fregean sense is to be individuated in accordance with *the intuitive criterion of difference* – two senses are distinct if it is possible for someone rationally to take differing epistemic attitudes to thoughts which differ only in that the one contains the one sense while the other contains the other (as in the example of Venus and The Evening Star just given).

On the Fregean account, sense is supposed to *determine* reference. It is supposed to be impossible that any term or thought-component should share the very same sense as the term 'Venus' and yet differ in reference. (Reference, on the other hand, does not determine sense – there are many different ways of referring to, or thinking of, the planet Venus.) So it is sufficient to individuate the content of a thought, or the meaning of a sentence, that one should specify its sense, since the reference will thereby have been fixed.

Difficulties for the Fregean system began to arise when it was noticed that there are many terms which do not appear to differ in the manner in which they *present* their referents (from a subjective point of view, at least), and yet which refer to different things. For example, the indexical term 'I' seems to have the same sense for each one of us, but picks out a different person in each case. So either (1) we have to say that sense does not determine reference, or (2) we have to say that the actual reference belongs amongst the individuation-conditions of a sense.

Defenders of narrow, or 'internalist', content take the first option. They say that the thought, 'I am cold' has the same sense (the same narrow content) for each one of us. But those senses are *about* different things, and different tokens of the very same (narrow) thought can have different worldly truth-conditions. Defenders of wide, or 'externalist', content take the second option. They say that since the token thoughts expressed by 'I am cold' have different truth-conditions in the case of each one of us (and can in some cases be true while in other cases being false), those thoughts belong to different types, with different contents. So we do not think the same thing when we each of us think 'I am cold'. The thoughts are distinct because the referents are.

2 Arguments for wide content

In this section of the chapter we shall consider some of the arguments which have been offered in defence of wide content, concluding with the argument that narrow content is actually incoherent. Then in section 3 we respond to this challenge, arguing that it is at least *possible* that psychology should be narrow; and in section 4 we shall argue that explanatory psychology *is* narrow.

2.1 Externalist intuitions

Putnam (1975a) devised a new type of philosophical thought-experiment to demonstrate that meanings 'ain't in the head'. We are to imagine that there is, or could be, an exact duplicate of Earth (Twin Earth, often written 'Twearth'), where everything is exactly as it is on Earth, except for some minor respect which can be varied depending upon the type of example. Imagine, in particular, that everything on Twearth is exactly as it is on Earth, down to the smallest detail, *except* that on Twearth water $\neq H_2O$. Rather, on Twearth water $= XYZ$, where the two substances can only be distinguished from one another in a chemistry laboratory. Putnam argues that if a person on Earth, $Peter_e$, asserts 'Water is wet' and his twin on Twearth $Peter_{tw}$ makes the same utterance, then their thoughts differ in content (and their sentences differ in meaning) because the substances they respectively refer to are different.

Suppose that neither $Peter_e$ nor $Peter_{tw}$ initially knows the composition of water/twater. Then each of them is told in similar circumstances 'Water is H_2O', and believes it. Surely, Putnam argues, they cannot have formed *the very same* belief, since $Peter_e$'s belief is *true* while $Peter_{tw}$'s belief is *false*. And how can the very same thought-content be both true and false at one and the same time? Yet every aspect of their brains and of their internal (non-relationally described) psychology is, by hypothesis, exactly the same. Conclusion: the contents of thoughts about natural kinds (and the meanings of sentences referring to natural kinds) depend upon the *actual* internal constitution of the kinds in question. Where that actual internal constitution differs, then so does the content of the thought. That is to say: thought-content is *wide* in its individuation-conditions, involving properties (often unknown) in the thinker's environment.

Similar arguments have been developed by Burge (1979, 1986a), in connection with non-natural kinds, this time turning on linguistic division of labour. (This latter phenomenon was also discovered by Putnam – I can say 'There is an elm in the garden' and *mean* that it is an elm, even though I personally cannot tell elms from beeches, because I speak with the intention of deferring to the judgements of those who *can* distinguish them.) Burge's well-known arthritis example is designed to show that thought-content depends for its identity partly on *social* facts about one's linguistic community, which can differ even when nothing internal to two thinkers is different. So, again, the moral is that 'meaning ain't in the head'.

The example (slightly adapted) is this: $Peter_e$ and $Peter_{tw}$ are identical in all physical and non-relationally described respects; and each believes that arthritis is a painful condition affecting the joints *and bones*. The difference between them is that $Peter_e$ lives in a community where people use the term 'arthritis' just to designate a certain kind of inflammation of the joints (his false belief results from some sort of misinformation or confusion); whereas $Peter_{tw}$ lives in a community where people use the term 'arthritis' rather more broadly, to refer to a range of painful conditions (by hypothesis, $Peter_{tw}$ formed his belief through a causal route exactly mirroring the way in which $Peter_e$ formed his). But now when each of them asserts, 'I have arthritis in my thigh', one of them ($Peter_e$) says something *false*, whereas the other ($Peter_{tw}$) expresses a belief which is *true*. This is then supposed to motivate us to think that $Peter_e$ and $Peter_{tw}$ entertain beliefs with different contents, merely by virtue of living in different linguistic communities. So, it is argued, those beliefs must be externally individuated.

Yet another set of externalist intuitions is invoked by Evans (1982) and McDowell (1984, 1986, 1994), who focus especially on singular thoughts. They maintain that singular thoughts are both *Russellian*, in that they involve, as constituents, the actual individual things thought about, and *Fregean*, in that they also involve a *mode of presentation* of those things. Bertrand Russell had maintained that thoughts are relations between persons and propositions, where a proposition is a complex consisting of the actual objects of thought themselves (individuals and properties). So if I entertain the thought 'Pavarotti is fat', this consists of a relation between me, the singer Pavarotti himself, and the property of fatness. Such a view at least has the virtue of simplicity.

The problem for Russell's account is that it is too austere to do all the work that we need a notion of thought to perform. In particular, we surely think that there can be many *different* thoughts about the singer Pavarotti and the property of fatness. Whereas on Russell's account there is only one (not involving any other elements, such as negation – Russell of course allows that the thought 'Pavarotti is *not* fat' is different). Thus the thoughts 'Pavarotti is fat' and '*That* man is fat' – where the *that* is a demonstrative element, picking out a particular person seen on TV or on the stage – are surely different. For if I do not know what Pavarotti looks like, I might believe the one to be false while believing the other to be true. And so those thoughts would guide my behaviour differently too – I would say 'No' in response to a question about the first, but would say 'Yes' in answer to the same question about the second. Yet they both involve the very same Russellian proposition: both ascribe the property of being fat to the very same man.

Evans and McDowell believe that singular thoughts are individuated, in part, by the objects they concern. But they allow that thoughts may also differ by differing in the way in which one and the same object is presented. (It is a consequence of this view that in the absence of an appropriate individual, there is no singular thought there to be had. So someone who is merely hallucinating the presence of an individual is incapable of thinking any singular thought about that – putative – thing. We shall return to this consequence below.) On this account, then, although a singular thought contains two different aspects (the object in the world, and its mode of presentation), these are not supposed to be fully separable. In particular, there is supposed to be no possibility of the singular mode of presentation either existing, or being characterisable, independently of the object presented.

In what follows, we shall focus on the case of singular thought in particular, for two reasons. The first is that all the issues which concern us arise here in their sharpest relief. Our main conclusions should generalise from this relatively simple case to thought about both natural and non-natural kinds. The second is that the externalist intuitions stimulated by Twin Earth thought-experiments are usually felt most strongly in the case of natural kinds like water. Resisting those intuitions is liable to involve arguments sketching elaborate scenarios – transportation between Earth and Twin Earth, migrant interplanetary plumbers who may or may not suffer from amnesia, a Twix Earth where the liquid in the Atlantic is XYZ while that in the Pacific is H_2O, and such like. Diverse variations on the original thought-experiment may dilute the strength of the intuitions, but usually allow some way out for the externalist who stubbornly clings to Putnam's model of the indexical introduction of natural kind concepts, according to which one means by '*water*' (say) something like: 'Stuff which is the same as *this* in its basic composition'. So the most incisive line of attack will be directed against singular thoughts such as those about ostended samples, on which indexical concepts must ultimately depend.

2.2 Arguments for externalist folk psychology

What reason is there to believe that singular thoughts are Russellian (constitutively involving the object thought about) as well as Fregean? That is, why should one believe (roughly) that *same content = same reference + same mode of presentation*? One bad argument, which is nevertheless frequently to be found in the literature, is that we routinely *describe* such thoughts in terms of their objects. We say 'John thinks that *that* cat is dangerous'; 'Mary thinks that *John* is a coward'; and so on.

Now, this certainly does not show anything very much by itself. For the fact that we individuate, describe, or pick out, something by its relation to another does not show that the latter figures amongst the *identity conditions* of the thing in question. Thus, I might pick out Big Ben tower in London for you by saying, 'It is the clock-tower which stands next to the Houses of Parliament'. But this does not make the Parliament building constitutive of the identity of Big Ben. On the contrary, we think that the former could be destroyed, for example, while leaving the latter the very same as it was. So, the fact that I individuate John's thought for you by indicating the particular cat he is thinking about, does not show that the cat in question is a constitutive part of, or essential to the existence and identity of, his thought.

There are, however, cases in which we might be tempted to insist that distinct thoughts are entertained, where the only available distinguishing feature is the difference in their objects. For example, suppose that Mary and Joan walk into different but *exactly similar* burger bars, and sit down at identical tables in the corner. Each then thinks, 'This table is greasy.' Since one of these thoughts might be true while the other is false (in Joan's case the table may only be wet), it looks as if we need to insist that the thoughts belong to distinct types. But there is nothing in the mode(s) of presentation of the tables to distinguish them. The difference must then lie with their objects – that is to say, in the numerical difference between the two tables. So, in contrast with the Big Ben example above, it might be held that it is no mere accident that we would describe these thoughts by indicating which table is in question – by saying, for example, 'Mary is thinking that *that* table (the one in front of her) is greasy, whereas Joan is thinking that *that* table (the one in front of *her*) is greasy'.

But this argument just assumes, without defence, that it is thought-*types* rather than thought-*tokens* which are the primary bearers of truth-values. For recall that narrow-content theorists do not deny that thoughts have truth-conditions; they just deny that thoughts (as types) are to be individuated in terms of their truth-conditions. So if it is thought-tokens which are the bearers of truth-values, then we can say that Mary and Joan are both thinking thoughts of the very same type, with the very same (narrow) content; but since they entertain distinct *tokens* of that type, the one can be true while the other is false.

Another – more powerful – argument picks up on, and defends, the Russellian consequence that a singular thought must *fail to exist* in the absence of an appropriate object. (If singular thoughts are individuated by their relation to the object referred to, in such a way that the object is part of the identity of the thought, then if there is no object, there is no thought either.) Thus suppose that I hallucinate the presence of a cat, and think to myself, '*That* cat is lost.' On the Russellian view, I here attempt, but *fail*, to think a singular thought. It merely *seems* to me that I have thought a demonstrative thought, when I have not. Now if we wish to reject the Russellian view, we shall need to avoid this consequence. And that means finding a way of saying *what* thought I succeed in thinking in the case of the hallucinated cat. A further argument for externalism, then, is that none of the available alternatives seems successful.

In particular, the content of the (putative) singular thought, '*That* cat is lost' is not the same as the content of any *descriptive* thought, which would be available for me to entertain (but which would then be false) in the case of the non-existent cat. (For these purposes we assume the truth of Russell's Theory of Definite Descriptions, according to which a statement of the form 'The F is G' should be analysed as saying 'There exists one and only one [relevant] F and it is G'.)

E.g. (1): the thought ≠ 'The cat in my office is lost' (supposing that I am in my office at the time). For I may doubt this, while continuing to believe that *that* cat is lost, if I forget where I am. So the thoughts are distinct by the Fregean intuitive criterion of difference. Alternatively, I might believe that there are *two* cats in my office, and so deny that *the* cat in my office is lost, while continuing to believe that *that* cat is lost.

E.g. (2): the thought ≠ 'The cat over *there* is lost.' For again, since in a hall of mirrors I might wonder, 'Is *that* cat over *there*?', I might doubt whether the cat over there is lost while continuing to believe that *that* cat is lost.

E.g. (3): the thought ≠ 'The cat now causing *these* very experiences is lost' (*contra* Searle, 1983, ch.8). For while it seems implausible that I

could ever doubt whether *that* cat is causing *these* experiences
(that is, the experiences which now ground my demonstrative
reference to that cat), it seems quite wrong to make all demonstrative thoughts involve reference to one's current experiences.
For my experiences are not, normally, an object of attention in
such cases. And indeed, it surely seems possible for someone (a
young child, or an autistic person, say) to entertain the thought,
'*That* cat is lost' who does not yet *have the concept of* experience.

These points give rise to an argument against the very coherence of narrow
content. For narrow contents are supposed to be available to be thought,
whether or not their putative worldly objects exist or are present. But if it
turns out that in the absence of an object there is no way of stating the
content of the putative singular thought, then it seems that there can be no
such world-independent content.

3 The coherence of narrow content

In this section we take up the challenge presented by the argument outlined
above. Note that it is a suppressed premise of the argument that if a
thought-content exists at all, then it can be specified by means of a
that-clause. That is to say, it is assumed that, if a singular thought really is
entertained in the hallucination case, then it must be possible for us to *say*
what thought is entertained by means of a phrase of the form, 'He is
thinking *that such-and-such.*' This assumption is tacitly rejected in the
alternative proposals for specifying narrow content considered in section
3.1 below. It will then be explicitly examined and criticised in section 3.2.

3.1 Specifying narrow content

Fodor (1987, ch.2) acknowledges that we cannot *express* a narrow content directly, using a that-clause; because any such clause will automatically take on one or another *wide* content (that is, truth-condition). But
he thinks we can (as he puts it) *sneak up on* narrow contents, providing
such contents with an indirect characterisation. Fodor maintains, in fact,
that *narrow contents are functions from contexts to truth-conditions*. Thus
the narrow content which I and my twin share when each of us says,
'Water is wet', is that unique content which, when 'anchored' on Earth
has the truth-condition, H_2O *is wet*, and when anchored on Twearth has
the truth-condition, *XYZ is wet*. (Most of Fodor's discussion concerns
natural-kind examples.) Similarly, the narrow content which we share
when each of us says, '*That* cat is dangerous', is the unique content which,

when anchored in the context of Tiddles has the truth-condition, *Tiddles is dangerous*, and when anchored in the context of Twiddles has the truth-condition, *Twiddles is dangerous*.

Notice that Fodor's approach makes narrow contents entirely parasitic upon wide content – indeed, upon wide content conceived of purely in terms of truth-conditions, or worldly states of affairs. For Fodor will have no truck with Fregean senses, or *modes of presentation* of truth-conditions. In fact, there is nothing *more* to any given narrow content than its being that state which, when embedded in one context yields one truth-condition, and when embedded in another context yields another. Indeed, as we shall see in the next chapter, Fodor's project is to offer a naturalistic wide-content semantics, characterising meaning and reference in purely causal terms, and then to construct a notion of narrow content to ride piggy-back on that. Why is Fodor so minimalist about the nature of narrow content? In part because of an obsessive fear of *holism*, as we shall see in due course. If one said more, of an intra-cranial sort, about what makes any given narrow content the content that it is, this would presumably have to work by relating that content to others (what further beliefs that content may lead the thinker to by inference, for example). But then there may be no way of stopping short of saying that the (narrow) content of any one belief will implicate *all* the subject's other beliefs. This is a consequence Fodor is keen to avoid.

The main problem with Fodor's minimalist approach, however, is that it fails to give us a notion of content which satisfies the Fregean *intuitive criterion of difference*. Thus, let us return to an earlier example, comparing the two thoughts, 'Pavarotti is fat' and '*That man* is fat.' These are plainly distinct, by the intuitive criterion, since I might doubt the one while believing the other, or vice versa. But they come out as possessing the same narrow content, on Fodor's account (and so as having the same wide content too, of course). For, of *each* of these thoughts you can say that it is the thought which, when embedded in a context containing the singer Pavarotti, in such a way that the referential element of the thought is causally connected to that person, it has the truth-condition, *Pavarotti is fat*. Both thoughts end up with a truth-condition which attributes fatness to one and the same man. Similarly, consider the two thoughts one might express by saying, '*That* man is well paid' (both, again, involving reference to the singer Pavarotti), where the one is grounded in vision and the other in hearing. By the intuitive criterion these should come out as distinct, since one might of course doubt whether *that* man (seen) is *that* man (heard). But by Fodor's account they will come out as the very same, since the same function from contexts to truth-conditions is instantiated. The two thoughts are such that, whenever the demonstrative elements are caused by one and the same person, then they have the same truth-condition. Bad news for Fodor, we say.

Carruthers' (1987a) proposal is initially somewhat similar. It is that we can describe the narrow content entertained, in the case of hallucination (for example, of a dangerous cat), by exploiting the alleged identity of narrow content across contexts. We can say, in fact: 'He is entertaining a thought with the very same (narrow) content as he *would* have had if there had been a real cat there causing his experiences, and if he had entertained a demonstrative thought, concerning the cat, that *it* is dangerous'. And we can say what is common to Peter$_e$ and Peter$_{tw}$ when each entertains a thought they would express with the utterance, '*That* cat is dangerous', by saying: 'Each is entertaining the very thought they would have whenever there is a cat in front of them, causing their experiences in such a way as to ground a demonstrative thought, and they think, of the perceptually presented cat, that *it* is dangerous'. Notice that these accounts are not *reductive* – they do not attempt to reduce demonstrative thoughts to something else. Rather, they just describe the content of one token demonstrative thought by specifying it as being identical to the (narrow) content of another.

Now in one way, of course, this proposal can seem like a cheat. It merely *uses* a claimed identity of narrow content in order to describe the content of a target thought, without attempting to tell us what narrow content *is*, or what the conditions of narrow-content identity are. Nevertheless, the proposal is, we claim, sufficient to rebut the charge of incoherence levelled against narrow content – the charge that, in a case of hallucination, there is no way to describe the (putative) content of the singular thought entertained. On the contrary, there is such a way, and we have just given it. Moreover, the proposal leaves open the possibility of a more substantive account of narrow content (in a way that Fodor's proposal does not). It might be said, for example, that the narrow content of the demonstrative element *that man*, when grounded in a visual presentation, is given by the location in egocentric space at which the man is represented. So all tokenings of the thought, '*That man* is fat', provided they represent the man in question in the same position in the thinker's egocentric space, will count as having the very same narrow content, irrespective of any further differences between the men and their circumstances. Of course, this is just one highly debatable proposal. But it illustrates how the proposed approach to narrow content might admit of further supplementation.

Note, too, that on both of the above ways of characterising narrow content (Fodor's and Carruthers'), narrow content is not really a kind of *content* at all, if by that you mean something which has to have a unique semantic value (true or false). For narrow contents do not, in themselves, have truth-conditions, and are not, in themselves, *about* anything. And it makes no sense to ask whether a narrow content, as such, is true or false. Only when embedded in a particular context do narrow contents come to have truth-conditions. Nevertheless, an individual tokening of a given narrow content will normally have some particular truth-condition. Hallucinatory cases aside, every time someone thinks, '*That* cat is dangerous', their (narrow) thought comes to have some or other truth-condition, through its embedding in a particular context. So one way to put the point is that it is, properly, narrow content *tokens*, rather than narrow content types, which have truth-conditions, and which are the bearers of truth-values.

3.2 Contents and that-clauses: undermining an assumption

The assumption which was implicit in the argument for the Russellian (object-involving) status of singular thought which we discussed in section 2.2, is that any genuine content has to be specifiable in a that-clause. The responses of Fodor and Carruthers considered above take it for granted that this assumption is false. Here we shall *argue* that it is. But note, first of all, that the assumption is quite widespread in philosophy. Thus, you will find people arguing that dogs and cats do not really have beliefs (Davidson, 1975), on the grounds that we cannot *describe* their beliefs using *our* concepts – we cannot say, for example, 'The cat believes that the bird is edible', since the concept *bird* has many conceptual connections (for example, to 'living thing') which we might be loath to attribute to an animal. Yet the assumption in question appears to be wholly unmotivated.

Obviously this is so if (like us) you are a *realist* about propositional attitudes, thinking that beliefs and desires are what they are independently of our descriptions of them. But the same is surely true even if, like Davidson, you are an interpretationalist about the attitudes, maintaining that there is nothing *more* to being a believer/desirer than being a creature whose behaviour can be successfully predicted and explained by suitable attributions of beliefs and desires. For why insist that the descriptions used to generate predictions and explanations *have* to be couched in the form of a that-clause? We do agree that being able to specify the contents of others' intentional states in this way greatly enhances our predictive and explanatory powers. For, as we noted above in chapter 4 (section 3), attribution of a belief-content allows us to run a simulation on the content and so, by inferential enrichment, attribute many other beliefs – and we can only run a simulation when we have a complete content to insert into our own (off-line) inferential systems. By contrast, our mapping of the beliefs of animals and very young children is patchy and incomplete. But even if we cannot predict what they will *infer*, we can still predict and explain some of their *actions* on the basis of such a description of their beliefs and desires.

When it is claimed that any genuine thought must have a content specifi*able* in the form of a that-clause, there are three things which this might mean.

(1) It might mean specifiable *by someone, sometime*. But then this would be a principle without teeth, unless we simply beg the question against narrow content. For of course the people on Twearth can express their thought in a that-clause, by saying, 'We think that water is wet.' And the person hallucinating the presence of a cat can similarly say, 'I think that *that* cat is dangerous.' Unless we just *assume* that narrow contents do not exist, it is hard to see why this should not count as a genuine description of the content of their thought.

(2) It might mean specifiable *by us, now*. But then this conflicts with the obvious truth that there are people who entertain thoughts whose contents I cannot now share (and so whose contents I cannot now express in a that-clause), because I lack some of the requisite concepts. It is surely obvious that there will now exist many perfectly genuine thoughts whose contents I cannot now express, entertained, for example, by scientists in disciplines of which I am ignorant.

(3) It might mean specifiable *by us, in principle*. This answers the point about scientists in (2) above, since I can presumably learn their theories and acquire their concepts, and *then* I could describe their thoughts using a that-clause. But it still runs into trouble in connection with the thoughts of animals, since it seems likely that I cannot, even in principle (while retaining my status as a sophisticated thought-at-tributer) acquire the concepts which a cat uses to categorise its world. Since the common-sense assumption that cats do have thoughts works pretty well, there had better be some powerful independent argument if we are to give it up. But in fact there is none.

So none of the available proposals is at all attractive. In fact, as Fodor (1987) points out, the reason why we cannot describe the singular thought of our cat-hallucinator using a that-clause is simple, and trivial. It is that, since *we* do not believe in the existence of the cat, *we* cannot describe the hallucinator's thought by using a demonstrative within the scope of a that-clause (nor, indeed, by using *any* singular concept). *We* cannot say, 'He thinks that *that* cat is dangerous', since this would require us to entertain, ourselves, a demonstrative thought about the – putative – particular cat. Similarly, the reason why *we* cannot use the term 'water' within the scope of a that-clause to describe the thoughts of Peter$_{tw}$, is that the reference of that term, in our mouths, is of course tied to the constitution of the stuff on Earth. There is, surely, nothing of deep significance about the nature of content to be derived from these facts – and certainly not a refutation of the coherence of narrow content.

4 Explanation and causation

In this section we examine the respective roles of wide and of narrow content in psychological explanation, asking whether either or both might be causally relevant to behaviour, and concluding that only narrow content is genuinely causally explanatory. But we begin with an argument against wide content, from its failure adequately to explain the behaviour of a hallucinator.

4.1 Illusory demonstrative thoughts: the case against

The thoughts of our cat-hallucinator turn out to give rise to a powerful argument against the ubiquity of wide content. Recall that it is a consequence of the wide-content theory, as applied to the case of singular thought, that in a case where there exists no actual object of thought (for example, through hallucination or misinformation), then there exists no singular thought either. For singular thoughts are supposed to be Russellian, being partly individuated in terms of the objects thought about. In such cases people are said to *essay*, or attempt to entertain, a singular thought of a certain type, but to fail.

Thus, compare two examples: in the one case I am really confronted by a cat, which I perceive and believe to be vicious; I think, '*That* cat is dangerous,' and lash out at it with my foot. In the other case everything is, from my subjective perspective, exactly the same, and issues in an exactly similar bodily movement, except that there is really no cat there; I am merely hallucinating. Wide-content theorists will say that in the first case I do entertain, and act on, a singular thought, but in the second case I do not; it merely *seems* to me that I have done so. Narrow-content theorists will say, in contrast, that in each case I entertain the very same type of thought, which explains my action in virtue of instantiating the same psychological (content-involving) law – the law, namely, that whenever people take themselves to be confronted with something dangerous, then they will, *ceteris paribus*, take action to deflect or avoid that threat. This certainly accords well with the intuition that the two cases are, psychologically speaking, alike.

The immediate problem for the Russellian is to explain how, in the hallucination example, my movement is genuinely an intentional action, which admits of a rationalising (that is, content-involving) explanation. For how can an action which is not done for a reason (not caused by a thought) really be intentional? Yet, in the case in question, it surely is. My lashing out with my foot was certainly not a mere reflex, like a knee-jerk, but an *attempt to achieve something*. Now, the response usually made by Russellians is that there are plenty of *other* (non-singular) thoughts still available to me, grounded in my hallucination, which can still serve to rationalise my action. Thus, I will still have such general beliefs as, 'I am confronted by a dangerous cat', 'There is a cat over *there*', and so on. And I can then be said to act because of these beliefs, in order to deflect a believed threat.

There are two problems with this response. The first is that it rides rough-shod over the (putative) distinction between *actual* (or *core*) and *merely dispositional* beliefs. This distinction may be needed to explain how we can have infinitely many beliefs, consistent with our finite cognitive space. (I say something true of you when I say that you believe that 1 is less than 2, that 1 is less than 3, that 1 is less than 4, and so on indefinitely.) What may really be the case is that we have a finite number of actually existing beliefs, represented and stored in some fashion in the brain; and from these beliefs we are immediately disposed to deduce any number of further beliefs, as the situation demands. Now, in a case where I see a cat and think, '*That* cat is dangerous', it seems perfectly possible that beliefs such as, 'I am confronted by a dangerous cat' are merely dispositional. That is, I would immediately assent to them if asked, but have not actually computed and stored them. The Russellian, however, must deny this. For a belief which remains merely dispositional cannot be a cause. If the general (non-singular) belief, 'I am confronted by a dangerous cat' is to explain my behaviour, then it must first have become actual. So the Russellian must maintain that we routinely actualise a great many more beliefs than we appear to – which, although possible, is otherwise unmotivated.

The second – and stronger – objection to the Russellian response is this. Even if the belief, 'I am confronted by a dangerous cat' was in some way activated, it certainly did not figure as a conscious judgement. The only (putative) thought which I *consciously* entertained was the singular one, '*That* cat is dangerous'. So, if the Russellian is right, my act of kicking was caused by non-conscious thoughts only. And now (quite apart from the intuitive implausibility of this suggestion) the Russellian has a real problem. For it must then be said that in the veridical case too, where there really is a cat present, my action is caused by non-conscious thoughts only. (Either that, or it is causally overdetermined.) And then it is hard to see how we can avoid the consequence that my actions are *never* caused by conscious singular judgements, but *only ever* by non-conscious general ones. And that, surely, would be absurd.

The only other option, for the Russellian, is to claim that it is not really thoughts, but rather *thought-signs* (sentences, or sentence-like objects) which cause actions. And then the pattern of causation in the two cases can be the same. For in the hallucination case it need not be in doubt that I do entertain a thought-*sign* of some sort. For example, I might entertain in auditory imagination the English words, '*That* cat is dangerous' (see chapter 8). Or as Fodor has claimed in another context (1994), it may be that it is signs of Mentalese which are the only intra-cranial components of (widely individuated) thoughts. The Russellian merely claims that, in context, these signs do not express any complete content. But the trouble with this is that it pitches the explanation of my actions at the wrong level. Even if, at some level of description, our actions are caused by sentence-processings (as the computational model of the mind maintains, indeed; see Fodor, 1980), we *also* think that they are caused, at a higher level of description, by thoughts – psychological states with intentional content. And it is this that Russellians cannot accommodate, if they take this final option.

(Although Fodor was once a champion of narrow content, in his 1994 he proposes to use wide content plus 'modes of presentation' – in the shape of sentences of Mentalese – to do the explanatory work he had previously assigned to narrow content. But, despite the case in favour of a language of thought – for which see chapter 8 below – this manoeuvre fails to preserve the right sort of psychological explanation. Oedipus was not horrified that he had made love to Jocasta, but now he is horrified that he has made love to his mother. The explanation for why he puts out his eyes must surely advert to the fact that he has *realised that* Jocasta is his mother, and thus realised that he has committed incest – not just that he has come to have some new sentences of Mentalese which refer to his mother tokened in his brain.)

Thus far in this chapter we have defended the coherence of the notion of narrow content, and have argued that the examples of singular thought attempted in cases of hallucination present a powerful challenge to a wide-content theorist. We now turn explicitly to questions concerning the respective roles of wide and narrow content in psychological explanation (both folk and scientific).

4.2 Same behaviour, same causes?

Return to the Twin Earth examples. Someone might argue thus: since, by hypothesis, the behaviours of Peter$_e$ and Peter$_{tw}$ are exactly the same, we should look for the same explanations of those behaviours too – that is, we should ascribe to both Peters the very same behaviour-determining thoughts. Thus suppose that each of the two Peters is confronted by a glass containing a colourless liquid, and that each thinks a thought they would express with the words, 'There is still some water left in that glass', and consequently lifts the glass to drink from it. Since the behaviour is the same in each case, we might think that the explanations we advance of that behaviour should be the same too – which means *not* individuating the thoughts in terms of the inner structure of the natural kinds in question, but rather narrowly, independently of the actual environment.

Of course the background principle appealed to here is not a hard-and-fast one. For we know that there can be cases of convergent causation. That is, there can be cases where instances of the very same event-types are caused by quite different routes. This is especially familiar in the case of human action, since examples where people behave similarly but for very different reasons are rife. Thus, consider the variety of reasons people might have for writing to apply for a particular job – one because he needs a job, and any job would do; another because she wants that particular job; another because he wants to please his mother; and so on. Yet the behaviour in each case is of an identical type (in some respects).

All the same, whenever two systems are changing and evolving in such a way as to follow exactly similar trajectories, we surely have powerful reason to believe that the underlying causal processes must be the same. Thus imagine two ropes being tested in a company's testing laboratory: each begins to fray in the same place after exactly the same amount of time, and then each snaps in the same place, again at the same time. Surely these facts would give us reason to believe that the intrinsic properties of the two ropes were the same, and that they were subjected to the same forces throughout. Otherwise we would have to believe that the similar effects were a mere coincidence. Moreover, the more complex the effects in a pair of parallel sequences, the more unlikely the coincidence. And remember that in the Twin Earth examples, *all* the behaviours of the two Peters are the same over an *indefinite* time-span!

There is an obvious reply that defenders of wide content can make to the above argument. They can deny that the *behaviours* of $Peter_e$ and $Peter_{tw}$ are the same (under an intentional description). And if they do not really behave in the same way, then there need be no presumption that their behaviours should be caused by thoughts of identical types. Thus, consider what it is that they do when they lift and drink from the glass: while $Peter_e$ drinks *water* (H_2O), $Peter_{tw}$ drinks *twater* (XYZ). And these can be counted as belonging to two different action-types. So it can, in effect, be objected that the argument above presupposes content-neutral (non-intentionally described) descriptions of behaviour – arm-movings, glass-liftings, and so on, but not water/twater-drinkings. In which case that argument seems just to beg the question at issue. For if thoughts are widely individuated, then so too will a person's intentions be; and then so will their intentional behaviour.

A similar point holds in connection with singular thought. Consider the case where Mary and Joan think, '*That* table is greasy', and each reaches for a tissue to wipe it. Or consider the case where I and my twin each sees a cat, thinks, '*That* cat is dangerous', and lashes out at it with a foot. While it might initially seem that in the two types of case we are dealing with two instances of the same behaviour (table-wiping and cat-kicking respectively), which should then receive the same (narrow) explanations, in fact the behaviours *can* be categorised as different. For Mary wipes *this* table while Joan wipes *that* one. And Peter$_e$ kicks Tiddles while Peter$_{tw}$ kicks Twiddles. So if singular thought is relationally individuated, in such a way as to embrace the actual objects thought about, then actions guided by such thoughts, under an intentional description, will come out as relationally individuated too. And then the argument above collapses.

Notice, however, that this response by the externalist places questions of sameness and difference of behaviour, and of sameness and difference of psychological explanation, in hock to scientific discovery, in a way which may seem unpalatable. For suppose it had turned out that water (somewhat like jade) is differently constituted in different parts of the globe. In that case Mary, in England, and Kylie, in Australia, might have been engaged in *different behaviours* when reaching for a glass of water, even in advance of the discovery of the difference. (We assume that the externalist must say that if water in England is H_2O, but in Australia is XYZ, then the word 'water' refers to different substances when used by Mary and Kylie respectively.) And when we explain those behaviours by saying, 'She wanted a drink of water', the explanations would have been different too, attributing thoughts of a different type. So the question of how many types of psychological explanation there are depends on the question of how many types of water (and other natural kinds) there are – which is possible, perhaps, but somewhat hard to swallow!

People sometimes assume that if content is individuated narrowly, then we would have to resort to individuating *behaviour* in terms of the bodily movements involved. But this is not so. There are a variety of ways of classifying behaviour, depending upon purpose and context. Sometimes we need to classify behaviour in terms of agents' intentions, *narrowly construed* – as, for example, to distinguish the pursuits of knights in search of the Grail, alchemists in search of the Philosopher's Stone, and contemporary hunters of the Loch Ness monster, even if all alike are on a wild-goose chase. Our cat-hallucinator and someone actually confronted by a fearsome feline may equally run away out of fear of a dangerous cat, for all that one cannot distance oneself from something which is not there.

Parts of our vocabulary for describing actions have wide commitments, other parts do not. So you cannot *mine* gold unless gold gets mined; although you can *try to* mine gold in a place where there is nothing but fool's gold, and you could *prospect for* gold in a world in which there was no such stuff at all. The vocabulary appropriate for classification of behaviour will depend upon whether our interest is focused on the agents or on their environment, on psychological explanation and prediction, or on the acquisition and communication of other facts (see section 5 below, for the related distinction between *explanatory* and *semantic* content).

4.3 Do mental states supervene on local facts?

Let us try another tack. Consider the way in which physicalism about the mental is often expressed: by claiming that mental states supervene upon brain states. It is often said that there can be no differences at the level of the mental, without some corresponding differences in the brain. If two people have distinct mental states, then there must – it is alleged – be some *other* (physical) difference between them (presumably in their brains) which explains the difference. In contrast with mental/physical dualism, we no longer accept that mental facts can 'float free' of physical facts. On the contrary, almost everyone today is a physicalist.

This now gives rise to an argument for narrow content. For brain states are surely *not* individuated relationally. No one would want to maintain that $Peter_e$ and $Peter_{tw}$ are in two different brain states, merely on the grounds that the one has water in his environment whereas the other has twater in his. Equally, no one would want to say that Mary and Joan must be in distinct brain states, merely on the grounds that the tables confronting them are numerically distinct. So, if brain states are non-relationally (that is, narrowly) individuated, and mental states supervene on brain states, then mental states must be narrowly individuated as well. For otherwise there would be (relational) mental differences without any corresponding brain difference.

On reflection, however, this argument, too, just begs the question in favour of narrow content. For if mental states 'ain't (entirely) in the head', as wide-content theorists maintain, then, plainly, mental states will not supervene on brain states alone. Rather, they will supervene on brain states *together with relational facts*. This can still be fully consistent with physicalism, provided that those relational facts are themselves physical ones (as, indeed, they are).

A more promising strategy for a narrow-content theorist is to appeal to the thought that *mental states should supervene upon causal powers*. For from the standpoint of explanatory psychology, we are only going to be interested in differences amongst mental states which reflect differences in their causal powers. And where the causal powers of two token mental states are identical, we shall therefore want to regard them as being of the very same type. (We understand 'causal powers' here to include the potential *causes* as well as the potential *effects* of the state in question. We also assume that psychology is not – unlike geology, for example – an historical science; that is, it does not individuate the kinds with which it deals in terms of their actual causal history. See chapter 7 for further discussion.)

Now the notion of a causal power is counterfactual-involving. To talk of the causal powers of state S is to talk, not just of what S actually causes, but also of what S *would* cause (or be caused by) in various hypothetical and counterfactual circumstances. Seen in this light, it is obvious that the causal powers of the states of the two twins are the same. For if $Peter_e$ were to be on Twin Earth, then he would behave exactly as $Peter_{tw}$ does (even under an intentional description); and if $Peter_{tw}$ were on Earth, he would behave exactly as $Peter_e$ does. Similarly, if Mary were to be sitting where Joan is, then she would be behaving as Joan does, and vice versa. In fact, it is the causal powers of mental states which supervene on (non-relationally described) brain states. Then if we insist that mental state types should supervene on causal powers, it will follow that content is narrow. For otherwise there would be (relational) differences between mental states (widely individuated) which would not reflect differences in their causal powers.

This looks as if it might become a powerful argument in support of narrow content. But why should one accept that mental states are only distinct where their causal powers are? This will follow if we think that mental states are, basically, the theoretical posits of an explanatory proto-science (that is, if we accept some or other version of the 'theory-theory' of mental states, as we argued in chapter 4 we should). For science, in general, types entities and states by their causal powers, taking no interest in differences between states not reflected in differences in their causal powers. (At least, this is true of sciences which are a-historical.)

No doubt folk-psychology may be *more than* a proto-science, and may also take an interest in (merely relational) differences amongst mental states not reflected in their causal potential. (Indeed, we will argue as much in section 5 below.) But to the extent that folk psychology is *at least* attempting to do the work of a scientific theory – typing states by their causal powers, and explaining events as caused by the states so distinguished – to that extent we have reason to categorise thoughts narrowly, in terms of a non-relationally individuated notion of content. Moreover, if we are to extract from folk psychology a notion of content fit to subserve a content-based scientific psychology, then it would appear, from the arguments above, that the notion extracted had better be a narrow one.

Supposing that there are some psychological (content involving) *laws* (or *nomic tendencies*, at least), what can be concluded about the notion of content likely to figure in those laws (or tendencies)? Much, of course, depends upon what kinds of law may be in question. Some putative psychological laws operate by *quantifying over* content, for example; in which case nothing much can be concluded about the nature of such content. Thus, consider the practical reasoning syllogism:

$(\forall x)(\forall P)(\forall Q)$(if x wants that P, and x believes that, by bringing it about that Q, x can succeed in bringing it about that P, and x believes that it is now within x's power to bring it about that Q, then – *ceteris paribus* – x will act in such a way as to try to bring it about that Q).

It does not seem as if this can throw any light on the nature of the contents *P* and *Q*. But some putative psychological laws will involve particular contents or types of content – such as the law that the moon looks bigger near the horizon; or that people have an aversion to mother–son incest; or that people will (*ceteris paribus*) act so as to avoid or deflect a perceived threat. Here, plainly, the contents involved had better be typed narrowly, if the laws are to achieve the requisite generality. For example, if the law of threats involves a content such as, '*That* is a threat to me', then this content will need to be individuated non-relationally, so that many different thinkers, entertaining demonstrative thoughts about many different things, can nevertheless be encompassed by the law. So to re-iterate: if there is a notion of content which gains its life and significance from the way in which it figures in (putative) psychological laws, then there is good reason to expect that notion to involve narrow (non-relational) principles of individuation.

It may be objected that at least some scientific laws appeal to properties which are individuated relationally. Consider the scientific discovery that malaria is caused by mosquito bites, for example. Here we have a law (or nomic tendency) relating the property of suffering from malaria, on the one hand, to the property of *having a bite which was caused by a mosquito*, on the other – that is to say, a property which is individuated by its relation to another thing (the mosquito). So why should not psychology, similarly, formulate its laws in terms of properties of the agent individuated by relation to things external to the agent? But in fact there is no nomic connection between mosquito bites and malaria. The relevant law will relate malaria to the presence of a certain sort of parasite in the bloodstream. And it just so happens that the normal causal route by means of which those parasites enter the bloodstream is a bite from a mosquito. But it is a real possibility that in the course of evolution those parasites might come to be transmitted by other secondary hosts, apart from mosquitoes. The relationally formulated 'law' is not really a law at all, but rather a generalisation which lines up more-or-less usefully with the genuinely (and non-relationally individuated) nomically connected properties.

4.4 Content in explanation: how can reasons be causes?

It is deeply embedded in our common-sense, or folk, psychology that our reasons are causes of our actions. We think we normally act as we do *because* we believe this and desire that, or *because* we intend to achieve the other. But reasons, of course, are propositional attitudes with content, partly individuated in terms of their content. A belief is always a belief *that P*, and a desire is (arguably – there is an issue as to whether desires for particular *objects* can always be analysed as desires for the truth of some corresponding proposition) a desire *that Q*. So when we believe that reasons are causes we believe that *states individuated in terms of their content* are causes.

But now the problem for the wide-content theorist is this: if contents, in turn, are relationally individuated, in terms of objects and properties external to the subject, then how can the content of a mental state be a causally relevant feature of it? For surely causation is, in general, *local*, mediated by intrinsic (non-relational) properties of the events and states in question. How can the fact that a state stands in a certain relation to something, which may be distant from that state in space and time, be a causally relevant feature of it, partly determining its causal powers? Admittedly, there do exist examples of relationally individuated properties which are causally relevant. We have just discussed the causal relevance of the relationally individuated property, *being a mosquito-bite*. Now consider the property, *being a planet*. This is, plainly, a relational property: to be a planet is to stand in a certain relation to a sun. Yet standing in that relation is one of the determinants of the causal powers of planets. This case is easy to understand, since the relation in question is correlated with the existence of a causal *force* (namely gravity) which acts on any planet *qua* massive object. There is nothing similar to help us in connection with widely individuated mental states. How can the mere fact that the stuff in the lakes and rivers in my environment is composed of H_2O rather than XYZ, for example, make any difference to the causal powers of my belief that water is wet?

Some naturalistic accounts of wide content (particularly the version of informational semantics due to Dretske, 1988) are designed, in part, to overcome this problem. On Dretske's account, mental states have the contents which they do in virtue of the information that they carry about the environment (where *information* is a causal notion). Content can then come to be of causal relevance, provided that the mental state in question becomes harnessed to the control of a particular type of behaviour (either through evolution or through learning) *because of* the information that it carries. But it is obvious that this solution to the present problem must be unsuccessful. One reason is that the behavioural success of my water-thoughts, for example, has nothing to do with the fact that they carry information about H_2O (as opposed to XYZ), but rather with the fact that they carry information about water's properties of potability, solvency, and so on – properties, note, which are equally shared with XYZ. Another reason is that many singular thoughts (widely individuated) are one-off. If I think '*That* cat is dangerous' and act accordingly, then there can be no historical explanation of the causal powers of the thought in terms of the information which it carries about that particular cat, since I may never before have encountered that cat, nor entertained that thought.

Some wide-content theorists have replied that there is really no problem here for them to answer (Klein, 1996). For on most accounts of wide content, the relation in question, in terms of which the content of a state is partly individuated, is itself a *causal* one. (This is true in connection with all varieties of what McGinn calls 'strong externalism'. See his 1989.) Thus, when I think, '*That* cat is dangerous', for example, my thought comes to have the wide content which it does in virtue of the *causal* relationship which obtains between my tokening of the thought and that particular cat. In fact, to individuate thoughts widely is to individuate them in terms of their causes, on most accounts. And then, it may be said, the (wide) content of a thought must, after all, be causally relevant. For the cause of a cause must be causally relevant to the latter's effects. If my thought about the cat explains my attempt to kick it, and my thought is caused by the presence of a particular cat, then that particular cat is causally relevant to my kicking. And then to individuate my thought in terms of its causation by that particular cat is to individuate it in a way which must be causally relevant to the kicking.

This reply fails, however. For it does not show that wide content is relevant to the distinctive causal powers of (as opposed to the mere existence of) a thought. Individuating states in terms of their causes does not automatically mean (indeed, will normally *not* mean) individuating them in a manner relevant to their causal powers. (Note that by a causal power, here, we mean a capacity to bring about certain *effects*. Our topic now is whether reasons, as such, are causes; not whether reasons *have* causes.) Consider, for comparison, the concept *chair*. To oversimplify somewhat, this, too, individuates items in terms of their causal history: to be a chair is to be an object which was caused to exist by someone's intention to produce something for sitting upon. Does this mean that *chairhood* is causally relevant to the effects which any given chair has? Surely not. If I trip over a chair in the dark and break my leg, then it is not *because it is a chair* that I break my leg – it is not because the object I trip over was created with a certain intention in mind. Rather, the cause of the break is that I caught my foot on an object of a certain mass, rigidity, and shape. The fact that it was a *chair* which had those properties is causally irrelevant. (The point, here, is essentially the same as the one made above concerning the causal relevance of the mosquito in relation to malaria – the causal powers of the bite depend upon its intrinsic properties, not its causation by the mosquito.) Then so too, it seems to us, in connection with wide content. The fact that my thought was caused by one particular cat rather than another, or by a sample of H_2O rather than of XYZ, is irrelevant to its causal powers. And then to individuate mental states widely, in terms of their extra-cranial causes, is to individuate them in a way which is irrelevant to the causal status of the mental.

Peacocke (1993) has argued that what wide contents (contents relationally described) explain, are *relational properties of movements*. Thus, one and the same movement of my hand can be both a movement *towards someone in the garden*, and a movement *northwards*. But only the former is explained by saying that I wanted to draw your attention to that person's presence. For different counterfactuals are sustained. If that person had been in a different position in the garden then I would still have pointed towards him (given that I perceive him), but I would no longer have pointed northwards. Peacocke claims that only wide contents can give us this pattern of explanation of relationally described movements by relationally described mental states; only wide contents give us the right set of counterfactuals.

We have two points to make. The first is that sustaining counterfactuals is not the same thing as being a cause. For example, imagine a wave breaking on the seashore, destroying as it does so a particular sand-castle. And suppose that breaking waves always produce *surf* (a film of bubbles on their breaking edge). Then the following counterfactuals are true: (a) if the surf had not been present, then the sand-castle would not have broken; (b) if the sand-castle had not been broken, then the surf would not have been present. But the surf is not the cause of the destruction. Rather, the sand-castle is destroyed by the wave, which also causes the surf. So, the fact that wide contents sustain counterfactuals does not show that such contents are causes. Rather, the wide content may just supervene in a law-like way on what really does do the causing (that is, a narrow content which happens to have a particular worldly cause).

Our second point (see also Segal, 1989a) is that a narrow-content explanation, supplemented by relational facts, can sustain the *same* set of counterfactuals. Set out in more detail, the Peacocke example is this:

(1) I see a person in the garden;
(2) I want to draw your attention to him;
(3) so I move my hand in his direction.

And his point is that this explanation works whether or not anything more is known of the spatial relationship between myself and the person in question (for example, whether or not you know where I was in the room at the time). And it is true that if he had been in a different position in the garden then, provided that (1) and (2) remain true, I would have moved my hand in that direction instead.

Yet these features of the explanation can, surely, be replicated in a narrow-content account. A narrow-content explanation of the case would be this:

(i) I experience a person-as-represented in a particular direction in ego-centric space (a content I can entertain whether or not it is really that particular person, or indeed anyone, who is there);
(ii) I want to draw your attention to the presence of the person I represent;
(iii) a particular person is in fact the veridical cause of the experience in (i);
(iv) so I move my hand in his direction.

Here, too, the explanation works whether or not anything further is known about where the person and I are. And here, too, the right counterfactuals are sustained: if he had been in a different position then, provided that (i), (ii) and (iii) remain true, I would have moved my hand in that direction.

The advantage, indeed, is firmly with the narrow-content explanation of the case. For Peacocke will be forced to postulate three psychologically distinct explanations for the cases where (a) I perceive the person in the garden, (b) I perceive not him but his identical twin brother, and (c) where I am hallucinating; for I shall be said to entertain different thoughts in each case. But the narrow-content theorist can advance exactly the same form of explanation for (a) and (b) – the only difference being that a different person will be picked out in clause (iii). Moreover, explanation (c) will only differ in that clause (iii) is dropped altogether – which gives us just the right counterfactuals, since all that is then relevant is where my experience *represents* a person as being. So on a narrow-content account the *psychological* aspect of the explanation will be the same for all three cases.

A wide-content theorist may reply to the difficulties we have been raising, by saying that there is no *special* problem in explaining how wide contents, *qua* contents, can be causes, since essentially the same problem will arise in connection with all conceptions of content. For after all, as physicalists we must believe that all bodily movements will have sufficient causes at a neurological level – brain events causing brain events, causing muscles to contract, causing arms to move in certain directions, and so on. So how can there be any space for reasons to be causes as well, unless reason-descriptions are just *alternative ways of describing* brain events? In which case it will not be *qua* reason that a given brain event is a cause.

There are a number of different possibilities for responding to the allegation that all content must be epiphenomenal. The most direct (and, to our minds, the most convincing) is to point out (1) that reasons will be causes in virtue of their content if they figure in a distinctive set of content-involving causal *laws*; and (2) to claim that there are, indeed, such laws. The first part of this response is relatively uncontroversial. For there are few who are prepared to claim that the only real causes which exist are at the level of sub-atomic physics. Yet there is exactly the same sort of reason to claim that all processes – of whatever level, and whatever degree of complexity – must be realised in sub-atomic physical ones. At any rate, the second part of the above response, if true, would show that reasons have the same sort of causal status as genes, or H_2O molecules, or any other natural kind above the level of basic physics. So: *is* claim (2) true? It would certainly appear that there are many content-involving laws, ranging from the highly particular ('The moon looks bigger near the horizon'; 'People have an aversion to the thought of mother–son incest') to the general ('People try, *ceteris paribus*, to get what they want' – and note that *all* laws above the level of basic physics are *ceteris paribus*). And if the arguments above are sound, such laws will only employ, and vindicate, contents which are narrowly individuated.

5 Folk-psychological content

Suppose it had turned out that folk-psychological content is wide, whereas scientific-psychological content would have to be narrow; and suppose, too, that it had turned out that narrow content is actually incoherent; then this would have meant that the prospects for an intentional scientific psychology were bleak. It would have meant that folk psychology is the only kind of intentional psychology we could ever have. Although we have, indeed, argued that scientific-psychological content should be narrow, we have denied that the notion of narrow content is incoherent. So there is no threat to scientific psychology from this quarter. But is there, now, an eliminativist threat to folk psychology? If folk psychology is committed to wide content, but science tells us that content is narrow, does that mean that folk psychology is in error, and should be replaced? That all depends, plainly, on what it is that folk psychology is trying to *do*.

What, then, is our common-sense notion of content? Many of those who defend narrow content do *not* think that it is, or is a component of, our common-sense conception. Thus Fodor (1987) thinks that the folk-psychological notion is *wide* – indeed purely referential, dealing only in worldly properties and individuals. (This is then a notion of content which Russell himself would have been entirely at home with.) But he also thought (he is no longer so sure; see his 1994) that it is imperative that we should be able to *construct* a notion of narrow content to serve as the basis for a scientific psychology. Others (Burge, 1991) think that a notion of narrow content is indeed *legitimate*, but forms no part of our actual common-sense psychology – maintaining that our actual notion of content is a Russellian hybrid of reference plus Fregean mode of presentation. *We* think, in contrast, that narrow content does (or should) form one strand in our common-sense notion (a strand which Carruthers has elsewhere labelled 'cognitive content' – see his 1989; here we adopt the terminology of 'explanatory content'), the other being purely referential (labelled 'semantic content').

5.1 Two kinds of content

We claim that there are two very different perspectives which we can, and regularly do, take towards the contents of people's thoughts – that there are two distinct kinds of *interest* which we can and do take in descriptions of thought-content, each of which motivates a different set of identity constraints. Sometimes our interest in thoughts and thought-ascriptions is either *explanatory* or *predictive*. Often our main interest in the thoughts of other people is to use them in such a way as to explain what those people have done, or to predict what they will do. And often, from this perspective, it will be crucial to know the precise way in which the thinker conceptualises the subject matter – it can make all the difference in explaining Oedipus' remorse whether the content of his thought is described as 'I am married to Mother' or as 'I am married to Jocasta'. So our principles of individuation will at least need to be Fregean, requiring identity of mode of presentation for identity of thought-content. But equally, from this explanatory and predictive perspective we are generally *not* interested in the truth or falsity of the thoughts ascribed. So the principles of individuation can abstract away from the actual worldly referents of the component concepts of the thought – such content can be *narrow*.

Sometimes, on the other hand, our interest in the thoughts of others is *communicative*, or *belief-acquisitive*. Often our perspective on the thoughts of others is that their thoughts may give us something which we ourselves may wish to believe or deny. And here Fregean modes of presentation are of no relevance, we maintain. All that matters is that we should get hold of *which* worldly objects and properties the person's thoughts concern. So such contents are purely Russellian. It seems to us that the popular view that our common-sense conception of content is a Russellian/Fregean hybrid comes from *conflating* these two perspectives, and/or from living on a diet of examples which vacillate ambiguously between them.

Would we have to maintain, then, that our common-sense notion of content is itself ambiguous? Are the identity conditions of the contents ascribed in statements of the form, 'A believes that P', sometimes purely referential, and sometimes narrow, depending upon the context? Not necessarily. It may be that we have an unambiguous, unequivocal, notion of content, but in such a way that the purpose-relativity of content is written into the notion itself. Thus, 'A believes that P', may mean something like, 'The content of A's belief is similar enough to the content *I* would express by the assertion P for the purposes in hand'. Where the purposes in hand are psychological (explanatory or predictive), the constraints imposed give us narrow content. But where the purposes are communicative, then the constraints give us a purely truth-conditional notion. But the content-sentence itself would mean the same both times.

It does seem to us quite likely that we *do* employ a notion of narrow content when our main interest is psychological; and that where examples are presented clearly in this light, they will evoke intuitions supporting narrow content. Imagine a case where two ticket-holders in a local lottery – Peter and Paul – are clamouring at the ticket-booth, shouting and hammering on the door. We ask, 'Why? Why are they both behaving like that?' Answer: 'Each believes the very same thing: that he has won the lottery.' Here we feel no compunction in attributing the *same* thought to them both, despite the fact that each of their thoughts (of course) concerns a different subject – namely, himself. We are, therefore, apparently quite happy to individuate the thoughts narrowly, abstracting from the differences in subject matter for purposes of psychological explanation. Now extend the example in such a way that truth becomes relevant. We ask, 'Who has won? Have they both won, or only one of them?' Answer: 'Only Peter has won; Paul misread his ticket number.' Now, I think, our intuitions switch. We are inclined to insist that they thought different things, because one was right while the other was wrong. This is just as the position sketched above would predict.

It seems likely, then, that one strand in our folk-psychological notion of content is *explanatory*, conforming to narrow principles of individuation. This is just as it should be if, as we suggested in chapter 2, our folk psychology embodies a set of more-or-less explicit psychological *laws* or *nomic tendencies*, which would then require a notion of narrow content for their proper formulation, if the arguments given above are correct. If this is right, then we do not have to revise or reconstruct folk psychology in order to get something which might serve as an appropriate basis for scientific psychology. On the contrary, it is *already* of the right form, and we might expect folk and scientific psychologies to merge seamlessly into one another.

It is worth stressing, however, that the identity-conditions of the thoughts we attribute is one thing, the surface form of the sentences we use in doing it may be quite another. We rely on a variety of conventions and dodges in communicating explanatory content, often leaving the latter to be garnered from the context. Thus in the example above we explained the behaviour of the lottery-ticket holders by saying, 'Each believes that *he* has won.' But of course they themselves would not employ a third-person singular mode of presentation in their thought. Here we know *which* (narrow) thought is being entertained – it is the same thought *I* would express by saying, 'I have won' – but we use an indirect means of describing it.

5.2 Semantic content

It seems to us likely that we also employ a notion of content which is purely referential, or Russellian; and that we do so when our interest in thoughts and thought-descriptions is basically belief-acquisitive. First, let us make a point about linguistic communication. It seems to us that successful communication, in many contexts, does *not* require mutual knowledge of modes of presentation, or of Fregean senses. All that is necessary is that there should be mutual knowledge of *what* is being said *about what*. Consider the following example. You are a security guard in a museum, to which a new sculpture has recently been delivered. You are sitting outside the room where the sculpture is the only work of art on display, but you have not, as yet, seen it yourself. You now hear a visitor in the room say, 'That sculpture wasn't worth what they paid for it.' Do you understand this remark? It seems to us that you plainly do (*contra* Evans, 1982). You know *which* thing is being talked about, and you know what is being said about it. But you neither *share* with the speaker a mode of presentation of the referent of their demonstrative, nor know anything about what that mode of presentation may be like (after all, for all you know the speaker may be blind, and feeling the sculpture with their hands; this makes not a bit of difference to your success in understanding them).

Why is it that the conditions for successful communication, in general, are as they are, requiring only mutual knowledge of worldly truth-conditions? By way of answer, reflect on what communication is basically *for*. Communication is an important channel for the acquisition of new beliefs, second only to vision in our cognitive economy. When people tell me things, in general I believe them. This works because, when people believe things, in general they believe truly. And then all that really matters, in order to make linguistic communication a reliable method of belief-acquisition, is that the *truth-conditions* of the beliefs at either end of the process should be the same. When you assert something of the form, 'a is F', then provided that I know *which* thing you refer to by 'a' and *which* property you designate by 'F', it doesn't matter how differently these things may be presented to you – if your thought is true, then so too will mine be.

Very often communication takes place at one remove, by us being told what someone else believes. To continue with the museum example given above: suppose that Mary is a famous art-critic, and that you tell me, 'Mary thinks that the new sculpture wasn't worth what was paid for it.' This gives me reason to believe what Mary believes, just as if I had heard her *say*, 'That sculpture wasn't worth it.' And the same conditions for understanding apply. In order for your statement to serve as a reliable channel for the acquisition of a new belief, all that matters is that I should get hold of *which* sculpture Mary's belief is about, and what she thought about it. Mary's modes of presentation matter not at all. So where our *interest* is basically belief-acquisitive, the constraints on a correct description of Mary's thought are simply that it should preserve the original truth-conditions. And this gives us a notion of thought-content which is purely truth-conditional.

This explains, we think, the strong pull of intuitions towards wide content. Since there is, indeed, a notion of content – *semantic content* – which is individuated by worldly truth-condition, we are apt, if we fail to notice the different perspectives on content-description, to think that *the notion of content must be Russellian, or world-involving*. But the truth is that we also employ a notion of content – *explanatory content* – which is narrowly individuated, where our interest is in psychological explanation.

Although it does seem to us likely that common sense employs *both* a notion of narrow content *and* a notion of wide content for different purposes, this is not really the crucial point. It would not matter to us if it should turn out to be *indeterminate* whether common sense employs two distinct notions of content, or just one hybrid notion. What is important is that, once we see that there are two quite different perspectives we can take on the notion of content, and two distinct purposes for which we employ that notion, we see that we *should* employ two distinct notions (or one context-sensitive one, with varying application-conditions). Here, as so often in philosophy, what matters is not what notion we actually do have; but rather what notion we *should* have, given our purposes (see Carruthers, 1987b; see also Craig, 1990).

6 Conclusion

In this chapter we have rebutted arguments for the ubiquity of wide content and against the coherence of narrow content. We have argued that narrow content is not only coherent, but is also the notion which should be employed for purposes of psychological explanation, whether folk or scientific. We have also allowed that we should employ a notion of content which is wide, in communicative contexts where our interests are belief-acquisitive.

SELECTED READING

In defence of wide content: Putnam, 1975a; Burge, 1979, 1986a, 1986b; Evans, 1981, 1982; McDowell, 1986, 1994; McCulloch, 1989.

In defence of narrow content: Fodor, 1980, 1987, 1991; Blackburn, 1984, ch.9; Block, 1986; Noonan, 1986, 1993; Segal, 1989a, 1989b, 1991.

7 Content naturalised

In this chapter we review the three main types of current project for naturalising semantics – informational (or causal co-variance) semantics; teleological semantics; and functional-role semantics. There are severe problems for each, though perhaps least for the last. We then argue that the natural status of content does not, in fact, require a fully reductive semantics, but can rather be vindicated by its role in scientific psychology.

1 Introduction

Recall from chapter 2, that one of the main realistic commitments of folk psychology is to the existence of states with representational *content* or *meaning*. This is then the source of what is perhaps the most serious eliminativist challenge to folk psychology (which is also a challenge to any content-based scientific psychology). This comes from those who doubt whether *meaning* and *representation* have any real place in the natural world. The problem is this: how can any physical state (such as a pattern of neural firing) represent some aspect of the world (and so be true or false) in its own right, independent of our interpretation of that state? The contemporary project of naturalising semantics is best seen as a response to this problem. In various ways, people have attempted to spell out, in purely natural terms (that is, terms either drawn from, or acceptable to, the natural sciences) what it is for one state to represent, or *be about*, another.

(The notion of the *natural*, here, is parasitic upon the notion of natural *science*. A natural property is one which is picked out by some term derived from some or other (true) theory of natural science, or which is referred to by a term which can be defined in terms of the terminology of natural science, including terms of general scientific coinage, such as 'cause'. So the property of being a mother is a natural one, since terms referring to it are indispensable in scientific biology. And the property of being a second-cousin-once-removed is also natural, since although terms referring to it do not figure in any scientific theory, they can be constructed by definition out of terms which *do* figure in such theories.)

Being a realist about propositional attitudes means believing that the differences between the *belief* that P and the *desire* that P, or between the belief *that P* and the belief *that Q*, are real, forming part of the fabric of the world independently of our theories, interpretations, and systems of classification. In which case, we had better also believe that such properties can be naturalised. For the only real mind-independent properties that there are – which are not mere reflections of our systems of classification – are those which science may discover and describe (Armstrong, 1978). But must that mean believing that those properties can be *reduced* to other terms? Notice that the various forms of naturalised semantics which we shall be considering are *reductive*, attempting to say what it is for a state to mean *that P* in terms of causal co-variance, selectional history, or functional role. Indeed, most versions of these theories attempt to lay down necessary and sufficient conditions for a state to mean *that P* in natural terms – the exception being Fodor (1990) who tries to provide sufficient conditions only (a point we will return to in sections 2 and 5 below).

We shall return to the question whether *naturalisation* requires *reduction* in section 5 (arguing that it does not). For the next three sections we shall be exploring the strengths and weaknesses of the three main naturalisation programmes on offer. Each of these shares the assumption that defending the reality of content-bearing propositional attitudes means saying what it is (or at least, what it can be) for a belief to mean *that P* in terms which do not themselves presuppose semantic notions.

It should be noted, before we begin, that the naturalisation issue is orthogonal to the debate between wide and narrow content which we discussed in chapter 6, since even narrow-content theorists insist that (tokens of) narrow contents do have truth-conditions, and are about things in the world; they merely claim that they are not *typed in terms of* their truth-conditions. So the *aboutness* of our thoughts is something which will have to be accounted for in any case. While most of those who have tackled the naturalisation issue have been wide-content theorists (see below), narrow-content theorists should be equally concerned to show that semantic relations (reference, truth, and the like) exist as part of the natural order of the world. For it is essential to narrow contents that they should be the kinds of state, tokens of which generally possess semantic properties. And since we may want to explain the success of a given action in terms of the *truth* of a thought (say), or failure in terms of falsehood, these are not optional properties of thought-contents, even for a narrow-content theorist.

2 Informational semantics

Informational, or causal co-variance, semantics is one version of naturalistic semantics. Semantic theories of this type claim that meaning is carried by the causal connections between the mind and the world. Roughly, the idea is that for a mental term 'S' to mean *S*, is for tokenings of 'S' to causally co-vary with Ss – that is, Ss, and only Ss, cause tokenings of 'S'. So, the idea is that for the term 'mouse' (or its Mentalese equivalent, which we shall henceforward write as MOUSE) to mean *mouse*, is for tokenings of the term MOUSE in belief to be reliably caused by the presence of mice, and only by the presence of mice. Such an account is plainly naturalistic, since the only terms which figure in it are 'cause', together with terms referring to worldly properties on the one hand and physical word-tokens and sentence-tokens on the other.

Informational theories of mental content are modelled on the sense of 'represent' which is appropriate whenever there are causal co-variance relations in the natural world, and so whenever one state of the world *carries information about* another (see Dretske, 1981). Thus we say, 'Seven tree rings *means* (represents) that the tree was seven years old', 'Heavy clouds mean rain', 'Those spots mean measles' (that is, 'Spots of that type causally co-vary with the presence of measles'), and so on. But why would anyone want to begin a *semantic* theory here? Since it is obvious that there is no real *intentionality*, or *aboutness,* present in these examples, why should we take them as our model? There are at least two distinct lines of attraction.

One comes from noticing that this very same causal co-variance sense of 'represent' is apparently employed by neuropsychologists studying the brain. They will say, for example, 'The firing of this cell *represents* the presence of an upright line in the visual field', on the grounds that the cell is caused to fire when, and only when, an upright line is present. The hope is then that we may be able to build up to a full-blown notion of mental representation from this simple starting point, just as the neuropsychologist hopes to build up an account of the visual system from such simple materials.

The second source of attraction is particularly emphasised by Fodor (1987, 1990). It is that the account is *atomistic*, as opposed to *holistic*, in form. That is, it attempts to deliver the meaning of each mental term one by one, without mentioning the meaning of any other mental state of the thinker. Fodor believes that any acceptable naturalistic, realistic, account of intentional content should be atomistic. His reasoning is that, once any degree of holism is admitted into the account, then there is no principled way of stopping short of saying that *all* the thinker's actual beliefs partly contribute to the content of any given representation. This would then entail that no two thinkers ever entertain a belief with the very same content, since there will always in fact be some differences in belief between the two. So content would become *idiosyncratic*, which would render it unfit to serve as the basis for a scientific psychology. For the latter surely seeks *general* intentional laws to apply across *all* the thinkers in the population. We shall return to the issue of holism in section 4.4.

2.1 Misrepresentation and the disjunction problem

The obvious problem that informational theories have to overcome, is to make room for the possibility of (normal) *mis*representation. For plainly it is possible – indeed, quite common – for our beliefs and thoughts to misrepresent the world. But it appears *im*possible for one state to carry *misinformation* about another, in the objective causal sense of information which is in question (except by violation of the *ceteris paribus* clause governing co-variation). Thus if heavy clouds do not just co-vary with rain, but also with strong winds, then heavy clouds which are not followed by rain do not misrepresent the state of the weather (although *we*, as observers, may draw a false inference from them); rather, what heavy clouds *really* represent (that is, causally co-vary with), is rain-or-strong-winds. Similarly, if the spots normally caused by measles can also be caused by, say, toxic metal poisoning, then the presence of those spots in the latter sort of case does *not* mean (that is, carry information about) measles (although they may lead a doctor into a misdiagnosis); rather, what spots of that sort really mean is measles-or-toxic-metal-poisoning.

Applied to the case of mental states, then, the difficulty for informational theories is to avoid what is sometimes called 'the disjunction problem'. Suppose that I reliably mistake certain kinds of shrew for mice. That is, not only does the presence of a mouse in my environment reliably cause me to think MOUSE, but so too does the presence of a certain kind of shrew cause me to think MOUSE. What, then, does MOUSE represent, for me? If mental symbols mean what they reliably co-vary with, then it looks as if MOUSE must mean *shrew-or-mouse* rather than *mouse*. So I am not, after all, mistaken when I think MOUSE in the presence of a shrew. Indeed, if this problem generalises, it looks as if, according to informational semantic theories, it is going to be impossible for *anyone ever* to be mistaken (other than through breakdown of the mechanisms mediating perception)! And that, of course, is absurd.

The best-developed approach to this problem has been presented by Fodor (1987, 1990). His preferred solution is to formulate his theory in terms of *asymmetric causal dependence*. That is, he claims that a Mentalese

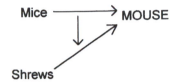

Figure 7.1 Asymmetric causal dependence (the arrows represent causation or causal dependence)

term 'S' will refer to Ss, and only Ss, provided that the causal connections between 'S' and any other (non-S) objects which may happen to cause tokenings of 'S' are asymmetrically causally dependent upon the causal connection between tokenings of 'S' and Ss. So if any other types of object besides Ss cause tokenings of 'S', they will only do so *because* Ss cause tokenings of 'S'. The account, then, is this (also represented diagrammatically in figure 7.1 above):

MOUSE will mean *mouse* (and so shrews will be *mis*represented by MOUSE) if:

(i) mice cause tokenings of MOUSE, and
(ii) if mice had not caused tokenings of MOUSE, shrews would not have, and
(iii) if shrews had not caused tokenings of MOUSE, mice still would have.

Thus (i)–(iii) capture the idea that the *shrew*-to-MOUSE connection is asymmetrically causally dependent upon the *mouse*-to-MOUSE connection.

Note that what Fodor offers is only a *sufficient* condition for MOUSE to mean *mouse*, not a *necessary and* sufficient condition (that is, what immediately precedes clauses (i)–(iii) is an 'if', not an 'if and only if'). This is in line with his (1974) conception of what naturalisation should involve. In general, he thinks, we cannot hope for a *reduction* of some problematic term T into purely natural terminology (which would involve a statement of necessary and sufficient conditions for T to apply). For most higher-level properties admit of multiple instantiation in lower-level facts. The most that we can hope for is a statement, in natural terms, of one of the *realising conditions* for T to apply. That is to say, the most we can hope for is a statement of *sufficient* conditions for its application. So it is no good looking to refute Fodor's account by finding cases where MOUSE means *mouse* but conditions (i)–(iii) do not collectively apply. Rather, we should need to find a case where conditions (i)–(iii) apply, but MOUSE does not, intuitively, mean *mouse*. Can this be done?

Here is a possibility to think about. Consider any term T with *marginal cases* (for example, 'red', or 'sport'). Call the central cases where T applies Cs, and the marginal cases Ms. (Note that the Ms *are* cases of T, only marginal ones.) Does it not seem plausible that the application of T to the marginal cases is asymmetrically dependent upon its application to the cases in the centre? That is, might it not be plausible that (i) Cs cause tokenings of T, and (ii) if Cs had not caused tokenings of T, Ms would not have, and (iii) if Ms had not caused tokenings of T, Cs still would have? In which case Fodor's theory would tell us that the marginal cases are not really cases of Ts at all! In fact, it would tell us that Ms are *mis*classified as Ts! So orangey-reds are *not* red (as opposed to marginal reds), and synchronised swimming is *not* a sport (as opposed to a marginal one).

Let us run this objection through for the case of colour in a little more detail, to see how it might go. Let crimson be our representative central red, and let the marginal case be an orangey-red which speakers would still categorise as 'red' in a forced choice, or when speaking carefully. Plainly, the equivalent of (i) is true – crimson objects cause us to think RED. Now what would it take for crimson objects *not* to cause us to think RED? – that is, for the antecedent of (ii) to be true? One possibility is that we be colour-blind. Another possibility is that the Mentalese term RED be harnessed to some other meaning (for example, *blue*, or *mouse*) while crimson causes the tokening of a distinct Mentalese item – say, XYZ. But in either case, orangey-reds would not have caused us to think RED either – that is, (ii) is true. Then what would it take for orangey-reds not to cause us to think RED? – that is, for the antecedent of (iii) to be true? Plausibly, it would be enough if English were to introduce and make salient a distinct term (like 'oranred') for just that shade of orangey-red. But in such circumstances, crimson would still have caused us to think RED, and so (iii) is true. So conditions (i)–(iii) are all fulfilled, and Fodor's account entails that orangey-red (by hypothesis, a marginal case of red) is *not* now red. And then we have our counterexample.

2.2 The problem of causal chains

Perhaps the biggest problem for any informational semantics, however, is this: where in the causal chain which leads to the tokening of a mental symbol do you stop, to fix on the meaning of the latter? Any mental symbol will always carry information about events further out, and events further in, from what we would intuitively take to be its referent. For example, any term which reliably co-varies with *mouse* will also reliably co-vary with *mouse-mating*, since the world is such that, whenever there is a mouse, there has also been a mating between mice in the past. (We ignore the possibilities of artificial insemination, cloning and test-tube reproduction for simplicity – they would just render the background causal conditions for *mouse* disjunctive, while allowing essentially the same point to go through.) So what shows that MOUSE means *mouse* and not *mouse-mating*?

It is doubtful whether an appeal to asymmetric causal dependence can help Fodor here. For it appears that we have a *symmetric* dependence between the *mouse*-to- MOUSE connection and the *mouse-mating*-to-MOUSE connection – that is, if mice had not caused me to think MOUSE, then nor would matings of mice; but if mice-matings had not caused me to think MOUSE, then nor would mice. Examples of this sort provide powerful support for some form of teleological semantics or for some form of functional-role semantics (see sections 3 and 4 below, respectively). Thus one might say that what makes MOUSE mean *mouse*, is that its *function* is to co-vary with mice and not mouse-matings – that is, the role of MOUSE in cognition is to focus our behaviour differentially upon mice. Or one might say that what makes MOUSE mean *mouse*, is the kinds of *inference* which the subject is inclined to make – for example, from MOUSE to LIVING THING, and not from MOUSE to TEMPORAL EVENT.

A similar problem arises in respect of causal co-variance with events further in. Suppose that by electrically stimulating just the right spot in my cortex, an experimenter can make me think MOUSE. Then what shows that MOUSE means *mouse* and not *immediate neural cause of* MOUSE? But in this case we appear to have asymmetric dependence the wrong way round – if mice had not caused me to think MOUSE (for example, because the Mentalese term XYZ gets harnessed to do the job instead), then still the (actual) immediate neural cause of MOUSE would have caused me to think MOUSE (where MOUSE would now be harnessed to mean something else); and if the (actual) immediate neural cause of MOUSE had not caused me to think MOUSE (but some other neural event had), then nor would mice have caused me to think MOUSE (rather, MOUSE would have been harnessed to some other meaning). And here, too, the solution would appear to be to move to a form of teleological, or perhaps functional role, semantics. At any rate, we predict that if there is any way of securing the asymmetric dependence of the *immediate-neural-cause-of*-MOUSE-to-MOUSE connection upon the *mouse*-to-MOUSE connection, it will have to make at least covert appeal to the *role* of MOUSE in normal cognition.

3 Teleo-semantics

As we have already seen, one way to motivate a form of teleological semantics is to come to regard it as necessary to rectify the deficiencies with informational semantics (this is Dretske's view, 1988). But there are a number of other ways in which one might try to motivate the attempt to naturalise semantics into teleological, biological terms.

3.1 The case for teleo-semantics

One source of attraction is to note that the mind is an evolved system as well as the body. Since the mind, like the body, has been shaped and selected by evolution, we should expect to find within it systems and mechanisms with *proper functions* – that is, systems which are *supposed* to act in one way rather than another, in the sense that they only exist at all because they *have* acted in one way rather than another in the past, and proved successful. And some of these systems will be those which process information, set goals, and execute plans. Indeed, it seems natural to think that propositional attitudes – beliefs and desires, in particular – will have proper functions, being supposed to operate in one way rather than another within our cognition. Desires are *supposed* to get us to act, and beliefs are *supposed* to guide those actions towards success, in any given environment, by providing correct representations of the state of reality. And then it is but a small step from this to the thought that the *contents* of propositional attitudes will have functions too.

(Note that this small step is resistible, however; as Fodor – 1990, ch.3 – points out. From the fact that hair has a function – to protect the scalp from sunburn, say – it certainly does not follow that any individual hair has a unique function, distinct from that of the others; indeed, it seems most unlikely that it has. So from the fact that beliefs in general have a function, it does not follow that the *belief that P* has a function distinct from that of the *belief that Q*.)

This gives us the project of teleo-semantics. If we could say what it is for a state to have the content that P in terms of what that state is *supposed* to achieve in cognition, then we would have effected a naturalistic reduction, provided that the notion of proper function appealed to in the account is a genuinely biological one. Roughly, the idea will be that the content (truth-condition) of a belief is that state of the world which enables the belief to achieve those effects (namely, successful action) which it is *supposed* to achieve (that is, which it is its function to achieve).

Another way of motivating this sort of teleological account, is to notice that many naturally occurring signs employed by biological systems only rarely co-occur with the phenomena which (one wants to say) they represent. For an evolved feature does not have to be always or often successful in order to be selected for. It just has to confer *some* advantage on organisms which possess it (without incurring any significant disadvantage). For example, suppose that a particular species of ground-squirrel uses a series of alarm-calls to warn of potential predators (somewhat like the vervet monkey, only rather less discriminating) – one call for *eagle*, one for *snake*, and one for *big cat*. It is quite possible that the call which means *eagle* should mostly be a false alarm, triggered by any large bird flying overhead. For the costs to the squirrels of taking cover under a tree are small, whereas the gains, on those occasions when there *is* an eagle approaching, are very large. Better to hide unnecessarily many times, than to risk not hiding when you should, and be eaten. So in terms of *information carried* it looks like the alarm call would just mean 'big bird'. But when we consider the *function* of the alarm call in the lives of the squirrels, we see that it has been selected for in virtue of those occasions, and only those occasions, when it carries the information that an eagle is above. And then this, according to teleo-semantics (and in accordance with intuition), is what it means.

3.2 Two distinctions

In developing her version of teleo-semantics, Millikan (1984) draws an important distinction between the *producers* and *consumers* of mental representations. And she claims that it is the consumers which are primary when it comes to determining intentional contents. In the case of a visual percept, for example, the producer system will be the visual module which constructs that representation out of the information striking the retina. And the consumer system will be the various practical reasoning and action-control systems which *use* (or can use) that percept in the course of their normal functioning. (See figure 3.3, for example. Note that what is a consumer system for one type of mental state can be a producer system for another. An inferential system which generates beliefs from percepts is a consumer system relative to the latter, but is itself a producer system for the practical reasoning faculty.) Now the function of any given mental state lies in its evolved effects (the effects it is *supposed* to have) on the consumers of that state. So it is to the latter that we need to look in fixing the content of the state in question.

It seems to us that Millikan has an important point here, which is independent of teleological approaches as such, and which embodies a significant criticism of informational (or 'indicator') semantics. The point is that the meaning of a sign, *for a system*, can only be the meaning which it has for the processes within that system which consume, or make use of, that sign. It is no good a sign carrying information about some worldly state of affairs if, so to speak, the rest of the system doesn't know that it does! This now holds out some hope of making progress with the disjunction problem. If we ask why MOUSE does not mean *shrew-or-mouse* – given that I frequently misrecognise shrews as mice, and so given that MOUSE often carries information about shrews – the answer can be that it is because the rest of the system only operates in ways appropriate to mice, and not to shrews-or-mice. Thus from MOUSE the system infers NOT SHREW, and also perhaps CAN BE AN INDOOR PEST. And it will lead me to answer 'Yes' if asked whether there is a mouse and not a shrew nearby, and so on. So MOUSE representations have a variety of further effects, on inference and action, whose success requires the presence of a mouse, and not of a shrew. So if MOUSE is to have the effects which it is *supposed* to have, it needs to carry the information *mouse*, and not *shrew-or-mouse*. And that, accordingly, can be said to be its truth-condition.

It is important to note that most of those who opt for some version of teleo-semantics, such as Millikan (1984, 1989), Dretske (1988), and Papineau (1987, 1993), are explicit in endorsing an *evolutionary, selectionist*, notion of *function*. On this account, the functions of any property F are those effects of F which explain why the system in question *has* that property – that is, in terms of which we can explain how the property was selected for and/or has been sustained in systems of that type. So functions, on this account, are essentially historical. To know the function of a thing or property, it is not enough to observe what it *presently* does. Rather, you must discover which effect, from amongst the things which it presently does (perhaps only rarely), explains why that thing or property exists. Thus, to know the function of the peacock's tail, you have to ask which of the effects of such tails in ancestral peacocks (presumably, in this case, attractiveness to female peacocks) explains why they were selected for and/or preserved.

The contrasting notion of function, *not* adopted by defenders of teleo-semantics, is an a-historical one. On this account, the functions of any property F are those effects of F which are beneficial to some wider system or process of which F forms a part, or which play a role in sustaining the capacities of that wider system. So on this account, whether or not a property has a function is entirely independent of the question of how that property came to be possessed in the first place. To ask, in this sense, about the function of the peacock's tail is to ask what the tail *does for* the peacock (what benefit it confers), in a way which just brackets off as irrelevant the question of how the peacock came to have such a tail. This notion of function is generally rejected on the grounds that it is not scientifically respectable, and that its application might be vague and observer-relative (but see Cummins, 1975, for replies). For:

(1) How are we to determine the boundaries of the system of which the target property forms a part? Unless some principled way can be found of picking out systems, then just about any effect of a thing can count as its function. (Consider the sound made by the heart when it beats: this, surely, is *not* its function. But now take the 'system' to be the

doctor–patient relationship. Since it is the beat of the heart which enables the doctor to diagnose heart disease, that beat will confer benefits on that 'system', and so come to be picked out as a function of the heart, after all!)

(2) How are we to determine, objectively, what counts as *benefit* to the system so defined?

The objection is that there is no principled way of answering these two questions (we return to answer this objection in section 3.5). In contrast, the evolutionary notion of function is held to be objective in its application, and just as well defined as any other notion in scientific biology. For whether or not a property F has some evolved function ϕ comes down to the question whether it was the fact that instances of F caused ϕ in the past which has caused it to be the case that F is now instanced. And this is a matter of objective causal fact. (In fact, given poly-functionality, this is not so clear. Almost any morphological feature or behaviour will have a complex cost-benefit profile. So is there then any objective way of selecting an element from that profile as *the* function? But if not, then the problem of indeterminacy of content may return.)

3.3 The disjunction problem strikes again?

Plainly, teleological semantics can make *some* progress with the disjunction problem. If, in the half-light of evening, I mistake a tiger-in-the-distance for a nearby tabby cat, then, one presumes, we can say that my perceptual state *mis*represents the tiger as a tabby, on the grounds that it is the making of just this sort of discrimination which my perceptual mechanisms were selected for. A tabby-cat-representation is *supposed* to lead to actions of stroking and feeding, or at least ignoring the presence of, its object. These actions are (needless to say) not appropriate in respect of the tiger. All the same, Fodor argues that teleological semantics must still be fatally infected with a version of the disjunction problem (1990, ch.3). For, since teleology cannot distinguish between properties which are *reliably co-instantiated* in the organism's environment, it will have to be left indeterminate which of these properties is represented.

Consider the snapping-reflex of the frog. This is normally made in response to a fly flying by, but it can in fact be induced by any small black thing moving across the frog's field of vision, such as a shot-gun pellet thrown by an experimenter. We are inclined to say that the frog's perceptual state *misrepresents* the shot-gun pellet as a fly. But can we vindicate this by an appeal to function? Can we demonstrate that the function of the frog's percept is to represent *flies* as opposed to *small black things*, or as opposed to *flies-or-shot-gun-pellets*? Fodor argues not, since in the environments in which the frog's perceptual system has evolved and been maintained, something is a fly if and only if it is a small black thing, and if and only if it is a fly-or-shot-gun-pellet. And from the point of view of evolution, it does not matter which way you tell the story. You can either say that the function (and hence the content) of the frog's state is *to represent flies*, since that state has evolved because of its effect in causing snappings which have led (given the nature of the frog's digestive system) to enhanced survival; or you can say that its function is to represent *small black things*, since that state has evolved because of its effect in causing snappings which have led (given the fact that all the small black things are flies) to enhanced survival; or you can even say that its function is to represent *flies-or-shot-gun-pellets*, since it evolved to cause snappings which led (given that all the flies-or-shot-gun-pellets have been flies) to enhanced survival.

Fodor goes on to claim that the notion of *function* can only be used to discriminate between these cases if we move to a version of it framed in terms of counterfactuals, rather than in terms of actual selectional history. That is, we can ask whether the state in question *would have been* selected for had the frog lived in an environment where all the moving small black things were shot-gun-pellets. Plainly, the answer is 'No'. Then if the function of a state is those of its effects which ensure its existence in actual *and counterfactual* circumstances, we can say that the function of the frog's movement-detector is to represent *flies* and *not* either *small black things* or *flies-or-shot-gun-pellets*. (Actually, pursuit of this sort of approach to functional identity would lead us to the conclusion that the frog's percept represents *ambient food*, since it would still have evolved as it did in environments where all the small moving things were bees, or wasps, or bits of beef thrown by human experimenters. This seems right.)

We shall return to the idea that semantics is best approached by employing an a-historical notion of function below. But first it is worth noting an alternative response to the form of disjunction problem raised here, suggested by our earlier discussion of MOUSE. A teleo-semanticist might concede the indeterminacy in the content of the frog's representation which causes it to snap, because the mechanism in question is such an immediate and simple one. But in more complex cases, where the representation feeds into a distinctive pattern of inferences, these further effects can be used to resolve the indeterminacy. Thus, what shows that *my* state represents *fly* and not *fly-or-shotgun-pellet*, on this account, is that I am prepared unequivocally to infer from it LIVING THING and HAS WINGS. If these are amongst the effects which the state is supposed to have, then they can help to triangulate the correct function. On this approach, then, a teleo-semanticist would be conceding that determinate functions – and so determinate contents – only appear as one moves up the phylogenetic scale, to include organisms capable of increasingly complex and sophisticated inferences. This seems intuitively quite plausible.

3.4 The Swampman objection

Perhaps the strongest objection to teleo-semantics is that it entails that creatures (and/or parts of creatures) which have *not* evolved (and so whose properties and parts fail to have *proper functions*) must lack any intentional states. Davidson's (1987) example of *Swampman*, who is accidentally configured out of an old tree stump in a swamp by a bolt of lightning, in such a way as to be molecule-for-molecule identical to an actual living person, is often used to make the point. Swampman acts and responds to questions just as the normal person does, since his accidentally configured brain has provided him with a complete set of 'beliefs', 'goals', and 'memories'. But according to the teleo-semanticist, Swampman in fact lacks any beliefs, or any other states with intentional content, because, having come to exist by accident, he lacks states with proper functions. This is highly counterintuitive. Would we not be strongly inclined to say that Swampman *believes* (wrongly) that he is 44 years old, and that he *desires* (embarrassingly) to move in with someone else's wife, for example? But according to the teleo-semanticist we cannot say these things. Rather, it is only *as if* Swampman has such beliefs and desires. In fact he has none, because none of his states have proper functions.

Papineau (1987) faces this objection, and replies that on this matter our intuitions need to be reformed. For he points out that he, and teleo-semanticists generally, are not in the business of offering a *conceptual analysis* of the notion of content. Rather, what is being offered is a naturalistic theory of the *nature* of content. And it is perfectly possible that our concepts may be poor reflections of, or have gotten out of line with, reality. So our *concept* of content would lead us to say that Swampman has thoughts with content, but the *nature* of content is such that, in fact, he does not. But this reply, although acceptable so far as it goes, does not address the real problem. For the difficulty for teleo-semantics is not just that we feel pre-theoretically *inclined* to say that Swampman has beliefs and desires. Rather, it is that Swampman's behaviour is subsumed by just the same psychological (content-involving) laws as may be used to explain and predict the behaviour of normal people. Not only *can* we explain Swampman's behaviour by attributing to him beliefs and desires, but so we *should*, it seems to us; for it is beliefs and desires which do cause his behaviour, just as they do other people's. In which case beliefs and desires cannot have their contents individuated in terms of evolutionary function, contrary to what the teleo-semanticist claims.

The point just made can also be put by saying: *psychology is not a historical science* – psychology is interested in the present, and the way in which our minds *now* operate, not in the past, or the way in which our minds got that way. (Even so-called 'evolutionary psychology' looks to the past primarily to gain clues as to the modular structure of present mental functioning. See Barkow *et al.*, 1992. The fact that a science employs historical methods or arguments does not make it a historical one in the sense of employing *historical principles of individuation*.) So the notion of function employed in psychology should be an a-historical, non-evolutionary one. Equally, one can say that physiology is not a historical science either; its interest in hearts is an interest in what hearts *now* do. And note that those who think that all functions are evolutionary will have to say that Swampman lacks a heart too!

If teleo-semanticists insist that the content of a representation can derive only from a function which has been selected for, then they are landed with further awkward consequences. It is, for example, a matter of considerable controversy within psychology and linguistics, whether our innate language faculty was selected for and has a (historical) function – with Chomsky and others lining up on one side, and Pinker and others on the other. (Chomsky, 1988, thinks that our capacity for language may be some sort of by-product of having a big brain; see Pinker and Bloom, 1990, and Pinker, 1994, for the contrary case.) Yet both sides in this debate insist that the language faculty contains innate *representations*. Now on this matter our own sympathies are very firmly with Pinker, that the language-system *has* evolved. But it would be strange indeed, if what looked like a substantive scientific debate turned out to be trivially resolvable by philosophers, on the grounds that the very property of *being a representation* presupposes a historical function.

Note that this objection does not involve a covert return to the idea that teleo-semantics is being put forward as a piece of *a priori* conceptual analysis. No, we allow that teleo-semantics is produced by philosophical reflection in the light of substantive background beliefs, also – and crucially – involving reflection on the commitments of scientific practice in the area. Our point is that since there is a substantive scientific debate over the question whether the innate representations of the language-faculty have evolved, those engaged in this debate cannot be believing that representational content is individuated in terms of selectional history, on pain of irrationality. The debate on this issue suggests that the *scientific* notion of content cannot be a teleo-functional one, any more than is the folk-psychological notion teleological.

What these points suggest, then, is that the most promising way to develop an analysis of content in terms of function would bring it much closer to functional*ism* in the philosophy of mind than is generally recognised. Functionalists think that mental states are to be individuated in terms of their normal causal role, or *function* in cognition. Teleo-semanticists think that the contents of mental states are to be individuated by their distinctive *functions* (normally historical, or evolutionary). But if, as we have suggested, the latter view is best developed in terms of an a-historical, contemporary, notion of function, then the two positions will become much harder to tell apart. It may be, indeed, that teleo-semantics, properly understood, is a variety of functional-role semantics – on which see the discussions in section 4 below.

3.5 A-historical functions revisited

If teleo-semantics is to employ a notion of function which is *not* evolutionary, then how are we to answer the attendant charges of arbitrariness and observer-relativity? One possible route is that sketched by Fodor, and discussed briefly above, in terms of evolution under counterfactual scenarios. For it is, surely, an objective matter of fact whether or not the frog's motion-detectors would have evolved and been sustained in a variety of counterfactual environments. So, one way to objectify what the frog's motion-detector does for the frog (that is, its contemporary function) is to cash it in terms of the range of counterfactual circumstances in which that detector would have enhanced survival and/or reproductive success.

Another way to rebut the charge of arbitrariness, is to point out that functions understood in terms of beneficial contributions to some wider system can be perfectly objective, provided that the system in question is a *natural kind*, whose processes are governed by *causal laws*. So provided that the mind is a natural kind, in the way that psychology takes for granted, and provided that the various psychological transitions into which contents can enter are lawful (again, as psychology supposes), then there can be no principled objection to the use of the notion of *function within the psychological system* in characterising the contents of our intentional states. Or so, at any rate, it seems to us.

But how, on this approach, are we to distinguish between the effects of a mental state which are its functions, and those which are not? We think this will have to be done in terms of the effects of the state which partly explain the continued operations of its containing-system – function-effects are those effects which form part of the *explanation* of the operations of the wider containing-system. Compare: the function of the heart, now, is to pump blood (whether or not it ever evolved to do that) and *not* to cause a rhythmical sound. But both are equally effects of the heart. What is the difference? The difference is that it is (in part) *because* the heart pumps blood that the containing system (the living body) continues to exist. If the heart did not pump blood then the system of which it is a part (the living organism) could not operate as it does. In contrast, the making of a heart-beat is not causally relevant to the continued functioning of the organism. So we could say that the function of a particular belief in cognition is given by those of its effects which it is supposed to have, which partly explain how the cognitive system continues to operate successfully – for example, not leading to predictions which are falsified, or not leading to actions which fail.

4 Functional-role semantics

Teleological semantics faces pretty severe difficulties. One of these difficulties is that it does not seem plausible to account for the semantic properties of thoughts in terms of an historical, or selectionist, notion of *function*. We suggested, on the contrary, that psychology (both scientific and, especially, common-sense) is primarily interested in the present. Our content-based psychology is concerned with the laws and principles governing *present* cognitive functioning, not necessarily with the question of how those laws and principles came to be the way they are. This suggested that the best way forward for teleo-semantics might be to analyse content in terms of a notion of *current* function – where the current function of a property F is that effect of F within the system which partly explains the continued functioning of the system.

But maybe it still remains implausible that all thoughts should *have* a function in this sense. For example, the content of my belief that the universe is finite does not play any role in explaining why my cognitive system continues to operate, since the only reason I continue to have it is that I have not found reason to reject it (it is certainly not something that I need to *act upon!*). So what we might then do is thin down the notion of function still further, in such a way that the function of a state is just its functional, or causal, *role* within the system – where to characterise the causal role of a state is just to describe the characteristic pattern of causes and effects which it normally has within the system, without any commitment to the idea that some of the effects of the state play a role in sustaining the existence of the system itself. And this is, then, the project of functional-role semantics.

4.1 In support of functional-role semantics

One argument in support of functional-role semantics is an argument from functionalism about mental states *in general*. As we saw in chapter 1, the majority of philosophers now think that the way to avoid dualism about the mental, and to understand the relationship between mind and brain, is by accepting that mental states are individuated by their causal role, conceptualised at some level of abstraction from the physical mechanisms in the brain which instantiate those roles. Indeed, we have accepted (in chapter 2) that folk psychology embodies an implicit *theory* of the causal structure and functioning of the mind, in such a way that different mental state types can be individuated by their position within the theory. The argument is then, that when we extend this approach to states like *the belief that P* we get functional-role semantics. But precisely *which* of a state's normal causes and effects are to be used to individuate it? *All* of them? And only the *actual* causes and effects within a particular thinker? We shall argue that the answer to both of these questions should be 'No'.

To see the latter point (that it is not just actual causes and effects which count), notice that functionalism about the mind claims to individuate mental states in terms of their *potential* causal interactions with bodily stimuli, with other mental states, and with behaviour. Causal relations with other *actual* states of the subject do not always play a defining role. For example, no functionalist would claim that my pain must be a distinct kind of mental state from yours, merely because I happen to have a desire to appear brave whereas you do not. On the contrary, functionalists will insist that our states are the same, provided that they *would* have the same effects *if* all our other mental states were similar. In the same way, although functionalists should accept that *some* causal connections with other actual mental states (namely, the unmediated connections) play a defining role in individuating some types of mental state, they should deny that mental state identity is transitive across chains of such connections. Surely no functionalist would want to deny that blind people have desires, for example (that is, action-determining states of the same type that sighted people have), merely because of the differences in the remote causal connections of those states! (Standing-state desires tend to be activated by the belief that the thing desired is now available, and such beliefs are often caused, in the normal case, by visual experience of the desired object.)

When the argument is extended to *the belief that P*, then, it is obvious that it will not be all of the causal connections between that state and the agent's other actual beliefs and desires which individuate it, but rather the potential connections. It will not be the *actual* causal liaisons of a belief with other beliefs and desires which constitute its content, but rather the set of conditionals about what the subject *would* think or do in the presence of (some but not all) other – hypothetical – beliefs and desires. (This point goes a considerable distance towards answering Fodor's charge of *idiosyncrasy* of content; for the same conditionals can be true of different thinkers, despite wide variations in their actual beliefs. See Carruthers, 1996c, ch.4.)

A second argument for functional-role semantics is a kind of 'what else?' argument from those working on the semantics of beliefs and statements. It is generally maintained that we cannot individuate contents (explanatory as opposed to semantic ones, that is – see chapter 6) purely in terms of reference, since this will slice them *too thick*. That is, it will fail to distinguish from one another thought-contents which are, intuitively, distinct. For example, Oedipus' belief, 'Jocasta is more than forty years old', differs in content from his belief, 'Mother is more than forty years old', even though Jocasta is, in fact, his mother. For, not knowing that Jocasta is his mother, it would be possible for him to have the one belief without the other. Yet if the reference is the same, what *else* can distinguish these beliefs *except* their differences of causal role? For example, Oedipus' belief that he is thirty years old will tend to cause him to have the second of the above beliefs in the presence only of the belief that a girl of ten cannot have a child, whereas the first of the above beliefs will only be caused if he *also* believes that Jocasta is his mother.

It is worth also considering a slightly more elaborate example, lest someone should respond (as Fodor does, 1994, ch.2) by appeal to compositionality, pointing out that JOCASTA and MY MOTHER can be distinguished by virtue of the fact that the latter contains the concept MOTHER, whereas the former does not. The example is as follows. Imagine that I have learned to use colour-terms normally, by sight, but have also learned to use a hand-held machine which *in fact* (unknown to me) responds to colour – perhaps vibrating in the hand with an intensity proportional to the dominant wavelengths it receives. And suppose that I have been trained, ostensively, to use a set of terms, 'der', 'wolley', 'neerg', and so on; where these terms are *in fact* co-extensive with the colour-terms, 'red', 'yellow', 'green', and so on. Then, plainly, there are circumstances in which I might believe that the tomato is red without also believing that it is der, or vice versa. And this despite the fact that it is the very same worldly property, surely, which my thought concerns. Here, as before, the argument is: what *else* can distinguish the contents of the beliefs, 'The tomato is red' and 'The tomato is der', except their functional roles? For there is, by hypothesis, no overt compositional or syntactic difference between them. What makes the two beliefs different, in fact, are such things as that, for example, (unless I *also* believe that anything der is red) it is only the former which will cause me to point to the tomato if asked to exhibit something red; and if I want to check on the truth of the former I shall open my eyes, whereas if I want to check on the truth of the latter I shall pick up my vibrating-machine.

4.2 Elaborating functional-role semantics

How best should functional-role semantics be developed? One question is whether or not the identity of a content-bearing state should be made to turn on *all* kinds of characteristic causes and consequences of that state with an explanatory role. Thus suppose that my psychology happens to be such that the thought, 'There is a snake nearby' always causes me to have a panic attack – where it does not have this effect because I *believe* that snakes are dangerous, but rather because of some association set up in my childhood. Does this effect contribute to the identity of the thought which I thereby entertain, in such a way that if the thought which you would express in the same words does *not* cause panic attacks in you, then we do not entertain one and the same type of thought? Or suppose that the thought, 'Madonna is to visit Sheffield' causes my hands to shake, but not yours. Does this mean that we do not entertain thoughts with the very same content, because our thoughts differ slightly in their functional roles? If we answer 'Yes' to these questions then we are proposing that content should be analysed in terms of crude, undifferentiated, causal role, where *any* cause and *any* effect – whether cognitive, affective, or brute physical – can count in the individuation of content. If we answer 'No', then we need to find some principled way of drawing a ring around the set of causes and effects we are interested in.

It does seem implausible that you and I should count as entertaining distinct thoughts (which we would nevertheless express in the very same words), merely because the 'emotional colouring' or the physical effects of those thoughts are different. But how, then, are we to characterise the relevant subset of a thought's causes and effects, which goes to make up its content-defining functional role? One obvious way forward, is to say that it is only those causes and effects which are *inferential* in character which count towards identity of content. But this then raises another problem: what *is* an inferential process? How do we distinguish inferences from other sorts of cognitive transition? We obviously cannot say that a transition is inferential just in case it can be broken down into intermediate steps, since this would bring it out that the transition from 'P & Q' to 'P' is *not* an inferential one! But then nor can we say that a process is inferential just in case it is *valid*, or (more plausibly, since not all inferences are deductive ones) just in case it *reliably generates truth from truth*. For this would be to introduce semantic notions into our attempt to naturalise content, in a way which would be tantamount to abandoning the project altogether.

There would appear to be two possible ways forward for functional-role semantics, here. One would be to borrow a leaf from the teleo-semanticist's book, and say that a process is inferential just in case it occurs when our cognition operates in the way that it is *supposed* to. Then the transition from 'P & Q' to 'P' will come out as inferential, whereas the transition from the thought, 'Madonna will visit Sheffield' to shaking hands will not, just as intuition dictates. For the first transition is either innate (and selected for) or at least maintained in cognition because of its success; whereas the second is neither. But notice that this need not commit us to saying that thoughts themselves have functions. Rather, we would be saying that thoughts are individuated in terms of those of their normal causes and effects which happen in accordance with properly functioning cognition.

The other way forward would be to characterise as inferential those processes which happen in accordance with psychological *laws*, and/or which are counterfactual supporting. This approach would probably cover much the same ground as the previous proposal, but has the advantage that content-involving psychology can then be characterised entirely a-historically. So, provided it is a *law* (or nomic tendency, at least) that people who believe 'P & Q' will also come to believe 'P' *ceteris paribus*, then this transition can be used to characterise the functional role of the former. But since it is presumably *not* lawful that thoughts of Madonna visiting Sheffield should cause shaking hands, this effect will not form part of the functional role of that thought.

4.3 Two-factor functionalism

Another point is that it can easily seem that functional-role semantics is not really a *competitor* to informational semantics or to teleological se-mantics, in that it is not really addressing the same questions. For how can the reference, or worldly truth-condition, of a thought be a matter of how that thought functions intra-cranially? – how can it be a matter of the network of inferences into which that thought can enter? It can seem inevitable, in fact, that functional-role semantics is only a naturalised account of *narrow* content, and that it cannot be extended to account for *wide* content. In which case someone might claim to be an informational or teleological semanticist (about wide content) *and* a functional-role seman-ticist (about narrow content), and there is no real competition.

It is certainly true that some versions of functional-role semantics have been intended as accounts of narrow content only. And it is equally true that defenders of narrow content might be well advised to look to some such form of functional-role semantics if they seek a naturalised account of their target notion. But it is important to see that functional-role semantics does not *have* to be narrow. For the functional-role of a mental state can be characterised in such a way as to embrace the worldly causes and effects of that state – these are then 'long-armed', or world-involving, as opposed to 'short-armed', or in-the-head, functional roles (Block, 1986). Thus we might say that it is part of the functional role of the belief, 'Madonna will visit Sheffield' to be caused by events involving Madonna herself, and to cause me (given my desires) to stand all night in the rain outside the Sheffield Arena in order to see her.

Functional-role semantics might well appeal to some form of causal co-variance, or informational, account in order to characterise the world-involving element of functional role. So we might say that a MOUSE thought is one which carries information about mice (which is caused, *inter alia*, by the presence of mice), appealing to the ways in which that thought interacts inferentially with others in order to solve the disjunction problem, and to distinguish it from other thoughts which might concern the same worldly property. So MOUSE has the content *mouse*, and not *shrew-or-mouse*, in virtue of the fact that it tends to be caused by the presence of a mouse, and because I am apt to infer from it NOT SHREW, and CAN INTERBREED WITH OTHER MICE, and so on. (For a number of different proposals concerning the development of a two-factor semantics, see Field, 1977; Loar, 1982; McGinn, 1982; Block, 1986.)

4.4 The charge of holism

Plainly, there is a sense in which functional-role semantics is holistic. For in specifying the functional-role of one state – say, *the belief that P* – we will have to mention others with which it may causally interact; and many of these, too, will be states with semantic contents (*the belief that Q; the desire that R*; and so on). And it might seem that this then raises a difficulty for the project of *naturalising* content. For how can one successfully reduce into purely natural, causal, terms the content *P*, if the statements that attempt to do so have to mention yet other contents? It can easily seem that this is not *reducing* content, but merely passing the buck from one content to another. In reality, however, there is no difficulty here, and this (weak) sense in which functional-role semantics is holistic raises no problem for the naturalisation project. In fact it is a ubiquitous feature of scientific (and other) theories, that they should contain terms which only get their significance from their relationship to the other terms in the theory. But as Lewis has shown (1970), one *can* still define each of these terms by *quantifying over* the entities they concern. We will not pursue this further here.

Fodor has argued, however, that functional-role semantics must give rise to a much stronger form of holism than this, and claims that scientific psychology can have no use for such a strongly holistic notion of content (1987, ch.3; Fodor and Lepore, 1992). In which case, since attempts to naturalise content are ultimately driven by a desire to defend the reality of the propositional attitudes by showing that they can be incorporated into science, we had better not pursue that goal by adopting functional-role semantics. Fodor's claim is that functional-role semantics must make the identity of any given belief-content dependent upon *all* of the beliefs with which it is inferentially connected. In which case content will turn out to be radically idiosyncratic, and rarely, if ever, will two people share beliefs with the very same content. For there will always be enough differences in their belief systems to ensure that there are *some* differences in the inferential connections of the candidate belief. But if content is idiosyncratic, then it must, it seems, be useless for purposes of scientific psychology. For what such a psychology seeks are laws which will subsume all of the individuals in a population.

There are various ways for adherents of functional-role semantics to respond to the alleged problem of strong holism. One has already been mentioned, which is that functional role is really functional *potential* – and the same set of conditionals can be true of people who differ in their actual beliefs. There are also a number of further proposals to draw limits to those of the inferential connections of any given belief which count towards the identity of its content (see Carruthers, 1996c, ch.4; Devitt, 1996). While the problem is difficult, there are no reasons to think that it must be insuperable, in our view. Here, however, we will concentrate on showing that even if our folk-psychological notion of content proves to be strongly holistic, and so idiosyncratic, this need not mean that scientific psychology should abandon the notion of content altogether.

The first point to be made, is that much of psychology could operate perfectly well even with an idiosyncratic notion of content. For many psychological generalisations *quantify over* content, in a way which does not require it to be true that any two thinkers ever entertain the *same* content. Thus the practical reasoning syllogism tells us that anyone who desires Q, and who believes *if P then Q*, and who believes *P is within my power*, will try to bring it about that P, *ceteris paribus*. This generalisation can remain true, and can retain its predictive and explanatory power, even if no two thinkers ever instantiate the *same* instance of it (with particular contents substituted for P and for Q). But clearly this point by itself cannot draw all of the teeth from the charge of idiosyncrasy. For it is also true that a great many psychological generalisations relate to *particular* contents or types of content.

Consider the claim that there exist various kinds of incest taboo, for example. If I say that people have an aversion to the thought of sexual intercourse between mother and son, then I have expressed a generalisation in relation to a thought which no one else but myself can share, if strong holism is true. Since no one else can have an aversion to *that* thought (a thought individuated by the totality of the inferential connections which it has, for me), then my attempted generalisation fails.

One way of trying to respond to this objection would be to take up Stich's (1983) suggestion, that scientific psychology should operate with a graded *similarity measure* for intentional contents. Psychological laws might then be formulated for contents which are more or less similar to one another, even if no two people ever share thought-contents which are strictly speaking identical. However, as Fodor (1998) points out, *similarity* of contents has to be cashed in terms of the extent of overlap in the sets of thoughts with which a given pair of contents is inferentially connected. And this in turn presupposes that we can *identify* (absolutely, not merely as similar) the thoughts in question. So this approach looks unpromising.

To see the possibility of a rather different way of responding to the objection, notice that not all of the inferential connections of the concept *incest between mother and son* are likely to be equally relevant to the existence of the incest taboo. In order to feel aversion at the thought, 'Jocasta is committing incest with her son' there are probably various beliefs which you have to have, and various inferences which you must be prepared to make – such as the inference that Jocasta is considerably older, for example. But remote inferential connections with beliefs about average family size, say (let alone with beliefs about famous female novelists) are unlikely to have any impact. What this then suggests is that there may be a subset of the total inferential connections of a given thought-content which bear on the truth of the law-like generalisations in which it figures. In which case psychological science could identify the content in question by means of the relevant subset.

(This might lead to a situation in which one and the same mental representation – such as, JOCASTA IS COMMITTING INCEST WITH HER SON – would be assigned contents with *different* identity-conditions in different contexts, depending on which psychological laws were in question. But there need not be anything particularly surprising in this, let alone subversive of the very idea of content-based psychology.)

A real example might help here. As we saw in chapter 4, psychologists have discovered that there is a watershed in normal development which occurs around the age of four, prior to which many of the generalisations which are true of us in virtue of our possession of a folk psychology are inapplicable. And most psychologists say, in consequence, that prior to the age of four children lack the concept *belief*, and are incapable of belief-thoughts. (Perner, 1991, says that three year olds possess the distinct concept *prelief*, which is a kind of pared-down amalgam of *pretence* and *belief*.) Yet they also say that *after* the age of four we all possess the same concept of belief, despite the many minor differences which may exist between individuals in their beliefs concerning beliefs. Plainly, then, their idea may be that the concept *belief* is to be individuated by just those inferential connections (such as the one from 'A believes that P' to 'A is in a state which may be false') which are necessary and sufficient for the relevant psychological generalisations to be true of us.

A general moral can be extracted from this sort of case. Fodor objects to functional-role semantics on the grounds that it has no 'principled' way of marking out the inferences which are constitutive of meaning; so all inferences would have to be counted as meaning-constitutive; so content becomes holistic and idiosyncratic; and so, disastrously, there would be no contentful psychological laws. We maintain that Fodor has got the dialectics of content back-to-front. The first thing to assert is that there are, undeniably, contentful psychological causal tendencies of a lawlike character. (Indeed, note how we rely upon them all the time – in order to communicate, pragmatically, far more than we need explicitly state, for example.) But then, given that there are such lawlike connections, a notion of functional-role content can always be constructed – namely, from whatever inferences are necessary for the laws to apply. Whatever is idiosyncratic is *precisely what is omitted* from the functional-role that constitutes content. And there we have the required principle.

5 Naturalisation versus reduction

All three of the main semantic theories considered here (informational semantics, teleological semantics, and functional-role semantics) are driven by a desire to *naturalise* semantic properties, such as meaning, truth, and reference. And this desire, in turn, is underpinned by the need to avoid *eliminativism* about content-based psychology, as we noted in section 1. But in order to see whether a *naturalised* semantics would have to be a *reductive* semantics, we need to get a little clearer about what, exactly, a reductive account of some phenomenon *is*.

5.1 Reduction and reality

Reductions come in (at least) two forms – *conceptual* and *metaphysical*. Conceptual reductions are generally attempted *a priori*, and purport to state, in terms not involving the target concept, the conditions necessary and sufficient for something to satisfy that concept. Conceptual reductions are part of the staple fare of analytic philosophy. Thus, the attempted analysis of knowledge as *justified true belief*, is an attempted reduction of our notion of knowledge to other terms. The historical record of analytic philosophy does not hold out very much hope of success in finding conceptual reductions of any but a very few concepts. Despite the collective labour of several generations of analytical philosophers, there is hardly a single case where a reductive definition is generally agreed upon. Typically, the search for reductive definitions has followed the same depressing pattern. First, a definition is proposed (as in 'knowledge = justified true belief'); then counterexamples to the proposal are found (as in the Gettier-cases for knowledge); then the analysis is patched up to accommodate these counterexamples; but then further counterexamples to the new analysis are found; and so on. So we appear to have quite good inductive grounds for saying that *there are no conceptual reductions to be found* (or at least none which are informative). And so, *a fortiori*, it is unlikely that there are any conceptual reductions of semantic concepts to be had, either.

A possible explanation for the general unavailability of reductive conceptual analyses is provided by recent work in cognitive psychology, as both Stich (1992) and Tye (1992) point out. A variety of experimental data suggest that concepts are stored, not in the form of statements of necessary and sufficient conditions, but rather as *prototypes*. A prototype is a representation of a prototypical member of the kind, including a (weighted) set of prototypical properties, and perhaps also including a perceptual *paradigm* derived from acquaintance with one or more members of the kind. A prototype for the concept *dog*, for example, would include *chases cats, has dogs as parents, eats bones, barks when angry or afraid, is a mammal, wags its tail when happy*, and so on, together with a perceptual template, or paradigm, derived from experience of one or more examples. But there is no suggestion that dogs must necessarily have all of these features. Rather, deciding whether something is a dog is a matter of judging whether it is sufficiently similar to the prototypical dog. (And judgements of 'sufficient similarity', in turn, may be context-sensitive, and vary with background purposes.) If the concept *knowledge* has a similar sort of structure, then it is obvious why all attempts to give a reductive analysis of the concept, in a statement of necessary and sufficient conditions for knowledge, have failed. And if semantic concepts, too, share prototype structure, then it looks unlikely that any reductive analysis can be provided for them, either.

Metaphysical reductions, in contrast, focus on the worldly properties in question, rather than on our conceptions of them. The classic form of such reductions is inter-theoretic, as when the gas temperature–pressure laws are reduced to statistical mechanics. Boyle's Law states this: $PV = kT$. So if the volume (V) of a gas is kept constant, an increase in temperature (T) will cause a corresponding increase in pressure (P). This law can in fact be derived from statistical mechanics, together with the 'bridge principles' that pressure is force per unit area, and temperature is mean molecular momentum. For as the average momentum of the molecules (the temperature) is increased, so the force per unit area exerted on the surface of the container (the pressure) will also increase, if that surface area remains constant.

Just as there have been very few successful analytic reductions, so, too, there exist few successful inter-theoretic reductions. The reason, in this case, lies with the phenomenon of *multiple realisability*. It appears to be quite common for laws in the special sciences (chemistry, biology, neurology, psychology, and so on) to be multiply realised in lower-level mechanisms. If there are a variety of different physical mechanisms, involving a variety of different physical properties P_i, any one of which is sufficient to realise a property T in a special-science law, then it will not be possible to *identify* the special-science property T with any single physical property. This sort of situation is especially likely to arise in the case of biology and psychology, where we know that evolution can come up with a number of different mechanisms to perform the same function. In which case we should not expect to be able to find reductive accounts of psychological properties, including semantic properties. So, if realism requires naturalisation, it becomes crucial to know whether naturalisation, in turn, must require reduction.

5.2 Naturalisation without reduction

Plainly, belief in the reality of some property cannot, *in general*, require a successful reduction of that property into other terms, on pain of vicious regress. Nor is it very plausible to maintain that all properties *above the level of basic physics* need to be reduced to the terms of that physics in order to be shown to be real. For then we may have to deny the reality of chemical and biological kinds, as well as the reality of psychological ones. For there are very few successful inter-theoretic reductions to be found at all, let alone reductions to the vocabulary of basic physics. Rather, we should accept that the existence of a variety of special sciences is a permanent, irreducible, part of our world-view, reflecting the way in which the natural world is organised in terms of laws and principles operating at different levels of generality. And then all we need do in order to *naturalise* some property, is show that it figures in the laws of some or other special science, in whose persistence we have good reason to believe.

In which case, for those of us who believe in the scientific status of psychology, there is nothing more that we need do, in order to naturalise intentional content, than to point out that such contents figure within the laws of psychology. So those who have been seeking a naturalised *reduction* of intentional content have not only been chasing something which may in fact be unattainable, but they have been doing so unnecessarily. All they really ever needed to do was defend the scientific status of intentional psychology directly, without seeking any sort of reduction.

What becomes of the supposed *unity* of science, however, on the picture being sketched here? Can we really allow all the various special sciences to float free of one another? Can we allow that natural science just consists of 'one more damn law after another', with no requirements of ordering or integration between them? If so, then there would be no principled objection to dualism, since the laws of psychology would not be required to stand in any particular relation to laws governing brain-processes. But plainly, belief in the irreducibility and reality of the special sciences need not entail anything nearly so strong. On the contrary, we can continue to insist on token identities between special-science occurrences and physical events. That is, whenever a property is tokened which falls under some special-science law (of psychology, as it might be), we can (and surely should) require that the token be identical with (be none other than) the tokening of some lower-level (and, ultimately, physical) property happening at the same time. So, belief in the irreducibility of the special sciences is at least consistent with our well-motivated physicalism.

It may be, indeed, that we can (and should) believe in a weakened version of the doctrine of the unity of science, without succumbing to reductionism, as Smith (1992) argues. Roughly, the idea is that it must be possible to seek *explanations* of special-science laws in terms of lower-level mechanisms. That is, it should be possible to render it *unmysterious* that a given special-science law obtains, given the ways in which the properties involved in that law can be realised in physical mechanisms, and given the lower-level laws which govern such mechanisms. Put slightly differently: it may be reasonable to believe that each *token* process which happens in accordance with a special-science law must be realised in a token process describable in the vocabulary of some lower-level science, which is also lawful at that lower level. In which case, in order to be realists (and naturalists) about psychology, we must be able to believe that in connection with each token psychological process, there is some process describable in the vocabulary of physics and/or chemistry and/or neurology, whose occurrence is *sufficient for* (because it is the *realiser of*) the occurrence of the psychological process in question.

But there is surely no requirement that we must already be able to *point to*, or provide an account of, such lower-level processes, before we can believe in the reality of the psychological. We just have to be able to have a *reasonable belief* that they can be found. And even less is it required that such realising processes should be specifiable more-or-less *a priori*, as a result of philosophical reflection in the light of our background beliefs. On the contrary, surely, the interface(s) between psychology and neurology are for science to discover and elucidate. So there is no requirement that we should, as philosophers, be able to state, in non-psychological vocabulary, a condition which would be sufficient for the occurrence of any given content-bearing psychological state.

It would seem that the reality, and natural status, of content is assured by the existence of a content-based scientific psychology, provided that the latter can in principle be unified with the remainder of science. So if one believes in the reality (and quasi-scientific status) of folk psychology, and in the prospects for content-based scientific psychology more generally (as does Fodor, 1987, and as do we), then there is nothing more which needs to be done to naturalise content, beyond showing that psychological processes are implementable in mechanisms which can, ultimately, be physical mechanisms. And it would appear that the computational theory of cognition (also championed by Fodor, 1980) can at least make a good start on doing that.

It remains true that we are committed, sometime, to providing a reductive explanation of some content-involving psychological phenomena – that is, to detailing the implementing mechanisms so as to explain, in detail, how the higher-level process is instantiated in them. And it is also true, if we believe in at least a weak form of the unity of science, that we are committed to finding neurological or other lower-level theories which should render it unmysterious why our psychological science works as well as it does – that is, theories of underlying mechanisms in terms of which we can see why the content-involving phenomena cluster together in the ways that they do. But these are emphatically *not* tasks to be undertaken by philosophers from their armchairs. The task of seeking the requisite degree of unity in science, and of offering reductive explanations, is a scientific one, not to be attempted by *a priori* reflection.

Our view, then, is that much of what has gone on under the banner of 'naturalising content' has been misguided, or at least misdirected. Even Fodor – Mr Special Sciences himself (see his 1974) – is at fault here. Admittedly, although Fodor at one time attempted what looked like fully reductive accounts of content (see his 1984, 1985b, and 1987), he has now given up seeking *necessary and* sufficient conditions for someone to entertain a given content; he now seeks only sufficient conditions (1990). And this might seem to be at least a gesture in the direction of multiple realisability. The idea seems to be that although we cannot be required to provide natural conditions which are *necessary* for a given content (since that content might be realised in a variety of *different* conditions), still it must at least be possible to find natural conditions *sufficient* for a given content, which play the realising role. But he still seems to think that the reduction has to be some sort of conceptual one, since he allows that it can be refuted by appeal to purely imaginary examples. And he still seems to think that the sufficient conditions in question can be discovered by *a priori* reflection. But why on earth would one expect that such an enquiry could be conducted *a priori*, or that the sufficiency in question should be conceptual?

5.3 The future of naturalised semantics

Does this then mean that there is no truth whatever in the various reductive accounts of intentionality proposed by philosophers which we have considered? No, we do not insist on that. For one thing, there is a puzzle about the origin of content. The world did not always contain representations. So representations must somehow have evolved in the natural order. We are happy to agree that the question of how that can have happened can be answered by appeal to the basic elements of teleosemantics – specifically, a system of reliably sensitive indicator states coming to be selected for purposes of behavioural control. (Compare a modest account of the origins of monetary exchange – as against the unpromising attempt to provide a reductive analysis of every species and quantity of monetary value.)

For another thing, it may be that what can, indeed, be plausibly provided from the philosopher's armchair are *necessary conditions* for intentionality, or for entertaining any given intentional content. This is surely to be expected if concepts are represented in the form of prototypes, in the way discussed earlier. For notice that amongst the prototypical features of dogs listed above were two – *has dogs as parents* and *is a mammal* – which are at least plausible necessary conditions for a creature to be a dog. So one might predict that in the case of semantic concepts, too, there are necessary conditions which can be articulated more-or-less *a priori*. (See Williamson, 1995, who makes just this point in connection with our concept of knowledge.)

What we propose, then, is that philosophers should start to explore variants of the naturalistic programmes discussed in this chapter – perhaps with special emphasis on functional-role accounts, either in their 'long-armed' form, or supplemented by causal co-variance constraints – with a view to providing, from the armchair, not a *reductive* account of intentional properties, nor even a set of *sufficient* conditions for intentional content, but rather a set of *necessary* conditions. These would provide constraints on what it takes to be a creature with intentional contents in general, and on what is required to entertain any given content *P* in particular. And of course there is plenty of scope, too, for interdisciplinary work with psychologists, in seeking accounts of the necessary conditions for a given body of psychological generalisations to have application, such as were discussed in section 4.4 above in connection with the concept of belief.

6 Conclusion

In this chapter we have explored the strengths and weaknesses of three different naturalisation programmes in semantics, arguing that, of the three, some form of functional-role semantics stands the best chance of success. But we have also argued that the reductive pretensions of these programmes are misguided, especially when undertaken as a *philosophical* exercise. Although it may be a requirement on the natural status of intentional properties that the content-involving laws of scientific psychology should be explicable in the light of realising mechanisms, such explanations are for natural scientists to discover *a posteriori*. Philosophers should, at best, propose and defend some necessary conditions for creatures to entertain intentional contents.

SELECTED READING

On informational semantics: Dretske, 1981, 1986; Fodor, 1987, 1990; Loewer and Rey, 1991.

On teleo-semantics: Millikan, 1984, 1986, 1989; Papineau, 1987, 1993; Dretske, 1988.

On functional-role semantics: Loar, 1981, 1982; McGinn, 1982; Block, 1986; Peacocke, 1986, 1992.

On naturalisation: Fodor, 1974; Smith, 1992; Stich, 1992; Tye, 1992.

On concepts in philosophy and in psychology: Margolis and Laurence, 1999. (See especially the long introductory essay by the editors.)

8   Forms of representation

Over the last two chapters we have been considering the nature of psychological content. In the present chapter we take up the question of how such content is *represented* in the human brain, or of what its *vehicles* might be. Following a ground-clearing introduction, the chapter falls into two main parts. In the first of these, the orthodox Mentalese story is contrasted with its connectionist rival. Then in the second, we consider what place natural language representations may play in human cognition. One recurring question is what, if anything, folk psychology is committed to in respect of content-representation.

1 Preliminaries: thinking in images

One traditional answer to the questions just raised, concerning the vehicles of our thoughts, is that thinking consists entirely of mental (mostly visual) *images* of the objects which our thoughts concern, and that thoughts interact by means of *associations* (mostly learned) between those images. So when I think of a dog, I do so by virtue of entertaining some sort of mental image of a dog; and when I infer that dogs bark, I do so by virtue of an association which has been created in me between the mental images of *dog* and of *barking*. This view has been held very frequently throughout the history of philosophy, at least until quite recently, particularly amongst empiricists (Locke, 1690; Hume, 1739; Russell, 1921). Those who hold such a view will then argue that thought is independent of language on the grounds that possession and manipulation of mental images need not in any way involve or presuppose natural language.

In fact the imagist account is that thinking consists in the manipulation of mental images, and that thoughts inherit their semantic properties from the representative powers of the images which constitute them. There may be something importantly correct in the first part of this claim, as we will argue in section 3 of this chapter. It may be that our conscious thinking presupposes imagination, and that mental images (particularly images of natural language sentences) are implicated in all of our conscious thoughts. But the second – semantic – part of the claim is definitely incorrect, as we will now briefly argue.

Images, of themselves, unsupplemented by much prior knowledge (and hence thought) on the part of the thinker, are confined to representations of appearance. To have a visual mental image is to represent to oneself how something would look; to have an auditory mental image is to represent to oneself how something would sound; and so on. This gives rise to an immediate problem for the imagist theory of thought, since many of our words and concepts do not stand for the kinds of thing which *have* an appearance. For example, and more or less at random, consider logical concepts like *and, or, not*; temporal concepts like *tomorrow, yesterday, year*; concepts for abstract properties like *inflation* (of money), *prime* (of numbers); and number-terms like *sixteen*, or *sixty-four*. In none of these cases is there any mental image which seems even remotely appropriate to express what we mean.

Moreover, we have many concepts which represent things which do *have* an appearance, but which do not represent them *in virtue of* their appearance. Consider, for example, the concept *bus-stop*. Bus-stops do, of course, have a characteristic appearance (though different in different parts of the country, let alone in different parts of the globe). But if I steal a bus-stop sign and erect it in my garden as an ornament, that does not turn my garden into a bus-stop. Rather (very roughly), a bus stop is *a place where buses are supposed to stop*. How is this to be expressed in an image? Even if my image is of a bus stopping at a bus-stop sign, with people getting on and off, this does not attain to the generality of the idea of a place where buses (in general) stop; nor does it touch the normativity implicit in the idea *supposed to stop*.

In the light of points such as these, it is plain that no image, or sequence of images, can, of itself, carry the content of even a simple thought such as, 'All grass is green', let alone of a complex proposition such as, 'Life may be discovered on Mars in the next ten or twelve years.' Yet it may be replied that there can be nothing to stop people using images as *signs* to express their thoughts, somewhat as words are used. However, it will not, then, be the representational content of the image, as such, which determines the content of the thought. Of course it is true that someone may employ images of objects with conventionally determined conditions of application, somewhat like a hieroglyphic or ideographic script. But then this is not really distinct from the claim that thought involves some sort of language, since such an image-system would presumably mirror the structural properties and combinatorial powers of a language.

Despite the points just made, we certainly do not want to claim that mental images can never play a part in anything which might properly be called 'thinking'. Sometimes, surely, our thoughts can consist in a mixture of sentences and mental images. Thus, when reasoning about some practical problem, I might entertain a mixed thought like the following: 'If I put this stool on the table *like so* [insert image], then by climbing on top of it I shall be able to reach up *like that* [insert image].' (Note that we do not mean to beg any questions about the *language in which* such a thought is partly entertained. The non-imagistic components of the thought might very well be expressed in Mentalese, for all that we mean to imply here.) Moreover, sometimes our conscious thoughts can consist *entirely* of images of objects (and not of images used as conventional symbols). The thoughts of composers may sometimes consist entirely of auditory images, as they manipulate images of melodies and chord patterns, trying out different possibilities until hitting upon something which satisfies them. The thoughts of an engineer, or of someone trying to pack a set of suitcases into the luggage compartment of a car, may consist entirely of visual images of arrangements of objects. And someone's thoughts as she tries to find her way round a room in the dark might consist simply in an evolving image of the room's layout in egocentric space, becoming updated in accordance with her movements.

Our focus in this chapter, however, will be exclusively on *propositional* or *fully conceptual* thinking – that is, on the kind of thought whose content may properly and correctly be described by means of a propositional that-clause. Many of us feel intuitively that our imagistic thoughts are not properly described in the that-clauses which we are forced to use if we want to express them in language. For example, if I have been planning my route from my home to the railway station by mapping it out in my head, using an image of the layout of the city, then I would feel pretty lame to have to describe that thought by saying, 'I was thinking that I should start towards the city centre, and then turn right.' For this does not begin to approximate to the richness of what I had actually thought. Moreover, as we pointed out above, mental images cannot begin to capture the content of even a relatively simple proposition such as, 'All grass is green.' This suggests that there exist two distinct kinds of thinking – imagistic thinking, on the one hand, and propositional thinking, on the other.

It can be disputed just how distinct these forms of thinking really are. In particular, cognitive psychologists argue about whether visual images are picture-like, carried by representations with the analog properties of maps, or whether they are description-like, being subserved by complex descriptions of their subject matter. This is the dispute between *pictorial* and *descriptivist* theories of the nature of mental images. (See Tye, 1991, for an account.) This is not a debate we propose to join. We shall confine our attention to those forms of thought which are unequivocally propositional, reserving judgement on whether imagistic thinking, too, is covertly propositional in form.

2 Mentalese versus connectionism

How, then, are propositional thoughts carried in cognition? How is content represented? Recall that the realist's view is that propositional attitudes – beliefs, desires, and the like – interact with one another causally to produce behaviour in ways which respect their semantic contents. The belief that it is dark down in the cellar combines with the desire to see my way around down there, not randomly, but in such a way as to produce the intention to find some means of illumination. This in turn may combine with the belief that a torch is available, so as to cause me to carry that torch in my hand when I go down. How is this possible? How can propositional attitudes have causal powers which reflect their *relatedness to the world*, as well as their logical relations with one another, which is distinctive of their possessing a semantic content? There are really three different, but closely related, problems in need of solution here.

First, propositional attitudes are *systematic*, having contents which are systematically related to one another, in such a way that anyone capable of believing (or otherwise thinking) a given content will be capable of believing or thinking a number of closely related contents. Anyone capable of believing *that Jane loves John* will also be capable of the thought *that John loves Jane*. Why should this be so? How is this fact about propositional attitudes to be explained?

Second, propositional attitudes are *productive*, in the sense that anyone capable of thinking at all will be capable of entertaining unlimitedly many (or at least, a *very great* many) thoughts. If you can think that Jane has a mother, then you can think that Jane's mother has a mother, and that Jane's mother's mother has a mother, and so on (subject, of course, to limitations of memory and other cognitive space). There is no end to the new thoughts which thinkers are capable of entertaining. This fact, too, is in need of explanation.

Third, propositional attitudes interact causally with one another in ways which respect their semantic contents and component concepts. This was the point which was closest to the surface in our initial statement of the problem three paragraphs back. Beliefs and desires interact to cause intentions, and beliefs interact with other beliefs to generate new beliefs, in ways which are closely responsive to the *contents* of those states, and by means of transitions which are generally rational ones. How can this happen? How can patterns of causality respect semantic relations of entailment and evidential support?

2.1 The case for Mentalese

The classical solution to these three problems has been that beliefs are relations to internal sentences, as Fodor has consistently argued (1975, 1978, 1987 Appendix; see also Field, 1978; Davies, 1991). For sentences have contents which are systematically determined from the contents of their component words, together with rules of combination. If you understand the words, and know the rules of syntax, then you must be capable of understanding new combinations of those words, never before encountered. And by the same token, of course, sentences are productive, in virtue of the fact that rules of syntax are recursive. So the sententialist hypothesis provides us with solutions to the problems of systematicity and productivity: thought is systematic and productive because there is *a language of thought* (LoT).

Moreover (and providing us with a solution to the third problem also) sentence tokens can have causal powers, by virtue of being physical particulars. If beliefs and desires consist of sentences, or sentence-like structures, encoded in some distinctive way in the brain, then there will be no difficulty in explaining how beliefs and desires can be causes. (By way of analogy, think of the manner in which sentences can be stored in magnetic patterns on an audio-tape. These sentence tokens then *cause* the sound-waves which result when the tape is played.) And if we suppose, in addition, that the mind is arranged so as to effect computations on these sentences in ways which respect their syntax, then the causal roles of the sentences will respect their semantic properties. For semantics is, in part, a reflection of syntax. And then we shall have explained successfully how beliefs and desires can have causal roles which depend upon their semantic contents.

For example, a logical concept like *and* or *not* can be carried by a lexical item of some sort, distinguished by its capacity to enter into certain characteristic patterns of inference. Roughly, '&' means *and* provided that the computational system within which it belongs ensures that it is governed by the following forms of inference: $(P \& Q) \rightarrow P$; $(P \& Q) \rightarrow Q$; and $P, Q \rightarrow (P \& Q)$. And a concept such as *bus-stop*, too, can be constituted by some lexical item (BUS-STOP, as it might be) characterised both by its causal connections with worldly objects (bus-stops), and by the way in which it figures in distinctive patterns of inference (such as *bus-stop* $\rightarrow$ *buses should stop*) involving yet other lexical items from other parts of the language of thought.

It is worth noting that the argument for Mentalese can be considerably strengthened, by asking just *why* propositional attitudes should be systematic. Is it merely a brute fact about (some) cognisers, that if they are capable of entertaining some thoughts, then they will also be capable of entertaining structurally related thoughts? Horgan and Tienson (1996) argue not, and develop what they call *the tracking argument* for Mentalese. Any organism which can gather information about, and respond flexibly and intelligently to, a complex and constantly changing environment must have representational states with compositional structure, they claim.

Consider early humans, for example, engaged in hunting and gathering. They would have needed to keep track of the movements and properties of a great many individuals – both human and non-human – updating their representations accordingly. While on a hunt, they would have needed to be alert for signs of prey, recalling previous sightings and patterns of behaviour, and adjusting their search in accordance with the weather and the season, while also keeping tabs on the movements, and special strengths and weaknesses, of their co-hunters. Similarly while gathering, they would have needed to recall the properties of many different types of plants, berries and tubers, searching in different places according to the season, while being alert to the possibility of predation, and tracking the movements of the children and other gatherers around them. Moreover, all such humans would have needed to track, and continually update, the social and mental attributes of the others in their community. (This point will prove important in our discussion of Dennett's views on consciousness in chapter 9.)

Humans (and other intelligent creatures) need to collect, retain, update, and reason from a vast array of information, both social and non-social. There seems no way of making sense of this capacity except by supposing that it is subserved by a system of compositionally structured representational states. These states must, for example, be formed from distinct elements representing individuals and their properties, so that the latter may be varied and updated while staying predicated of one and the same thing. But then states which are compositionally structured are *ipso facto* systematic (and also productive) – if the state representing aRb is composed of distinct representations for a, R, and b, then of course it will be possible for the thinker to build out of those representations a representation of bRa. And to say that propositional-attitude states are compositionally structured *is* just to say that they have syntax-like properties, and hence that there is – in the intended sense – a language of thought.

In the classical account, not only are thoughts carried by Mentalese sentences, but the transitions amongst those sentences are *computational*, involving rule-governed causal transitions which serve to realise the intentional laws of common-sense and scientific psychology; and those sentences, and those computational transitions amongst sentences, are somehow realised in neural states of the brain. The picture, here, is best understood in terms of Marr's (1982) three levels of analysis: first there is the (top) *functional* level, at which mental-state transitions are characterised *as such*, and at which intentional laws are discovered and formulated; then there is the (middle) *algorithmic* level, at which the rules for transforming Mentalese sentences may be specified; and then finally there is the (bottom) *implementational* level, where physical processes sufficient to execute those algorithmic steps may be described.

This classical picture of the way in which cognitive processes are realised in the brain has been challenged by recent progress in connectionism. But it is important to distinguish between connectionism as a claim about the mere lower-level *implementation* of cognitive processes (Marr's bottom level), on the one hand, and attempts to use connectionism to usurp altogether either the level of algorithmic explanation (middle) or the level of psychological description (top), on the other. The former is no threat to the classical computational account of cognition: it is possible for a symbol-crunching program to run on a connectionist machine, just as connectionist networks are in fact modelled by programs running on orthodox digital computers. It is the extension of connectionism into the cognitive – algorithmic – domain which is controversial, whether it be to propose type-identities with psychological properties, or to substitute replacements for them.

2.2 Some common (mostly bad) arguments for connectionism

As we explained in chapter 1 (section 2.5), connectionism is often defended on grounds of neurological plausibility. It is said that the fact that nerve cells in the cortex each connect with many hundreds of other such cells, often with extensive 'feed-back' as well as 'feed-forward' connections, suggests that representations are likely to be *distributed* across such neural networks. But this is not so: there is simply no relationship between the one idea and the other. And from what little is known of representation within actual neural systems it seems that it is generally local, rather than distributed.

For example, the area of primary visual cortex known as 'V1' (the area which is distinctively damaged in the case of blindsight; see figure 3.1) appears to be a retinotopic map, in such a way that stimulation of different areas of the retina maps directly onto stimulation of similarly spatially-related areas of the cortex – so if you could see the pattern of stimulation in V1, you could, quite literally, see what the subject was seeing. And although the visual system then bifurcates into a number of different streams of processing – of which the 'what-stream' and the 'where-stream' are the most salient – it is still possible to find individual cells, or small groups of cells, responding differentially to particular features, such as the presence of a colour, or an upright line in a particular region of the visual field. In fact on the basis of what is known so far, it seems quite likely that neural processing, in general, proceeds by means of the logical operations of addition and subtraction, in such a way that the representational status of individual neurons is preserved. So neurons representing straight edges in different portions of the visual field will sum together (minus any input from neurons representing curvature) to cause a cell to fire which represents the presence of a straight line, say.

Connectionism is also often supported by pointing out that processing in the brain is carried out in parallel, not serially as in a conventional computer. But this is a muddle. *Parallel* processing should not be confused with *distributed* processing; and only the latter is inconsistent with some sort of Mentalese-based account of cognition. In fact, anyone who believes in modularity should accept parallel processing. If the visual system subdivides into a number of distinct modules, for example, each of which processes its input independently of the others before passing on an output for integration, then the visual system will process inputs in parallel. But it is quite another matter to claim that the processing which takes place *within* a given module or sub-module contains no states which represent independently of the others.

So it is important to distinguish between *parallel* processing and *distributed* processing. If there is a contrast to be drawn between symbolic and connectionist systems, that contrast should *not* be seen as one between linear and parallel forms of processing. The fact that the brain is known to process contents in parallel, in many domains, provides no particular support for the connectionist approach. It is perfectly possible for symbolic systems to process contents in parallel, by devolving processing to a variety of modules or sub-modules, each of which operates independently of the others. As we saw in chapters 3 and 4, the case for a modular structure to cognition (including central cognition) is a powerful one. So we are happy to allow that processing of perceptual inputs will be conducted in parallel; and that central processes of thought and reasoning, too, are often conducted in parallel, devolved to a variety of conceptual modules. All this is quite consistent with those processes involving computations upon symbols, or symbol-like structures. Matters are otherwise, however, if connectionism is understood as proposing that processing is distributed across a network, computing patterns of activation across the nodes, in such a way that none of the computations in question can be described as transformations of symbols.

Connectionism is also sometimes supported by pointing out that human memory systems degrade gracefully, with gradual loss of function, in a

way that only connectionist models can explain. Now, it may be that a
little tampering with the hidden nodes within a network will still leave a
system which can produce imperfect but acceptable output, whereas damage to a serial processor is liable to result in the whole program crashing.
But does this mean that connectionism provides the best model of how
memory functions, malfunctions, and declines? If dissociation in cognitive
performance in other areas is best explained by postulating modules, then
there is clearly an alternative hypothesis. So we think it worth exploring
whether this effect might not be explained by postulating a memory
system structured out of many sub-modules, which can be independently
damaged.

We do not mind conceding that *some* human memory systems may
operate by *superpositional storage*. This is particularly plausible where
memory can consist in recognitional capacities of one sort or another. For
connectionist systems are at their strongest when it comes to pattern-
recognition. (For example, there has been some success in devising connectionist programmes for face-recognition – see O'Toole *et al.*, 1994.) We
suspect that there is nothing in the folk-psychological account of recog-
nition-memory which requires such memories to be individually represented. But we *do* think that folk psychology is committed to the idea that
cognitive *processes* (for example, of practical inference or of belief-formation) involve individual (and individually contentful) events – see section 2.3 below. Moreover, if there is anything in *the tracking argument*
outlined above, then memory will need to be continually updated with
information supplied in a language of thought, and will also itself inform
decision-making processes which require the representational power of
such a language.

In general, too, we would advise caution over allowing that any distributed connectionist system which can be trained-up to mimic human
performance in some domain of recognition or memory can therefore be
treated as explanatory – that is, as providing a *correct* account of human
performance in that domain. It is also crucial that the system should share
the same human learning trajectory. So if humans can do one-off learning
in the domain in question, for example, then so too must any connectionist network which adequately models the human capacity. This constraint
is very commonly ignored or glossed over by connectionist modellers, with
information about training-trials either not given at all, or confined to an
obscure footnote. But in fact it is vital. Recall from chapter 3 that one of
the main arguments in support of the modularist and nativist research
programme in cognitive science is the *speed* of human learning in many
domains, following a common developmental trajectory over highly variable environmental inputs. To the extent that a connectionist system in

one of these domains requires an implausibly high number of training runs, or an implausible degree of structure imposed upon the sequencing of its inputs, to that extent it will fail as a model of human cognition in the domain in question. The moral is: in order to assess any connectionist claim, you first need to know the details of the training regime.

2.3 Connectionism and folk psychology

To what extent is connectionism consistent with folk psychology? Obviously that depends upon the commitments of the latter, and on the nature, and fineness of grain, of the former. As will be clear from our discussions in chapters 1, 2 and 4, we believe that folk psychology conceives of the mind as a structured system which can be subjected to various levels of functional analysis. So perception (in a number of different modalities) feeds into, but is distinct from, long-term belief; which in turn is called upon to produce activated beliefs, judgements, and memories; actions are produced by intentions and guided by beliefs and perceptions; and intentions are the product of reasoning processes involving both activated beliefs and activated desires, which are distinct kinds of state from one another; and so on.

One way in which connectionism might be inconsistent with folk psychology, then, would be by failing to replicate, to any significant degree, the right functional architecture. For example, the proposal that the brain is a single large distributed network, within the operations of which it is impossible to distinguish between perceptions, judgements and goals, would surely be inconsistent with folk psychology. But then no one seriously makes any such claim. Since it is known that the brain is subdivided into a huge variety of separate, functionally characterisable, subsystems, no connectionist should propose anything inconsistent with this. In which case there will, to this extent, be no inconsistency with folk psychology either.

To put these points somewhat differently: suppose we represented the functional commitments of folk psychology boxologically, in a flow-chart of different processing systems. Then anyone (connectionists included) can make proposals inconsistent with folk psychology by proposing functional architectures which differ from the commitments of the folk. But everyone will surely agree to the minimal claim that there is some (complex) functional architecture there to be described. And it would be possible for connectionists to confine their claims to the internal processes of the various boxes in the diagram of folk belief.

Consider any one box within folk psychology's postulated functional organisation – the box for 'practical reasoning', say. Is folk psychology committed to anything about the inner organisation of the box, or could it just as well be a distributed connectionist network? Consider what we think takes place when someone engages in a simple piece of practical reasoning: they want to eat an apple, see an apple in the fruit-bowl, and so form and execute the intention to pick it up to eat it. Using the abbreviations BEL, DES and INT to represent belief, desire, and intention respectively, and the square-bracket notation to represent contents, it would seem that the folk are committed to the occurrence of at least the following sequence of states:

> DES [I eat an apple]
> BEL [*there* is an apple]
> → INT [I eat what is *there*]

There is first of all a commitment, here, to the *co*-occurrence of distinct states of belief and desire which interact with one another to produce the intention. But there seems no particular difficulty for connectionism in this. It could be modelled by having two distinct banks of input nodes for the network – one for belief-inputs and one for desire-inputs.

Second, there is a commitment to common conceptual components between the states – it is because the desire is for *apples* and my perceptual belief represents an *apple* to be *there* that I form the intention to eat *that* object (namely, the object which is *there*). It seems unlikely that a distributed-connectionist system could preserve these properties. It seems unlikely, in particular, that any given pattern of activation amongst the input nodes will be preserved in the output nodes, such as would be required for there to be a common conceptual component in the BEL and in the INT state, representing the location of the apple. Or rather, if there is such a pattern, it will be entirely accidental, whereas folk psychology considers this to be integral to, and necessary for the rationality of, the inference. For if it were not the *same* representation figuring in the BEL and in the INT states, then we think that it would not be rational for me to act.

Admittedly, what folk-psychological explanation is committed to, in the way of identity of representation, is sameness of conceptual content, *not* necessarily sameness of representational vehicle (as in a particular sentence of Mentalese). Our argument is that robust and dependable ways of processing identical conceptual contents are required. This effectively presents the advocate of connectionist cognitive architectures with a dilemma. If a system of connectionist networks *cannot* deliver these shared conceptual contents in a dependable way, then it cannot model the functional organisation of cognition – at least in so far as this is known to folk psychology. On the other hand, if a system of such networks *can* deliver such conceptual contents, then it becomes unclear why one would maintain that it is a distinctively connectionist architecture, rather than a connectionist implementation of a system which can also be described in terms of representations and processing rules.

Consider now an instance of theoretical reasoning (loosely described, to include any system which can generate new beliefs from old). Again folk psychology would seem to be committed to the existence of *trains of thinking* and reasoning, within which discrete thoughts are tokened, and where, once again, common conceptual components are shared between consecutive thoughts in the sequence. Suppose that I return home from work to hear the cat meowing. Then using BEL to represent new beliefs grounded in perception or inference, and MEM to represent old, the following sequence may occur:

> BEL [the cat is meowing]
> MEM [when cats meow, it is often because they are hungry]
> → BEL [the cat is probably hungry]
> MEM [food removes hunger]
> → BEL [feeding the cat will probably remove its hunger]
> → BEL [feeding the cat will probably stop it meowing]

We believe that the various steps in this sequence of thought are distinct from one another. And it seems crucial to the rationality of the sequence that there should be common conceptual elements shared between the states – for example, that *cat* should figure in all four BEL states, and that *hunger* should figure in the two MEM states. And again it seems unlikely that a distributed-connectionist network would replicate these features of theoretical reasoning.

Is our folk-psychological belief in the causal systematicity of cognitive processes derivative from natural language in some way? Is it because the folk believe that thinking is conducted in natural language, or because they *report* acts of thinking in natural language, that they come to believe that thought is systematic? Well, as we shall see later in this chapter, we do think that one way of instantiating systematicity is to have conscious thought-processes involve imaged natural language sentences, in such a way that conscious thinking is conducted in 'inner speech'. If the vehicles of conscious propositional thoughts are natural language sentences, then the systematicity of conscious thought can be derivative from the systematicity of language. But we are doubtful whether this is why the folk believe in systematicity. If it were, then they should be happy to allow connectionists free rein in the domain of non-conscious thought, or in respect of non-linguistic creatures – and this would then mean that animals and infants fail to engage in genuine inference. In fact our folk-commitment to causal systematicity seems rather to derive from our folk-belief in systematic inference.

While we doubt whether there is anything in folk psychology which commits us to believing that occurrent propositional thoughts are tokened in natural language sentences, the folk do at least find this idea quite natural. Whether this is because, in reporting thoughts, we slip easily between the use of a that-clause ('Mary thought that it was about to break') and the use of indirect speech ('Mary thought, "It is about to break"'); or whether, rather, our use of indirect speech reflects our belief in the role of natural language in thinking, is moot. In fact we are inclined to suspect the latter, since 'inner speech' is a familiar – indeed ubiquitous – introspectible phenomenon (Hurlburt, 1990, 1993), and since the patterns in inner speech seem to mirror so closely the inferential and causal roles distinctive of thought. (We return to this issue in sections 3.4 and 3.5 below.)

Does all this mean that connectionism is a threat to folk-psychological beliefs about the mind? Should the modest successes so far enjoyed by connectionist models lead us to wonder whether our folk-beliefs about the mind might be radically mistaken? Do those successes even provide us, perhaps, with sufficient reason to think that those beliefs probably *are* mistaken? Here we are inclined to take a tough line. Since we *know* that human inference involves tokenings of discrete states, and since we *know* that many of these states share common conceptual components, it is a constraint on any adequate connectionist model of human inference that it should be able to replicate these facts. If connectionist networks are incapable of generating systematic relations amongst their states – except by accident – of the sort displayed above, then so much the worse for connectionism, we say.

2.4 Connectionism and systematicity

Some connectionists seem, at least tacitly, to accept the point just made, and devote their energies to showing that connectionist systems *can* exhibit systematicity (Smolensky, 1988, 1991, 1995). For example, it is often noticed that distributed connectionist systems which have been trained-up on some domain (concerning hot drinks and drink-containers, say) will show certain complex *patterns* in their outputs corresponding to certain components of their inputs. These activation-vectors will generally cross-cut traditional conceptual boundaries – with vectors corresponding to *mug-containing-coffee* or *mug-containing-tea-with-milk* (between which there would be no common element corresponding to *mug*), rather than what we think of as the more usual atomic concepts of *mug* or *coffee*. But they can nevertheless be thought of as conceptual components of the output.

So connectionists sometimes claim that they can accommodate the systematicity of contentful events in terms of the way in which activation-patterns can display a distinctive 'clustering' appropriate to different concepts. But firstly, this just seems to be a brute fact about (some) connectionist networks. There seems to be nothing in connectionism, as such, which guarantees it, or even makes it likely. And secondly, these patterns seem causally epiphenomenal. It is not a particular clustering of node-activations which explains the output and further effects of a system, but rather the level of activation across all of the nodes. Thus Fodor has argued that while such activation vectors may exist, they do not play any *causal* role in the activity of a connectionist network; whereas we *do* think that conceptual components play a causal role in reasoning (Fodor and Pylyshyn, 1988; Fodor and McLaughlin, 1990).

Some have accused Fodor of committing a sort of *reductionist fallacy* here (Matthews, 1997). The suggestion is that Fodor must be reasoning as follows: since the real causal work in a connectionist network is done by the activation levels of the individual nodes, together with the weighting with which each node transmits its activation to other nodes, a *pattern* of activation cannot itself be causally efficacious; rather, it just supervenes on what does the real 'pushing and pulling' within the system, namely the activities of the individual nodes. Such an argument is fallacious because the causal activity within such complex systems may operate, and be correctly describable, at many different levels. Would not the same line of argument applied to a chemical system, for example, show that chemical properties must be causally irrelevant, because the real 'pushing and pulling' is done by the underlying sub-atomic mechanisms? (There is some irony in attributing such a fallacy to Fodor, of course, since he is famous for defending the reality of, and the causal efficacy of, the 'special sciences' – see his 1974.)

In fact the argument need not presuppose that the real causal work must be done at a mechanistic level. We (and Fodor) are quite happy to allow that there is real causality wherever there are events linked together by causal law, or by dependable nomic (productive) tendency, as we saw in chapter 7. So we are quite happy to allow that a pattern of activation might, in principle, be the sort of thing which can causally produce an effect, provided that there are some *ceteris paribus* laws linking the pattern with its effects. The crucial point is that in distributed connectionist systems there is no reason to believe there are any such laws linking activation-clusters with outputs. In general such clusterings are unstable and liable to shift when the system is presented with a new range of inputs.

And even if an activation-cluster remains sufficiently stable to support some generalisation linking patterns of activation with outputs, this is a fact about how a particular network is functioning, rather than a regularity of connectionist processing which might have law-like status. For the patterns of clustering are a product of the inputs in the training set and the method of adjusting weights and biases in response to information about the output, and what the patterns are is *highly sensitive* to the exact inputs and method of adjustment. So here too one needs to consider the details of the training regime, rather than just the performance of a single specimen of a trained-up network.

2.5 Connectionism, holism and the frame problem

Horgan and Tienson (1996) draw an important distinction between two different, and partially independent, commitments of classical (that is, symbolic; *non*-connectionist) approaches to cognitive science. On the one hand, classicists are committed to the idea that propositional attitudes have *syntactic structure* – that is, to the idea that there is a language of thought (LoT). And on the other hand, they are committed to the claim that cognitive processing is *rule-governed*, operating in accordance with strict (albeit probabilistic) algorithms. It seems very likely that the second of these ideas entails the first – that is, that algorithmic processing must operate on structured states. But the first does not entail the second – while cognitive states are syntactically structured, it could be that transitions amongst such states are not rule-governed but rather, in some sense, 'chaotic'. Horgan and Tienson argue at length for the claim that propositional attitudes are syntactically structured states. As we have seen, they argue that we cannot make sense of complex intelligent cognition without supposing that mental states are systematically built out of conceptual components. But they also argue at length against the classical assumption of *algorithmicity*. Rather, they think that the correct way to model and explain mental-state transitions will be by using some or other form of *dynamical systems theory*.

We are happy to endorse this distinction. And we, too, want to insist that propositional attitudes are compositionally structured states. This in itself is enough to ensure the reality of the states postulated by folk psychology, since the folk are certainly not committed to anything concerning the algorithmic nature of the processes which transform and generate such states. Moreover, it does seem to us to be an open – and entirely empirical – question whether cognitive processing is algorithmic, or would be better modelled by a different branch of mathematical theory, such as dynamical systems theory. But we do think that the *argument* which Horgan and Tienson offer in support of non-algorithmic processing (following Putnam, 1988) is unsound.

Horgan and Tienson premise their argument on *epistemic holism*, focusing especially on science and scientific method. In science, anything can, potentially, be relevant to anything else. As they put it:

Are whales and dolphins relevant to questions about human evolution? Not if the task is to produce a Darwinian history of *Homo sapiens*. But if the question is the role of tool use in the evolution of human intelligence, then it could be relevant to compare whale and dolphin cognition with human and (so far as possible) early hominid cognition, given that whales and dolphins are said to be pretty intelligent among nonhuman animals and that they are not tool users. (1996, p.38)

It is now a familiar and well-documented phenomenon in the history of science, indeed, that what seem like completely independent questions in domains of enquiry remote from one another, have a way of turning out to be relevant to each other after all. This motivates the Quinean idea of a 'web' of scientific belief (Quine, 1951), in which relations of epistemic support are distributed right across the system, and in which an alteration in any one part of the web can, in principle, be accommodated by making adjustments in remote regions.

Given the truth of epistemic holism, Horgan and Tienson then argue that it is very unlikely that central cognition – and, in particular, belief-fixation – should be subserved by strict processing algorithms, whether probabilistic or not. For it seems impossible to devise algorithms which would allow *any* belief or piece of evidence to be relevant to the fixation of a given belief. Indeed, those working within classical approaches to cognitive science face a dilemma, which has come to be known as the 'frame problem'. *Either* they try to allow everything to be relevant to everything, in which case it is hard to avoid combinatorial explosion – thus it is plainly impossible to search through each of your beliefs, together with their logical consequences, every time you make a decision. *Or* they place a 'frame' around the information which is deemed to be relevant for a particular processing task, in which case they can no longer do justice to the holistic nature of belief-fixation. The only way out of this dilemma, Horgan and Tienson argue, is to abandon the search for processing algorithms altogether, and to try to model central cognition in terms of dynamical systems theory, which might then be instantiated in a connectionist network.

One fallacy in this argument, however, is the same as that committed by Fodor (1983), and discussed at length in chapter 3 above. It is that the argument involves the move from *epistemic* holism in science to *cognitive* holism, or holism about belief-fixation within the minds of ordinary individual thinkers. Science is, of course, a collective and inter-subjective enterprise. New empirical results and new theories are normally arrived at through collaboration and discussion between a number of investigators; and, once published, they are subject to criticism and debate within the scientific community as a whole, often over extended periods of time. The fact that theory-confirmation under these circumstances is strongly holistic, provides no particular reason to think that the same will be true of the cognition of ordinary thinkers, who have to make up their minds in real time – often seconds or minutes rather than years – and often without any opportunity for public debate.

Another point against Horgan and Tienson's argument is that it is hard to get it to marry with the sort of modularism about central cognition which we have defended in this book. Their picture seems definitely to be of a *single* central system – a seamless web of belief – within which forces and influences flow back and forth in dynamical fashion. Our view, in contrast, is that central cognition probably contains a wide variety of conceptual modules which are each dedicated to processing information about particular domains.

Of course, it somehow has to be possible for individual thinkers, with their modularised minds, to engage in science. But it may be that this possibility depends crucially upon (and is 'scaffolded' by) the external – public – resources provided by spoken and written natural language, mathematics, libraries, computers, and such like, as well as the cognitive resources of the individual (Clark, 1998, and section 3.2 below). It is also true, surely, that the various central modules have to be able to pool together their information in some fashion, and communicate with one another in such a way as to fix belief. Here, too, it may be that natural language has an important part to play, as the sort of *lingua franca* by means of which modular central systems interact (Carruthers, 1998a, and section 3.6 below). Or it may be that the central 'pool' where the outputs of different modular systems can interact is provided by *conscious* thought (see Mithen, 1996, and sections 3.4 and 3.5 below).

These are, however, very much matters for future inter-disciplinary research – at the moment we can only speculate. And we certainly do not want to close off the possibility that some form of dynamical systems theory may be needed to explain the fixation of belief in ordinary cognition, even given the truth of modularism. But we do think that it would be premature to abandon the algorithmic paradigm at this stage. Investigators should explore what can be done to model processing within a variety of modular conceptual systems, and also the ways in which such systems can interact, in algorithmic (but almost certainly probabilistic) terms.

3 The place of natural language in thought

When the question of the place of natural language in cognition has been debated by philosophers the discussion has, almost always, been conducted *a priori* in universalist terms. Various arguments have been proposed for the claim that it is a conceptually necessary truth that *all* thought requires language (for example: Wittgenstein, 1921, 1953; Davidson, 1975, 1982b; Dummett, 1981, 1989; McDowell, 1994). But these arguments all depend, in one way or another, upon an anti-realist conception of the mind – claiming, for instance, that we cannot *interpret* anyone as entertaining any given fine-grained thought in the absence of linguistic behaviour (Davidson, 1975). Since the view adopted in this book – and shared by most cognitive psychologists – is quite strongly realist, we do not propose to devote any time to such arguments.

Notice, too, that Davidson *et al.* are committed to denying that any non-human animals can entertain genuine thoughts, given that it is very doubtful whether any such animals are capable of understanding and using a natural language (in the relevant sense of 'language', that is – see Premack, 1986). This conclusion conflicts, not just with common-sense belief, but also with what can be discovered about animal cognition, both experimentally and by observation of their behaviour in the wild (Walker, 1983; Allen and Bekoff, 1997). So not only are the arguments of Davidson *et al.* unsound, but we have independent reasons to think that their conclusion is false.

We propose, therefore, to take it for granted that thought is *conceptually* independent of natural language, and that thoughts of many types can *actually* occur in the absence of such language. But this leaves it open as a possibility that *some* types of thought may involve language as a matter of natural necessity, given the way in which human cognition is structured. It is on this, weaker, claim that we shall focus. Such claims seem to us to have been unjustly under-explored by researchers in the cognitive sciences – partly, no doubt, because they have been run together with the *a priori* and universalist claims of some philosophers, which have been rightly rejected. We shall refer to all forms of this weaker claim as (versions of) the *cognitive conception of language*, since they have in common that they assign to natural language some constitutive place in central cognitive processes of thinking and reasoning. The contrasting standard-cognitive-science view of language as a mere input/output system of the mind – that is, as a mere *conduit* for passing beliefs from mind to mind – we shall refer to as the (exclusively) *communicative conception of language*. Of course, on any view language is going to be used for purposes of communication. The question is: what else can it do for us?

3.1 The options

What place can be found for sentences of natural language in central cognitive processes? The orthodox cognitive science answer is: 'None'. One part of the reason for this has just been given. It is that researchers have assumed that any sort of positive answer would commit them to views which they regard as absurd, such as that it is conceptually impossible for animals and infants to entertain genuine thoughts. But another point is that language is, almost universally, believed to be a distinct input and output module of the mind; which might seem to make it difficult to see how it could, at the same time, be crucially involved in central cognition. And yet another reason is that, since non-linguistic creatures are believed by most to share at least some of their cognitive functions with us (practical reasoning, say), natural language sentences cannot be crucially required to execute such functions (even if the modality of 'required' here is just that of natural, rather than conceptual, necessity).

The first of these reasons collapses as soon as the requisite distinctions are drawn. To claim that some thought implicates natural language, either as a matter of fact or out of natural necessity, is perfectly consistent with denying that it is *conceptually* necessary that *all* thought should involve language. So we can reject the strong claims of some philosophers, while continuing to maintain that natural language is crucially implicated in at least some forms of central thought-process.

The second reason is also weak, as the analogy with the visual system makes clear. This is the very paradigm of a modular input-system. Yet, as noted in chapter 3, it is known to share mechanisms with imagination, which is surely a central process, implicated both in reasoning and in the fixation of belief (Kosslyn, 1994). Just as central cognition can recruit the resources of the visual module in visual imagination for purposes of visuo-spatial reasoning, so it may also be able to recruit the resources of the language module, in 'inner speech', for purposes of conceptual or propositional reasoning. This point is worth elaborating on further.

According to Kosslyn (1994), visual imagination exploits the top-down neural pathways (deployed in normal vision to direct visual search and to enhance object recognition) in order to generate visual stimuli in the occipital cortex, which are then processed by the visual system in the normal way, just as if they were visual percepts. Normal visual analysis proceeds in a number of stages, on this account. First, information from the retina is mapped into a visual buffer in the occipital lobes. From here, two separate streams of analysis then take place – encoding of spatial properties (position, movement, and so on) in the parietal lobes, and encoding of object properties (such as shape, colour, and texture) in the temporal lobes. These two streams are then pooled in an associative memory system (in the posterior superior temporal lobes), which also contains conceptual information, where they are matched to stored data. At this stage object recognition may well take place. But if recognition is not immediately achieved, a search through stored data, guided by the partial object-information already available, then occurs. Object-representations are projected back down through the visual system to the occipital lobes, shifting visual attention, and asking relevant questions of the visual input. This last stage is subserved by a rich network of backward-projecting neural pathways from the 'higher', more abstract, visual areas of the brain to the occipital cortex. And it is this last stage which is exploited in visual imagination, on Kosslyn's account. A conceptual or other non-visual representation (of the letter 'A', as it might be) is projected back through the visual system in such a way as to generate activity in the occipital cortex (just as if a letter 'A' were being perceived). This activity is then processed by the visual system in the normal way to yield a quasi-visual percept.

Note that hardly anyone is likely to maintain that visual imagery is a mere epiphenomenon of central cognitive reasoning processes, playing no real role in those processes in its own right. On the contrary, it seems likely that there are many tasks which cannot easily be solved by us without deploying a visual (or other) image. Thus, suppose you are asked (orally) to describe the shape which is enclosed within the capital letter 'A'. It seems entirely plausible that success in this task should require the generation of a visual image of that letter, from which the answer ('a triangle') can then be read off. So it certainly appears that central cognition functions, in part, by co-opting the resources of the visual system to generate visual representations, which can be of use in solving a variety of spatial-reasoning tasks. And this then opens up the very real possibility that central cognition may *also* deploy the resources of the *language* system to generate representations of natural language sentences (in 'inner speech'), which can similarly be of use in a variety of *conceptual* reasoning tasks.

The third reason mentioned above for denying that natural language is constitutively involved in central cognition – namely that non-linguistic animals are in fact capable of thought – also establishes little. For everyone is prepared to allow that there are thought-processes distinctive of humans. (One candidate would be *explicit* as opposed to *implicitly entertained* thoughts, tokened in such a way as to be promiscuously available to other cognitive processes; another would be *conscious* as opposed to *non-conscious* thoughts, which are available to higher-order reflection; and there are presumably also a number of particular domains which can only be thought about by humans, with their distinctive conceptual resources and high degree of cognitive sophistication.) In which case the claim of natural-language-involvement can be confined to just those types of thought which are distinctive of us.

In fact we can distinguish at least four different strengths of cognitive conception of language – that is, four different grades of potential involvement of natural language in cognition – ordered from the weakest to the strongest (but all weaker than the universal conceptual claims rejected above):

1 Language is used to scaffold and enhance some kinds of thinking – verbally learned instructions can be repeated aloud or sub-vocally by those acquiring new skills (Vygotsky, 1934–86); signs and text (whether in sub-vocal 'inner speech' or publicly produced) can be used to off-load the demands on memory, and to provide objects of further leisured reflection (Clark, 1998); and new forms of symbolism (such as the decimal numbering system) can reduce the computational demands on certain forms of thought. Almost everyone will sign up to this role for language in thought, to a greater or lesser degree.

2 Language is the vehicle for *conscious* thought, at least in its propositional, or fully conceptual (as opposed to visual-image-based or auditory-image-based) guises (Carruthers, 1996c, thesis NN_w, and 1998b). This view can allow that thought as such is conducted in sentences of Mentalese. But when thoughts are tokened consciously – in such a way, that is, for them to be reflexively available to further, higher-order, thought (see chapter 9) – they are so by virtue of receiving expression in an imaged natural language sentence. Such imaged sentences can count as constitutive of conscious thinking provided that the further effects within cognition, distinctive of such thoughts, depend upon the occurrence of the imaged sentence in question.

3 Language is the vehicle for *explicit* (that is, *promiscuous*) propositional/conceptual thought, serving as the *lingua franca* underpinning interactions between a number of quasi-modular central systems (Mithen, 1996; Carruthers, 1996c, thesis NN_s, and 1998a). On this account, imaged sentences of inner speech would be just the conscious variety of a more general phenomenon; for non-conscious thought, too, could be carried by natural language representations, perhaps sentences of Chomsky's 'Logical Form' or LF. Despite natural language retaining the status of an input/output module, some sort of evolutionary story can be told about how it came to underpin and make possible promiscuously available conceptual thinking.

4 Language is what creates and makes possible the concept-wielding mind, transforming the parallel-process architecture of the brain into a

serial processor, and providing it with the majority of its contents. One variant of this idea is Dennett's (1991a) vision of the conscious mind as a *Joycean machine*, according to which it is the colonisation of the brain by *memes* (ideas, concepts – mostly borne by natural language lexical items) which utterly transforms the brain's powers and capacities. Another variant is Bickerton's (1990, 1995) idea that the evolution of language involved a massive re-organisation of the neural connectivity of the brain, in such a way as to support conceptualised thought for the first time. On either of these views, it is not just *conscious* and/or *explicit* conceptual thought which is dependent upon language, but rather it is the very capacity for conceptual thought as such which involves language.

Cognitive scientists have, in general, barely considered (1) – presumably on the grounds that it is a peripheral aspect of human cognition – although they would mostly concede its truth. And they have mostly rejected (4), on the grounds that it is overly extreme, unjustifiably down-playing the cognitive powers of young children and other animals. Hypotheses (2) and (3), insofar as they are ever considered, are generally conflated with (4) and rejected for that reason. We shall begin to discuss the strengths and weaknesses of these theses in the sections which follow. This discussion must inevitably be tentative and exploratory, given the extent to which the questions are under-researched. Our hope will be to convince our readers that there are issues here worthy of further inter-disciplinary investigation.

3.2 Linguistic scaffolding

Everyone should agree that natural language is a necessary condition for human beings to be capable of entertaining at least some kinds of thought. For language is, at least, the conduit through which we acquire many of our beliefs and concepts, and in many of these cases we could hardly have acquired the component concepts in any other way. So concepts which have emerged out of many years of collective labour by scientists – such as *electron*, *neutrino*, and *DNA* – would *de facto* be inaccessible to someone deprived of language. This much, at any rate, should be obvious. But all it really shows is that language is *required for* certain kinds of thought; not that language is actually *involved in* or is the *representational vehicle of* those thoughts.

It is often remarked that the linguistic and cognitive abilities of young children will normally develop together. If children's language is advanced, then so will be their abilities across a range of tasks; and if children's language is delayed, then so will be their cognitive abilities. To cite just one item from a wealth of empirical evidence: Astington (1996) reports finding a high correlation between language-ability and children's capacity to pass false-belief tasks, whose solution requires them to attribute, and reason from, the false belief of another person. Do not these and similar data show that language is constitutively involved in children's thinking? In the same spirit, we may be tempted to cite the immense cognitive deficits which can be observed in those rare cases where children grow up without exposure to natural language. Consider, for example, the cases of so-called 'wolf children', who have survived in the wild in the company of animals, or of children kept by their parents locked away from all human contact (Malson, 1972; Curtiss, 1977). Consider, also, the cognitive limitations of profoundly deaf children born of hearing parents, who have not yet learned to sign (Sachs, 1989; Schaller, 1991). These examples might be thought to show that human cognition is constructed in such a way as to require the presence of natural language if it is to function properly.

But all that such data really show is, again, that language is a *necessary condition for* certain kinds of thought and cognition; not that it is actually *implicated in* those forms of cognition. And this is easily explicable from the standpoint of someone who endorses the standard cognitive-science-conception of language, as being but an input/output system for central cognition. For language, in human beings, is a necessary condition of normal enculturation. Without language, there are many things which children cannot learn; and with delayed language, there are many things which children will only learn later. It is only to be expected, then, that cognitive and linguistic development should proceed in parallel. It does not follow that language is itself actually *used in* children's central cognition.

Stronger claims may be extracted from the work of Vygotsky (1934/1986), who argues that language and speech serve to *scaffold* the development of cognitive capacities in the growing child. Researchers working in this tradition have studied the self-directed verbalisations of young children – for example, observing the effects of their soliloquies on their behaviour (Diaz and Berk, 1992). They found that children tended to verbalise more when task demands were greater, and that those who verbalised most tended to be more successful in problem-solving. But this claim of *linguistic scaffolding* of cognition admits of a spectrum of readings. At its weakest, it says no more than has already been conceded above, that language may be a *necessary condition for* the acquisition of certain cognitive skills. At its strongest, on the other hand, the idea could be that language forms part of the functioning of the highest-level executive system – which would then make it a variant of the ideas to be discussed in sections 3.4 and 3.5 below.

Clark (1998) argues for a sort of intermediate-strength variant of the Vygotskian idea, defending a conception of language as a cognitive *tool*. According to this view – which he labels the *supra-communicative conception* of language – certain extended processes of thinking and reasoning constitutively involve natural language. The idea is that language gets used, not just for communication, but also to augment human cognitive powers. Thus by writing an idea down, for example, I can off-load the demands on memory, presenting myself with an object of further leisured reflection; and by performing arithmetic calculations on a piece of paper, I may be able to handle computational tasks which would otherwise be too much for me (and my short-term memory).

The main difference between the supra-communicative account and the kinds of stronger view to be considered later in this chapter, should *not* be expressed by saying that for the former, sentence-tokens serve to augment but do not constitute thought, whereas for the latter the sentence-token *is* the thought. For no one should want to claim that a tokened natural language sentence *is* (or is sufficient for) a thought. (Consider a monolingual speaker of Russian uttering a sentence of English, for example.) Indeed, defenders of all forms of cognitive conception of language should accept that the content of an inner tokened sentence will depend upon a host of more basic connections and sub-personal processes. Rather, the stronger claim will be that the sentence is a *necessary component of* the thought, and that (certain types of) reasoning necessarily involve such sentences.

The difference between the two sorts of view can be put as follows. According to stronger forms of the cognitive conception, a particular tokening of an inner sentence is (sometimes) an inseparable part of the mental episode which carries the content of the token thought in question; so there is no neural or mental event at the time which can exist distinct from that sentence, which can occupy a causal role distinctive of that sort of thought, and which carries the content in question; and so language is constitutively involved in (certain types of) cognition, even when our focus is on token thinkings. For the supra-communicative account, however, the involvement only arises when we focus on an extended *process* of thinking or reasoning over time. So far as any given token thought goes, the account can (and does) buy into the standard input/output conception of language. It can maintain that there is a neural episode which carries the content of the thought in question, where an episode of that type can exist in the absence of any natural language sentence and can have a causal role distinctive of the thought, but which in the case in question causes the production of a natural language representation. This can then have further benefits for the system of the sort Clark explores (for example, off-loading memory demands).

The supra-communicative account can provide quite a convincing explanation for the use of language (especially written language) in soliloquy, as when one writes notes to oneself, or performs a calculation on a piece of paper. It is less obvious what account it can give of *inner* speech. Since there is here no medium of representation outside the mind, we certainly cannot say that the function of 'inner speech' is to *off*-load the demands on memory. What we can perhaps say, however, is that 'inner speech' serves to *enhance* memory (Varley, 1998). For it is now well established that the powers of human memory systems can be greatly extended by *association* (Baddeley, 1988). If asked to memorise a list of items, for example, it will be more efficient to associate them with something else, rather than simply repeating the names to yourself (even repeating them many times over). Thus, you might imagine walking around the rooms of your house, placing a distinct item in each room. This then gives you an independent fix on those items in memory – you can either recall them directly, or you can recall the rooms, from which you might extract the associated item.

Something similar might very well take place in the case of inner verbalisation. By translating an underlying (non-natural-language) thought into its imaged natural language equivalent, we might get an independent fix on that thought in memory, so making it more likely that it will be available to enter into our reasoning processes as and when the need arises. This might then greatly enhance the range and complexity of the thoughts and sequences of reasoning which are available to us. While this memory-enhancement proposal may not necessarily provide the *best* explanation of inner speech (see Carruthers, 1996c, chs.6 and 8), it is certainly a possible one.

In this section we have introduced two fairly weak claims concerning the place of natural language in central cognition. The first is that language is a necessary condition for us to entertain at least certain kinds of thought. This thesis ought to be acceptable to everyone, and is too weak even to count as a form of cognitive conception of language. The second claim is that certain complex and/or extended processes of thinking are only possible for us when scaffolded by language. This supra-communicative view *can* be counted as a form of cognitive conception of language; but it is still weak enough that some or other variant of it ought already to be acceptable to most cognitive scientists. The remainder of this chapter will be concerned to explore a variety of stronger and more challenging variants of the cognitive conception.

3.3 Language and the conceptual mind: Dennett and Bickerton

Dennett (1991a) argues that human cognitive powers were utterly transformed following the appearance of natural language, as the mind became colonised by *memes* (ideas, or concepts, which are transmitted, retained and selected in a manner supposedly analogous to genes – see Dawkins, 1976). Prior to the evolution of language, on this picture, the mind was a bundle of distributed connectionist processors – which conferred on early hominids some degree of flexibility and intelligence, but which were quite limited in their computational powers. The arrival of language then meant that a whole new – serial – cognitive architecture could be programmed into the system. This is what Dennett calls the *Joycean machine* (named after James Joyce's 'stream of consciousness'). The idea (to which we shall return in chapter 9) is that there is a highest-level processor which runs on a stream of natural-language representations, utilising learned connections between ideas, and patterns of reasoning acquired in and through the acquisition of linguistic memes. On this account, then, the concept-wielding mind is a kind of social construction, brought into existence through the absorption of memes from the surrounding culture, which is both dependent upon natural language and constitutively involves natural language.

Bickerton's (1990, 1995) proposals are somewhat similar, but more biological in flavour. He thinks that, before the evolution of language, hominid cognition was extremely limited in its powers. He thinks that these early forms of hominid cognition consisted largely of a set of relatively simple computational systems, underpinning an array of flexible but essentially behaviouristic conditioned responses to stimuli. But then the evolution of language some 100,000 years ago involved a dramatic re-wiring of the hominid brain, giving rise to distinctively human intelligence and conceptual powers. Bickerton, like Dennett, allows that subsequent to the evolution of language the human mind underwent further transformations, as the stock of socially transmitted ideas and concepts changed and increased. But the basic alteration was coincident with, and constituted by, a biological alteration – the appearance of an innately structured language-faculty. For Bickerton is a nativist about language (indeed, his earlier work on the creolisation of pidgin languages – 1981 – is often cited as part of an argument for the biological basis of language; see Pinker, 1994). And it is language which, he supposes, conferred on us the capacity for 'off-line thinking' – that is, the capacity to think and reason about topics and problems in the abstract, independent of any particular sensory stimulus.

These strong views seem to us unlikely to be correct. This is so for two reasons. First, because they undervalue the cognitive powers of pre-linguistic children, animals, and earlier forms of hominid. Thus *Homo erectus*, for example, was able to survive in extremely harsh tundra environments (presumably without language: see below). It is hard to see how this could have been possible without a capacity for quite sophisticated planning and a good deal of complex social interaction (as argued by Mithen, 1996). And second, the views of Dennett and Bickerton are inconsistent with the sort of central-process modularism defended in chapters 3, 4 and 5 above. Our view is that the mind contains a variety of conceptual modules – for mind-reading, for cheater-detection, and so on – which are probably of considerable ancestry, pre-dating the appearance of a modular language-faculty. So hominids were already capable of conceptual thought, and of reasoning in a complex, and presumably 'off-line', fashion *before* the arrival of language (we return to this point in chapter 9).

Why do we think that language evolved *after* the central-process conceptual modules? Why could not Dennett and Bickerton claim that language evolved first, with the various central modules making their appearance thereafter? Well, there does seem to be an emerging consensus, grounded in a variety of kinds of evidence (and accepted by Bickerton), that the evolution of language coincided with the appearance of *Homo sapiens sapiens* about 100,000 years ago in Southern Africa (see Mithen, 1996, for reviews). In which case it is very unlikely that there would have been time for a number of complex modular systems to emerge between then and the human dispersal around the globe just a few tens of millennia later. And it is, moreover, hard to understand anyway how language could have evolved in the absence of quite highly developed mind-reading abilities (Gomez, 1998), which in any case we have reason to believe are present, in primitive form, in the common ancestor of ourselves and the other primates (Byrne, 1995).

3.4 Conscious thinking 1: learning and inferring

Even if language is not what underpins *conceptual* thinking, as such, it may be that it is the vehicle for *conscious* conceptual thinking. It may be that imaged natural language sentences, in 'inner speech', are the primary vehicles for our conscious propositional (as opposed to visuo-spatial) thoughts (Carruthers, 1996c; Mithen, 1996). On this view, a variety of modular central-systems – crucially including a mind-reading module – would have been in place prior to the evolution of language; as would have been a capacity for various forms of sensory imagination (Wynn, 1993). At this stage, hominids would have been capable of attributing thoughts to themselves more-or-less reliably on the basis of self-interpretation, rather than having the sort of non-inferential access to their own thinkings necessary for those thoughts to count as conscious ones.

(Gazzaniga – 1992, 1994 – thinks that this is the only kind of access to our own thoughts which we modern humans enjoy. He believes that there is a specialist theory-of-mind system – which he dubs *the interpreter* – located in the left frontal lobe, whose business it is to construct, by self-interpretation, a meta-narrative about the course of the subject's own mental life. Our view is that in that case there is no such thing as conscious thinking. We return to this point below.)

With the arrival of language, we humans would then have been capable of entertaining imaged sentences of natural language, in 'inner speech', to whose forms and contents we would have had non-inferential access, by virtue of their availability to our mind-reading faculty – hence qualifying them as 'conscious' (see chapter 9). If these sentences had then somehow come to occupy the causal roles distinctive of thought, then this would have meant both that we became capable of conscious conceptual thinking for the first time and that natural language sentences would have been constitutive of such thinkings.

At issue here is the question of the causal role of 'inner speech'. The *phenomenon* of inner speech is not in doubt. Nor should be the claim that we have non-inferential access to the events in inner speech, hence allowing them to qualify as 'conscious'. The question is whether or not sentences in inner speech *themselves* occupy the causal roles which are distinctive of the thoughts which those same sentences express. One view is that they do. On this account, it is *because* I token in auditory imagination the sentence, 'The world is getting warmer, so I must use less fuel', for example, that I may thereafter be found walking rather than driving to work. The other view is that they do not. On this account the thought itself is carried by a sentence of Mentalese, say, and it is the Mentalese vehicle which has the further effects in cognition and action distinctive of a thought with that content. But even on this weaker view the imaged sentence need not be epiphenomenal – it may, for example, play a role in enhancing memory, thus rendering possible sequences of thought which would otherwise be too complex to entertain (Jackendoff, 1997; Clark, 1998; Varley, 1998).

It is by no means easy to adjudicate between these two views of the causal role of 'inner speech'. But one point in support of the 'thinking in language' hypothesis, is that it may turn out to be a presupposition of our belief that we do engage in *conscious* propositional thinking at all. If 'inner speech' does not count as thinking, then probably we only ever know of our own thoughts by swift self-interpretation. This conditional conclusion is strongly supported by a rich body of data coming out of the social psychology literature, where it has been found that there are many circumstances in which subjects will confabulate self-explanations which are manifestly false, but without realising that this is what they are doing (Nisbett and Wilson, 1977; Nisbett and Ross, 1980; Wilson *et al.*, 1981; Wilson, 1985; Wilson and Stone, 1985). For example, when asked to select from a range of *identical* items (shirts, say), identically presented, people show a marked preference for items on the right-hand-side of the display. But their explanations of their own choices never advert to position, but rather mention superior quality, appearance, colour, and so on. These explanations are plainly confabulated. (Remember, there is really no difference at all between the items.) And note that people's explanations, here, can be offered within seconds of the original choice. So the problem is unlikely to be one of memory (contrary to the suggestion made by Ericsson and Simon, 1980). Moreover, although the explanations are in fact elicited by experimenter questioning, there is every reason to think that they could equally well have been spontaneously offered, had the circumstances required.

The best explanation of these and similar data (and the explanation offered by Nisbett and Wilson) is that subjects in such cases lack any form of conscious access to their true thought-processes. (See also Gopnik, 1993, for a range of developmental data which are used to argue for the same conclusion.) Rather, lacking immediate access to their reasons, what people do is engage in a swift bit of retrospective self-interpretation, attributing to themselves the thoughts and feelings which they think they *should* have in the circumstances, or such as make sense of their own behaviour. In fact, looking across the full range of the experimental data available, the one factor which stands out as being common to all those cases where individuals confabulate false self-explanations, is simply that in such cases the true causes of the thoughts, feelings, or behaviours in question are *unknown to common-sense psychology*. The best explanation of the errors, then, is that in *all* cases of unverbalised thought individuals are actually *employing* common-sense psychology, relying on its principles and generalisations to attribute mental states to themselves. The distinguishing feature of the cases where confabulation occurs is simply that in these instances common-sense psychology is itself inadequate.

This account is also supported by neuropsychological data, in particular the investigations of split-brain patients undertaken by Gazzaniga and colleagues over many years (Gazzaniga, 1992, 1994). For in these cases self-attributions are made in a way which we *know* cannot involve access to the thought-processes involved, but are made with exactly the same phenomenological immediacy as normal. And yet these self-attributions can involve the most ordinary and everyday of thoughts, being erroneous in a way which manifestly does *not* depend upon the inadequacies of common-sense psychology, as such, nor upon any special features of the case – rather, these are just cases in which the mind-reading faculty lacks sufficient data to construct an accurate interpretation. So, if unwitting self-interpretation can be involved here, it can be involved anywhere. Let us briefly elaborate.

As is well known in connection with split-brain (commissurotomy) patients, information can be presented to, and responses elicited from, each half-brain independently of the other. In the cases which concern us both half-brains have some comprehension of language, but only the left-brain has access to the language-production system; the right-brain, however, is capable of initiating other forms of activity. When an instruction, such as, 'Walk!', is flashed to the right-brain alone, the subject may get up and begin to leave the room. When asked what he is doing, he (that is: the left-brain) may reply, 'I am going to get a Coke from the fridge'. This explanation is plainly confabulated, since the action was actually initiated by the right-brain, for reasons to which, we know, the left-brain lacks access.

As we noted above, these and similar phenomena lead Gazzaniga to postulate that the left-brain houses a special-purpose cognitive sub-system – a mind-reading module, in fact – whose function is continually to construct rationalising explanations for the behaviour of oneself and other people. And it then seems reasonable to suppose that it is this same sub-system which is responsible for the confabulated self-explanations in the data from normal subjects discussed by Nisbett and Wilson. Indeed, it is reasonable to suppose that this sub-system is responsible for *all* the access, or *apparent* access, which we have to our unverbalised thoughts. So if 'inner speech' does *not* have the causal role of thought, then it seems quite likely that there is really no such thing as conscious thinking. (For more extended discussion, see Carruthers, 1998b.)

Some further indirect support for the 'thinking in language' hypothesis can also be derived from our discussion of the reasoning data in chapter 5. Recall that Evans and Over (1996) argue that human reasoning processes need to be understood as operating on two distinct levels – an implicit, non-conscious level, governed by a variety of hard-wired heuristics and principles of relevance; and an explicit, conscious level, at which subjects attempt to conform to various norms of reasoning. And recall, too, that this latter kind of reasoning is held to be crucially dependent upon language. Then we need only add that explicit reasoning may be conducted in sequences of imaged natural language sentences, to get the view that 'inner speech' is constitutive of conscious thought.

It is easy to understand how some such two-level version of central cognition may come into existence, if we suppose that norms of reasoning are social constructs of some kind, taught and transmitted via language. Consider, as a kind of simple model, what happens when someone attends a course in logic at college or university – they learn to make certain sorts of transition amongst sentences of certain forms, refraining from making those which they learn to recognise as invalid. Then at the end of the course – one hopes! – they have a set of inferential dispositions which differ from those they had before, and which are dispositions to make transitions amongst *sentences*. If these same inferential dispositions thereafter govern (some of) the transitions they make amongst sentences in inner speech, then we have a vindication of the view that sentences of inner speech can occupy the causal role distinctive of thought. For, by hypothesis, these would be inferences which would not occur at all at a nonconscious level.

We should stress that this picture of the role of language in conscious cognition is *not* a *computational* one. The idea is not that there are processes which operate on and transform sentences in inner speech purely in virtue of the syntactic properties of the latter. For an imaged natural language sentence comes to us already laden with its content, in the normal case. The phenomenology of inner speech is that meanings-clothed-in-forms pass before our minds, just as the phenomenology of listening to other people speaking is that *we hear meaning in* the words that they use. Because of this, the two-level story being sketched here is not in competition with a Fodorian computational account of mind. For all that we have said, it may well be that underlying each imaged natural language sentence is a sentence of Mentalese which confers on it its meaning. It can still be the case that the imaged sentences are constitutive of some kinds of thought, if there are inferences which we are only inclined to make at all when certain contents are tokened in natural language form.

3.5 Conscious thinking 2: two-level theories

We have sketched one way in which natural language sentences may have come to be constitutive of conscious conceptual thinking, by mediating socially-learned and constructed *norms* of good reasoning. Another possibility – which is orthogonal to, but consistent with, this one – has recently been developed by Frankish (1998, forthcoming; see also Cohen, 1992), building on some early ideas of Dennett's (1978c). The idea is that language – whether overt or sub-vocal – forms the object of various forms of higher-order mentalising, which together give rise to a whole new level of cognition, which Frankish dubs 'the virtual mind'. This is the level at which we can consciously *make up* and *change* our minds, deciding to adopt a certain opinion in the light of the evidence for it, say, or deciding to adopt a certain goal in the light of the considerations which make it seem attractive.

On this account, low-level cognition is essentially *passive* in nature. Beliefs get formed non-reflectively by a variety of sub-personal processes of perception and inference. But this is not to say that low-level cognition is incapable of entertaining quite sophisticated thought-contents. On the contrary, in Frankish's view anything which we can think consciously in the virtual mind, we can also think non-consciously. And in the background to the virtual mind are language, imagination, and a mind-reading system, whose co-ordinated interaction gives rise to the new level of cognition, which is, by contrast, *active* in nature. At this level, we can formulate a sentence in 'inner speech', using auditory, visual, or even manual (for sentences of Sign) imagination. The occurrence and content of that sentence is then available to us to reflect upon – we can wonder about its likely truth, seek evidence in its support, and finally *make up our minds* to accept or reject it.

High-level *acceptance*, on this view, is a kind of policy-adoption. When I decide to accept a sentence I have been considering, I thereby adopt the policy of reasoning and acting exactly as if I believed it. In order to do this, I need to have a conception of just how someone who believed it would reason and act, which is why acceptance crucially implicates and depends upon a theory of mind. This is not to say that I *consciously* think of myself as adopting a certain policy, of course. It is the formation and execution of the policy which constitutes the high-level, virtual, belief – which does not mean that I have to conceive of myself *as* forming and executing a policy. On the contrary, I just think of myself as making up my mind. But to make up my mind *is* to commit myself to a policy, on Frankish's account. And it is crucially dependent upon a capacity to image the sentences which I accept – which is what gives natural language a constitutive position at the heart of the 'virtual mind'.

Suppose I think to myself, 'I wonder whether P'. After reflection on the content of 'P', and the evidence for and against it, suppose I then decide to accept it, thereby committing myself to think and reason as I believe a P-believer would. Provided that my beliefs about the inferences and actions distinctive of P-believing are sufficiently accurate; and provided, too, that I manage in the future to recall and execute my commitments; then we can see how acceptance constitutes a kind of virtual belief. For in acting out my commitments I shall mirror the states and activities of someone who believes (low-level) that P.

Notice that this account of the place of natural language in conscious thought is different from – albeit compatible with – the previous one. According to the account sketched in section 3.4, we learn to make certain inferential transitions between natural language sentences, where we previously lacked any disposition to make similar transitions amongst thoughts. So when we activate our acquired inferential dispositions, tokens of those sentences form an indispensable part of the process of thinking in question; hence vindicating some form of cognitive conception of language. On Frankish's account, in contrast, we *commit* ourselves to making certain inferential transitions whenever we make up our minds; hence bringing an aspect of our mental lives under our own intentional control. But here, too, language has a constitutive role to play.

3.6 Explicit conceptual thought: LF and inferential promiscuity

The final possibility to be explored is that at least some central-process conceptual representations might already consist of (*non*-imagistic, *non*-conscious) natural language symbols. For example, Chomsky (1995a, 1995b) has maintained that there is a level of linguistic representation which he calls 'logical form' (LF), which is where the language faculty interfaces with central cognitive systems. It might then be claimed that some (or all) conceptual, propositional, thinking consists in the formation and manipulation of these LF representations. In particular, it could be that tokening in an LF representation is what renders a given content *explicit* (in the sense of Karmiloff-Smith, 1992) – that is to say, this format serves to make it generally inferentially available (or 'promiscuous') outside its given cognitive domain, thus conferring the potential to interact with a wide range of central cognitive operations. On this account, it would not just be some (conscious) thought *tokens* which constitutively involve natural language representations; but certain explicit thoughts, as *types* (whether conscious or non-conscious), would involve such sentences.

The hypothesis can thus be that central-process thinking often operates by accessing and manipulating the representations of the language faculty. Where these representations are *only* in LF, the thoughts in question will be non-conscious ones. But where the LF representation is used to generate a full-blown phonological representation (a sentence in auditory imagination, or an episode of 'inner speech'), the thought will be a conscious one. But what, now, is the basic difference between the hypothesis that (many forms of) central-process thinking and reasoning operate, in part, by deploying sentences of LF, and the hypothesis that they are conducted entirely in Mentalese? The important point, here, is that sentences of LF are *not* sentences of Mentalese – they are not pure central-process representations, but rather depend upon resources provided by the language faculty; and they are not universal to all thinkers, but are always drawn from one or another natural language.

(Philosophers and logicians should note that Chomsky's LF is very different from what *they* are apt to mean by 'logical form'. In particular, sentences of LF do not just contain logical constants and quantifiers, variables, and dummy names. Rather, they consist of lexical items drawn from the natural language in question, syntactically structured, but regimented in such a way that all scope-ambiguities and the like are resolved, and with pronouns cross-indexed to their binding noun-phrases and so on. And the lexical items will be semantically interpreted, linked to whatever structures in the knowledge-base secure their meanings.)

Moreover, the proposal is not that LF is the language of all central processing (as Mentalese is supposed to be). For, first, much of central cognition may in any case employ visual or other images, or cognitive models and maps (Johnson-Laird, 1983). Second, and more importantly, our proposal is that LF serves only as the intermediary between a number of quasi-modular central systems, whose internal processes will, at least partly, take place in some other medium of representation (perhaps patterns of activation in a connectionist network, or algorithms computed over sentences of Mentalese). This idea will be further elaborated below. But basically, the thought is that the various central systems may be so set up as to take natural language representations (of LF) as input, and to generate such representations as output. This makes it possible for the output of one central module (mind-reading, say) to be taken as input by another (the cheater-detection system, for example), hence enabling a variety of modular systems to co-operate in the solution of a problem, and to interact in such a way as to generate trains of thinking.

But how can such an hypothesis be even so much as *possible*? How can a modular central system interpret and generate natural language representations, except by first transforming an LF input into a distinct conceptual representation (of Mentalese, as it might be), then using that to generate a further conceptual representation as output, which can then be fed to the language system to build yet another LF sentence? But if *that* is the story, then the central module in question does not, itself, utilise the resources of the language system. And it also becomes hard to see why central modules could not communicate with one another by exchanging the sentences of Mentalese which they generate as outputs and take as immediate inputs. Let us briefly outline an evolutionary answer to the question how LF, rather than Mentalese, could have come to be the medium of intra-cranial communication between central modules. (For more extended development, see Carruthers, 1998a.)

Suppose that the picture painted by Mithen (1996) of the mind of *Homo erectus* and the Neanderthals is broadly correct. Suppose, that is, that their minds contained a set of more-or-less isolated central modules for dealing with their different domains of activity – a mind-reading module for social relationships and behavioural explanation and prediction; a cheater-detection module for mediating co-operative exchange; a natural history module for processing information about the lifestyles of plants and animals; and a physics module, crucially implicated in the manufacture of stone tools. When a language module was added to this set it would, very naturally, have evolved to take as input the outputs of the various central modules, so that hominids could talk about social relationships, co-operative exchange, the biological world, and the world of physical objects and artefacts. (We think it unlikely that language would have evolved *only* for talking about social relationships, as Mithen, 1996, suggests, following Dunbar 1996. For given that mind-reading would already have had access to non-social contents – as it would have to if it was to predict and explain non-social behaviour – there would then have been a powerful motive to communicate such contents. See Gomez, 1998.) It also seems plausible that each of those modules might have altered in such a way as to take linguistic as well as perceptual *in*puts, so that merely being told about some event would be sufficient to invoke the appropriate specialist processing system.

With central modules then taking linguistic inputs and generating linguistic outputs, the stage was set for language to become the intra-cranial medium of communication between modular systems, hence breaking down the barriers between specialist areas of cognition in the way Mithen characterises as distinctive of the modern human mind. All that was required was for humans to begin exercising their imaginations on a regular basis, generating sentences internally, in 'inner speech', which could then be taken as input by the various central modular systems. This process might then have become semi-automatic (either through over-learning, or through the evolution of further neural connections), so that even without conscious thought, sentences of LF were constantly generated to serve as the intermediary between central cognitive systems.

4 Conclusion

In this chapter we have considered how propositional thought-contents are represented in the human mind/brain. We have argued that some version of the hypothesis of a 'language of thought', as against any strong form of connectionism, is the most likely. This language may be an innate and universal 'Mentalese', as Fodor has long argued (1975). Or it may, at least in part, be sentences of natural language which are the vehicles of our (conscious and/or explicit) thoughts. If this latter possibility proves to be the case, as we suspect it will, then we have yet another vindication of our folk-psychological self-image. For it certainly *seems* to us that we entertain propositional thoughts which are conscious, and that the stream of 'inner speech' is constitutive of such thinking.

SELECTED READING

On connectionism versus LoT: Fodor, 1975, 1978, and 1987, Appendix; Bechtel and Abrahamsen, 1991; Davies, 1991; Macdonald and Macdonald, 1995b (contains papers by Smolensky, Fodor and Pylyshyn, Fodor and McLaughlin, and Ramsey *et al.*); Horgan and Tienson, 1996.

On the place of natural language in cognition: Vygotsky, 1934/1986; Weiskrantz, 1988 (a collection of papers by psychologists); Dennett, 1991a; Pinker, 1994; Bickerton, 1995; Carruthers, 1996c; Mithen, 1996; Carruthers and Boucher, 1998 (contains papers by Carruthers, Clark, Dennett, and Frankish).

9   Consciousness: the final frontier?

Many people have thought that consciousness – particularly phenomenal consciousness, or the sort of consciousness which is involved when one undergoes states with a distinctive subjective phenomenology, or 'feel' – is inherently, and perhaps irredeemably, mysterious (Nagel, 1974, 1986; McGinn, 1991). And many would at least agree with Chalmers (1996) in characterising consciousness as the 'hard problem', which forms one of the few remaining 'final frontiers' for science to conquer. In the present chapter we discuss the prospects for a scientific explanation of consciousness, arguing that the new 'mysterians' have been unduly pessimistic.

1 Preliminaries: distinctions and data

In this opening section of the chapter, we first review some important distinctions which need to be drawn; and then discuss some of the evidence which a good theory of consciousness should be able to explain.

1.1 Distinctions

One of the real advances made in recent years has been in distinguishing between different notions of consciousness (see particularly Rosenthal, 1986; Dretske, 1993; Block, 1995; and Lycan, 1996) – though not everyone agrees on quite *which* distinctions need to be drawn. All are agreed that we should distinguish *creature*-consciousness from *mental-state*-consciousness. It is one thing to say *of an individual person or organism* that it is conscious (either in general or of something in particular); and it is quite another thing to say *of one of the mental states* of a creature that it is conscious.

It is also agreed that within creature-consciousness itself we should distinguish between *intransitive* and *transitive* variants. To say of an organism that it is conscious *simpliciter* (intransitive) is to say just that it is awake, as opposed to asleep or comatose. There do not appear to be any deep philosophical difficulties lurking here. But to say of an organism that it is conscious *of such-and-such* (transitive) is normally to say at least that it is *perceiving* such-and-such. So we say of the mouse that it is conscious of the cat outside its hole in explaining why it does not come out; meaning that it *perceives* the cat's presence. To provide an account of transitive creature-consciousness would thus be to attempt a theory of perception. No doubt there *are* many problems here; but we shall proceed as if we had the solution to them.

Two points about perception are worth making in this context, however. The first is that perceptual contents can be – and often are, to some degree – *non-conceptual*. While perception often presents us with a world of objects categorised into kinds (tables, chairs, cats and people, for example) sometimes it can present a world which is unconceptualised, but rather presented as *regions-of-filled-space* (and in the case of young children and many species of animal, presumably often does do so). Perception presents us with a complex array of surfaces and filled spaces, even when we have no idea *what* we are perceiving, and/or have no concepts appropriate to what we perceive.

The second – related – point is that perceptual contents are *analog* as opposed to digital, at least in relation to the concepts we possess. Thus perceptions of colour, for example, allow us to make an indefinite number of fine-grained discriminations, which far outstrip our powers of categorisation, description and memory. I perceive just *this* shade of red, with just *this* illumination, for instance, which I am incapable of describing in terms other than, 'The shade of *this* object now'. Here is at least part of the source of the common idea that consciousness – in this case, transitive creature-consciousness – is *ineffable*, or involves indescribable properties. But it should be plain that there is nothing especially mysterious or problematic involved. That our percepts have sufficient fineness of grain to slip through the mesh of any conceptual net does not mean that they cannot be wholly accounted for in representational and functional terms.

There is a choice to be made concerning transitive creature-consciousness, however, failure to notice which may be a potential source of confusion. For we have to decide whether the perceptual state in virtue of which an organism may be said to be transitively conscious of something must itself be a conscious one (state-conscious – see below). If we say 'Yes' then we shall need to know more about the mouse than merely that it perceives the cat if we are to be assured that it is conscious of the cat – we shall need to establish that its percept of the cat is itself conscious. If we say 'No', on the other hand, then the mouse's perception of the cat will be sufficient for it to count as conscious of the cat. But we may have to say that although the mouse is conscious of the cat, the mental state in virtue of which it is so conscious is not itself a conscious one! We think it best to by-pass all danger of confusion here by avoiding the language of transitive creature-consciousness altogether. Nothing of importance would be lost to us by doing this. We can say simply that organism O *observes* or *perceives* X; and we can then assert explicitly, if we wish, that its percept is or is not conscious.

Turning now to the notion of *mental-state*-consciousness, there is a further major distinction to be made between *phenomenal* consciousness – which is a property of states which it is *like something* to be in, and which have a distinctive 'feel' – and various functionally definable notions, such as Block's (1995) *access*-consciousness. (Block defines an access-conscious mental state as one which is available to processes of belief-formation, practical reasoning, and rational reflection; and – derivatively – to expression in speech.) Most theorists believe that there are mental states – such as occurrent thoughts or judgements – which are conscious (in whatever is the correct functionally definable sense), but which are not phenomenally conscious. (One exception here is Carruthers, 1996c, ch.8, who argues that occurrent propositional thoughts can only be conscious – in the human case at least – by being tokened in imaged natural language sentences, which will then possess phenomenal properties.) But there is considerable dispute as to whether mental states can be phenomenally conscious without also being conscious in the functionally definable sense – and even more dispute about whether phenomenal consciousness can be *explained* in functional and/or representational terms.

It seems plain that there is nothing deeply problematic about functionally definable notions of mental-state consciousness, from a naturalistic perspective. For mental functions and mental representations are the staple fare of naturalistic accounts of the mind. But this leaves plenty of room for dispute about the form that the correct functional account should take. Some claim that for a state to be conscious in the relevant sense is for it to be poised to have an impact on the organism's decision-making processes (Kirk, 1994; Dretske, 1995; Tye, 1995), perhaps also with the additional requirement that those processes should be distinctively *rational* ones (Block, 1995). Others think that the relevant requirement is that the state should be suitably related to higher-order representations (HORs) – higher-order thoughts (HOTs), higher-order descriptions (HODs), and/or higher-order experiences (HOEs) – of that very state (Armstrong, 1984; Rosenthal, 1986; Dennett, 1991a; Carruthers, 1996c; Lycan, 1996).

What *is* often thought to be naturalistically problematic, in contrast, is phenomenal consciousness (Nagel, 1986; McGinn, 1991; Block, 1995; Chalmers, 1996). For how can any physical state or event (for example, a particular pattern of neural firing) possess *phenomenal properties*? There is something distinctive that a conscious experience, or a conscious feeling, or a conscious visual image, *is like*. And it seems that no one except those who have enjoyed such states can ever *know* what they are like. How can this phenomenal aspect of our conscious mental lives ever be explained or accounted for within a physicalist framework? There are those who respond by saying that, indeed, conscious states are *not* physical (Jackson, 1982); and there are those who say that we can never *understand* how conscious states *can be* physical, while continuing to believe that they are (Nagel, 1974, 1986; McGinn, 1991).

Equally, phenomenal consciousness presents a challenge to any claim of functionalism and theory-theory to provide *comprehensive* accounts of the mental. For it seems that we can describe systems which would be functionally and theoretically equivalent to the human mind, but which we would not, intuitively, want to say were conscious, or were subjects of phenomenal feelings. And 'inverted qualia' and 'absent qualia' thought-experiments seem to show that the phenomenal qualities of our experiences cannot be given a functional characterisation. For if a person could be functionally equivalent to me while having their red and green experiences inverted, or absent altogether, then it seems that the felt quality of my experience of redness cannot be any sort of functional characteristic (Block, 1978, 1990; Shoemaker, 1986; Searle, 1992).

More generally, phenomenal consciousness can be seen as a challenge to science. Indeed, many scientists regard consciousness (together with the question of the origin of the universe) as one of the 'final frontiers' – a last bastion of mystery which is yet to fall to the onslaught of scientific explanation. And some, like Penrose (1989, 1994), have thought that the solution of the problem might provide the key to problems elsewhere in science, particularly in fundamental physics. Our task will be to see whether there are any reasons of principle why phenomenal consciousness can never be explained; and (following a negative answer) to see what progress has actually been made in explaining it.

We thus have distinctions between *creature*-consciousness (intransitive and transitive), on the one hand, and *mental-state*-consciousness on the other. And then within the latter, we have distinctions between *phenomenal* consciousness and various forms of functionally defined state-consciousness (first-order access-consciousness, higher-order-consciousness, and so on). Our main task will be to consider whether phenomenal consciousness can be explained in terms of some or other functionally definable notion. But there is one further distinction to be placed on the map, lest it be confused with any of the notions already discussed – and that is *self-consciousness*.

Self-consciousness admits of both weaker and stronger varieties, where each is a dispositional property of the agent. In the weak sense, for a creature to be self-conscious is just for it to be capable of awareness of itself as an *object* distinct from others (and perhaps also capable of awareness of itself as having a past and a future). This form of self-consciousness is conceptually not very demanding, and arguably many animals will possess it. Roughly, it just involves knowing the difference between one's own body and the rest of the physical world. But the stronger sense of self-consciousness involves higher-order awareness of oneself *as* a self, as a being with mental states. This is much more demanding, and arguably only human beings (together, perhaps, with the great apes) are self-conscious in this sense. For an organism to be self-conscious in this manner, it has to be capable of awareness of itself as an entity with a continuing *mental* life, with memories of its past experiences, and knowledge of its desires and goals for the future. This is even more demanding than higher-order thought (HOT) consciousness, since it involves not just HOTs about one's current mental states, but a conception of oneself as an on-going entity with such states – that is, with a past and future mental life.

1.2 Conscious versus non-conscious mental states

Our main focus will be on the adequacy of various functional (and/or representational) accounts of state-consciousness, especially on the question whether any such account can give a satisfying explanation of phenomenal consciousness. But there is one other crucial *desideratum* of such theories, and that is that they should be able to explain the distinction between conscious and non-conscious mental states. Here we argue that all types of mental state admit of these two varieties.

Consider routine activities, such as driving, walking, or washing up, which we can conduct with our conscious attention elsewhere. When driving home over a route I know well, for example, I will often pay no conscious heed to what I am doing on the road. Instead, I will be thinking hard about some problem at work, or fantasising about my summer holiday. In such cases it is common that I should then – somewhat unnervingly – 'come to', with a sudden realisation that I have not the slightest idea what I have been seeing or physically doing for some minutes past. Yet I surely must have been seeing, or I should have crashed the car. Indeed, my passenger sitting next to me may correctly report that I *saw* the vehicle double-parked at the side of the road, since I deftly turned the wheel to avoid it. Yet I was not conscious of seeing it, either at the time or later in memory. My perception of that vehicle was not a conscious one.

This example is at one end of a spectrum of familiar phenomena, all of which deserve to be classed as examples of non-conscious perception. For there are, in addition, many cases in which, while continuing to enjoy conscious experience, I also display sensitivity to features of my environment which I do *not* consciously perceive. For example, while walking down the street, and having conscious perceptions of many aspects of my surroundings, I may also step up and down from the kerb and make adjustments for various irregularities and obstacles in my path of which I have no conscious awareness. Since all the phenomena along this spectrum involve sensitivity to changing features of the environment, and since – most importantly – they fit neatly into the practical reasoning model of explanation, they deserve to be described as perceptual experiences which are non-conscious. For it may truly be said of me that I stepped up onto the kerb because I *wanted* to avoid falling, *saw* that the kerb was there, and *believed* that by stepping higher I should avoid tripping. So this is a case of genuine *seeing* which is non-conscious.

(Some people – for example, Dennett, 1991a – have attempted to explain such phenomena in terms of instantaneous memory loss, rather than in terms of non-conscious experience. On this account, my percept of the kerb *was* conscious, but since no space was devoted to it in memory, I can neither report nor remember it. Yet this explanation seems ruled out by the existence of cases where one can respond non-consciously to changes – such as the slowing down of a metronome – which happen too gradually to be perceivable at an instant, and so which must presuppose an intact memory.)

Consider, also, the striking phenomenon of *blindsight*. It has been known for some time that patients who have had certain areas of the striate cortex damaged (area V1) will apparently become blind in a portion of their visual field. They sincerely declare that they are aware of seeing nothing in that region. It was then discovered that some such patients nevertheless prove remarkably good at guessing the position of a light source, or the orientation of a line, on their 'blind' side. When their high rate of success is pointed out to them, these patients are genuinely surprised – they really thought they were guessing randomly. But the data show convincingly that they are capable of at least simple kinds of non-conscious perceptual discrimination – see Weiskrantz (1986) for details. Indeed, it has been shown that some patients are capable of reaching out and grasping objects on their blind sides with something like 80 or 90 per cent of normal accuracy, and of catching balls thrown towards them from their blind sides, again without conscious awareness (Marcel, forthcoming).

In addition to absent-minded activity and blindsight, there are also such phenomena as sleep-walking, where subjects must plainly be perceiving, to some degree, but apparently without consciousness. And Block (1995) describes cases of epileptics who continue their activities when undergoing a mild fit, but who do so without conscious awareness. Indeed, the psychological literature is now *rife* with examples of non-conscious perceptual processing, including the equivalent of blindsight in other sense-modalities – 'deaf-hearing', 'insensate-touch', and so on (see Baars, 1988, and Weiskrantz, 1997, for reviews).

Furthermore, it seems highly likely that beliefs and desires can be activated without emerging in conscious thought processes. Consider, for example, a chess-player's beliefs about the rules of chess. While playing, those beliefs must be activated – organising and helping to explain the moves made and the pattern of the player's reasoning. But they are not consciously rehearsed. Chess-players will not consciously think of the rules constraining their play, except when required to explain them to a beginner, or when there is some question about the legality of a move. Of course the beliefs in question will remain *accessible* to consciousness – players can, at will, recall and rehearse the rules of the game. So considered as standing states (as dormant beliefs), the beliefs in question are still conscious ones. We have nevertheless shown that beliefs can be non-consciously activated. The same will hold for desires, such as the desire to avoid obstacles which guides my movements while I drive absent-mindedly. So thoughts as events, or mental episodes, certainly do not have to be conscious.

Essentially the same point can be established from a slightly different perspective, by considering the phenomenon of non-conscious problem-solving. Many creative thinkers and writers report that their best ideas appear to come to them 'out of the blue', without conscious reflection (Ghiselin, 1952). Consider, also, some more mundane examples. I might go to bed unable to solve some problem I had been thinking about consciously during the day, and then wake up the next morning with a solution. Or while writing a paper you might be unable to see quite how to construct an argument for the particular conclusion you want, and so might turn your conscious attention to other things. But when you come back to it after an interval, everything then seems to fall smoothly into place. In such cases you must surely have been thinking – deploying and activating the relevant beliefs and desires – but not consciously.

One thing which a good theory of state-consciousness needs to do, then, is to provide a satisfying explanation of the distinction between conscious and non-conscious mental states, explaining what it is about the various phenomena in question which makes them fall on one or other side of the divide.

2 Mysterianism

In this section we review all the major arguments which have been presented in defence of *mysterianism* – the doctrine that phenomenal consciousness is, and must forever remain, a mystery. We propose to show that none of these arguments is compelling. This is in itself no positive argument *against* mysterianism, of course. We shall then turn to the positive project in section 3, considering various proposed explanations of phenomenal consciousness.

2.1 Perspectival and subjective facts?

Nagel (1986) has emphasised how, when we do science, we try to represent the world from no particular point of view. When we seek an objective characterisation of the world and the processes which take place within it, we try to find ways of describing the world which do not depend upon the particular structure of our sense-organs, or upon our limited, and necessarily partial, perspectives. We also try to describe our own relationship to the world in essentially the same objective, perspectiveless, vocabulary. So when we do science, instead of talking about colours we talk about the reflective properties of surfaces and wavelengths of light; and we try to explain colour perception in terms of the impact of light rays on the rods and cones in the retina, and the further neural events which are then caused to take place in the brain. In Nagel's phrase, the scientific view of the world is *the view from nowhere*.

Nagel argues, however, that there are some facts which are, and must be, *invisible* to science. And since they are invisible to science, they must inevitably be *inexplicable by* science, as well. These are perspectival and subjective facts. Science can provide (or at least allow for) a perspectiveless description of the layout of objects in my office, for example, but it cannot account for the fact that the desk is over *there* while I am sitting *here*. For such facts are inherently perspectival, Nagel thinks. They characterise places, not objectively, but from the standpoint of a particular perspective – namely, in this case, mine. Equally, science may one day be able to provide a complete objective description of what takes place in my brain when I perceive a red tomato. But what it cannot account for, Nagel maintains, is what it is *like* to see a red tomato – the *subjective feel*, or the *phenomenology*, of the experience itself. Science can hope to describe the processes of perception objectively, from the outside, but this leaves out what these processes are like *for the subject*, from the inside.

These claims are not convincing as stated. For they conflate the level of *reference* (the domain of facts) with the level of *sense* (the domain of concepts, and modes of presentation of those facts). In addition to the facts concerning the spatial layout of objects in my office, there is not any *further* fact in the world, namely that the desk is *there* while I am *here*. Rather, these are just further ways of representing, from the standpoint of a particular subject, some of the very same worldly facts. Equally, it might be thought, there may be no facts in addition to those concerning the brain-processes of someone perceiving red, namely the facts of what that experience *is like*. Rather, the subjective feel of the experience may merely be the mode of presentation of those brain-events to the subject. There need not be *two* facts here (the brain-event and the phenomenal feel), but only one fact variously represented – namely, objectively, from the standpoint of science, and subjectively, from the standpoint of the subject to whom the brain-event occurs.

Now admittedly, representations, or the existence of modes of presentation, are themselves a species of fact. Besides facts about the world, represented by us in various different ways, there are also facts about our representation of the world. So in addition to the facts about the spatial layout of the room, there *are* further facts concerning how I represent that layout from my particular perspective. But no reason has yet been given why these cannot be characterised objectively. An observer can describe the standpoint from which I perceive the room, and the way in which the room will appear to me from that standpoint. (In one sense, this is really just a question of geometry.) There is nothing here to suggest the existence of a special category of fact which must be invisible to science.

(Note that essentially the same response, to that given here, can be made to Nagel's claim that there are also irreducible and inexplicable *myness*-facts, involved in characterising perspectives and mental states as *mine* (1986, ch.4). Nagel may be correct that I-thoughts are irreducible to other types of representation, feeding into behaviour-control, in particular, in a distinctive and irreplaceable way. But this shows nothing about the existence of any special category of fact.)

2.2 What Mary didn't know

We have replied to an argument purporting to show that the different perspectives on the world adopted by different subjects must elude any objective description or scientific explanation. Jackson (1982, 1986) has presented a variation on this argument, designed to show that the subjective aspect of experience (the phenomenal feel), in particular, is a genuine *fact* about experience which cannot be captured in either physicalist or functionalist terms.

Jackson imagines the case of Mary, who has lived all her life in a black-and-white room. At the point where he takes up the story, Mary has never had any experience of colour; but, we may suppose, there is nothing wrong with her visual system – she still has the *capacity* for colour vision. Now, Mary is also a scientist, living in an era much more scientifically advanced than ours. So Mary may be supposed to know *all there is to know* about the physics, physiology and functional organisation of colour vision. She knows exactly what takes place in someone's brain when they experience red, for example, and has full understanding of the behaviour of the physical systems involved. So she knows all the objective, scientific facts about colour vision. But there is one thing she does *not* know, surely, and that is what an experience of red *is like*. And on being released from her black-and-white room there is something new she will *learn* when she experiences red for the first time. Since knowledge of all the physical and functional facts does not give Mary knowledge of *all* the facts, Jackson argues, then there are some facts – namely, facts about subjective experiences and feelings – which are not physical or functional facts, and which cannot be explicable in terms of physical or functional facts, either.

One influential reply to this argument is developed at length by Lewis (1988). It turns on a distinction between two different kinds of knowledge. On the one hand there is *propositional* knowledge (often called 'knowledge *that*'), which is knowledge of facts; and on the other hand there is *practical* knowledge (often called 'knowledge *how*'), which is knowledge of how to do something. Thus your knowledge of British history is propositional (you know *that* the Battle of Hastings was fought in 1066, for example), whereas your knowledge of shoe-lace-tying is (largely) practical – there are very few *facts* which you know about tying your shoe-laces, and you would be at a loss to *tell* me how to do it (except by running a description of what to do off a memory-image of the appropriate sequence of actions); rather you just *can* do it; you have the ability to do it. With this distinction in place, the reply to Jackson can be that knowing what an experience is like is not propositional knowledge, but rather practical knowledge.

What Mary lacks in her black-and-white room, on this account, is an *ability* – the ability to recognise, remember and imagine experiences of red. And what experience teaches her, on her release from the room, is just that – an ability to recognise experiences of red (without having to rely on any inference from physiological facts), and abilities to recall and visualise such experiences. So there need be no *facts* over and above the physical and functional facts which Mary already knew. For she does not *learn* any new facts when she comes out of her room. Rather, she acquires some new skills which she did not have before. And this need cause us no problem. For no one would want to maintain that mere knowledge of facts can confer practical abilities on someone – knowledge of all the facts about skiing would not make you into a skier, for example.

It may be objected that Mary surely does acquire some new propositional knowledge on her release from the room (Loar, 1990). For example,
she may learn something she would express by saying, '*This* colour [point-
ing at something red] is warmer than *this* one [pointing at something
yellow]'. The knowledge she thereby expresses is surely the knowledge *that*
one colour is warmer than the other. But this is knowledge which she
cannot have had before, since it involves recognitional concepts of colour
('*this* colour') which she did not possess when in her black-and-white
room. But now this is just a dispute about how one *types* facts. Are facts
different if the *concepts* used to describe them are different? Or are facts
only different if the worldly objects and properties involved in them differ?
The objection to the Lewis argument assumes the former. But then that
just returns us to the confusion between sense and reference discussed
above. As Loar points out, that there are some *concepts* which you can
only possess in virtue of having had certain experiences (namely, recognitional concepts of experience) does not show that *what is recognised*
(namely the experiences themselves) in any way transcends physical or
functional description.

2.3 Cognitive closure?

McGinn (1991) has argued that the solution to the problem of phenomenal consciousness (the problem, that is, of understanding how phenomenal consciousness can be, or be explained in terms of, physical events in
the brain) is *cognitively closed to us*. He argues, first, that it is a corollary
of the Chomskian claim that we have a variety of innate special-purpose
learning-mechanisms, specialised for particular domains such as natural
language or folk psychology, that there may be *some* domains which are
cognitively closed to us. These would be domains which might actually
contain facts sufficient to answer the questions which we can frame about
them, but where the innate structure of our minds means that we shall
forever be incapable of discerning those answers. So these will be domains
which, while not *intrinsically* (metaphysically) mysterious, must always
remain mysterious *to us*. He then presents reasons for thinking that the
realisation of phenomenal consciousness in physical brain-events is one
such domain.

Now, we are certainly inclined to quarrel with the first premise of this
argument. From the fact that our minds contain specialised learning-
mechanisms which make the acquisition of knowledge of certain domains
particularly *easy* for us, it does not follow that there are any domains which
are cognitively *closed* to us. It only follows that there are domains where
learning will be *less easy*. Provided that our special-purpose learning-
mechanisms can also be deployed, somewhat less effectively, outside of

their home domain; or provided that in addition to these mechanisms we also have some *general*-purpose learning-mechanisms (and surely one or other of these possibilities *must* be the case, or else cognitive closure would be a familiar fact of everyday life); then it may well be that *all* domains can yield, eventually, to systematic enquiry. But what really matters, for our purposes, is McGinn's second premise. For even if we thought (*contra* the first premise) that there is no good reason to *expect* to find areas of cognitive closure, we should still need to look at his case for saying that, as a matter of fact, phenomenal consciousness, in particular, must forever remain mysterious to us.

McGinn suggests that the problem of phenomenal consciousness lies in an explanatory gap between the subjective, or *felt*, qualities of experience, on the one hand, and the underlying neural events in our brains, on the other. And there are, he argues, just two ways in which we might hope to close this gap. *Either* we can use introspection to dig deeper into the phenomenal properties of our experiences, perhaps seeking a more sophisticated set of phenomenal concepts with which to categorise and describe the subjective qualities of those experiences. *Or* we can work from the other end, investigating the physical events in our brains, hoping to achieve from there (perhaps by means of some sort of inference to the best explanation) an understanding of phenomenal consciousness.

But we can see in advance that neither of these strategies stands any chance of being successful. For there is plainly no prospect that further introspective investigation of our experiences could ever lead us to see how those very experiences could be neurological events in our brains. Nor does it seem possible that further scientific investigation of our brains could ever lead us to postulate that those events possess phenomenal characteristics. For our only mode of access to brain states (when characterised as such – remember, McGinn allows that conscious states *probably are* brain states) is observational, from a third-person perspective. And it is hard to see how any sequence of inferences to the best explanation, starting from the observed properties of such states, could ever lead us to something which is inherently subjective, namely the felt characteristics of our experiences. So although McGinn allows that phenomenal consciousness is almost certainly a physical characteristic of our brains, he thinks it must forever remain mysterious just how it can be so.

There are at least two major faults in this argument. The first is that McGinn seems entirely to forget that there may be many different levels of scientific enquiry and description between neuroscience and common-sense psychology, including a variety of forms of computationalism, together with the kinds of functional description characteristic of much cognitive psychology. For it can easily seem mysterious how *anything* in nature can be physical, if you try to jump over too many intermediate stages at once. For example, it can easily seem mysterious how a living organism can maintain itself as an integrated whole, if we just focus on the fact that any such organism must consist, ultimately, of sub-atomic wave-particles governed by indeterministic principles, forgetting about all the intermediate levels of description in between. And as we shall see in section 3, the most plausible explanations of phenomenal consciousness on the market are *cognitive* in nature, attempting to use some or other functionally definable notion of state-consciousness to explain the subjective qualities of our experiences.

But the second, and truly major, fault in McGinn's argument is that he ignores the possibility that we might succeed in closing the explanatory gap between consciousness and the brain by operating with inference to the best explanation on phenomenal consciousness itself. Indeed it is obvious, when one reflects on it, that this is the direction in which enquiry should proceed. For in science it is rarely, if ever, the case that we have to seek higher-level explanations of lower-level phenomena. We do not, for example, turn to biology to explain why chemical reactions work as they do. Rather, we seek to understand higher-level phenomena in terms of their realisation in lower-level processes. And no reason has yet been given why this strategy should not work when applied to phenomenal consciousness, just as it does elsewhere in nature. To adopt this strategy would be to seek to explain phenomenal consciousness in terms of some postulated underlying cognitive mechanisms or architectures, which one might then hope to explain, in turn, in terms of simpler computational systems, and so on until, ultimately, one reaches the known neural structures and processes of the brain. While we perhaps have, as yet, no particular cause for *optimism* about the likely success of this strategy, McGinn's sort of principled pessimism seems certainly unfounded.

2.4 More explanatory gaps?

Chalmers (1996) argues that almost all states and properties of the natural world (with the exception of phenomenal consciousness, and of states in one way or another involving phenomenal consciousness, including secondary qualities such as colours and sounds) supervene *logically* on the total micro-physical state of the world. That is, he thinks it is conceptually impossible, or inconceivable, that there could be a universe exactly like ours in respect of its total micro-physical description, and sharing our basic physical laws, but differing in respect of any of its chemical, geological, geographical, meteorological, biological, psycho-functional, or economic properties. For once the properties, position, and motion of every last microscopic particle in the universe has been fixed, there is simply no *room* for any further variation (except by conservative addition – Chalmers allows that a world might differ from ours in having something *extra*, such as angels constituted out of non-physical ectoplasm, provided that they make no difference to the distribution of micro-physical particles).

In contrast, Chalmers claims, phenomenal consciousness does *not* supervene logically on the physical world. For it is easy to imagine a world which is micro-physically identical to ours, but in which there is nothing which it feels like to be one of the organisms (including the human beings) in that world. This is the *zombie* world. And it is the conceivability of zombie worlds (and/or *inverted qualia* worlds – see below) micro-physically identical to our own which makes the problem of phenomenal consciousness so *hard*, Chalmers thinks – indeed, which makes it insoluble from within a physicalist and/or functionalist framework.

Chalmers also maintains that only those natural properties which supervene logically on physical ones can admit of any sort of reductive explanation. (By reductive explanation he means explanation by instantiation in, or composition by, lower-level mechanisms and processes; so reductive *explanation* is to be distinguished sharply from ontological or theoretical reduction, of the sort discussed above in chapter 7, section 5.) According to Chalmers, our concept of any given higher-level process, state, or event, specifies the conditions which any reductive explanation of that phenomenon must meet. For example, our concept *life* contains such notions as *reproduction* and *energy generation by metabolic processes*, which are amongst the functions which any living thing must be able to perform. And then a reductive explanation of life will demonstrate how appropriate chemical changes and processes can constitute the performance of just those functions. The phenomenon of life is explained when we see how those lower-level chemical events, suitably arranged and sequenced, will instantiate just those functions which form part of our concept *living thing*. In fact it is science's track-record of success in providing such reductive explanations which warrants our belief that physics is closed in our world, and which provides the grounds for the claim that all natural phenomena supervene on micro-physical facts.

Since concepts of chemical, geological, geographical, meteorological, biological, psycho-functional and economic states and processes are broadly functional ones, it is possible for events of those kinds to admit of reductive explanations. But our concepts of phenomenally conscious states are different, as evidenced by the conceivability of zombie (and inverted qualia) worlds. If we can conceive of states which are functionally identical to our conscious experiences while being phenomenally distinct, then we cannot be conceptualising the latter in terms of functions. Rather our concepts, here, are presumably bare *recognitional* ones, consisting in our possession of immediate recognitional capacities for phenomenal states of various kinds. It is this which sets up the explanatory gap between neurological or cognitive functions, on the one hand, and phenomenal consciousness on the other. Chalmers claims, indeed, that we can see in advance that any proposed reductive explanation of phenomenal consciousness into neurological or cognitive terms is doomed to failure. For what such 'explanations' provide are mechanisms for instantiating certain *functions*, which must fall short of the *feel* possessed by many types of conscious state. Since we do not conceptualise our conscious states in terms of function, but rather in terms of feel, no explanations of function can explain them. Hence the existence of the 'hard problem' of phenomenal consciousness.

Now, much of this is roughly correct. We agree that reductive explanations normally work by specifying lower-level mechanisms for fulfilment of some higher-level function. And we agree that we have available to us purely recognitional concepts of phenomenally conscious states. But we disagree with the conclusions Chalmers draws from these facts. His mistake is to assume that a given property or state can only be successfully reductively explained if the proposed mechanisms are what we might call 'immediately cognitively satisfying', in the sense that they mesh with the manner in which those states are conceptualised. While the 'explanatory gap' is of some cognitive significance, revealing something about the manner in which we conceptualise our experiences, it shows nothing about the nature of those experiences themselves. Or so, at any rate, we maintain.

A good reductive explanation of phenomenal consciousness (of the sort offered by higher-order thought theories, for example – see section 3.3 below) can explain a variety of features of our conscious experiences, while also explaining the nature and existence of our recognitional concepts themselves. And a good cognitive architecture can explain why subjects instantiating it should have a natural tendency to make many of the claims traditionally made by philosophers concerning *qualia* – that qualia are non-relationally defined, ineffable, private, and known with certainty by the subject, for example. Admittedly, it will still remain possible, by *employing* our recognitional concepts of experience, to imagine zombie versions of just such an architecture. But that will be revealed as *not* posing any additional explanatory problem. It is not something about the nature of conscious experience which makes such zombie architectures conceivable, but merely something about the way in which we (can) *conceptualise* those experiences. In fact there is no worldly property or phenomenon which need go unexplained. For even this freedom to conceptualise can *itself* be explained on such an account, as we shall see.

So, we agree that absent or inverted phenomenal feelings are conceptually possible. Thus we can conceive of the possibility of undetectable zombies. These would be people who are *functionally* indistinguishable from ourselves, who act and behave and speak just as we do; but who are entirely lacking in any inner phenomenology. Equally, we can conceive of the possibility of inverted phenomenologies (see figure 9.1 below). We can conceive that other people, when they look at something red, have the kind of subjective experience which I should describe as an experience of green; and that when they look at something green, they have the sort of experience which *I* get when I look at a ripe tomato. But because *they* describe as 'an experience of green' what *I* describe as 'an experience of red' (and vice versa), the difference never emerges in our behaviour. We both say that grass is green, and causes experiences of green, and that tomatoes are red, and cause experiences of red. Do these facts about *conceivability* show that the subjective aspects of our experiences themselves must be both non-representational and not functionally definable?

No. The best response to these arguments is to allow that absent and inverted feelings are *conceptually* possible, but to point out that it does not follow from this that they are logically (*metaphysically*) possible – even less that they are *naturally* possible; and to claim that only the latter would establish the actual existence of qualia. In fact the argument falls prey to essentially the same weakness as the 'what Mary didn't know' argument. We can allow that there are recognitional concepts of experience and of the way subjective states distinctively feel, and we can allow that those *concepts* are not relationally or causally defined, while insisting that the properties which those concepts pick out *are* relational ones. It is because the concepts are recognitional that absent and inverted feelings are conceptually possible. But it is because the properties which those concepts pick out are actually relational ones, that absent and inverted feelings are, arguably, neither naturally nor metaphysically possible.

To elaborate this thought is, in fact, to develop a higher-order thought (HOT) account of phenomenal consciousness, to be discussed in section 3. The idea is, that it is by virtue of having HOTs about our perceptual states – and in particular, by deploying recognitional concepts of experience – that those states come to possess their phenomenal properties. To a first approximation: any creature which can perceive red and which can make all the visual discriminations which I can, and which can recognise its own perceptual representations of red as and when they occur, will *ipso facto* be a subject of just the same phenomenal feelings as me, on such an account.

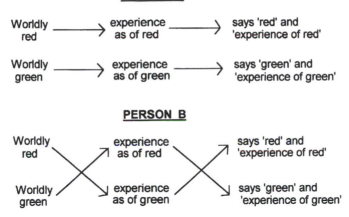

Figure 9.1 A case of inverted phenomenology

2.5 Real inversions?

Unfortunately for the above line of reply to Chalmers, there are variants of the inverted-spectra arguments (but not of the absent-qualia arguments) which seem to show that undetectably inverted phenomenologies are not just conceivable, but *naturally* possible – in which case it cannot be metaphysically necessary that all percepts of red are similar in respect of *feel*. Here, for example, is a possible case of intra-personal spectrum inversion (Shoemaker, 1981; Block, 1990):

(1) We take a normal person and insert colour-inverting lenses into his eyes (or we insert a neural-transformer into his optic nerve, which transposes the sort of neural activity normally characteristic of seeing red, into the sort of activity normally characteristic of seeing green, and so on round the colour-circle). He says that grass looks red and blood looks green.

(2) After a period of confusion and deviant usage, the person brings his colour-concepts into line with the rest of us – for example, he says (and thinks) that grass is green and that blood is red. But he still *remembers* that grass used to look the way blood now looks to him.

(3) Everything remains as in (2), except that he undergoes amnesia. Then we have someone who is functionally indistinguishable from a normal person. But surely what colour-experience is *like* for him is still inverted from normal – in which case *what it is like* cannot be functionally characterisable.

Some people respond to this sort of argument by saying that the case is such a deviant one that we have no good reason to rely upon the subject's memory-reports at stage (2) – see Dennett, 1988b. If we do not rely on the person's memory, then there is no reason why we should not insist that the colour-feels shift with the shift in concepts and language which takes place in (2). In which case there is no inversion.

Block (1990) replies with a case which does not involve confusion or memory-loss – *Inverted Earth*. This is a case of *functional* and *intentional* inversion, but where (arguably) *feel* remains the same. In which case the same conclusion follows, that the latter must be distinct from the former.

(a)   There is a place – either an inverted duplicate of Earth, or some sort of restricted artificial environment, like a room – where the colours of everything are inverted from normal. In this place, the sky is yellow, bananas are blue, grass is red, blood is green, and so on. But the language-use of the inhabitants is also inverted. So they *say*, 'The sky is blue', 'Bananas are yellow', and so on.

(b)   A normal Earthling is kidnapped, rendered unconscious, has colour-inverters inserted into his eyes (or optic nerve), and is transported to Inverted Earth. When he wakes up he notices no difference – he sees the sky as blue, bananas as yellow, and so on. And that is the way he describes things – *falsely*, so far as his own colour-concepts are concerned, because the sky is *not* blue, it is yellow.

(c)   After a long enough period on Inverted Earth, his concepts (and the intentional contents of his colour-thoughts) shift into line with those of his co-locutors, so that when he says, 'The sky is blue', he means the same as the people in the speech-community to which he then belongs (namely, that the sky is yellow); and he then says something true.

By stage (c) we have someone who is functionally and intentionally inverted from a normal person on Earth. But surely what his experiences are *like* for him have remained the same! So when he looks at a yellow sky and thinks the true thought which he would express by saying, 'The sky is blue', it is, subjectively for him, just as it was when he looked at a blue sky back on Earth.

However, this Inverted Earth argument assumes that meaning and concepts have to be individuated *widely*, in terms of the objects and properties in the thinker's environment (as also does the more traditional intra-personal inversion argument). So it is because the person says 'blue' in the presence of yellow things, in a language community where all speakers normally refer to yellow things as 'blue', that he means *yellow* and expresses the concept *yellow* by 'blue'.

But there are those who think that concepts and intentional contents can also be individuated *narrowly*, in abstraction from the actual objects and properties of the thinker's environment, particularly when contents are being individuated for the purposes of psychological explanation. Indeed, the legitimacy and appropriateness of narrow content for psychology was defended at length in chapter 6 above. And if it turns out that the person *retains* (narrow) colour-concepts and intentional colour-contents unchanged on Inverted Earth, then it is not true that he is completely inverted in respect of intentional contents. And so the argument for the distinctness of *feel* from intentional contents will collapse. For it will not *just* be the feel which remains the same on Inverted Earth; it will also be his narrowly individuated colour-concepts and narrowly individuated perceptual states.

The person on Earth began with a recognitional concept of *blue*, among others. This concept can be individuated widely for some purposes, involving a relation to worldly blueness, or it can be individuated narrowly. The narrow concept can be specified thus: it is the recognitional concept which he could apply whenever undergoing analog colour-experiences of a sort which, in normal circumstances in the actual world, are caused by blue objects. On Inverted Earth, even after the wide-content of his concepts has shifted to take account of his new external surroundings, he still deploys that very same narrowly individuated concept. We can say that if he were transported back to Earth and had the colour-inverters removed from his eyes, it would be that very recognition-concept which he would apply in relation to percepts of blue sky. And we can now identify the *feel* of an experience of blue as that *representational* perceptual state which would activate a recognitional application of the narrowly individuated concept *blue*. So there is nothing in the Inverted Earth argument to force us to recognise qualia as non-representational properties of experience.

In the case of Inverted Earth, it is the person's behaviour and widely individuated mental states which are inverted. But as we have seen, that need not stop us from characterising the *feel* of his experiences as the same in (narrowly individuated) intentional terms. In the case of intra-personal inversion, in contrast, the person's behaviour and widely individuated states remain the same, post amnesia, as they were prior to the insertion of the colour-inverters. But a functionalist can think that there are functional differences which do not show up on the outside – in this case differences in the narrow-content of the intervening perceptual states. So we can say that it is the contents (narrowly individuated) of his perceptual experiences which have undergone inversion, despite there being no difference in his behaviour.

2.6 Are there any non-representational properties of experience?

Those who think that the existence of phenomenal consciousness raises insuperable problems for functionalist accounts of the mental, and/or those who think that phenomenal consciousness is, and must remain, ineradicably mysterious, are almost certain to believe in *qualia*. Now, almost everyone accepts that conscious experiences have distinctive phenomenal feels, and that there is something which it is *like* to be the subject of such an experience. And some people use the term 'qualia' to refer just to the distinctive subjectivity of experience – which then makes it indisputable that qualia exist. But believers in qualia in any stronger sense maintain that the distinctive feel of an experience is due, at least in part, to its possession of subjectively available *non*-representational, *non*-relationally defined, properties. On this view, then, in addition to the distinctive ways our experiences represent the world as being, our experiences *also* have properties which are intrinsic, and which do not represent anything beyond themselves. It is also often claimed that qualia are *private* (unknowable to anyone but their subject), *ineffable* (indescribable and incommunicable to others), as well as knowable with complete *certainty* by the person who has them.

Plainly, if our experiences do possess qualia (in this strong sense), then naturalistic accounts of the mind are in trouble. For there will then exist aspects of our mental lives which cannot be characterised in functional or representational terms. Equally, if there are qualia, then the task of explaining how a physical system can possess phenomenal consciousness looks hard indeed. For it is certainly difficult to understand how any physical property or event in our brains could be, or could realise, a phenomenal state which is intrinsic, private, ineffable, and known with certainty.

The most direct response to this argument is to *Quine* qualia ('to Quine = to deny the existence of'; see Dennett, 1988b; Harman, 1990; Tye, 1995). This is to maintain that *there are no* non-representational properties of experience (or not ones which are available to consciousness, anyway – of course there will be intrinsic physical properties of the realising brain-states). The best way to do this is to claim that perceptual states are *diaphanous* or *transparent*. Look at a green tree or a red tomato. Now try to concentrate as hard as you can, *not* on the colours of the *objects*, but on the quality of your *experience* of those colours. What happens? Can you do it? Plausibly, all that you find yourself doing is paying closer and closer attention to the colours in the outside world, after all. A perception of red is a state which represents a surface as having a certain distinctive quality – *redness*, of some or other particular shade – and paying close attention to your perceptual state comes down to paying close attention to the quality of the world *represented* (while being aware of it *as* represented – this will become important later). Of course, in cases of perceptual illusion or hallucination there may actually be no real quality of the world represented, but only a represent*ing*. But still, plausibly, there is nothing to your experience over and above the way it represents the world as being.

But what about bodily sensations, like itches, tickles, and pains? Are these, too, purely representational states? If so, *what* do they represent? It might seem that all there really is to a pain, is a particular sort of *non*-representational quality, which is experienced as unwelcome. In which case, if we are forced to recognise qualia for bodily experiences, it may be simpler and more plausible to allow that outer perceptions possess qualia as well. But in fact, the case for qualia is no stronger in connection with pain than with colour (Tye, 1995). In both cases our experience represents to us a particular perceptible property – in the one case, of an external surface, in the other case, of a region of our own body. In the case of colour-perception, my perceptual state delivers the content, '*That* surface has *that* quality.' In the case of pain, my state grounds an exactly parallel sort of content, namely '*That* region of my body has *that* quality.' In each case the *that quality* expresses a recognitional concept, where what is recognised is not a quale, but rather a property which our perceptual state represents as being instantiated in the place in question.

If the above is correct, then qualia can no more be vindicated by the deliverances of introspection, than by the 'what Mary didn't know' argument and the 'inverted qualia' argument (discussed and defeated in, respectively, section 2.2 and sections 2.4–2.5 above).

3 Cognitivist theories

As we have seen, the arguments offered in support of mysterianism are less than convincing. The remainder of this chapter will now be devoted to exploring the strengths and weaknesses of a variety of attempts to explain phenomenal consciousness in cognitive terms. The main contrast which we shall consider is between theories which offer their accounts in terms of first-order representations (FORs) and those which make appeal to higher-order representations (HORs) of some sort. But we can represent all the various attempts to provide a reductive explanation of phenomenal consciousness on a branching tree-structure, as in figure 9.2 below.

The first choice to be made (choice-point (1) in figure 9.2), is whether to attempt a reductive explanation of phenomenal consciousness in physical (presumably neurobiological) terms, or whether to seek an explanation which is cognitive and/or functional. For example, Crick and Koch (1990)

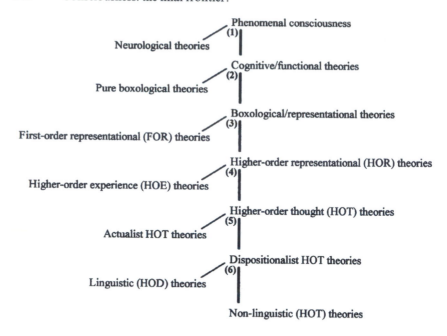

Figure 9.2 The tree of consciousness theories

propose that phenomenal consciousness may be identified with syn-chronised 35- to 75-hertz neural oscillations in the sensory areas of the cortex. Given the points made in section 2.3 above, however, in our discussion of McGinn, it seems unlikely that any reductive explanation into neurobiological terms can be successful – this is trying to jump over too many explanatory levels at once.

A number of different functional theories have been proposed which incorporate some sort of 'phenomenal-consciousness box'. In some of these the consciousness box is located in relation to other aspects of cognition, but no attempt is made to explain those features of phenomenal consciousness which seem most puzzling. For want of a better term, we label these 'pure boxological theories' (the term 'obviously non-explana-tory boxological theories' might be descriptively more accurate). For example, in a model due to Schacter et al. (1988), there is a conscious awareness system (or CAS) defined by its relations with a number of specialist modules, on the one hand, and the executive and verbal memory systems on the other. The model is designed to explain a variety of dissociation data – for example, that people with prosopagnosia can lack any conscious recognition of faces, while recognition can nevertheless be demonstrated (for instance, by galvanic skin responses) to be taking place at some level.

But no attempt is made at explaining *why* a box located as the CAS is located in cognition should contain states which are phenomenally conscious. Why could there not be a system whose function was to make its contents available for executive decision and for reporting in speech, but whose contents lacked *feel*? In fact, this is one of those places where Block's (1995) distinction between phenomenal consciousness and *access-consciousness* starts to bite. That there is some system which makes its contents *accessible* in various ways, does not in itself explain why those contents should be *like anything* for their subjects to undergo. In fact, all the proposed theories which we shall be concerned with attempt to explain the subjective aspect of phenomenally conscious states in terms of the distinctive sort of *content* possessed by such states – that is, all these theories opt for the vertical branch at choice-point (2).

We shall now work through the four remaining choice-points in figure 9.2, contrasting: first-order with higher-order theories (3); higher-order experience (or 'inner sense') theories with higher-order thought theories (4); actualist as against dispositionalist forms of higher-order thought theory (5); and forms of the latter which do or do not implicate natural language (6). Our goal will be to convince you, by the end of the chapter, of the merits of dispositionalist, non-language-involving, higher-order thought theory.

3.1 FOR theories

Dretske (1995) and Tye (1995) independently develop very similar first-order representationalist (FOR) theories of phenomenal consciousness. In both cases the goal is to characterise all of the phenomenal – 'felt' – properties of experience in terms of the analog (non-conceptual) representational *contents* of experience. So the difference between an experience of green and an experience of red will be explained as a difference in the properties represented – reflective properties of surfaces, say – in each case. And the difference between a pain and a tickle is similarly explained in representational terms – the difference is said to reside in the different properties (different kinds of disturbance) represented as located in particular regions of the subject's own body. The main argument in support of first-order theories is that they can explain the *transparency* of conscious experience, discussed in section 2.6 above. If some such theory is correct, then it is obvious why, in trying to concentrate on my conscious *experience*, I end up concentrating on the states which my experience *represents* – it is because there is nothing *more* to a phenomenally conscious

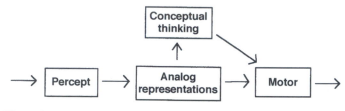

Figure 9.3 First-order representationalism

experience than having a certain sort of representational content poised and accessible to concept-wielding thought (as represented in figure 9.3).

Dretske and Tye differ from one another mainly in the accounts which they offer of the representation-relation. For Dretske, the content of a representational state is fixed teleologically, in terms of the objects/ properties which that state is *supposed* to represent, given the organism's evolutionary and learning histories. For Tye, in contrast, the content of a state is defined in terms of causal co-variance in normal circumstances – where the notion of *normal* circumstances may or may not be defined teleologically, depending upon cases. But both are agreed that content is to be individuated *externally*, in a way which embraces objects and properties in the organism's environment. We shall begin our discussion by suggesting that they have missed a trick in going for an externalist notion of content, and that their position would be strengthened if they were to endorse a *narrow*-content account instead.

We have already seen, in section 2.5 above, that it is legitimate to respond to the Inverted Earth argument for qualia by invoking a narrowly individuated notion of perceptual content. Externalists can respond rather differently, however, by placing further (teleological) constraints on content-individuation. In fact, both Dretske and Tye are in a position to claim that the content of the person's experiences remains the same, uninverted, on Inverted Earth. For the state the person is in when looking at the yellow sky is the state which is *supposed* to represent blueness, or which would *normally* co-vary with blueness, given their Earthly evolutionary history. However, there are cases which they cannot explain so easily.

Consider, again, Davidson's (1987) example of *Swampman* (discussed in chapter 6 above), who is accidentally created by a bolt of lightning striking a tree-stump in a swamp, in such a way as to be molecule-for-molecule identical to an existing person. Dretske is forced to deny that Swampman and that person are subject to the same colour experiences (and indeed, he must deny that Swampman has any colour experiences at all), since his states lack *functions*, either evolved or learned. As Dretske admits, this consequence is highly counterintuitive; and the intuition is one which he has to chew on pretty hard to force himself to swallow. Tye, on the other hand, believes that he is better off in relation to this example, since he says Swampman's circumstances can count as 'normal' by default. But then there will be other cases where Tye will be forced to say that two individuals undergo the same experiences (because their states are such as to co-vary with the same properties in circumstances which are normal for them), where intuition would strongly suggest that their experiences are different. So imagine that the lightning-bolt happens to create Swampman with a pair of colour-inverting lenses as part of the structure of the corneas in his eyes. Then Tye will have to say, when Swampman looks at green grass, that he undergoes the same experiences as his double does (who views the grass *without* such lenses). For in the circumstances which are normal for Swampman, he is in a state which will co-vary with greenness. So he experiences *green*, just as his double does. This, too, is highly counterintuitive. We would want to say, surely, that Swampman experiences *red*.

Some may see sufficient reason, here, to reject a first-order representationalist account of phenomenal consciousness straight off. We disagree. Rather, such examples just motivate adoption of a narrow-content account of representation in general, where contents are individuated in abstraction from the particular objects and properties in the thinker's environment. Our case in support of narrow-content was made in chapter 6. Given those arguments, it should be obvious that one could adopt a first-order naturalisation of phenomenal consciousness while rejecting externalism.

3.2 Distinctions lost

This is not to say, of course, that we think first-order approaches to consciousness are unproblematic. One major difficulty for such theories is to provide an account of the distinction between conscious and non-conscious experience, outlined in section 1.2 above. For in some of these cases, at least, we appear to have first-order representations of the environment which are not only poised for the control of behaviour, but which are actually controlling it. So how can first-order theorists explain why our perceptions, in such cases, are not phenomenally conscious? There would seem to be just two ways for them to respond – either they can accept that absent-minded driving experiences are *not* phenomenally conscious, and characterise what additionally is required to render an experience phenomenally conscious in (first-order) functional terms; or they can insist that absent-minded driving experiences *are* phenomenally conscious, but in a way which makes them inaccessible to their subjects.

Kirk (1994) apparently exemplifies the first approach, claiming that for a perceptual state with a given content to be phenomenally conscious, and to acquire a 'feel', it must be present to the *right sorts* of decision-making processes – namely those which constitute the organism's highest-level executive. But this is extremely puzzling. It is utterly mysterious how an experience with one and the same content could be sometimes phenomenally conscious and sometimes not, depending just upon the overall role in the organism's cognition of the decision-making processes to which it is present – how could mere height in a hierarchy of control make such a difference?

Tye (1995) takes the second approach. In cases such as that of absent-minded driving, he claims there is experience, which is phenomenally conscious, but which is 'concealed from the subject'. This then gives rise to the highly counterintuitive claim that there are phenomenally conscious experiences to which the subject is blind – experiences which it is *like* something for the subject to have, but of which the subject is unaware. And in explaining the aware/unaware distinction, Tye then goes for an actualist form of higher-order thought (HOT) theory. He argues that we are *aware* of an experience and its phenomenal properties only when we are actually applying phenomenal concepts to it. The dilemma then facing him is *either* that he cannot account for the immense richness of experience of which we are (can be) aware; *or* that he has to postulate an immensely rich set of HOTs involving phenomenal concepts accompanying each set of experiences of which we are aware – the same dilemma faced by any actualist HOT theorist, in fact (see section 3.7 below).

Not only is Tye's position counterintuitive, but it is surely also incoherent. For the idea of the *what-it-is-likeness* of experience is intended to characterise those aspects of experience which are *subjective*. But there surely could not be properties of experience which were subjective without being *available to* the subject, and of which the subject was unaware. An experience of which the subject is unaware cannot be one which it is *like something* for the *subject* to have. On the contrary, an experience which it is *like something* to have, must be one which is available to the subject of that experience – and that means being a target (actual or potential) of a suitable higher-order state.

It may be objected that 'subjective' just implies 'grounded in properties of the subject', and that we are quite happy with the idea that someone's prejudices, for example, might reflect evaluations which are subjective in this sense without being available to the subject. But in the case of perception it is already true that the subjectivity of the world, for a subject, is grounded in properties of the perceiver. In what could the further subjectivity *of the experience* consist, except its availability to the subject?

This point prompts us to raise another – closely related – general difficulty for such first-order accounts, which is that they cannot distinguish between what the *world* (or the state of the organism's own body) is like for an organism, and what the organism's *experience of the world* (or of its own body) is like for the organism. This distinction is very frequently overlooked in discussions of consciousness. Tye, for example, will move (sometimes in the space of a single sentence) from saying that his account explains what *colour* is like for an organism with colour-vision, to saying that it explains what *experiences of colour* are like for that organism. But the first is a property of the world (or of a world-perceiver pair, perhaps), whereas the latter is a property of the organism's experience of the world (or of an experience-experiencer pair). These, we would argue, should be distinguished.

It is commonplace to note that each type of organism will occupy a distinctive point of view on the world, characterised by the kinds of perceptual information which are available to it, and by the kinds of perceptual discriminations which it is capable of making (Nagel, 1974). This is what it means to say that bats (with echolocation) and cats (without colour vision) occupy a different point of view on the world from ourselves. Put differently but equivalently: the world (including subjects' own bodies) is subjectively presented to different species of organism somewhat differently. And to try to characterise this is to try and characterise what the world for such subjects *is like*. But it is one thing to say that *the world* takes on a subjective aspect by being presented to subjects with differing conceptual and discriminatory powers, and it is quite another thing to say that the subject's *experience of the world* also has such a subjective aspect, or that there is *something which the experience is like*. So, by parity of reasoning, this sort of subjectivity would seem to require subjects to possess information about, and to make discriminations amongst, their own states of experience. And it is just this which provides the rationale for higher-order representationalist (HOR) as against first-order representationalist (FOR) accounts, in fact.

According to HOR theories, first-order perceptual states alone may be adequately accounted for in FOR terms. The result will be an account of the point of view – the subjective perspective – which the organism takes towards its world (and the states of its own body), giving us an account of what *the world*, for that organism, *is like*. But the HOR theorist maintains that something else is required in accounting for what *an experience is like* for a subject, or in explaining what it is for an organism's *mental states* to take on a subjective aspect. For this, we maintain, higher-order representations – states which meta-represent the subject's own mental states – are required. Since the way the world appears – subjectively – to a subject depends upon the way properties of the world are made available to the subject, grounded in properties of the subject's perceptual system, it is hard to see in what else the subjectivity of the subject's experience of the world could consist but *its* availability to the subject in turn, through some type of higher-order representation (HOR).

3.3 The explanatory power of HOR theories

We now propose to argue that phenomenal consciousness will emerge in any system where perceptual information is made available to HORs in analog form, and where the system is capable of recognising its own perceptual states, as well as the states of the world perceived. For by postulating that this is so, we can explain why phenomenal feelings should be so widely thought to possess the properties of *qualia* – that is, of being non-relationally defined, private, ineffable, and knowable with complete certainty by the subject. (In fact we focus here entirely on the question of non-relational definition. For the remaining points, see Carruthers, 1996c, ch.7.) We claim that any subjects who instantiate such a cognitive system (that is, who instantiate a HOR-model of state-consciousness) will normally come to form just such beliefs about the intrinsic characteristics of their perceptual states – and they will form such beliefs, not because they have been explicitly programmed to do so, but naturally, as a by-product of the way in which their cognition is structured. This then demonstrates, we believe, that a regular capacity for HORs about one's own mental states must be a sufficient condition for the enjoyment of experiences which possess a subjective, phenomenal, feel to them.

Consider, in particular, the thesis of non-relational definition for terms referring to the subjective aspects of an experience. This is a thesis which many people find tempting, at least. When we reflect on what is essential for an experience to count as an experience *as of red*, for example, we are inclined to deny that it has anything directly to do with being caused by the presence of something red. We want to insist that it is conceptually possible that an experience of that very type should normally have been caused by the presence of something green, say. All that is truly essential to the occurrence of an experience *as of red*, on this view, is the way such an experience feels to us when we have it – it is the distinctive feel of an experience which defines it, not its distinctive relational properties or causal role (see Kripke, 1972).

Now any system instantiating a higher-order model of consciousness will have the capacity to distinguish or classify informational states according to the manner in which they carry their information, not by inference (that is, by self-interpretation) or description, but immediately. The system will be capable of recognising the fact that it has an experience *as of red*, say, in just the same direct, non-inferential, way that it can recognise red. (This is just what it means to say that perceptual states are available to higher-order thoughts, in the intended sense.) The system will, therefore, readily have available to it purely recognitional concepts of experience. In which case, absent and inverted subjective feelings will immediately be a conceptual possibility for someone applying these recognitional concepts. If I instantiate such a system, I shall immediately be able to think, '*This* type of experience might have had some quite other cause', for example.

We have conceded that there are concepts of experience which are purely recognitional, and so which are not definable in relational terms. Does this then count against the acceptability of the functionalist conceptual scheme which forms the background to cognitive accounts of consciousness? If it is conceptually possible that an experience *as of red* should regularly be caused by perception of green grass or blue sky, then does this mean that the crucial facts of consciousness must escape the functionalist net, as many have alleged? We think not. For higher-order accounts are not in the business of conceptual analysis, but of substantive theory development. So it is no objection to those accounts, that there are some concepts of the mental which cannot be analysed (that is, defined) in terms of functional and/or representational role, but are purely recognitional – provided that the nature of those concepts, and the states which they recognise, can be adequately characterised within the theory.

According to higher-order theories, the properties which are in fact picked out (note: not *as such*) by any purely recognitional concepts of experience are not, themselves, similarly simple and non-relational. When I recognise in myself an experience *as of red*, what I recognise is, in fact, a perceptual state which represents worldly redness, and which underpins, in turn, my capacity to recognise, and to act differentially upon, red objects. And the purely recognitional concept, itself, is one whose normal cause is the presence of just such a perceptual state, tokenings of which then cause further characteristic changes within my cognition. There is nothing, here, which need raise any sort of threat to a naturalistic theory of the mind.

Since any organism instantiating a higher-order model of state-consciousness will naturally be inclined to make just those claims about its experiences which human 'qualia-freaks' make about theirs, we have good reason to think that higher-order (HOR) theory provides us with a *sufficient* condition of phenomenal consciousness. But is there any reason to think that it is also *necessary* – that is, for believing that HOR-theory gives us the truth about what phenomenal consciousness *is*? One reason for doubt is that a first-order (FOR) theorist, too, can avail himself of the above explanation, as Tye (1995) does. For FOR-theorists need not deny that we humans are in fact capable of HORs. They can then claim that FOR-theory gives the truth about phenomenal consciousness, while appealing to HORs to explain, for example, the conceptual possibility of inverted spectra. To put the point somewhat differently – it may be claimed that what *underpins* the possibility of inverted spectra (that is, phenomenal consciousness itself) is there, latent, in FOR systems; but that only a creature with the requisite concepts (HORs) can actually *entertain* that possibility.

This suggestion can be seen to be false, however, in light of the first-order theorists' failure to distinguish between worldly subjectivity and mental-state subjectivity, discussed in section 3.2 above. In fact a system which is only capable of FORs will have the raw materials to underpin only a much more limited kind of possibility. Such a system may contain, let us say, FORs of *red*. Its states will then represent various surfaces as covered with a certain uniform property, for which it may possess a recognitional concept. This provides the raw materials for thoughts such as, '*That* property [*red*] may in fact be such-and-such a property [pertaining to reflective powers]'. But there is nothing here which might make possible thoughts about spectral inversion. Lacking any way of distinguishing between *red* and *the experience of red*, the system lacks the raw materials necessary to underpin such thoughts as, 'Others may experience *red* as I experience *green*' – by which we mean not just that a FOR-system will lack the concepts necessary to frame such a thought (this is obvious), but that there will be nothing *in the contents of the system's experiences and other mental states* which might warrant it.

3.4 Conscious states for animals?

Having argued for the superiority of higher-order (HOR) theory over first-order (FOR) theory, we turn now to the question of how widely distributed conscious mental states will be, on a HOR-account. For both Dretske (1995) and Tye (1995) claim – without any real argument – that this provides a decisive consideration in favour of their more modest FOR approach. We will argue that they are correct to claim that HOR-theories must deny phenomenal consciousness to the mental states of animals, but wrong that this provides any reason for accepting a FOR account.

Gennaro (1996) defends a form of higher-order thought (HOT) theory. And he acknowledges that if possession of a conscious mental state M requires a creature to conceptualise (and entertain a HOT about) M *as M*, then probably very few creatures besides human beings will count as having conscious states. Let us focus on the case where M is a percept of green, in particular. If a conscious perception of a surface as green required a creature to entertain the HOT, 'I am perceiving a green surface', then probably few other creatures, if any, would qualify as subjects of such a state. There is intense debate about whether even chimpanzees have a conception of perceptual states as such (see Povinelli, 1996, for example); in which case it seems very unlikely that any non-apes will have one. So the upshot might be that state-consciousness is restricted to apes, if not exclusively to human beings.

This is a consequence which Gennaro is keen to resist. He tries to argue that much less conceptual sophistication than the above is required. In order for M to count as conscious one does not have to be capable of entertaining a thought about M *qua M*. It might be enough, he thinks, if one were capable of thinking of M as *distinct from* some other state N. Perhaps the relevant HOT takes the form, '*This* is distinct from *that*'. This certainly appears to be a good deal less sophisticated. But appearances can be deceptive – and in this case we believe that they are.

What would be required in order for a creature to think, of an experience of green, that it is distinct from a concurrent experience of red? More than is required for the creature to think *of green* that it is distinct from red, plainly – this would not be a HOT at all, but rather a first-order thought about the distinctness of two perceptually presented colours. So if the subject thinks, '*This* is distinct from *that*', and thinks something higher-order thereby, *something* must make it the case that the relevant *this* and *that* are colour *experiences* as opposed to just colours. What could this be?

There would seem to be just two possibilities. Either, on the one hand, the *this* and *that* are picked out as experiences by virtue of the subject deploying – at least covertly – a concept of *experience*, or some near equivalent (such as a concept of *seeming*, or *sensation*, or some narrower versions thereof, such as *seeming colour* or *seeming red*). This would be like the first-order case where I entertain the thought, '*That* is dangerous', in fact thinking about a particular perceptually presented cat, by virtue of a covert employment of the concept *cat*, or *animal*, or *living thing*. But this first option just returns us to the view that HOTs (and so phenomenal consciousness) require possession of concepts which it would be implausible to ascribe to most species of animal.

On the other hand, the subject's indexical thought about their experience might be grounded in a non-conceptual *discrimination of* that experience as such. We might model this on the sort of first-order case where someone – perhaps a young child – thinks, '*That* is interesting', of what is in fact a coloured marble (but without possessing the concepts *marble*, *sphere*, or even *physical object*) by virtue of their experience presenting them with a non-conceptual array of surfaces and shapes in space, in which the marble is picked out as one region-of-filled-space amongst others.

Taking this second option would move us, in effect, to a *higher-order experience* (HOE) account of consciousness. Just such a view has been defended recently by Lycan (1996), following Armstrong (1968, 1984).

How plausible is it that animals might be capable of higher-order experiences (HOEs)? Lycan faces this question, arguing that HOEs might be widespread in the animal kingdom, perhaps serving to integrate the animal's first-order experiences for purposes of more efficient behaviour control. But a number of things go wrong here. One is that Lycan seriously underestimates the computational complexity required of the internal monitors necessary to generate the requisite HOEs. In order to perceive an experience, the organism would have to have the mechanisms to generate a set of internal representations with a content (albeit non-conceptual) representing the content of that experience. For remember that both HOT and HOE accounts are in the business of explaining how it is that one aspect of someone's experiences (of movement, say) can be conscious while another aspect (of colour, for example) can be non-conscious. So in each case a HOE would have to be constructed which represents just those aspects, in all of their richness and detail. But when one reflects on the immense computational resources which are devoted to perceptual processing in most organisms, it becomes very implausible that such complexity should be replicated, to any significant degree, in generating HOEs.

Lycan also goes wrong, surely, in his characterisation of what HOEs are *for* (and so, implicitly, in his account of what would have led them to evolve). For there is no reason to think that *perceptual integration* – that is, first-order integration of different representations of one's environment or body – either requires, or could be effected by, second-order processing. So far as we are aware, no cognitive scientist working on the so-called 'binding problem' (the problem of explaining how representations of objects and representations of colour, say, get bound together into a representation of an object-possessing-a-colour) believes that second-order processing plays any part in the process.

Notice, too, that it is certainly not enough, for a representation to count as a HOE, that it should occur downstream of, and be differentially caused by, a first-order experience. So the mere existence of different stages and levels of perceptual processing is not enough to establish the presence of HOEs. Rather, those later representations would have to have an appropriate cognitive role – figuring in inferences or grounding judgements in a manner distinctive of second-order representations. What could this cognitive role possibly be? It is very hard to see any other alternative than that the representations in question would need to be able to ground judgements of *appearance*, or of *seeming*, helping the organism to negotiate the distinction between appearance and reality. But that then returns us to the idea that any organism capable of mental-state-consciousness would need to possess *concepts* of experience, and so be capable of higher-order thoughts (HOTs).

We conclude that higher-order theories will entail (when supplemented by plausible empirical claims about the representational powers of non-human animals) that very few animals besides ourselves are subject to phenomenally conscious mental states. Is this a decisive – or indeed any – consideration in favour of first-order accounts? Our view is that it is not, since we lack any grounds for believing that animals have phenomenally conscious states. Of course, most of us do have a powerful intuitive belief that there is something which it is *like* for a cat or a rat to experience the smell of cheese. But this intuition is easily explained. For when we ascribe an experience to the cat we quite naturally (almost habitually) try to form a first-person representation of its content, trying to imagine what it might be like 'from the inside'. (There is at least this much truth in the *simulationist* theories discussed in chapter 4.) But when we do this what we do, of course, is imagine a *conscious* experience – what we do, in effect, is represent one of our *own* experiences, which will bring its distinctive phenomenology with it. All we really have reason to suppose, in fact, is that the cat *perceives* the smell of the cheese. We have no independent grounds for thinking that its percepts will be phenomenally conscious ones. (Certainly such grounds are not provided by the need to explain the cat's behaviour. For this purpose the concept of perception, *simpliciter*, will do perfectly well.)

3.5 Two objections

Notice that it is not only animals, but also young children, who will lack phenomenal consciousness according to higher-order thought (HOT) accounts. For as we saw in chapter 4, the evidence is that children under, say, the age of three lack the concepts of *appearance* or *seeming* – or equivalently, they lack the idea of perception as involving *subjective* states of the perceiver – which are necessary for the child to entertain HOTs about its experiences. Dretske (1995) uses this point to raise an objection against HOT-theories, which is distinct from the argument from animals discussed above. He asks whether it is not very implausible that three year olds, on the one hand, and younger children, on the other, should undergo different *kinds* of experiences – namely, ones which are phenomenally conscious and ones which are not. Granted, the one set of children may be capable of more sophisticated (and higher-order) thoughts than the other. But surely their experiences are likely to be fundamentally the same?

In reply, we may allow that the *contents* of the two sets of experiences are very likely identical; the difference being that the experiences of the younger children will lack the dimension of *subjectivity*. Put differently: *the world* as experienced by the two sets of children will be the same, but the younger children will be blind to the existence and nature of their own experiences. This looks like a pretty fundamental difference in the mode in which their experiences figure in cognition! – Fundamental enough to justify claiming that the experiences of the one set of children are phenomenally conscious while those of the other are not, indeed.

A related worry, though, is developed by Tye (1995). As we saw earlier, he maintains that conscious experiences, even in adults, have the quality of *transparency*. If you try to focus your attention on your experience of a bright shade of colour, say, what you find yourself doing is focusing harder and harder on the colour itself. Your focus seems to go right *through* the experience to its objects. This might seem to lend powerful support to first-order accounts of phenomenal consciousness. For how can any form of HOT-theory be correct, given the transparency of experience, and given that all the *phenomena* involved in phenomenal consciousness seem to lie in *what is represented*, rather than in anything to do with the mode of representing it?

Now in one way this line of thought is correct – for in one sense there is nothing in the content of phenomenally conscious experience beyond what a first-order theorist would recognise. What gets added by the presence of a higher-order system is a dimension of *seeming* or *appearance* of that very same first-order content. But in another sense this *is* a difference of content, since the content *seeming red* is distinct from the content *red*. So when I focus on my experience of a colour I can, in a sense, do something other than focus on the colour itself – I can focus on the way that colour *seems* to me, or on the way it *appears*; and this is to focus on the subjectivity of my experiential state. It is then open to us to claim that it is the possibility of just such a manner of focusing which confers on our experiences the dimension of subjectivity, and so which renders them for the first time phenomenally conscious, in the way that we suggested in section 3.3 above. (See section 3.7 below for further elaboration of this point.)

3.6 HOE versus HOT accounts

With the superiority of higher-order over first-order accounts of phenomenal consciousness now established, the dispute amongst the different forms of higher-order theory is apt to seem like a local family squabble. Accordingly, our discussion over the next two sections will be brisk. In this section we consider choice-point (4) in figure 9.2, between higher-order experience (HOE, or 'inner sense') theories, on the one hand, and higher-order thought (HOT) theories, on the other.

The main problem for HOE-theories, as opposed to HOT-theories, is the problem of *function*. One wonders what all this re-representing is *for*, and how it could have evolved, unless the creature were already capable of entertaining HOTs. In fact this point has already emerged in our discussion of Lycan (1996) above: a capacity for higher-order discriminations amongst one's own experiences could not have evolved to aid first-order perceptual integration and discrimination, for example. (Yet as a complex system it would surely have had to evolve, rather than appearing by accident or as an epiphenomenon of some other selected-for function. The idea that we might possess a faculty of 'inner sense' which was not selected for in evolution is surely almost as absurd as the suggestion that *vision* was not selected for – and that is an hypothesis which no one now could seriously maintain.) It might be suggested that HOEs could serve to underpin, and help the organism to negotiate, the distinction between *appearance* and *reality*. But this is already to presuppose that the creature is capable of HOTs, entertaining thoughts about its own experiences (that is, about the way things *seem*). And then a creature capable of HOTs would not *need* HOEs. It could just apply its mentalistic concepts directly to, and in the presence of, its first-order experiences (see section 3.7 below).

In contrast, there is no problem whatever in explaining (at least in outline) how a capacity for HOTs might have evolved. Here we can just plug in the standard story from the primatology and 'theory-of-mind' literatures (Humphrey, 1986; Byrne, 1995; Baron-Cohen, 1995) – humans might have evolved a capacity for HOTs because of the role such thoughts play in predicting and explaining, and hence in manipulating and directing, the behaviours of others. And once the capacity to think and reason about the beliefs, desires, intentions, and experiences of others was in place, it would have been but a small step to turn that capacity upon oneself, developing recognitional concepts for at least some of the items in question. This would have brought yet further benefits, not only by enabling us to negotiate the appearance/reality distinction, but also by enabling us to gain a measure of control over our own mental lives. Once we had the power to recognise and reflect on our own patterns of thought, we also had the power (at least to a limited degree) to change and improve on those patterns. So consciousness breeds cognitive flexibility and improvement.

Another suggestion made in the literature is that the evolution of a capacity for HOEs might be what made it possible for apes to develop and deploy a capacity for 'mind-reading', attributing mental states to one another, and thus enabling them to predict and exploit the behaviour of their conspecifics (Humphrey, 1986). This idea finds its analogue in the developmental account of our mind-reading abilities provided by Goldman (1993) and some other simulationists. The claim is that we have introspective access to some of our own mental states, which we can then use to generate simulations of the mental activity of other people, hence arriving at potentially useful predictions or explanations of their behaviour.

The main difficulty for this proposal (quite apart from the implausibility of simulationist accounts of our mind-reading ability, that is – see chapter 4 above) is to understand how the initial development of 'inner sense', and its use in simulation, could ever have got going, in the absence of some mental *concepts*, and so in the absence of a capacity for HOTs. There is a stark contrast here with outer sense, where it is easy to see how simple forms of sensory discrimination could begin to develop in the absence of conceptualisation and thought. An organism with a light-sensitive patch of skin, for example (the very first stages in the evolution of the eye), might become wired up, or might learn, to move towards, or away from, sources of light; and one can imagine circumstances in which this might have conferred some benefit on the organisms in question. But the initial stages in the development of inner sense would, on the present hypothesis, have required a capacity to simulate the mental life of another being. And simulation seems to require at least some degree of conceptualisation of its inputs and outputs.

Suppose, in the simplest case, that I am to simulate someone else's experiences as they look at the world from their particular point of view. It is hard to see what could even get me started on such a process, except a *desire* to know what that person *sees*. And this of course requires me to possess a concept of *seeing*. Similarly at the end of a process of simulation, which concludes with a simulated intention to perform some action *A*. It is hard to see how I could get from here, to the prediction that the person being simulated will do *A*, unless I can conceptualise my result *as* an intention to do *A*, and unless I know that what people intend, they generally do. But then all this presupposes that mental concepts (and so a capacity for HOTs) would have had to be in place *before* (or at least coincident with) the capacity for HOEs (inner sense) and for mental simulation.

3.7 Actualist versus dispositionalist HOT-theories

Having argued for the superiority of higher-order thought (HOT) theories over higher-order experience (HOE) theories, we come now to choice-point (5) in figure 9.2. Our choice is between *actualist* forms of HOT-theory – which maintain that phenomenal consciousness requires the actual presence of a HOT targeted on the state in question – and *dispositionalist* forms, which explain phenomenal consciousness in terms of *availability* to HOT. Actualist HOT-theory is defended by Rosenthal (1986, 1991a, 1993). Dispositionalist HOT-theory is elaborated and defended by Carruthers (1996c – though note that this presents a form of the theory much more elaborate and complex than that to be defended here, in particular in requiring that the HOTs should themselves be conscious ones).

The main problem for actualist as opposed to dispositionalist HOT-theories (and note that this is a problem infecting HOE-theories, too, which are also actualist), is that of *cognitive overload*. There would appear to be an immense amount which we can experience consciously at any one time – think of listening intently to a performance of Beethoven's seventh symphony whilst watching the patterns of movement in the orchestra, for example. But there may be an equally large amount which we can experience *non*-consciously; and the boundaries between the two sets of experiences seem unlikely to be fixed. As I walk down the street, for example, different aspects of my perceptions may be now conscious, now non-conscious, depending upon my interests, current thoughts, and saliencies in the environment. Actualist higher-order theories purport to explain this distinction in terms of the presence, or absence, of a higher-order thought targeted on the percept in question. But then it looks as if our higher-order representations must be just as rich and complex as our conscious perceptions, since it is to be the presence of a higher-order state which explains, for each aspect of those perceptions, its conscious status. And when one reflects on the amount of cognitive space and effort devoted to first-order perception, it becomes hard to believe that a significant proportion of that cognitive load should be replicated again in the form of higher-order representations to underpin consciousness.

The only remotely plausible response for an actualist higher-order theorist would be to join Dennett (1991a) in denying the richness and complexity of conscious experience. But this is not really very plausible. It may be true that we can only (consciously) *think* one thing at a time (give or take a bit). But there is surely not the same kind of limit on the amount we can consciously *experience* at a time. Even if we allow that a variety of kinds of evidence demonstrates that the periphery of the visual field lacks the kind of determinacy we intuitively believe it to have, for example, there remains the complexity of focal vision, which far outstrips any powers of description we might have.

Dispositionalist forms of higher-order thought (HOT) theory can neatly avoid the cognitive overload problem. They merely have to postulate a special-purpose short-term memory store – hereafter called 'C' for

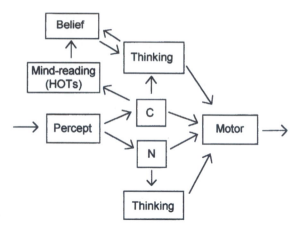

Figure 9.4 Dispositionalist HOT-theory

'conscious' – whose function is, *inter alia*, to make its contents available to HOT. See figure 9.4 above, which envisages two distinct routes for perceptual information through cognition – a non-conscious route, and a conscious route constituted as such by the availability of the perceptual states to higher-order thinking. So the perceptual states in C are available to two kinds of thinking – first-order thinking, generating beliefs and plans relating to the perceived environment; and second-order thinking, drawing on the resources of the mind-reading faculty, relating to the nature and occurrence of those perceptual states themselves. (Note that there are two distinct 'thinking boxes' in the diagram, to one of which conscious experiences are made available and to the other of which non-conscious experiences are available. In fact, as thorough-going modularists, we presume that there will be a variety of concept-wielding systems involved in each case; but we make no assumptions here about which reasoning systems will take input from C, which from N, and perhaps which from both.) The entire contents of C – which can, in principle, be as rich and complex as you please – can then be conscious in the absence of even a single HOT, provided that the subject remains *capable* of entertaining HOTs about any aspect of its contents. And note that the contents of the store are just first-order percepts, which can then be the objects of HOT – no re-representation is needed.

It is easy to see how a system with the required structure might have evolved. Start with a system capable of first-order perception, ideally with a short-term integrated perceptual memory store whose function is to present its contents, *poised*, available for use by various theoretical and practical reasoning systems. (For example, see Baars' vigorous defence of the idea of a *global workspace* – 1988, 1997.) Then add to the system a mind-reading faculty with a capacity for HOTs, which can take inputs from the perceptual memory store, and allow it to acquire recognitional concepts to be applied to the perceptual states and contents of that store. And then you have it! Each of these stages looks like it could be independently explained and motivated in evolutionary terms. And there is minimal meta-representational complexity involved.

But is not dispositionalism the wrong *form* for a theory of phenomenal consciousness to take? Surely the phenomenally conscious status of any given percept is an *actual* – categorical – property of it, not to be analysed by saying that the percept in question *would* give rise to a targeted HOT in suitable circumstances. In fact there is no real difficulty here. For presumably the percept is *really* – actually – contained in the short-term memory store C. So the percept is categorically conscious even in the absence of a targeted HOT, by virtue of its presence in the store in question. It is merely that what constitutes the store as one whose contents are conscious lies in its availability-relation to HOT.

It might still be wondered how the mere *availability* to HOTs could confer on our perceptual states the positive properties distinctive of phenomenal consciousness – that is, of states having a subjective dimension, or a distinctive subjective feel. The answer lies in the theory of *content*. As we noted in chapter 7, we agree with Millikan (1984) that the representational content of a state depends, in part, upon the powers of the systems which *consume* that state. It is no good a state carrying information about some environmental property, if – so to speak – the systems which have to consume, or make use of, that state do not know that it does so. On the contrary, *what* a state represents will depend, in part, on the kinds of inferences which the cognitive system is prepared to make in the presence of that state, or on the kinds of behavioural control which it can exert.

This being so, once first-order perceptual representations are present to a consumer-system which can deploy mental concepts, and which contains recognitional concepts of experience, then this may be sufficient to render those representations *at the same time* as higher-order ones. This is what confers on our phenomenally conscious experiences the dimension of subjectivity. Each experience is at the same time (while also representing some state of the world, or of our own bodies) a representation that we are undergoing just such an experience, by virtue of the powers of the mind-reading consumer-system. Each percept of green, for example, is at one and the same time a representation of *green* and a representation of *seems green* or *experience of green*. In fact, the attachment of a mind-reading faculty to the outputs of our perceptual systems completely transforms the contents which they carry.

3.8 HOD-theory

Dennett (1991a) argues for a form of dispositionalist higher-order theory similar to that defended above, differing from it in two main respects. *First,* Dennett thinks that our intuitions about phenomenal consciousness all derive, ultimately, from the availability of states to linguistic description, and that the insertion of *thoughts* between the states in question and our reports of them (in such a way as to give HOT-theory) is both unnecessary and ill-motivated. So conscious states get defined as those which are available to higher-order *description* (HOD).

Second, Dennett denies the existence of any short-term memory store (which he had once believed in – see his 1978b) whose function is to make its contents available to HODs. Rather, whether a state is *available* to report turns on whether it is true that it *would* be reported on in response to a suitable request or other probe. But then he thinks that the truth-value of such a counterfactual is likely to be indeterminate in many cases, since tiny differences in the timing and phrasing of any probe may deliver different results. (Compare the way in which people's opinions can be manipulated by appropriate phrasings of the questions, familiar to any pollster.) This then gives the famous thesis of the radical *indeterminacy of consciousness* – for most mental states, they are neither determinately conscious nor determinately non-conscious; rather, there is no fact of the matter either way.

In what follows we shall set to one side this second strand in Dennett's thinking, concentrating on the alleged connection between phenomenal consciousness and language. This is because Dennett's case for the indeterminacy of consciousness is for the most part built on his rejection of what he calls 'Cartesian Theatre' models of consciousness. But this notion, in turn, conflates a number of distinct ideas. Many of these are unobjectionable. And those which *are* objectionable are not ones to which the form of dispositionalist HOT-theory sketched above need be committed (see Carruthers, 1996c, ch.7). In addition, it seems very implausible that perceptual contents should be left fragmentary and distributed, as Dennett supposes, only being (partially) integrated in response to probing. For many of the purposes of perception require that perceptual contents should *already* be integrated. Think, for example, of a basketball player selecting, in a split-second, a team member to receive a pass. The decision may depend upon many facts concerning the precise distribution of team members and opponents on the court, which may in turn involve recognition of the colours of their respective jerseys. It is simply not plausible that all of this information should only coalesce in response to top-down probing of the contents of experience. ('Am I seeing someone in red to my right? Am I seeing someone in yellow coming up just behind him?' And so on.) Indeed in general it seems that the requirements of on-line planning of complex actions require an integrated perceptual field to underpin and give content to the indexical thoughts which such planning involves. ('If I throw it to him just *so* then I can move into *that* gap *there* to receive the return pass', and so on.)

So, why does Dennett think that phenomenal consciousness involves language? In his 1991a (ch.10) Dennett is first of all eulogistic about the virtues of higher-order thought (HOT) theory, but then argues that the insertion of *thought* between experience and its linguistic expression is an unnecessary shuffle. All we have reason to believe in, on the basis of introspection, is the existence of linguistic descriptions of our experiences, in 'inner speech'. And there is no good theoretical reason for postulating that those descriptions encode a separable set of thoughts.

There are two distinct issues here. One is whether we should endorse an 'encoding' (or purely communicative) conception of natural language, according to which we *first* entertain a thought which is *then* translated into a linguistic medium. It is possible to reject this picture (as we suggested in chapter 8 that we should) without endorsing a higher-order description (HOD) account of consciousness. One could allow that *conscious* propositional thought is constituted by the manipulation of natural language sentences, in inner speech, while denying that it is the availability of experiences to such sentences which constitutes them as phenomenally conscious. Rather, we can claim that the availability of experiences to *non*-conscious HOTs would be sufficient to render them phenomenally conscious, and we can claim that such HOTs are independent of language. And at least the first part of this claim is surely well motivated. For recall from section 3.3 above the salient features of our explanation of the distinctive, problematic, aspects of phenomenal consciousness. This consisted in *analog* experiential content being available to a concept-wielding system containing *recognitional concepts* of experience. This was then able to explain the conceivability of inverted and absent phenomenal properties, together with our temptation to insist that conscious experiences are private, ineffable, and knowable with complete certainty by the subject. Nothing in this explanation seems to require that the various HOTs involved (for example, in a recognition-judgement targeted on an experience) should themselves be conscious. What does the work in the explanation is the availability of experience to HOTs, not availability to conscious HOTs.

The second – and real – issue, then, is whether propositional thought, as such, must involve language. Here Dennett can (and does) run the following argument. At *some* point in cognition structured, content-bearing, states (whether thoughts or linguistic descriptions) need to be assembled in a way which does not involve any encoding from prior thought. Plainly this must be the case, on pain of vicious regress. So it is simpler to suppose that such assembling takes place at the level of language, rather than first for thought which is then encoded into language. Here Dennett (1991) endorses a *pandemonium model* of speech production, according to which there is a vast array of lower-level (thoughtless) 'word demons' who compete with one another by 'shouting out' a particular word or phrase. This competition goes on in semi-chaotic fashion, influenced by context and a variety of other factors (including the grammatical principles for the language in question, presumably), until some of the word-demons emerge as overall winners, and an assembled natural language sentence results.

We are also told that distinctively human thought was created when the human brain became colonised, as a result of enculturation and communication, by *memes* – that is, by ideas, or concepts, acquired both with and through natural language. These memes are carried by natural language expressions, and their role in this new form of (conscious) cognition results from the ways in which sentences act and react in the brain. And we are told that the stream of inner verbalisation constitutes a new kind of *virtual machine* in the computer which is the human brain. It is said to be a sequential, sentence-based, programme running in a connectionist, highly parallel, computer-architecture – a *Joycean* stream of consciousness *machine*, in fact. Moreover, it is only with the arrival of language in the hominid brain that we became capable of propositional thoughts *realistically construed* – that is, which consist of discrete, structured, content-bearing events having a causal role in virtue of their structure.

Dennett does not claim that the Joycean machine is wholly responsible for, and exhaustive of, what is distinctive of human intelligence, however. Rather, his position is that the Joycean machine is superimposed upon a cognitive architecture containing many specialist processors, each of which may have brought considerable adaptive benefits, and contributed to the success of earlier hominid species. Thus there may be specialist mind-reading systems; co-operative exchange systems; processors for dealing in naive physics and tool-making; processors for gathering and organising information about the living world; systems for selecting mates and directing sexual strategies; a faculty for acquiring and processing language; and so on – just as some evolutionary psychologists now suppose (see Barkow *et al.*, 1992; Mithen, 1996). Dennett's distinctive claim is that these processors not only operate in parallel, but that their internal operations are *connectionist* in nature, in such a way as *not* to legitimate robustly realist attributions of thought.

So Dennett can allow that hominids were capable of highly sophis-ticated social interactions prior to the appearance of language and the Joycean machine. In which case such hominids might have been *inter-pretable as* engaging in higher-order thought, from the standpoint of the Intentional Stance (see chapter 2 above). But this would not have been enough *actually* to transform the contents of these hominids' experiences in such a way as to render them phenomenally conscious – only the availability of experience to *real* (realistically construed) higher-order thought could do that. And this, in Dennett's view, had to wait upon the arrival of natural language and the stream of inner speech.

The question to be answered, then, in choosing between dispositionalist HOT-theory and dispositionalist HOD-theory (choice-point (6) in figure 9.1), is whether or not structured, discrete, higher-order thoughts are independent of language. If they are, then we shall have decisive reason to prefer HOT-theory to HOD-theory, it seems to us.

3.9 The independence of HOTs from language

The very same 'tracking argument' which we outlined in chapter 8 above applies – indeed, applies *par excellence* – to our capacity for higher-order thoughts (HOTs), strongly suggesting that our mind-reading faculty is so set up as to represent, process, and generate structured representations of the mental states of ourselves and other people. Then on the assumption that a mind-reading faculty would have been in place prior to the evolution of natural language, and/or that it can remain intact in modern humans in the absence of language, we get the conclusion that HOTs (realistically construed) are independent of language.

The central task of the mind-reading faculty is to work out and remem-ber who thinks what, who wants what, who feels what, and how different people are likely to reason and respond in a wide variety of circumstances. And all these representations have to be continually adapted and updated. It is very hard indeed to see how this task could be executed, except by operating with structured representations, elements of which stand for individuals, and elements of which stand for their mental properties; so that the latter can be varied and altered while keeping track of one and the same individual.

How plausible is it that such structured representations are independent of natural language? Many theories of the evolution of language – es-pecially those falling within a broadly Gricean tradition – presuppose that they are (Origgi and Sperber, forthcoming). On these accounts, language began with hominids using arbitrary 'one-off' signals to communicate with one another, requiring them to go in for elaborate higher-order reasoning concerning one another's beliefs and intentions. On a contrasting view, it is possible that there was only a fairly limited mind-reading capacity in existence prior to the evolution of language; and that language and a capacity for structured HOTs co-evolved (see Gomez, 1998, for an account of this sort). Even if this were so, however, it would remain an open question whether language would be implicated in the internal operations of the mature mind-reading faculty. Even if they co-evolved, it may well be that structured HOTs are possible for contemporary individuals in the absence of language.

In so far as there is evidence bearing on this issue, it supports the view that structured HOTs can be entertained independently of natural language. One sort of evidence relates to those deaf people who grow up isolated from deaf communities, and who do not learn any form of syntactically structured Sign until quite late (Sachs, 1989; Goldin-Meadow and Mylander, 1990; Schaller, 1991). These people nevertheless devise systems of 'home-sign' of their own, and often engage in elaborate pantomimes to communicate their meaning. These seem like classic cases of Gricean communication; and they seem to presuppose that a capacity for sophisticated HOTs is fully intact in the absence of natural language.

Another sort of evidence relates to the capacities of aphasics, who have lost their ability to use or comprehend language. Such people are generally quite adept socially, suggesting that their mind-reading abilities remain intact. And this has now been confirmed experimentally in a series of tests conducted with an a-grammatical aphasic man. Varley (1998) reports conducting a series of 'theory-of-mind' tests (which test for explicit grasp of the notions of belief and false belief) with an a-grammatic aphasic. This person had severe difficulties in both producing and comprehending anything resembling a sentence (particularly involving verbs). So it seems very unlikely that he would have been capable of entertaining a natural language sentence of the form, 'A believes that P'. Yet he passed almost all of the tests undertaken (which were outlined to him by a combination of pantomime and single-word explanation).

It seems, then, that a capacity for higher-order thoughts (HOTs) can be retained in the absence of language. But we also have the tracking-argument for the conclusion that a capacity for HOTs requires structured, discrete, representations. So we have the conclusion that higher-order thought, realistically construed, is independent of language, even in the case of human beings. And so there is reason to prefer a dispositionalist HOT-theory over Dennett's dispositionalist higher-order description (HOD) theory.

4 Conclusion

We have argued in this chapter that there is no good reason to think that consciousness – focusing particularly on phenomenal consciousness – is incapable of objective, scientifically grounded, explanation. And we have argued that such consciousness can be given a cognitive explanation in terms of its availability to higher-order thoughts. So here, too, what seemed like a potential conflict between common-sense psychology and science turns out to be illusory.

SELECTED READING

General: Block *et al.*, 1997, is an excellent collection of nearly 50 articles and book-parts, containing much of the seminal material in the area.

Mysterianism: Nagel, 1974, 1986; Jackson, 1982, 1986; McGinn, 1991; Chalmers, 1996.

First-order theories: Dretske, 1995; Tye, 1995.

Higher-order theories: Armstrong, 1968, 1984; Dennett, 1978b, 1991a; Rosenthal, 1986, 1991a, 1993; Carruthers, 1996c; Lycan, 1996.

References

Allen, C. and Bekoff, M. 1997. *Species of Mind: The Philosophy and Psychology of Cognitive Ethology.* MIT Press.

American Psychiatric Association. 1987. *Diagnostic and Statistical Manual of Mental Disorders*, 3rd revised edition. Washington DC.

Antell, E. and Keating, D. 1983. Perception of numerical invariance in neonates. *Child Development*, 54.

Aristotle. 1968. *De Anima.* Trans. Hamlyn, Oxford University Press.

Armstrong, D. 1968. *A Materialist Theory of the Mind.* Routledge.

1973. *Belief, Truth, and Knowledge.* Cambridge University Press.

1978. *Universals and Scientific Realism.* Cambridge University Press.

1984. Consciousness and causality. In D. Armstrong and N. Malcolm, *Consciousness and Causality*, Blackwell.

Asperger, H. 1944. Die autistischen Psychopathen im kindesalter. *Archive für Psychiatrie und Nervenkrankheiten*, 117.

Astington, J. 1996. What is theoretical about the child's theory of mind? In Carruthers and Smith, 1996.

Astington, J. and Gopnik, A. 1988. Knowing you've changed your mind: children's understanding of representational change. In J. Astington, P. Harris and D. Olson eds., *Developing Theories of Mind*, Cambridge University Press.

Atran, S. 1990. *Cognitive Foundations of Natural History.* Cambridge University Press.

Avis, J. and Harris, P. 1991. Belief-desire reasoning among Baka children: evidence for a universal conception of mind. *Child Development*, 62.

Baars, B. 1988. *A Cognitive Theory of Consciousness.* Cambridge University Press.

1997. *In the Theatre of Consciousness.* Oxford University Press.

Baddeley, A. 1988. *Human Memory.* Erlbaum.

Baillargeon, R. 1994. Physical reasoning in infancy. In M. Gazzaniga ed., *The Cognitive Neurosciences*, MIT Press.

Baker, R. and Bellis, M. 1989. Number of sperm in human ejaculates varies in accordance with sperm competition theory. *Animal Behaviour*, 37.

Barkow, J., Cosmides, L. and Tooby, J. eds. 1992. *The Adapted Mind.* Oxford University Press.

Baron-Cohen, S. 1995. *Mindblindness.* MIT Press.

Baron-Cohen, S. and Cross, P. 1992. Reading the eyes: evidence for the role of perception in the development of a theory of mind. *Mind and Language*, 7.

Baron-Cohen, S. and Ring, H. 1994a. A model of the mindreading system: neuropsychological and neurobiological perspectives. In C. Lewis and P. Mitchell eds., *Children in Early Understanding of Mind*, Erlbaum.

1994b. The relationship between EDD and ToMM: neuropsychological and neurobiological perspectives. In C. Lewis and P. Mitchell eds., *Children in Early Understanding of Mind*, Erlbaum.

Baron-Cohen, S. and Swettenham, J. 1996. The relationship between SAM and ToMM. In Carruthers and Smith, 1996.

Baron-Cohen, S., Cox, A., Baird, G., Swettenham, J., Drew, A., Nightingale, N., Morgan, K. and Charman, T. 1996. Psychological markers of autism at 18 months of age in a large population. *British Journal of Psychiatry*, 168.

Baron-Cohen, S., Leslie, A. and Frith, U. 1985. Does the autistic child have a theory of mind? *Cognition*, 21.

Baron-Cohen, S., Tager-Flusberg, H. and Cohen, D. eds. 1993. *Understanding Other Minds*. Oxford University Press.

Bechtel, W. and Abrahamsen, A. 1991. *Connectionism and the Mind*. Blackwell.

Bever, T. 1988. The psychological reality of grammar. In W. Hirst ed., *The Making of Cognitive Science*, Cambridge University Press.

Bever, T. and McElree, D. 1988. Empty categories access their antecedents during comprehension. *Linguistic Inquiry*, 19.

Bickerton, D. 1981. *Roots of Language*. Ann Arbor.

1984. The language bioprogram hypothesis. *Behavioral and Brain Sciences*, 7.

1990. *Language and Species*. University of Chicago Press.

1995. *Language and Human Behaviour*. University of Washington Press. (UCL Press, 1996.)

Blackburn, S. 1984. *Spreading the Word*. Oxford University Press.

1991. Losing your mind: physics, identity, and folk burglar prevention. In Greenwood, 1991.

Block, N. 1978. Troubles with functionalism. In C. Savage ed., *Minnesota Studies in the Philosophy of Science 9*. Excerpt reprinted in Lycan, 1990.

1986. Advertisement for a semantics for psychology. *Midwest Studies in Philosophy*, 10. Reprinted in Stich and Warfield, 1994.

1990. Inverted Earth. *Philosophical Perspectives*, 4.

1995. A confusion about a function of consciousness. *Behavioral and Brain Sciences*, 18.

Block, N. and Fodor, J. 1972. What psychological states are not. *Philosophical Review*, 81.

Block, N., Flanagan, O. and Guzeldere, G. eds. 1997. *The Nature of Consciousness*. MIT Press.

Botterill, G. 1994a. Recent work in folk psychology. *Philosophical Quarterly*, 44.

1994b. Beliefs, functionally discrete states and connectionist networks: a comment on Ramsey, Stich and Garon. *British Journal for the Philosophy of Science*, 45.

1996. Folk psychology and theoretical status. In Carruthers and Smith, 1996.

Boucher, J. 1996. What could possibly explain autism? In Carruthers and Smith, 1996.

Boyd, R. 1973. Realism, underdetermination, and a causal theory of evidence. *Nous*, 7.

1983. On the current status of the issue of scientific realism. *Erkenntnis*, 19.

Brown, D. 1991. *Human Universals*. McGraw-Hill.

Bruce, V. 1988. *Recognising Faces*. Erlbaum.

1996. *Unsolved Mysteries of the Mind*. Erlbaum.

Bruce, V. and Humphreys, G. eds. 1994. *Object and Face Recognition*. Erlbaum.

Bryant, P. and Trabasso, T. 1971. Transitive inference and memory in young children. *Nature*, 232.

Burge, T. 1979. Individualism and the mental. In French *et al.* eds., *Midwest Studies in Philosophy*. Reprinted in Rosenthal, 1991b.

1986a. Individualism and psychology. *Philosophical Review*, 95. Reprinted in Macdonald and Macdonald, 1995a.

1986b. Cartesian error and the objectivity of perception. In P. Pettit and J. McDowell eds., *Subject, Thought and Context*, Oxford University Press.

1991. Vision and intentional content. In E. Lepore and R. van Gulick eds., *John Searle and his Critics*, Blackwell.

Butcher, C., Mylander, C. and Goldin-Meadow, S. 1991. Displaced communication in a self-styled gesture system. *Cognitive Development*, 6.

Byrne, R. 1995. *The Thinking Ape*. Oxford University Press.

Byrne, R. and Whiten, A. eds. 1988. *Machiavellian Intelligence*. Oxford University Press.

Carey, S. 1985. *Conceptual Change in Childhood*. MIT Press.

Carruthers, P. 1986. *Introducing Persons: Theories and Arguments in the Philosophy of Mind*. Routledge.

1987a. Russellian thoughts. *Mind*, 96.

1987b. Conceptual pragmatism. *Synthese*, 73.

1989. *Tractarian Semantics*. Blackwell.

1992. *Human Knowledge and Human Nature*. Oxford University Press.

1996a. Simulation and self-knowledge. In Carruthers and Smith, 1996.

1996b. Autism as mind-blindness. In Carruthers and Smith, 1996.

1996c. *Language, Thought and Consciousness*. Cambridge University Press.

1998a. Thinking in language? Evolution and a modularist possibility. In Carruthers and Boucher, 1998.

1998b. Conscious thinking: language or elimination? *Mind and Language*, 13.

Carruthers, P. and Boucher, J. eds. 1998. *Language and Thought*. Cambridge University Press.

Carruthers, P. and Smith, P. eds. 1996. *Theories of Theories of Mind*. Cambridge University Press.

Casscells, W., Schoenberger, A. and Grayboys, T. 1978. Interpretation by physicians of clinical laboratory results. *New England Journal of Medicine*, 299.

Chalmers, D. 1996. *The Conscious Mind*. Oxford University Press.

Cheng, P. and Holyoak, K. 1985. Pragmatic reasoning schemas. *Cognitive Psychology*, 17.

Cherniak, C. 1986. *Minimal Rationality*. MIT Press.

Chomsky, C. 1986. Analytic studies of the Tadoma method: language abilities of three deaf-blind subjects. *Journal of Speech and Hearing Research*, 29.

Chomsky, N. 1959. Review of *Verbal Behavior* by B. F. Skinner. *Language*, 35.

1965. *Aspects of the Theory of Syntax*. MIT Press.

1975. *Reflections on Language*. Pantheon

1988. *Language and Problems of Knowledge*. MIT Press.

1995a. Language and nature. *Mind*, 104.

1995b. *The Minimalist Program*. MIT Press.

Christensen, S. and Turner, D. eds. 1993. *Folk Psychology and the Philosophy of Mind*. Erlbaum.

Churchland, P. 1979. *Scientific Realism and the Plasticity of Mind*. Cambridge University Press.

1981. Eliminative materialism and the propositional attitudes. *Journal of Philosophy*, 78. Reprinted in his *A Neurocomputational Perspective*, MIT Press, 1989; and in Lycan, 1990; Rosenthal, 1991b; and Christensen and Turner, 1993.

1988. *Matter and Consciousness*. MIT Press (revised edition: first edition 1984.)

Cioffi, F. 1970. Freud and the idea of a pseudo-science. In R. Borger and F. Cioffi eds., *Explanation in the Behavioural Sciences*, Cambridge University Press.

Clark, A. 1989. *Microcognition*. MIT Press.

1990. Connectionist minds. *Proceedings of the Aristotelian Society*, 90.

1998. Magic words: how language augments human computation. In Carruthers and Boucher, 1998.

Clements, W. and Perner, J. 1994. Implicit understanding of belief. *Cognitive Development*, 9.

Cohen, L.J. 1981. Can human irrationality be experimentally demonstrated? *Behavioral and Brain Sciences*, 4.

1982. Are people programmed to commit fallacies? *Journal for the Theory of Social Behaviour*, 12.

1992. *An Essay on Belief and Acceptance*. Oxford University Press.

Cook, V.J. 1988. *Chomsky's Universal Grammar*. Blackwell.

Copeland, J. 1993. *Artificial Intelligence*. Blackwell.

Corballis, M. 1991. *The Lopsided Ape*. Oxford University Press.

Cosmides, L. 1989. The logic of social exchange: has natural selection shaped how humans reason? Studies with the Wason selection task. *Cognition*, 31.

Cosmides, L. and Tooby, J. 1989. Evolutionary psychology and the generation of culture, part II. Case study: a computational theory of social exchange. *Ethology and Sociobiology*, 10.

1992. Cognitive adaptations for social exchange. In Barkow *et al.*, 1992.

Craig, E. 1990. *Knowledge and the State of Nature*. Oxford University Press.

Crick, F. and Koch, C. 1990. Towards a neurobiological theory of consciousness. *Seminars in the Neurosciences*, 2.

Cummins, R. 1975. Functional analysis. *Journal of Philosophy*, 72.

1989. *Meaning and Mental Representation*. MIT Press.

1991. Methodological reflections on belief. In R. Bogdan ed., *Mind and Common Sense*, Cambridge University Press.

Currie, G. 1996. Simulation-theory, theory-theory and the evidence from autism. In Carruthers and Smith, 1996.

Currie, G. and Ravenscroft, I. 1997. Mental simulation and motor-imagery. *British Journal for the Philosophy of Science*, 64.

Curtiss, S. 1977. *Genie: A Psycholinguistic Study of a Modern-day Wild Child.* Academic Press.

Dahlbom, B. ed. 1993. *Dennett and his Critics.* Blackwell.

Dale, P., Simonoff, E., Bishop, D., Eley, T., Oliver, B., Price, T., Purcell, S., Stevenson, J. and Plomin, R. 1998. Genetic influence on language delay in two-year-old children. *Nature Neuroscience*, 1.

Darwin, C. 1859. *The Origin of Species.*

Davidson, D. 1963. Actions, reasons, and causes. *Journal of Philosophy*, 60. Reprinted in Davidson, 1980.

    1970. Mental events. In L. Foster and J. Swanson eds., *Experience and Theory*, Duckworth. Reprinted in Davidson, 1980.

    1973. Radical interpretation. *Dialectica*, 27. Reprinted in Davidson, 1984.

    1974a. On the very idea of a conceptual scheme. *Proceedings of the American Philosophical Association*, 47. Reprinted in Davidson, 1984.

    1974b. Psychology as philosophy. In S. Brown ed., *Philosophy as Psychology*, Macmillan. Reprinted in Davidson, 1980.

    1975. Thought and talk. In S. Guttenplan ed., *Mind and Language*, Oxford University Press. Reprinted in Davidson, 1984.

    1980. *Essays on Actions and Events.* Oxford University Press.

    1982a. Paradoxes of irrationality. In R. Wollheim and J. Hopkins eds., *Philosophical Essays on Freud*, Cambridge University Press.

    1982b. Rational animals. In E. Lepore and B. McLaughlin eds., *Actions and Events*, Blackwell.

    1984. *Inquiries into Truth and Interpretation.* Oxford University Press.

    1987. Knowing one's own mind. *Proceedings and Addresses of the American Philosophical Association*, 60.

Davies, M. 1991. Concepts, connectionism, and the language of thought. In W. Ramsey, S. Stich, and D. Rumelhart, eds., *Philosophy and Connectionist Theory*, Erlbaum.

Davies, M. and Humphreys, G. 1993. Introduction. In M. Davies and G. Humphreys eds., *Consciousness*, Blackwell.

Davies, M. and Stone, T. eds. 1995a. *Folk Psychology: The Theory of Mind Debate.* Blackwell.

    1995b. *Mental Simulation: Evaluations and Applications.* Blackwell.

Dawkins, R. 1976. *The Selfish Gene.* Oxford University Press.

Dennett, D. 1971. Intentional systems. *Journal of Philosophy*, 68. Reprinted in Dennett 1978a.

    1975. Brain writing and mind reading. In K. Gunderson ed., *Minnesota Studies in the Philosophy of Science*, 7. Reprinted in Dennett 1978a.

    1978a. *Brainstorms.* Bradford Books.

    1978b. Toward a cognitive theory of consciousness. In C. Savage ed., *Minnesota Studies in the Philosophy of Science*, 9. Reprinted in Dennett 1978a.

    1978c. Why you can't make a computer that feels pain. *Synthese*, 38. Reprinted in Dennett 1978a.

    1978d. How to change your mind. In Dennett 1978a.

    1978e. Beliefs about beliefs. *Behavioral and Brain Sciences*, 1.

    1978f. Artificial intelligence as philosophy and as psychology. In M. Ringle ed.,

Philosophical Perspectives on Artificial Intelligence, Harvester. Reprinted in his 1978a.

1981. True believers: the intentional strategy and why it works. In A. Heath ed., *Scientific Explanation*. Oxford University Press. Reprinted in Dennett, 1987; Lycan, 1990; Rosenthal, 1991b; and Stich and Warfield, 1994.

1987. *The Intentional Stance*. MIT Press.

1988a. Précis of *The Intentional Stance*, followed by open peer commentary. *Behavioral and Brain Sciences*, 11.

1988b. Quining Qualia. In Marcel and Bisiach, 1988.

1991a. *Consciousness Explained*. Allen Lane.

1991b. Real patterns. *Journal of Philosophy*, 88.

1995. Consciousness: more like fame than television. Paper delivered at a Munich conference. Published in German as: Bewusstsein hat mehr mit Ruhm als mit Fernsehen zu tun. In C. Maar, E. Pppel, and T. Christaller eds., *Die Technik auf dem Weg zur Seele*, Munich: Rowohlt, 1996.

Dennett, D. and Kinsbourne, M. 1992. Time and the observer. *Behavioral and Brain Sciences,* 15.

Devitt, M. 1996. *Coming to our Senses: A Naturalistic Program for Semantic Localism*. Cambridge University Press.

Diaz R. and Berk, L. eds. 1992. *Private Speech: From Social Interaction to Self-Regulation*. Erlbaum.

Dretske, F. 1981. *Knowledge and the Flow of Information*. MIT Press.

1986. Misrepresentation. In R. Bogdan ed., *Belief*, Oxford University Press. Reprinted in Lycan, 1990; and Stich and Warfield, 1994.

1988. *Explaining Behavior*. MIT Press.

1993. Conscious experience. *Mind*, 102.

1995. *Naturalizing the Mind*. MIT Press.

Duhem, P. 1954. *The Aim and Structure of Physical Theory*. Trans. P. Wiener. Princeton University Press.

Dummett, M. 1981. *The Interpretation of Frege's Philosophy*. Duckworth.

1989. Language and communication. In A. George ed., *Reflections on Chomsky*, Blackwell.

Dunbar, R. 1993. Coevolution of neocortical size, group size and language in humans. *Behavioral and Brain Sciences*, 16.

1996. *Grooming, Gossip and the Evolution of Language*. Faber and Faber.

Elman, J. Bates, E. Johnson, M. Karmiloff-Smith, A. Parisi, D. and Plunkett, K. 1996. *Rethinking Innateness. A Connectionist Perspective on Development*. MIT Press.

Ericsson, A. and Simon, H. 1980. Verbal reports as data. *Psychological Review*, 87.

Erwin, E. 1996. The value of psychoanalytic therapy: a question of standards. In W. O'Donohue and R. Kitchener eds., *The Philosophy of Psychology*, Sage.

Evans, G. 1981. Understanding demonstratives. In H. Parret and J. Bouveresse eds., *Meaning and Understanding*, de Gruyter. Reprinted in G. Evans, *Collected Papers*, Oxford University Press, 1985; and in P. Yourgrau ed., *Demonstratives*, Oxford University Press, 1990.

1982. *The Varieties of Reference*. Oxford University Press.

Evans, J. 1972. Interpretation and 'matching bias' in a reasoning task. *British*

Journal of Psychology, 24.

1995. Relevance and reasoning. In S. Newstead and J. Evans eds., *Perspectives on Thinking and Reasoning*, Erlbaum.

Evans, J. and Over, D. 1996. *Rationality and Reasoning*. Psychology Press.

Farah, M. 1990. *Visual Agnosia: Disorders of Object Recognition and what they tell us about Normal Vision*. MIT Press.

Field, H. 1977. Logic, meaning, and conceptual role. *Journal of Philosophy*, 74.

1978. Mental representation. *Erkenntnis*, 13.

Flanagan, O. 1992. *Consciousness Reconsidered*. MIT Press.

Fodor, J. 1974. Special sciences. *Synthese*, 28. Reprinted in Fodor, 1981b.

1975. *The Language of Thought*. Harvester.

1978. Propositional attitudes. *The Monist*, 61. Reprinted in Fodor, 1981b; and in Rosenthal, 1991b.

1980. Methodological solipsism as a research strategy in cognitive psychology. *Behavioral and Brain Sciences*, 3. Reprinted in Fodor, 1981b.

1981a. The present status of the innateness controversy. In Fodor, 1981b.

1981b. *RePresentations*. Harvester Press.

1983. *The Modularity of Mind*. MIT Press.

1984. Semantics, Wisconsin style. *Synthese*, 59. Reprinted in Fodor 1990.

1985a. Précis of *Modularity of Mind*. *Behavioral and Brain Sciences*, 8. Reprinted in Fodor, 1990

1985b. Fodor's guide to mental representation. *Mind*, 94. Reprinted in Fodor 1990; and Stich and Warfield, 1994.

1987. *Psychosemantics*. MIT Press.

1989. Why should the mind be modular? In A. George ed., *Reflections on Chomsky*, Blackwell. Reprinted in Fodor, 1990.

1990. *A Theory of Content and Other Essays*. MIT Press.

1991. A modal argument for narrow content. *Journal of Philosophy*, 88. Reprinted in Macdonald and Macdonald, 1995a.

1992. A theory of the child's theory of mind. *Cognition*, 44.

1994. *The Elm and the Expert*. MIT Press.

1998. *Concepts: Where Cognitive Science went wrong*. Oxford University Press.

Fodor, J. and Lepore, E. 1992. *Holism: A Shopper's Guide*. Blackwell.

Fodor, J. and McLaughlin, B. 1990. Connectionism and the problem of systematicity. *Cognition*, 35. Reprinted in Macdonald and Macdonald, 1995b.

Fodor, J. and Pylyshyn, Z. 1988. Connectionism and cognitive architecture. *Cognition*, 28. Reprinted in Macdonald and Macdonald, 1995b.

Frankish, K. 1998. Natural language and virtual belief. In Carruthers and Boucher, 1998.

forthcoming. A matter of opinion. *Philosophy and Psychology*.

Frege, G. 1892. On sense and meaning. In his *Collected Papers*, ed. B. McGuinness, Blackwell, 1984.

Frith, U. 1989. *Autism*. Blackwell.

Gazzaniga, M. 1988. Brain modularity. In Marcel and Bisiach, 1988.

1992. *Nature's Mind*. Basic Books.

1994. Consciousness and the cerebral hemispheres. In M. Gazzaniga ed., *The Cognitive Neurosciences*, MIT Press.

Gelman, R. 1968. Conservation acquisition. *Journal of Experimental Child Psychology*, 7.

1982. Accessing one to one correspondence. *British Journal of Psychology*, 73.

Gennaro, R. 1986. *Consciousness and Self-Consciousness*. Benjamin Publishing.

Ghiselin, B. 1952. *The Creative Process*. Mentor.

Gleitman, L. and Liberman, M. eds. 1995. *An Invitation to Cognitive Science 1: Language* (2nd edition). MIT Press.

Goldin-Meadow, S. and Mylander, C. 1983. Gestural communication in deaf children: the non-effect of parental input on language development. *Science*, 221.

1990. Beyond the input given: the child's role in the acquisition of a language. *Language*, 66.

Goldin-Meadow, S., Butcher, C., Mylander, C. and Dodge, M. 1994. Nouns and verbs in a self-styled gesture system. *Cognitive Psychology*, 27.

Goldman, A. 1989. Interpretation psychologized. *Mind and Language*, 4.

1992. In defense of the simulation theory. *Mind and Language*, 7.

1993. The psychology of folk psychology. *Behavioral and Brain Sciences*, 16.

Gomez, J-C. 1996. Some issues concerning the development of theory of mind in evolution. In Carruthers and Smith, 1996.

1998. Some thoughts about the evolution of LADS, with special reference to TOM and SAM. In Carruthers and Boucher, 1998.

Gopnik, A. 1990. Developing the idea of intentionality. *Canadian Journal of Philosophy*, 20.

1993. How we know our minds: the illusion of first-person knowledge of intentionality. *Behavioral and Brain Sciences*, 16.

1996. Theories and modules; creation myths, developmental realities, and Neurath's boat. In Carruthers and Smith, 1996.

Gopnik, A. and Meltzoff, A. 1993. The role of imitation in understanding persons and in developing a theory of mind. In Baron-Cohen *et al.*, 1993.

Gopnik, A. and Wellman, H. 1992. Why the child's theory of mind really *is* a theory. *Mind and Language*, 7.

Gordon, R. 1986. Folk psychology as simulation. *Mind and Language*, 1.

1992. The simulation theory. *Mind and Language*, 7.

1995. Simulation without introspection or inference from me to you. In Davies and Stone, 1995b.

1996. Radical simulationism. In Carruthers and Smith, 1996.

Greenwood, J. ed. 1991. *The Future of Folk Psychology*. Cambridge University Press.

Grice, H. 1961. The causal theory of perception. *Proceedings of the Aristotelian Society*, supp. vol. 35.

Griggs, R. and Cox, J. 1982. The elusive thematic-materials effect in Wason's selection task. *British Journal of Psychology*, 73.

Grünbaum, A. 1984. *The Foundations of Psychoanalysis: A Philosophical Critique*. University of California Press.

1996. Is psychoanalysis viable? In W. O'Donohue and R. Kitchener eds., *The Philosophy of Psychology*, Sage.

Hacking, I. 1983. *Representing and Intervening*. Cambridge University Press.

280   References

Happé, F. 1994. Current psychological theories of autism. *Journal of Child Psychology and Psychiatry*, 35.
Harman, G. 1978. Studying the chimpanzee's theory of mind. *Behavioral and Brain Sciences*, 1.
    1990. The intrinsic quality of experience. *Philosophical Perspectives*, 4.
Harris, P. 1989. *Children and the Emotions*. Blackwell.
    1991. The work of the imagination. In A. Whiten ed., *Natural Theories of the Mind*, Blackwell.
    1992. From simulation to folk psychology. *Mind and Language*, 7.
    1993. Pretending and planning. In Baron-Cohen *et al.*, 1993.
    1996. Beliefs, desires and language. In Carruthers and Smith, 1996.
Heal, J. 1986. Replication and functionalism. In J. Butterfield ed., *Language, Mind and Logic*, Cambridge University Press.
    1995. How to think about thinking. In Davies and Stone, 1995b.
    1996. Simulation, theory, and content. In Carruthers and Smith, 1996.
Hirschfeld, L. and Gelman, S. 1994. *Mapping the Mind: Domain Specificity in Cognition and Culture*. Cambridge University Press.
Hogrefe, G., Wimmer, H. and Perner, J. 1986. Ignorance versus false belief: a developmental lag in the attribution of epistemic states. *Child Development*, 57.
Holm, J. 1988. *Pidgins and Creoles*. Cambridge University Press.
Horgan, T. and Tienson, J. 1996. *Connectionism and Philosophy of Psychology*. MIT Press.
Horgan, T. and Woodward, J. 1985. Folk psychology is here to stay. *Philosophical Review*, 94. Reprinted in Greenwood, 1991; and Christensen and Turner, 1993.
Hume, D. 1739. *A Treatise of Human Nature*.
    1751. *An Enquiry Concerning the Principles of Morals*.
Humphrey, N. 1986. *The Inner Eye*. Faber and Faber.
Humphreys, G. and Riddoch, M. 1987. *To See But Not To See: A Case Study of Visual Agnosia*. Erlbaum.
Hurlburt, R. 1990. *Sampling Normal and Schizophrenic Inner Experience*. Plenum Press.
    1993. *Sampling Inner Experience with Disturbed Affect*. Plenum Press.
Jackendoff, R. 1997. *The Architecture of the Language Faculty*. MIT Press.
Jackson, F. 1982. Epiphenomenal qualia. *Philosophical Quarterly*, 32. Reprinted in Lycan, 1990.
    1986. What Mary didn't know. *Journal of Philosophy*, 83. Reprinted in Rosenthal, 1991b; and Block *et al.*, 1997.
Jarrold, C., Carruthers, P., Boucher, J. and Smith, P. 1994b. Pretend play: is it metarepresentational? *Mind and Language*, 9.
Jarrold, C., Smith, P., Boucher, J. and Harris, P. 1994a. Comprehension of pretense in children with autism. *Journal of Autism and Developmental Disorders*, 24.
Johnson, M. and Morton, J. 1991. *Biology and Cognitive Development: The Case of Face Recognition*. Blackwell.
Johnson-Laird, P. 1982. Thinking as a skill. *Quarterly Journal of Experimental Psychology*, 34A.

1983. *Mental Models*. Cambridge University Press.

1988. A computational analysis of consciousness. In Marcel and Bisiach, 1988.

Johnson-Laird, P., Legrenzi, P. and Legrenzi, M. 1972. Reasoning and a sense of reality. *British Journal of Psychology*, 63.

Kahneman, D. and Tversky, A. 1972. Subjective probability. *Cognitive Psychology*, 3.

Kanner, L. 1943. Autistic disturbances of affective contact. *Nervous Child*, 2.

Karmiloff-Smith, A. 1992. *Beyond Modularity*. MIT Press.

Karmiloff-Smith, A., Klima, E., Bellugi, U., Grant, J. and Baron-Cohen, S. 1995. Is there a social module? Language, face processing, and theory of mind in individuals with Williams Syndrome. *Journal of Cognitive Neuroscience*, 7.

Kenny, A. 1963. *Action, Emotion and Will*. Routledge.

Kinsbourne, M. 1988. Integrated field theory of consciousness. In Marcel and Bisiach, 1988.

Kirk, R. 1994. *Raw Feeling*. Oxford University Press.

Klein, M. 1996. Externalism, content and causation. *Proceedings of the Aristotelian Society*, 96.

Koestler, A. and Smythies, J. eds. 1969. *Beyond Reductionism: the Alpbach symposium*. Hutchinson.

Kohler, W. 1925. *The Mentality of Apes*. Routledge.

Koslowski, B. 1996. *Theory and Evidence: The Development of Scientific Reasoning*. MIT Press.

Kosslyn, S. 1994. *Image and Brain*. MIT Press.

Kosslyn, S. and Osherson, D. eds. 1995. *An Invitation to Cognitive Science 2: Visual Cognition* (2nd edition). MIT Press.

Kripke, S. 1972. Naming and necessity. In G. Harman and D. Davidson eds., *Semantics of Natural Language*, Reidel.

Kühberger, A., Perner, J., Schulte, M. and Leingruber, R. 1995. Choice or no choice: is the Langer effect evidence against simulation? *Mind and Language*, 10.

Kuhn, T. 1970. Reflections on my critics. In I. Lakatos and A. Musgrave eds., *Criticism and the Growth of Knowledge*, Cambridge University Press.

Lakatos, I. 1970. Falsificationism and the methodology of scientific research programmes. In I. Lakatos and A. Musgrave eds., *Criticism and the Growth of Knowledge*, Cambridge University Press.

Lashley, K. 1951. The problem of serial order in behavior. In L. Jeffress ed., *Cerebral Mechanisms in Behaviour*, Wiley.

Lewis, D. 1966. An argument for the identity theory. *Journal of Philosophy*, 63.

1970. How to define theoretical terms. *Journal of Philosophy*, 67.

1980. Mad pain and Martian pain. In N. Block ed., *Readings in Philosophy of Psychology*, vol. 1, Methuen.

1988. What experience teaches. *Proceedings of the Russellian Society*, University of Sydney. Reprinted in Lycan, 1990.

Lewis, V. and Boucher, J. 1988. Spontaneous, instructed, and elicited play in relatively able autistic children. *British Journal of Educational Psychology*, 6.

Lillard, A. 1998. Ethnopsychologies: cultural variations in theory of mind. *Psychological Bulletin*, 123.

Loar, B. 1981. *Mind and Meaning*. Cambridge University Press.
   1982. Conceptual role and truth-conditions. *Notre Dame Journal of Formal Logic*, 23.
   1990. Phenomenal states. *Philosophical Perspectives*, 4.
Locke, J. 1690. *An Essay Concerning Human Understanding*.
Loewer, B. and Rey, G. eds. 1991. *Meaning in Mind: Fodor and his Critics*. Blackwell.
Luger, G. 1994. *Cognitive Science: The Science of Intelligent Systems*. Academic Press.
Luria, A. and Yudovich, F. 1956. *Speech and the Development of Mental Processes in the Child*. Trans. Kovasc and Simon, Penguin Books, 1959.
Lycan, W. 1987. *Consciousness*. MIT Press.
   1996. *Consciousness and Experience*. MIT Press.
Lycan, W. ed. 1990. *Mind and Cognition: A Reader*. Blackwell.
Macdonald, C. and Macdonald, G. eds. 1995a. *Philosophy of Psychology*. Blackwell.
   1995b. *Connexionism*. Blackwell.
MacDonald, M. 1989. Priming effects from gaps to antecedents. *Language and Cognitive Processes*, 5.
Malson, L. 1972. *Wolf Children and the Problem of Human Nature*. Monthly Review Press.
Manktelow, K. and Evans, J. 1979. Facilitation of reasoning by realism. *British Journal of Psychology*, 70.
Manktelow, K. and Over, D. 1990. *Inference and Understanding*. Routledge.
Marcel, A. 1983. Conscious and unconscious perception. *Cognitive Psychology*, 15.
   forthcoming. Blindsight and shape perception: deficit of visual consciousness or of visual function? *Brain*.
Marcel, A. and Bisiach, E. eds. 1988. *Consciousness and Contemporary Science*. Oxford University Press.
Margolis, E. and Laurence, S. eds. 1999. *Concepts: Core Readings*. MIT Press.
Marr, D. 1982. *Vision*. MIT Press.
Matthews, R. 1997. Can connectionists explain systematicity? *Mind and Language*, 12.
McCauley, R. 1986. Intertheoretic relations and the future of folk psychology. *Philosophy of Science*, 53. Reprinted in Christensen and Turner, 1993.
McCulloch, G. 1988. What it is like. *Philosophical Quarterly* 38.
   1989. *The Game of the Name*. Oxford University Press.
   1993. The very idea of the phenomenological. *Aristotelian Society Proceedings*, 93.
McCulloch, W. and Pitts, W. 1943. A logical calculus of the ideas immanent in nervous activity. *Bulletin of Mathematical Biophysics*, 5.
McDowell, J. 1977. On the sense and reference of a proper name. *Mind*, 86. Reprinted in A. Moore ed., *Meaning and Reference*, Oxford University Press, 1993.
   1984. *De re* senses. *Philosophical Quarterly*, 34. Reprinted in C. Wright ed., *Frege: Tradition and Influence*, Blackwell, 1984.
   1986. Singular thought and the extent of inner space. In P. Pettit and J. McDowell eds., *Subject, Thought and Context*, Oxford University Press.

1994. *Mind and World.* MIT Press.

McGinn, C. 1982. The structure of content. In A. Woodfield, ed., *Thought and Object*, Oxford University Press.

1989. *Mental Content.* Blackwell.

1991. *The Problem of Consciousness.* Blackwell.

Melden, A. 1961. *Free Action.* Routledge.

Meltzoff, A. and Moore, M. 1977. Imitation of facial and manual gestures by human neonates. *Science*, 198.

1983. Newborn infants imitate adult facial gestures. *Child Development*, 54.

Miller, G. 1956. The magical number seven, plus or minus two: some limits on our capacity for processing information. *Psychological Review*, 63.

Millikan, R. 1984. *Language, Thought, and Other Biological Categories.* MIT Press.

1986. Thoughts without laws: cognitive science with content. *Philosophical Review*, 95. Reprinted in Millikan's *White Queen Psychology and Other Essays*, MIT Press.

1989. Biosemantics. *Journal of Philosophy*, 86. Reprinted in Millikan's *White Queen Psychology and Other Essays*, MIT Press; in Stich and Warfield, 1994; and in Macdonald and Macdonald, 1995a.

1991. Speaking up for Darwin. In Loewer and Rey, 1991.

Minsky, M. and Papert, S. 1969. *Perceptrons.* MIT Press.

Mithen, S. 1996. *The Prehistory of the Mind.* Thames and Hudson.

Nagel, T. 1971. Brain bisection and the unity of consciousness. *Synthese*, 22. Reprinted in J. Glover ed., *The Philosophy of Mind*, Oxford University Press, 1976; and in T. Nagel, *Mortal Questions*, Cambridge University Press, 1979.

1974. What is it like to be a bat? *Philosophical Review*, 83. Reprinted in T. Nagel, *Mortal Questions*, Cambridge University Press, 1979; N. Block ed., *Readings in Philosophy of Psychology Vol I*, Harvard University Press, 1980: D. Hofstadter and D. Dennett, *The Mind's I*, Penguin, 1981; Rosenthal, 1991b; and Block *et al.*, 1997.

1986. *The View from Nowhere.* Oxford University Press.

Naito, M., Komatsu, S. and Fuke, T. 1995. Normal and autistic children's understanding of their own and others' false belief: a study from Japan. *British Journal of Developmental Psychology*, 13.

Newell, A. 1990. *Unified Theories of Cognition.* Harvard University Press.

Newell, A. and Simon, H. 1972. *Human Problem Solving.* Prentice-Hall.

Nichols, S., Stich, S., Leslie, A. and Klein, D. 1996. Varieties of off-line simulation. In Carruthers and Smith, 1996.

Nisbett, R. and Borgida, E. 1975. Attribution and the psychology of prediction. *Journal of Personal and Social Psychology*, 32.

Nisbett, R. and Ross, L. 1980. *Human Inference.* Prentice-Hall.

Nisbett, R. and Wilson, T. 1977. Telling more than we can know. *Psychological Review*, 84.

Noonan, H. 1986. Russellian thoughts and methodological solipsism. In J. Butterfield, ed., *Language, Mind and Logic*, Cambridge University Press.

1993. Object-dependent thoughts. In J. Heil and A. Mele eds., *Mental Causation*, Oxford University Press.

O'Brien, G. 1991. Is connectionism commonsense? *Philosophical Psychology*, 4.

O'Connell, S. 1996. Theory of Mind in Chimpanzees. Unpublished PhD thesis, University of Liverpool.

O'Toole, A., Deffenbacher, K., Valentin, D. and Abdi, H. 1994. Structural aspects of face recognition and the other-race effect. *Memory and Cognition*, 22.

Oakhill, J. and Johnson-Laird, P. 1985. The effect of belief on the spontaneous production of syllogistic conclusions. *Quarterly Journal of Experimental Psychology*, 37A.

Oakhill, J., Johnson-Laird, P. and Garnham, A. 1989. Believability and syllogistic reasoning. *Cognition*, 31.

Oaksford, M. and Chater, N. 1993. Reasoning theories and bounded rationality. In K. Manktelow and D. Over eds., *Rationality*, Routledge.

1995. Theories of reasoning and the computational explanation of everyday inference. *Thinking and Reasoning*, 1.

Origgi, G. and Sperber, D. forthcoming. Issues in the evolution of human language and communication.

Ozonoff, S., Pennington, B. and Rogers, S. 1991. Executive function deficits in high-functioning autistic children. *Journal of Child Psychology and Psychiatry*, 31.

Papineau, D. 1987. *Reality and Representation*. Blackwell.

1993. *Philosophical Naturalism*. Blackwell.

Peacocke, C. 1986. *Thoughts*. Blackwell.

1992. *A Study of Concepts*. MIT Press.

1993. Externalism and explanation. *Aristotelian Society Proceedings*, 93.

Penrose, R. 1989. *The Emperor's New Mind*. Oxford Univerity Press.

1994. *Shadows of the Mind*. Oxford University Press.

Perner, J. 1991. *Understanding the Representational Mind*. MIT Press.

1996. Simulation as explicitation of predication-implicit knowledge about the mind: arguments for a simulation-theory mix. In Carruthers and Smith, 1996.

Perner, J., Leekam, S. and Wimmer, H. 1987. Three year olds' difficulty with false belief. *British Journal of Experimental Psychology*, 5.

Perner, J., Ruffman, T. and Leekam, S. 1994. Theory of mind is contagious: you catch it from your sibs. *Child Development*, 65.

Perry, J. 1979. The problem of the essential indexical. *Nous*, 13. Reprinted in N. Salmon and S. Soames eds., *Propositions and Attitudes*, Oxford University Press, 1988; and in Q. Cassam ed., *Self-Knowledge*, Oxford University Press, 1994.

Peskin, J. 1992. Ruse and representations: on children's ability to conceal information. *Developmental Psychology*, 28.

Peters, R. 1958. *The Concept of Motivation*. Routledge.

Piaget, J. 1927. *The Child's Conception of Physical Causality*. Routledge.

1936. *The Origin of Intelligence in the Child*. Routledge.

1937. *The Construction of Reality in the Child*. Basic Books.

1959. *The Language and Thought of the Child*, 3rd edn. Routledge.

Piaget, J. and Inhelder, B. 1941. *The Child's Construction of Quantities: Conservation and Atomism*, trans. Pomerans. Basic Books.

1948. *The Child's Conception of Space*, trans. Langdon and Lunzer. Routledge.

1966. *The Psychology of the Child*. Routledge.

Pinker, S. 1994. *The Language Instinct.* Penguin.

Pinker, S. and Bloom, P. 1990. Natural language and natural selection. *Behavioral and Brain Sciences*, 13.

Pitts, W. and McCulloch, W. 1947. How we know universals: the perception of auditory and visual forms. *Bulletin of Mathematical Biophysics*, 9.

Place, U. 1956. Is consciousness a brain process? *British Journal of Psychology*, 47.

Pollard, P. 1982. Human reasoning: some possible effects of availability. *Cognition*, 12.

Popper, K. 1956. Three views concerning human knowledge. In his 1963. (First published in H. Lewis ed., *Contemporary British Philosophy, 3rd Series*, Allen and Unwin.)

   1957. Science: conjectures and refutations. In his 1963. (First published as 'Philosophy of science: a personal report' in C. Mace ed., *British Philosophy in Mid-Century*, Allen and Unwin.)

   1963. *Conjectures and Refutations.* Routledge.

   1971. Conjectural knowledge. *Revue Internationale de Philosophie*, 95–6. Reprinted in K. Popper, *Objective Knowledge*, Oxford University Press, 1972.

   1976. *Unended Quest: An Intellectual Autobiography.* Fontana/Collins.

Posner, M. 1978. *Chronometric Explorations of Mind.* Erlbaum.

Povinelli, D. 1996. Chimpanzee theory of mind? In Carruthers and Smith, 1996.

Premack, D. 1986. *Gavagai! Or the Future History of the Ape Language Controversy.* MIT Press.

Premack, D. and Woodruff, G. 1978. Does the chimpanzee have a theory of mind? *Behavioral and Brain Sciences*, 1.

Putnam, H. 1960. Minds and machines. In S. Hook ed., *Dimensions of Mind*, Harvard Press. Reprinted in his 1975b.

   1967. The nature of mental states. In W. Capitan and D. Merrill eds., *Art, Mind and Religion*, University of Pittsburgh Press. Reprinted in his 1975b; Lycan, 1990; and in Rosenthal, 1991b.

   1975a. The meaning of 'meaning'. *Minnesota Studies in Philosophy of Science*, 7. Reprinted in his 1975b.

   1975b. *Mind, Language and Reality.* Cambridge University Press.

   1988. *Representation and Reality.* MIT Press.

Quine, W.V. 1951. Two dogmas of empiricism. *Philosophical Review*, 60. Reprinted with additions in his *From a Logical Point of View*, Harvard University Press, 1953.

Radford, A. 1997. *Syntax: A Minimalist Introduction.* Cambridge University Press.

Ramsey, W., Stich, S. and Garon, J. 1990. Connectionism, eliminativism, and the future of folk psychology. *Philosophical Perspectives*, 4. Reprinted in Greenwood, 1991; and in Christensen and Turner, 1993.

Rapin, I. 1996. Developmental language disorders. *Journal of Child Psychology and Psychiatry*, 37.

Rey, G. 1997. *Contemporary Philosophy of Mind.* Blackwell.

Rosenblatt, F. 1958. The perceptron: a probabilistic model for information storage and organization in the brain. *Psychological Review*, 65.

   1962. *The Principles of Neurodynamics.* Spartan.

Rosenthal, D. 1986. Two concepts of consciousness. *Philosophical Studies*, 49. Reprinted in Rosenthal, 1991b.

1991a. The independence of consciousness and sensory quality. *Philosophical Issues*, 1.

1993. Thinking that one thinks. In Davies and Humphreys, 1993.

Rosenthal, D. ed. 1991b. *The Nature of Mind*. Oxford University Press.

Rumelhart, D. and McClelland, J. 1986. *Parallel Distributed Processing*, vol. 1. MIT Press.

Russell, B. 1921. *The Analysis of Mind*. Allen and Unwin.

Russell, J., Mauthner, N., Sharpe, S. and Tidswell, T. 1991. The 'windows task' as a measure of strategic deception in preschoolers and autistic subjects. *British Journal of Developmental Psychology*, 17.

Ryle, G. 1949. *The Concept of Mind*. Hutchinson.

Sachs, O. 1985. *The Man who Mistook his Wife for a Hat*. Picador.

1989. *Seeing Voices*. Picador.

Schacter, D., McAndrews, M. and Moscovich, M. 1988. Access to consciousness: distinctions between implicit and explicit knowledge in neuropsychological syndromes. In Weiskrantz, 1988.

Schaller, S. 1991. *A Man without Words*. Summit Books.

Schank, R. and Abelson, R. 1977. *Scripts, Plans, Goals and Understanding*. Erlbaum.

Searle, J. 1980. Minds, brains, and programs. *Behavioral and Brain Sciences*, 3.

1983. *Intentionality*. Cambridge University Press.

1992. *The Rediscovery of the Mind*. MIT Press.

Segal, G. 1989a. The return of the individual. *Mind*, 98.

1989b. Seeing what is not there. *Philosophical Review*, 98.

1991. Defence of a reasonable individualism. *Mind*, 100.

1996. The modularity of theory of mind. In Carruthers and Smith, 1996.

Selfridge, O. and Neisser, U. 1960. Pattern recognition by machine. *Scientific American*, 203.

Shallice, T. 1988a. *From Neuropsychology to Mental Structure*. Cambridge University Press.

1988b. Information-processing models of consciousness. In Marcel and Bisiach, 1988.

Shoemaker, S. 1986. Introspection and the self. *Midwest Studies in Philosophy*, 10.

Simon, H. 1979, 1989. *Models of Thought*, vols. 1 and 2. Yale University Press.

Skinner, B. 1957. *Verbal Behavior*. Appleton-Century-Crofts.

Smart, J.J.C. 1959. Sensations and brain processes. *Philosophical Review*, 68.

Smith, E. and Osherson, D. eds. 1995. *An Invitation to Cognitive Science 3: Thinking* (2nd edition). MIT Press.

Smith, N. and Tsimpli, I.-M. 1995. *The Mind of a Savant: Language-Learning and Modularity*. Blackwell.

Smith, P. 1992. Modest reductions and the unity of science. In D. Charles and K. Lennon eds., *Reduction, Explanation and Realism*, Oxford University Press.

Smith, P. and Jones, O. 1986. *The Philosophy of Mind*. Cambridge University Press.

Smith, P.K. 1996. Language and the evolution of mind-reading. In Carruthers and Smith, 1996.

Smolensky, P. 1988. On the proper treatment of connectionism. *Behavioral and Brain Sciences*, 11.

   1991. Connectionism, constituency and the language of thought. In Loewer and Rey, 1991.

   1995. Reply: constituent structure and explanation in an integrated connectionist/symbolic cognitive architecture. In Macdonald and Macdonald, 1995b.

Sodian, B. 1991. The development of deception in young children. *British Journal of Developmental Psychology*, 9.

Sodian, B. and Frith, U. 1992. Deception and sabotage in autistic, retarded and normal children. *Journal of Child Psychology and Psychiatry*, 33.

   1993. The theory of mind deficit in autism: evidence from deception. In Baron-Cohen, Tager-Flusberg and Cohen, 1993

Spelke, E. 1985. Preferential-looking methods as tools for the study of cognition in infancy. In G. Gottlieb and N. Krasnegor eds., *Measurement of Audition and Vision in the First Year of Postnatal Life*, Ablex.

Spelke, E., Phillips, A. and Woodward, A. 1995. Infants' knowledge of object motion and human action. In Sperber *et al.*, 1995b.

Spelke, E., Vishton, P, and von Hofsten, C. 1994. Object perception, object-directed action, and physical knowledge in infancy. In M. Gazzaniga ed., *The Cognitive Neurosciences*, MIT Press.

Sperber, D. 1996. *Explaining Culture*. Blackwell.

   1997. Relevance theory in an evolutionary perspective. Paper delivered at a workshop of the Hang Seng Centre for Cognitive Studies, University of Sheffield (September).

Sperber, D. and Wilson, D. 1986. *Relevance: Communication and Cognition*. Blackwell. (2nd Edition 1995.)

   1996. Fodor's frame problem and relevance theory. *Behavioral and Brain Sciences*, 19.

Sperber, D. Cara, F. and Girotto, V. 1995a. Relevance theory explains the selection task. *Cognition*, 57.

Sperber, D., Premack, D., and Premack, A. eds. 1995b. *Causal Cognition*. Oxford University Press.

Stein, E. 1996. *Without Good Reason: The Rationality Debate in Philosophy and Cognitive Science*. Oxford University Press.

Sternberg, S. and Scarborough, D. eds. 1995. *An Invitation to Cognitive Science 4: Conceptual Foundations* (2nd edition). MIT Press.

Stich, S. 1983. *From Folk Psychology to Cognitive Science*. MIT Press.

   1988. From connectionism to eliminativism. *Behavioral and Brain Sciences*, 11.

   1990. *The Fragmentation of Reason*. MIT Press.

   1991. Causal holism and commonsense psychology: a reply to O'Brien. *Philosophical Psychology*, 4.

   1992. What is a theory of mental representation? *Mind*, 101. Also in Stich and Warfield, 1994.

Stich, S. and Nichols, S. 1992. Folk psychology: simulation or tacit theory? *Mind and Language*, 7.

   1995. Second thoughts on simulation. In Davies and Stone, 1995b.

Stich, S. and Warfield, E. eds. 1994. *Mental Representation*. Blackwell.

Tager-Flusberg, H. 1994. Social-cognitive abilities in Williams syndrome. Paper presented at the conference on Williams syndrome, San Diego, CA (July).

Tardif, T. and Wellman, H. 1997. Acquisition of mental state language in Chinese children. Paper presented at the April meeting of the Society for Research in Child Development, Washington DC.

Thorndike, E. 1898. Animal intelligence: an experimental study of associative processes in animals. *Psychological Review, Monograph Supplement*, 2.

Turing, A. 1950. Computing machinery and intelligence. *Mind*, 59.

Tversky, A. and Kahneman, D. 1983. Extensional versus intuitive reasoning: the conjunction fallacy in probability judgement. *Psychological Review*, 904.

Tye, M. 1991. *The Imagery Debate*. MIT Press.

1992. Naturalism and the mental. *Mind*, 101.

1995. *Ten Problems of Consciousness*. MIT Press.

van Fraassen, B. 1980. *The Scientific Image*. Oxford University Press.

1989. *Laws and Symmetry*. Oxford University Press.

Varley, R. 1998. Aphasic language, aphasic thought. In Carruthers and Boucher, 1998.

Vygotsky, L. 1934. *Thought and Language*. Trans. Kozulin, MIT Press, 1986.

Walker, S. 1983. *Animal Thought*. Routledge.

Wason, P. 1968. Reasoning about a rule. *Quarterly Journal of Experimental Psychology*, 20.

1983. Realism and rationality in the selection task. In J. Evans ed., *Thinking and Reasoning*, Routledge.

Watson, J. 1924. *Behaviourism*. Norton and Company.

Weiskrantz, L. 1986. *Blindsight*. Oxford University Press.

1997. *Consciousness Lost and Found*. Oxford University Press.

Weiskrantz, L. ed. 1988. *Thought without Language*. Oxford University Press.

Wellman, H. 1990. *The Child's Theory of Mind*. MIT Press.

Whiten, A. and Byrne, R. 1988. Tactical deception in primates. *Behavioral and Brain Sciences*, 11.

Whorf, B. 1956. *Language, Thought, and Reality*. Wiley.

Wilkes, K. 1978. *Physicalism*. Routledge.

1991a. The long past and the short history. In R. Bogdan ed., *Mind and Common Sense*, Cambridge University Press.

1991b. The relationship between scientific psychology and common-sense psychology, *Synthese*, 89. Reprinted in Christensen and Turner, 1993.

Williamson, T. 1995. Is knowing a state of mind? *Mind*, 104.

Wilson, T. 1985. Strangers to ourselves: the origins and accuracy of beliefs about one's own mental states. In J. Harvey and G. Weary eds., *Attribution*, Academic Press.

Wilson, T. and Stone, J. 1985. Limitations of self-knowledge: more on telling more than we can know. In P. Shaver ed., *Self, Situations and Social Behaviour*, Sage.

Wilson, T., Hull, J. and Johnson, J. 1981. Awareness and self-perception: verbal reports on internal states. *Journal of Personality and Social Psychology*, 40.

Wimmer, H. and Perner, J. 1983. Beliefs about beliefs. *Cognition*, 13.

Winch, P. 1958. *The Idea of a Social Science*. Routledge.

Wing, L. and Gould, J. 1979. Severe impairments of social interaction and associated abnormalities in children: epidemiology and classification. *Journal of Autism and Developmental Disorders*, 9.

Wittgenstein, L. 1921. *Tractatus Logico-Philosophicus*. Routledge.

1953. *Philosophical Investigations*. Blackwell.

World Health Organisation. 1987. *International Classification of Diseases*, 9th edition. Geneva.

Wundt, W. 1912. *An Introduction to Psychology*, trans. R. Pintner. Allen and Unwin.

Wynn, T. 1993. Two developments in the mind of early Homo. *Journal of Anthropological Archaeology*, 12.

Index of names

Index of subjects

acceptance, 222
agnosia, 59
analog content, 228, 250, 267
analytic/synthetic distinction, 10–11, 115
animals, mental states of, 91–2, 141–2, 208,
    256–9, 261
anti-realism, 13, 15, 24, 26–30, 112, 208
aphasia, 59, 270
appearance/reality, 80, 93, 259, 261
atomism, semantic, 163
see also: causal co-variance semantics,
    holism
autism, 58–9, 95–103

behaviourism, 22, 57
    logical, 4–6, 9
    methodological, 15–17
blindsight, 232
brain scanning, 61–2

Cartesian theatre, 266
causal co-variance semantics, 163–7
causal role of mental, 35–7, 148–55, 204
central cognition, 65–72
cheater detection, 67–8, 120–3
cognitive closure, 237–8
cognitive conception of language, 208,
    214–15
cognitivism, 17–18
communicative conception of language,
    208, 267
competence/performance, 118
computationalism, 18–20, 188, 196–7,
    205–7, 221
concepts, 37–8, 115–16, 185, 201–2
connectionism, 19–22, 44, 55–6, 197–207,
    268
consciousness, 9, 50, 65, 131, 196, chapter 9
    passim
    access-, 229
    and subjectivity, 234–5, 253–4, 260, 265
    creature-, 227–9

different notions of, 227–231
first-order representational theory of,
    249–53, 255–6
higher-order description theory of,
    266–70
higher-order experience theory of, 258,
    260–2
higher-order representational theory of,
    253–6
higher-order thought theory of, 242, 252,
    256–70
of thought, 127, 144, 207, 210–11, 218–20
phenomenal, 4, 33, 227, 229–30, 234–42,
    252–60, 265
self-, 231
state-, 227, 229–30
transparency of, 246–7, 249–50, 260
see also: explanatory gap, inverted
    spectrum, knowledge argument,
    mysterianism, non-conscious, qualia,
    zombies
consumer semantics, 169, 265
content, intentional,
    and explanation of action, 145–55
    and interpretation, 27–30, 114–16
    as causal, 151–5
    explanatory versus semantic notions of,
    156–9
    in explanation of consciousness, 247–70
    in folk psychology, 37–8, 43, 131, 149,
    155–60
    in scientific psychology, 131, 155, 161
    narrow versus wide, chapter 6 *passim*
    naturalisation of, chapter 7 *passim*
    see also: analog content, causal
        co-variance semantics, concepts,
        functional-role semantics, Russellian
        thought, sense, teleo-semantics

demarcation criterion, 14
desires, 35, 74–5, 106
developmental rigidity, 54–8

295